The philosophy of
 pornography

The Philosophy of Pornography

The Philosophy of Pornography

Contemporary Perspectives

Edited by
Lindsay Coleman
Jacob M. Held

ROWMAN & LITTLEFIELD
Lanham • Boulder • New York • London

Published by Rowman & Littlefield
A wholly owned subsidiary of The Rowman & Littlefield Publishing Group, Inc.
4501 Forbes Boulevard, Suite 200, Lanham, Maryland 20706
www.rowman.com

16 Carlisle Street, London W1D 3BT, United Kingdom

British Library Cataloguing in Publication Information Available

Library of Congress Cataloging-in-Publication Data

The philosophy of pornography : contemporary perspectives / edited by Lindsay Coleman and Jacob M. Held.
p. cm.
Includes bibliographical references and index.
ISBN 978-1-4422-3596-0 (hardback : alk. paper) — ISBN 978-1-4422-3597-7 (ebook) 1. Pornography. 2. Pornography—Philosophy. I. Coleman, Lindsay, 1978– II. Held, Jacob M., 1977–
HQ471.P46 2014
363.4'7—dc23
2014014372

Printed in the United States of America

Contents

Acknowledgments

First and foremost I must thank Jacob Held, my partner in assembling this wonderful group of contributors, thinkers, and philosophers. It would have been impossible without him, in so many ways. He has taught me an immense amount about what genuine collaboration really means. Thank you. I must also give a huge amount of credit to our publisher, Rowman & Littlefield, for being patient, supportive, and for possessing infectious confidence in the thesis of this volume. I must also personally thank my partner Sarah and our baby Audrey for being very patient with Daddy while we were on holiday in New Zealand and he was editing drafts. I would also like to thank Katrien Jacobs. The road to this volume began, very much, with our serious discussions on the nature of pornography. Similarly, Jurgen Bruning's insights on the subject of erotica and pornography were immensely helpful. Above all I want to again thank every single one of the contributors to this book for agreeing to grapple with the reality of pornography as a part of modern life, and hence their responsibility to address its impact, each from the particular perspective of their own discipline or profession.

—Lindsay Coleman

Introduction

Why Pornography?

Lindsay Coleman and Jacob M. Held

Whenever the area of our research comes up, and we respond truthfully about what it is we do, we are immediately asked, "But, why pornography?" This question is incredibly hard to answer; in fact, this whole book is simply that, an answer to the question of why we should study pornography. But the question bears many meanings. It might be a question about why we, as individuals, study pornography. Of all the areas of philosophy, legal or political theory, film theory, or modern culture we could study, why choose pornography? Is there something lascivious lurking behind our ostensive rationale of furthering understanding? In this regard, the question appears to suspect our motives and impugn our characters. And oddly enough, porn studies seems to be the only field where knowing much more than others is perceived as a fault. Were we astrophysicists, you'd expect us to know everything, or pretty close to everything about physics, our field, the history of our field, and perhaps even a bit about the philosophy of science. In fact, you wouldn't lend credence to our position if it were demonstrated that we didn't know considerably more than most others about our field. Were we experts in war and public policy, you'd expect an encyclopedic knowledge of international law, treaties, conventions, as well a great deal about the history of war and warfare. You wouldn't find it at all odd or troubling that we were familiar with war atrocities and conventions regarding torture. But if we study pornography, knowing a great deal leads to suspicion, and gets back to the original meaning of the question: Is there something perverse lurking beneath the surface? Another meaning to the question is, why study porn in the sense of why study something that does not matter? Porn is taken to be innocuous.

So the person to whom you mention that you study porn might respond, "You must really enjoy your research." This respondent will also be wearing a smirk that seems to say, "I wish I could look at porn for a living." This is a harmless, albeit creepy, response. On the other end is the response that belittles this line of inquiry. This response is usually some variation on, "Wow, I should've gone into academia." This response is meant to diminish the value of academic work, implying that it's simply looking at porn. It also implies that pornography isn't worth thinking about seriously. Academics spend their time on worthless endeavors, like pornography. Rarely will the response an academic receives be proportionate to the seriousness of the work. Rarely does a researcher in porn studies hear, "That's fascinating, and important. What do you think about . . ." After all, it's just porn.

It is this attitude that often emotionally exhausts academics who work in porn studies, because it isn't just outsiders, family members, or random acquaintances who respond this way—it is coworkers, colleagues in academia. But porn does matter, and how we think about, respond to, and produce and consume it is both a window onto how we think about sex and sexuality as well as the active construction of our contemporary understanding of sex and sexuality. Anyone who is interested in what it means to be a human being in the twenty-first century should be interested in the issues surrounding and dealt with in the study of pornography.

But the study of pornography always begins from a position of justifying itself. And experts in the field must begin from a defensive posture, explaining why their studies are valuable and why they are not in some way profligate for pursuing this area of research. In this brief introduction, therefore, we will seek to offer such a defense—a defense of why it is important to study pornography.

First, let's begin from a simple truth: Pornography is a part of modern society, a considerable part of modern society. It is present on objects as essential and personalized as our iPhones and laptops and, thanks to Internet piracy, large amounts of commercially produced pornography are now completely free. In fact, when it comes to the Internet, you must go out of your way to protect yourself from the accidental slippage of pornography into your everyday life. One wrong key stroke, one wrong search term and immediately Google will present you with the best the adult entertainment industry has to offer, or a modest warning that you are about to venture into the red light district of the Internet. In addition, beyond traditional hard-core pornography, a pornographic sensibility can be seen permeating all aspects of culture, from tween and young teen fashions to television and commercially successful films. In fact, pornography is so prevalent that more often than not it is taken as a given in our modern social space. We assume that all people look at or know about pornography. Something this impactful, this definitive of modern culture needs to be laid open to scrutiny.

Beginning with the very idea of pornography's impact on contemporary popular culture, whether it is phrased as the "porning" or "pornification" of culture or the recognition of the existence of porno chic, the pervasive presence of porn in most of our lives is obvious. Pornography has infiltrated and informs contemporary culture. In this respect, we as individuals are also "porned" beings. Insofar as culture informs who we are, our self-understanding, and thus creates a feedback loop whereby we create the culture that in turn shapes our identities, a porned culture is indicative of porned individuals, and porned individuals express and recreate their porned culture. So whether we choose to accept it as a fact of modern culture or not, we are always already pornified, and thus as self-reflective, self-interpretative beings, it is our obligation to navigate a porned world as porned beings. To do otherwise is to neglect a fundamental aspect of ourselves, our culture, and our identity, and to forego our foremost duty to pursue reflective, examined lives. We need to understand pornography in order to understand our culture, in order to understand ourselves, so that as autonomous beings we can choose how, not if, we choose to engage our porned world, and how we wish to shape it and integrate ourselves into it.

The recognition that we are porned requires us to further contemplate the specific effects of such pornification. How does it impact our collective understanding of masculinity and femininity, does it lead to the promotion of unhealthy ideals, negatively impact our sense of self, body image, relationships, and so forth? Is there a connection between pornographic consumption and violence against women, the creation of a rape culture, or sexual harassment and discrimination? Nobody would balk at seriously considering relationships, mental health, body image issues, or violence against women. And pornography is a constitutive element in this discussion. Then there are the legal issues of free speech, hate speech, and the status of sex work. From sexuality to violence, from liberty to labor, how we address pornography speaks volumes to how we think about and respond to sex, sexuality, labor markets, rights, and multifarious issues that are significant in shaping our social world. Pornography is not innocuous background noise, a mindless pastime for the lonely, horny, or bored. Pornography is a multibillion dollar industry that forces us to engage and interrogate all those values that define who we are and who we dream of being, as individuals, as partners, and as a civilization.

Unfortunately, to date this debate has been anemic. On one side, anti-porn crusaders argue that porn leads to rape or sexual assault. Even when evidence is lacking, or argues to the contrary, they stick to their guns and reiterate the same talking points their predecessors authored in the 1970s and 1980s. Crucially these arguments depend on porn's history as taboo and the very lack of public debate and education that this book seeks, in part, to remedy. These anti-porn crusaders are not interested in a discussion of pornography, in understanding it as a phenomenon, as an element of culture. Frequently there is very little interest in the actual content found in contemporary pornography. Instead these authors, often focusing on a caricature of pornography or a far-from-representative sampling of what the adult industry has to offer, make sweeping generalizations about the content of porn, the working conditions of the actresses, and the responses of the viewers.[1] These generalizations don't speak to a deeper understanding of pornography or a bona fide interest in engaging it as a cultural phenomenon, but constitute a visceral reaction against pornography and the creation of an anti-porn ideology that speaks the language of "for or against" and seeks no further dialogue or investigation. In fact, the editors lost potential authors because they perceived the book as not being "balanced" enough. What they indicated was that a book including essays that find value in porn isn't "balanced." Apparently, when it comes to pornography, balance means "degrees of opposition."

On the other side of the debate are those who argue against the anti-porn crusaders. And their arguments are as well constructed as those they seek to refute. They dismiss the anti-porn crusaders, promote free speech, and in so doing actually denigrate the role pornography plays in our discourse. Most often, these theorists aren't pro-porn, they are anti-anti-porn. They deride the anti-porn crusaders as censors, they chide them for being "thought police," claim they misunderstand the legal basis of free speech, or impugn their character insofar as their positions align them with social conservatives. And in so doing they fail to appreciate and address the real role that porn plays in culture and in our lives.

So the debate goes back and forth, with each side preaching to its choir and speaking past the other. Occasionally someone breaks this mold and is immediately shouted down as a pseudopornographer by the anti-porn camp if they are not anti-porn enough, or they are decried as anti-liberal by the anti-anti-porn folks if they recognize a problem with pornography and seek legal or political means of redress. This structure of the discussion has led to very little progress being made in the past couple of decades in terms of furthering our understanding of pornography and its impact on and role in contemporary culture. It also leads to a stunted discussion. If we believe pornography to be a legitimate and important topic for research and discussion, if how we theorize and project sex and sexuality is important, then we need to be open to a dialogue on pornography, all forms of pornography, and all perspectives on pornography. Progress cannot be made if from the outset we condemn our opponents and reject all claims that don't sit nicely within our preconceived or ossified and orthodox position.

What perhaps leads to this ossified debate is the misapprehension of what is in fact being discussed. Any discourse on pornography is at root a discourse on sex. Sex, likewise, is a foundational human relationship, one transcribed by our social order, and built on constructed meanings of what it means to be male/female, masculine/feminine, and subject/object. So discussing pornography opens up a broader discourse on sex. But pornography is about more than just sex; it is about the production of sex, the production of media representations of sex and sexuality. So a discourse on pornography also affords us the ability to interrogate the effects that media have on our lives, in this case a specific aspect of our lives: sex and our sexual identities that form the basis of so many of our relationships and identities.

Beyond the reality that to discuss pornography is to discuss sex, it must be emphasized that a clear-eyed look at the actual content of pornographic videos and print throws up yet more issues that are relevant to any exploration of contemporary society. Randomly select any given pornographic video and you will, along with the straightforward record of people having sex, find an abundance of issues that reflect societal attitudes: sexism, racism, heterosexism, ageism, and so on. By interrogating pornography we interrogate a medium that plays out many of our innate hostilities and taboos, and in turn our social constructions of gender and sexuality. An ardent wish to stimulate debate surrounding this multiplicity of contentious issues found in pornography was behind the initial inception of the volume you now hold.

This anthology seeks to investigate the philosophical implications of pornography as a human phenomenon, as a part of how we now seek to conceive and express our sexuality in contemporary life and the myriad implications of this. In producing this volume we sought to bring together the best of contemporary theory on the subject from a variety of disciplines. In this way the reader is offered both a snapshot of the current discourse on pornography, and a window onto the world of pornography and its place in a variety of academic disciplines and discourses. Bias is naturally a reality in any discourse, yet we feel that in allowing for such a range of perspectives in a variety of disciplines, we have done our part to ensure a balanced discourse. Likewise, each position must fend for itself against alternatives placed directly next to, or at least within, this volume. No author is provided the safe cover of never having to meet and face an adversary, nor is the reader protected and shielded from positions he or she might find troubling or problematic. The philosophical project has always been an adversarial one where ideas meet and compete for acceptance, and where people dialogue in order to come to a better understanding of the world and in order to live their lives well. An investigation into pornography should be no different. Pornography demands this serious treatment, since its subject matter—sex, love, gender, interpersonal relationships, and so forth—is constitutive of who we are and what kind of society we want to create.

***

We are grateful to the many contributors who have happily engaged in this dialogue. We hope that this volume will promote a curiosity within the reader to seek out debates on the nature of pornography that extend beyond reassuring arguments that demonize or glorify porn.

NOTE

1. On a side note, at a conference at which Jacob Held was on a panel discussing pornography, a question was presented by an audience member regarding whether women could choose to pursue a career in porn and whether sex work is inherently exploitative. The audience member referenced Nina Hartley specifically, asking if her experience speaks against criticisms that sex work is inherently exploitative. Two of the panel members had to ask who Nina Hartley was. Experts on pornography did not know who Nina Hartley was. Consider the ramifications of allowing experts to direct a conversation on porn without knowing who Nina Hartley is. This episode is symptomatic of the problem with how this debate is traditionally carried out.

Part I

Pornification, Sexualization, and Society

Chapter One

Diagnoses of Transformation

*"Pornification," Digital Media, and the
Diversification of the Pornographic*

Susanna Paasonen

The cultural position of pornography has gone through evident and drastic transformations during the past decades. These transformations involve increased public visibility of all kinds of pornographies that since the 1990s have been increasingly distributed through online platforms, as well as a wave of academic and popular titles diagnosing the mainstreaming of porn and sex in contemporary culture, characterized as "pornified," "porned," and "raunchy."[1] This chapter addresses these recent developments within the pornographic, as well as diagnoses thereof, from two intertwining perspectives. It starts by asking whether the term "pornification" can be put into productive analytical use that would not efface the complexity of the cultural tendencies involved, nor truncate the potential meaning of the term "pornography" itself. This is followed by a brief discussion of the binary legacy of porn studies as it connects to diagnoses of pornification. The second part of the chapter investigates how the genre of porn has been transformed in the course of its digital production and distribution, and what challenges contemporary porn poses for scholarly analysis, which still remains largely rooted in studies of print media, film, and video productions distributed as material commodities (such as magazines and DVDs). In sum, this chapter asks how transformations in the visibility and ubiquity of pornography have been diagnosed, how the genre itself has been transformed, and what kinds of modifications within scholarly investigation all this may necessitate.

DIAGNOSES OF PORNIFICATION

Debates on the cultural role and meaning of pornography have been ongoing in academic, journalistic, political, and popular forums throughout the new millennium. The most often repeated arguments concerning the "pornification" of culture go roughly as follows: Pornography has become a pervasive element of contemporary culture and is increasingly accessible (and diverse) in its hard-core variants and ubiquitous in its soft-core forms. Pornography is accused of having grown increasingly violent, and this is seen to correlate with sexist and violent attitudes towards women among heterosexual men. Both of these developments are said to have crucial effects on people's conceptions and experiences of sexuality: porn addiction is arguably on the rise, and the imageries of porn are seen to affect children's development, young women's self-image, and women's sexual agency in harmful ways.

Such diagnoses seldom identify positive effects resulting from the "onscenity"[2]—that is, the increased public visibility—of pornography.[3] The term "pornification" may even evoke dystopian connotations of a culture in the throes of fornication, where sex and intimate ties are commodified and women are continuously, sometimes violently, objectified. Being conscious of such associations, Kaarina Nikunen, Laura Saarenmaa, and I contextualized and motivated the title of our 2007 anthology, *Pornification*, through three interconnected levels or strains of development, related to the changing position of pornography in contemporary media culture.[4]

First, we argued that technological transformations in the production, distribution, and consumption of media have affected an increase in and a diversification of porn production, and facilitated its ubiquitous consumption. In the 2000s, porn distribution has predominantly shifted to online platforms and users can search for, and browse through, virtually endless image, video, and text galleries in the comfort of their own home (or work station) without any need of visiting a specialty shop or paying for the experience. Online, porn usage is largely anonymous and the range of available selections is much broader than any adult shop catering print magazines and DVDs could ever hope to provide. As I discuss in more detail in the second part of the chapter, the landscape of pornography has been drastically transformed in just over a decade, both in terms of easy accessibility and diversity.

Second, we argued that developments in the jurisdiction and regulation concerning pornography, namely processes of liberalization and deregulation, have contributed to porn's increasing accessibility. The legal status of porn has clearly changed in most Western countries since the 1970s. While there is local oscillation between tighter and looser regulation, as has recently been the case in countries such as Australia and the United Kingdom,[5] pornography has been liberalized in most Western countries and adults can freely consume imageries formerly deemed illegal (with the exception of imageries deemed criminal, such as child pornography, violent pornography, and animal porn).

These two strands of development—namely transformations in both porn regulation and in its production and distribution—obviously converge, given the degree to which the centrality of the web as a distribution platform has impacted practices of media regulation. Traditional models of regulation based on centralized pre-examination and classification of locally produced or imported content, as deployed in the context of film and video, work poorly with networked communications for which content deemed illegal in one country can easily be hosted on a server operating under a different regional legal framework. Established practices of classification do not apply unless web access is subject to systematic local regulation, filtering, and censorship. This is the strategy adopted in countries such as China and Saudi Arabia and, lately, in the United Kingdom. Motivated by an interest to "protect children and their innocence," Prime Minister David Cameron's 2013 initiative aims at blocking access to pornographic and other disturbing content through filtering implemented by the largest Internet service providers in the country. Unless broadband users turn the filters off, pornographic material will be automatically filtered out. It is worth noting that such filters tend to conflate content ranging from sex education to erotic poetry to information resources for sexual minorities with pornography, filtering all of it. The example of the United Kingdom illustrates how pornography has re-emerged as a topic of public debate and policy with online distribution and its increasing "onscenity." Porn is framed as a topic of concern and risk in terms of children in particular, while the genre, its production, consumption, aesthetics, and economies are given little attention or definition: porn is assumed to be something that is always already known without further definition or study.

Third, our diagnosis of pornification addressed shifts in the cultural role and position of pornography. Advertising regularly cites and recycles the poses and gestures of soft-core and, in more covert and camp-oriented ways, the musical conventions and body styles of vintage hard-core porn. Nineteen seventies porn films are released as collector's editions available from mainstream vendors, select porn stars such as Ron Jeremy and Jenna Jameson have gained mainstream celebrity status, and contemporary porn stars—most notably Sasha Grey—have access to crossover stardom in so-called legitimate media.[6] Flirtation with the aesthetics of porn is not a novel trend in media culture as such. Advertising critic Rick Poynor argues that "by covering porn, the media borrows some of its dirty glamour and sense of danger, while in turn it confers legitimacy, making porn a topic of interest and discussion like any other."[7] Brian McNair discusses such aesthetic convergence as *porno-chic* that is not porn as such, "but the *representation* of porn in nonpornographic art and culture; the pastiche and parody of, the homage to and investigation of porn; the postmodern transformation of porn into mainstream cultural artifact for a variety of purposes."[8] Cutting through art and popular culture alike, porno-chic "aims to transfer the taboo, transgressive qualities of pornography to mainstream cultural production."[9]

Herein lies a paradox: given that the attraction of porn lies largely in its violations of public morality and taste, much of its power would be lost if it were indeed to become accepted, mainstreamed, and familiar as simply one media genre among others.[10] Following this argument, the cultural status of pornography draws on the scent of "forbidden fruit"—that is, on the acts of regulation, censorship, and outcries of moral dismay that accompany it.[11] As media scholar Annette Kuhn puts it, "in order to maintain its attraction, porn demands strictures, controls, censorship. Exposed to the light of day, it risks loss of power. Pornography invites policing."[12] It can therefore be argued that porn can only be mainstreamed or domesticated to a degree without the alluring scent of potential transgression being lost.

The three lines of development (transformations in porn production, regulation, and cultural visibility) addressed above are easy to identify. Nevertheless, the question remains whether "pornification" is an apt term for addressing them. One of the problems inherent in the term is the insufficient distinction that it affords between soft-core and hard-core pornographies, the public circulation of sexually suggestive imageries, and the explicitness of action shots.

The demarcation line between porn and more mainstream culture remains one of acceptability and unacceptability. While popular culture broadly flirts with partial nudity, sexually suggestive gestures and images, and the aesthetics of soft-core, this does not apply to the fleshy aesthetics, control scenarios, and minutely detailed displays of bodily fluids of hard-core porn. Explicit hard-core imagery does not become circulated in advertising, in music videos, or popular cinema but remains largely off-scene. In the case of UK regulation, it is also excluded from the palette of acceptable online content. The differences between the clearly distinct aesthetics and visibilities easily disappear under the umbrella term of pornification with the result that the actual topic under discussion becomes obscured. As an analytical concept, pornification risks giving rise to analytical muddiness.

A second—and possibly even more fundamental—defect related to the term is the implicit assumption that pornification involves a process in which pornography seeps into culture, as if from the outside in. Considering the process as one of the constant drawing of boundaries between the pornographic and the nonpornographic, the unacceptable and the acceptable, it can be argued that the flow in fact goes the other way, and that pornography is a product and part of culture that is constantly being filtered off and barred from the rest of culture proper. Consequently, diagnoses of pornification may work to uphold the perspective that marks porn as other to culture, rather than framing porn as the product of a culture.

A third set of problems inherent in the term is its vagueness in terms of cultural context. The most widely read diagnoses of pornification tend to address developments in the United States and United Kingdom, yet these analyses easily become general, generalized, and geographically indistinct. Discussions on the public visibility of porn and sex are indeed carried out across national borders, yet the specific tones and political investments involved vary drastically; a debate on pornification has different premises, investments, and implications in the United States than in Finland or India, for example. In Finland, the accessibility of porn among minors via smart phones is a public concern, yet one that needs to be seen in a context where conservative Christian voices remain subdued; pornography has been largely framed as an issue of social and gender equality, and public attitudes towards pornography are notably positive.[13] In India, again, media censorship and sexual representation remain topics of intense debate in relation to Western cultural influence and the threat it poses to traditional values, often in the framework set by Hindu nationalist politics. In this context, "The word 'pornography' has rarely been used to denote the *genre* of pornography, that is, sexually explicit material produced specifically for sexual arousal. It has been used to describe material that *connotes* sex, like film songs, advertisements, cover girls, rape sequences, consensual sex, and even beauty pageants."[14] Finally, in Indonesia, the "porn laws" of the 2000s are not about pornography per se but about the regulation of female clothing and demeanor, including public displays of affection.[15] Such examples help to make evident the risks involved in any general inter- or cross-continental diagnoses of pornification, given that the notion of porn is understood in drastically different ways across cultural contexts. Furthermore, such examples point out the obvious fact that while North American perspectives and concerns remain dominant in academic discussions, these are as particular and specific in their contexts and premises as any other regional debates.

It may well be that the ambiguities and imprecisions inherent in the term "pornification" cancel out its constructive uses as an analytical concept used for exploring transformations in the public accessibility and visibility of pornography. Rather than explaining or describing cultural tendencies in their complexity, pornification may create a fallacious impression of order and unity and obscure ruptures and mutually conflicting developments from view. Is it then possible to put the term into productive use, despite such shortcomings? Some years ago my answer would have been affirmative. I currently remain more skeptical.

A DUALISTIC LEGACY

Easy overarching diagnoses of "pornification," "porning," and the "main-streaming of porn" risk effacing distinctions between different pornographic styles and subgenres at the very moment when such distinctions are more pronounced than ever. Indeed, generalized debates on the "pornification of culture" risk crafting a master narrative out of diverse and often conflicting cultural tendencies. The range and volume of available pornography has expanded and commercial pornography has grown fragmented with the ubiquity of digital production tools and distribution platforms (a point addressed below in more detail). Consequently, the mainstream of porn is no longer what it used to be. This is a point—and perhaps one of the only points—on which authors identifying as anti-porn and anti-anti-porn can equally agree.

According to anti-porn criticisms, porn has grown increasingly violent, sexist, and generally nasty with the rise of gonzo porn and the plethora of available online pornographies since the 1990s.[16] Anti-anti-porn, pro-sex, and pro-porn authors again tend to argue that the spread of digital production tools and distribution platforms have fuelled the rise of marginal, experimental, and highly specific forms and markets of pornography that operate with aesthetics, ethics, and economies that differ from those of video production companies. This is seen to diversify the very notion of pornography.[17] In his recent book, *Porno? Chic!*, McNair returns to his earlier arguments concerning the mainstreaming of porn and argues that its increased cultural visibility, volume, and acceptability correlates with the democracy, openness, and gender equality of the said culture. In other words, the more liberal the porn legislation of a particular country is, the more liberal the culture is bound to be. Such optimistic diagnoses remain far less vocal than anti-porn views that link the mainstreaming of porn with violence against women, and the ubiquity of online pornography with its increasing acceptability.[18]

While the individual contributions to the so-called porn wars are far from lacking in complexity, ambition, or rigor, a simplistic tendency to frame pornography as either good or bad tends to resurface in discussions of the genre. As the term "war" implies, the scenario is one of opposing camps in active conflict, and no peace agreement has been reached between the two to date. And as the recurrent terminology—or labeling—of "anti," "anti-anti," and "pro" stances further suggests, the mode of interaction between these positions tends not to be generous and seldom amounts to critique as a "form of intellectual work that requires engaging closely with a range of work."[19] Rather, the framing of authors as "for or against" and strictly in opposition to one another impedes productive dialogue among scholars, activists, and practitioners with differing stances on the topic. Such bipolarity feeds selective, purposeful readings of other people's work and helps to efface nuances and complexities from the debate. Divergent opinions are easily dismissed, and people are labeled as either naïve or uncritical. The debate therefore risks being an exercise in thinking against and talking past, rather than an attempt at productive dialogue.[20] The categorical division of anti- and pro-porn works to pit authors against each other in a categorical manner and leaves the denominator of "pornography" afloat without closer definition.

I have personally found the continuing legacy of the sex wars something of a surprise. In the Finnish context in which I work, the dynamics of the sex wars are recognizable, yet they were never really waged in the Nordic countries.[21] Consequently, there is no assumption of scholars locating themselves as anti- or pro-pornography in order to study the genre. Regionally specific dynamics of the debate have nevertheless become, through the predominance of the English language as the lingua franca of academia, the general framework for contextualizing research done on pornography. At the same time, being for or against cultural phenomena, or specific images, before setting out to study them, strikes me simply as an untenable scholarly practice. For how is one to know a phenomenon before studying it? How is one to analyze the specificities of the materials studied if one presumably already knows what they are about, and has judged them accordingly?

When publishing in English, I have found my work interpreted within the dualistic framework of anti-porn and anti-anti-porn scholarship, despite my attempts to start somewhere different—namely, from a position of curiosity that does not presume mastery or categorical knowledge over what porn is, what it does, or what it can do. This simply means resisting the temptation to generalize at the expense of being sensitive to context. Rather than addressing pornography as a cultural, social, or political symbol and metaphor, I understand it as a historically evolved popular genre, which, like all genres, includes certain conventions and stock features, but is also volatile, contingent, and open to variation and change. Porn is among the most generic of popular genres, and while its conventions do not change overnight,[22] they gradually and continually do. New conventions are born and older ones open up to variation; body styles and audiovisual aesthetics alter; trends come and go; older porn imageries return as reflexive citations; and porn consumers remain suspended between the anticipation of the familiar and the titillation of novelty.[23] Porn involves both transformation and repetition, both difference and sameness: for Sarah Schaschek, this dual dynamic in fact underpins the serial nature of the genre.[24]

Not presuming to know that which one sets out to study beforehand, being open to surprises, and willing to account for the complexity of the phenomenon at hand is by no means a novel starting point for cultural analysis. If it comes across as such in the context of porn, this is solely due to the political and ideological investments involved.

INDEXES OF DIFFERENCE

The genre of porn currently involves more diversity than ever before. At the same time, the binary legacy of the "porn wars" continues to orient and limit the debate through dualistic conceptualizations of the politics and ideologies of the genre. This binary logic may lead to the framing of pornography (as a presumably singular entity) as a cultural metaphor, symbol, or symptom—of, for example, contemporary Western culture, late capitalism, cultural trans-formation, gender ideology, online cultures, the unruliness of desire, work-ing-class sensibility and anti-bourgeois aesthetics, or hegemonic forms of sexuality. "Pornification" can then be understood to intensify and accelerate such cultural tendencies and their public articulation. However, since general symptomatic and symbolic readings efficiently do away with the complexity, fragmentation, and instability of pornography as a genre, they fail to capture much of what they seek to address.

The dualistic framework of the porn debate contributes to the effacement of differences within the category of pornography by producing and resorting to overarching definitions of what the genre means, symbolizes, facilitates, or affects. Indeed, discussions on porn often involve the logic of synecdoche according to which any example (an isolated image, text, video, or website) can be invested with the power to stand and speak for the genre as a whole. When and if such isolated examples are taken as representative of "pornogra-phy" as a presumably coherent entity, the genre can be defined in endless ways and in accordance with a broad range of theoretical, ethical, and politi-cal passions and concerns. By choosing particular kinds of materials to study, it is possible to justify one's premise of what pornography arguably stands for. One can choose from the products of large and well-established compa-nies working cross-platform in a range of media, amateur videos, alternative porn sites featuring subcultural styles, porn produced for local (geographical, national, linguistic, or ethnic) markets, extreme, artful, vintage, or humorous porn, porn for straight men, women, or couples, gay porn and lesbian porn, transgender porn, queer porn, extreme fetish porn, shock porn, and many things beyond and besides. The plethora of available porn guarantees that virtually any stance on porn can be backed up with multiple examples sup-porting the specific argument to be outlined. Studying one set of materials nevertheless says little about the others, and any generalization made about pornography can be countered with numerous examples that point to some-thing different altogether—be this in terms of ethics, politics, sexual prefer-ences, economics, or any combination thereof.

Online, porn producers range from well-established video production stu-dios (such as Vivid or Private) to small companies, individual entrepreneurs, and amateurs sharing their work: porn may be distributed for a fee, in return for membership registration, openly, or illegally. Diverse porn niches and fringes have gained unprecedented visibility while digital media, and networked media in particular, have drastically impacted the forms and possibilities that porn consumption currently takes.[25] With their interaction options, webcam sites blur the boundaries between pornography and live sex entertainment and digital production tools have facilitated an explosion in amateur pornography, which has further contributed to the diversification of online porn while also challenging the hegemony of professionally produced visual and audiovisual material.

Distinctions are crucial in the contemporary production, promotion, and distribution of porn. Alternative and independent pornographers profile their imageries against the mainstream,[26] amateur porn challenges the overall plastic fakeness of commercial porn,[27] and porn produced for local markets is defined by its divergence from the U.S. porn that dominates the markets internationally[28] — to cite a few examples. In terms of niches and subgenres, distinctions involve much more than the general denominators of "straight," "gay," "BDSM," "anal," or "amateur," as made familiar in the video or DVD listings of the 1990s. The metasite www.gigagalleries.com quickly illustrates the point with its listing of the categories of porn images and videos for which it provides links. In the letter R, for example, one encounters the options "Raunchy," "Real Doll," "Rectal Exam," "Red Bottom," "Redhead," "Retro," "Revenge," "Reverse Gangbang," "Rich," "Riding," "Rimjob," "Rodox," "Rough," "Rubber," and "Russian." These tags and search terms define the acts performed, the body styles of the performers, the framework and style of the action, narrative framing, objects used, as well as national origins.

Porn distributed in pre-web newsgroups and BBSs (bulletin board systems) was difficult to index, whereas web portals, metasites, search engines, links, and tags have facilitated, and indeed necessitated, the use of specific subcategories, titles, and terms from which users can choose.[29] Indexing and tagging have opened up a seemingly endless range of distinctions that are used to identify and find a particular image, video, or text, as well as to mark these specific works apart from others. The degree of nuance available in contemporary porn browsing is first supported and fuelled by information architecture, namely the structure of files and hypertext links comprising any given website that renders files accessible to the user. Second, image and video files have to be searchable with the aid of metadata, textual information concerning their style and content. Labeling and tagging facilitates the classification of content that is very much a necessity on web platforms. Third, classification links to the attention economy of the web that necessitates the perpetual flow of specificities and novelties for users to discover. Novelties and curiosa generate clicks and visits that make the site more valuable for advertisers and increase the value of the site in question. To mark themselves apart from the competition, and to attract the attention, interest, or at least the curiosity of random users, porn sites aim to offer novelties and specialties. By doing so, they both form new micromarkets and increase the visibility of sexual fetishes and kinks that have previously been deemed marginal.[30] Due to the diversification of content driven by the more general attention economy of the web where clicks translate into value, the logic of synecdoche is likely to fail in accounting for the shapes and forms that pornography takes, the ways in which it is consumed, and the effects that it may have.

Video publishing and sharing sites following the operating principles of YouTube, but focusing on pornographic content excluded from that particular platform—such as YouPorn, RedTube, 8Tube, and PornoTube—have, since 2005, altered the accessibility and searchability of porn video clips and facilitated the increased accessibility of content produced by professionals, amateurs, professional amateurs, and semi-amateurs. Amateur porn has been produced for decades as written stories, photographs, films, and drawings, yet the affordability and ease of digital imaging—combined with the ease of online distribution—has marked a radical increase in its availability and volume.[31] With the avalanche of free content produced, or at least uploaded and circulated by users, the profit margins of porn are gradually shifting from production to distribution. Shifts in production tools and distribution platforms have, then, impacted shifts in how the very notion of the porn industry can be explored. While porn studios and institutions such as the Adult Video News awards remain, the notion of the porn industry as the generator and distributor of porn has become somewhat unstable. Users uploading their own pornographies to be shared with others are both pornographers and porn performers (if not necessarily "stars"). In this sense, the porn industry has expanded into something of a cottage industry of independent actors who often work for no pay at all. At the same time, access to online porn has been centralized as video clips are searched for and watched through tube sites, the largest of which are among the top 150 sites globally.[32]

The success of tube sites, enabled by the increase in affordable broadband connections and the ubiquity of Internet connectivity in the 2000s, has marked a shift not only towards amateur porn but also towards the format of the clip. This transformation has to do with both media formats—DVD disks versus .flv, .mpeg, .avi, or .swf files—and the form of the pornography consumed. Audiovisual porn produced on film, analog, and digital video has always been episodic. In films with a narrative framework, action routinely consists of "numbers" (oral, anal, girl-on-girl, masturbation, threesome), which, much like the dance numbers in musicals, tend to disrupt any narrative flow.[33] The episodic nature of porn films became increasingly pronounced in DVD releases of the 2000s that may be three hours long. In contrast, video clips produced for and distributed through file-sharing and video sites are detached from any broader narrative entity. They are generally short and lack a story beyond a possible establishing shot or textual description: in thousands and thousands of videos, people just get it on.

When writing about the "golden age" of porn in the 1970s, film scholar Linda Williams frames later developments in video porn and beyond in terms of loss: "pornography itself would devolve in the following decade into the parallel universe of mostly cheaply made, badly acted, and aesthetically impoverished sucking and fucking shots on video."[34] In Williams' account, the failure of pornography to become more like mainstream narrative cinema resulted in and contributed to its poor technical and aesthetic quality. Yet it can be argued that narrative has by no means been the most important feature of pornography that has, from its origins, focused on sucking and fucking shots. While such shots—these days distributed as clips—may tell a story,[35] this is not to say that the attraction of porn is about narrative, or that narrative is by necessity central to how porn scenes are organized and experienced. The tendency to see narrative feature film as an aesthetic norm in studies of pornography is problematic in that it renders all other developments in, and incarnations of, porn as inferior variations. Analysis focusing on the story is unlikely to capture much of the form or appeal of contemporary video porn. On a tube site, users search for specific acts, performers, and styles, and move from one clip to another on the basis of search hits and site recommendations. The act of watching is both continuous and discontinuous or fragmented.

The tendency to foreground narrative in studies of porn dovetails with the tendency to draw on models of spectatorship specific to the cultural form of cinema when studying all kinds of pornographies. The fact that pornography can be projected onto a cinema screen (of varying size), watched on a TV screen, computer screen, or the screen of a mobile device, does not mean that these different interfaces and the experiences they involve can be conceptualized with the same tools. These activities can be broadly defined as screen-based, yet there are obvious differences in watching a film on a cinema screen or on one's laptop at home (in terms of the social setting, privacy, and intimacy), watching a porn video on a DVD or VHS player attached to a TV screen, or browsing through websites with thousands of videos available for download and webcam sites to choose from. The forms that pornography takes, and the experiences it affords, are always mediated and conditioned by particular technical set-ups and media forms that need to be accounted for.

CONCLUSIONS

The dynamics of the academic porn debate are inseparable both from the threefold development outlined above (i.e., shifts in porn production/distribution, regulation, and cultural visibility) and the transformations within the pornographic to which they connect and contribute. These developments make evident that the influence of the web on the shapes and experiences of porn far exceeds the role of a passive channel or platform, and it is indeed impossible to understand contemporary porn outside the specificities of online platforms. The accumulation of different pornographies, combined with its easy and often free accessibility online, is a key reason for pornography having resurfaced as a topic of cultural debate. Rather than resorting to ready-tailored views of what pornography is or means, it is necessary to ask what shapes it currently takes and how scholarly perspectives can accommodate such transformations. As I have argued above, preconceived notions concerning the genre have limited validity in the sense that the diversity of current pornography makes it hard to reduce porn to familiar categorizations and to discuss it as a singular entity.

Scholarly investigations of pornography would do well to embrace the ethos of not already knowing: of being open to the phenomena studied without falling back on the dualistic legacy of the porn debates (as either for or against), and not making use of the readily available instruments derived from studies of other media forms without first conceptualizing the transformations that have occurred. Critical engagements with the imageries and economies of pornography cannot be built on categorical assumptions of the genre as a unified or fixed entity. "Pornification" is therefore not an explanation for the current developments addressed above, but rather something of a weak diagnosis concerning them. In order for analyses of "pornification"— or, perhaps better, the onscenity of porn—to have critical edge or political salience, they need to be specific and based on an understanding of both the dynamics of pornography as a contingent genre and of its (equally contingent) technological underpinnings.

NOTES

1. Brian McNair, *Striptease Culture: Sex, Media and the Democratization of Desire* (New York: Routledge, 2002); Brian McNair, *Porno? Chic! How Pornography Changed the World and Made It a Better Place* (London: Routledge, 2013); Feona Attwood, "Sexed Up: Theorizing the Sexualization of Culture," *Sexualities* 9, no. 1 (2006): 77–94; Feona Attwood, "Introduction: The Sexualization of Culture," in *Mainstreaming Sex: The Sexualization of Western Culture,* ed. Feona Attwood (London: I. B. Tauris, 2009), xiii–xxiv; Susanna Paasonen, Kaarina Nikunen, and Laura Saarenmaa, "Pornification and the Education of Desire," in *Pornification: Sex and Sexuality in Media Culture,* ed. Susanna Paasonen, Kaarina Nikunen, and Laura Saarenmaa (Oxford: Berg, 2007), 1–20; Pamela Paul, *Pornified: How Pornography Is Damaging Our Lives, Our Relationships, and Our Families* (New York: Owl Books, 2005); Ariel Levy, *Female Chauvinist Pigs: Women and the Rise of Raunch Culture* (New York: Free Press, 2005); Carmine Sarracino and Kevin M. Scott, *The Porning of America: The Rise of Porn Culture, What It Means, and Where We Go from Here* (Boston: Beacon Press, 2008); Ann C. Hall and Mardia J. Bishop, eds., *Pop-Porn: Pornography in American Culture* (Westport, CT: Praeger, 2007).

2. Linda Williams, *Screening Sex* (Durham, NC: Duke University Press, 2008); see also the Onscenity Research Network, http://www.onscenity.org/ (accessed 27 Aug. 2013).

3. For a notable exception, see McNair, *Porno? Chic!*

4. Paasonen, Nikunen, and Saarenmaa, "Pornification and the Education of Desire," 2–13.

5. Feona Attwood, Meg Barker, Sara Bragg, Danielle Egan, Adrienne Evans, Laura Harvey, Gail Hawkes, Jamie Heckert, Naomi Holford, Jan Macvarish, Amber Martin, Alan McKee, Sharif Mowlabocus, Susanna Paasonen, Emma Renold, Jessica Ringrose, Ludi Valentine, Anne Frances Watson, and Liesbet van Zoonen, "Engaging with the Bailey Review: Blogging, Academia and Authenticity," *Psychology and Sexuality* 3, no. 1 (2012): 69–94.

6. Emily Shelton, "A Star is Porn: Corpulence, Comedy, and the Homosocial Cult of Adult Film Star Ron Jeremy," *Camera Obscura* 17, no. 3 (2002): 115–46; Sarah Schaschek, *Pornography and Seriality: The Culture of Producing Pleasure* (New York: Palgrave, 2013).

7. Rick Poynor, *Designing Pornotopia: Travels in Visual Culture* (New York: Princeton Architectural Press, 2006), 132.

8. McNair, *Striptease Culture*, 61.

9. McNair, *Striptease Culture*, 70.

10. Consider, for example, the perennial popularity of incest scenarios in written erotica (e.g., Susanna Paasonen, "Good Amateurs: Erotica Writing and Notions of Quality," in *Porn.com: Making Sense of Online Pornography*, ed. Feona Attwood [New York: Peter Lang 2010], 138–54).

11. Walter Kendrick, *The Secret Museum: Pornography in Modern Culture*. Second Edition (Berkeley: University of California Press, 1999).

12. Annette Kuhn, *The Power of the Image: Essays on Representation and Sexuality* (London: Routledge, 1994), 23.

13. Susanna Paasonen, "Healthy Sex and Pop Porn: Pornography, Feminism and the Finnish Context," *Sexualities* 12, no. 5 (2009): 586–604.

14. Shohini Ghosh, "The Troubled Existence of Sex and Sexuality: Feminists Engage with Censorship," in *Gender and Censorship*, ed. Brinda Bose (New Delhi: Women Unlimited, 2006), 273.

15. Merlyna Lim, "Life Is Local in the Imagined Global Community: Islam and Politics in the Indonesian Blogosphere," *Journal of Media and Religion* 11, no. 3 (2012): 127–40.

16. Robert Jensen, *Getting Off: Pornography and the End of Masculinity* (Cambridge, MA: South End Press, 2007); Gail Dines, *Pornland: How Porn Has Hijacked Our Sexuality* (Boston: Beacon Press, 2011).

17. Katrien Jacobs, *Netporn: DIY Web Culture and Sexual Politics* (Lanham, MD: Rowman & Littlefield, 2007); Katrien Jacobs, Marije Janssen, and Matteo Pasquinelli, "Introduction," in *C'lick Me: A Netporn Studies Reader*, ed. Katrien Jacobs, Marije Janssen, and Matteo Pasquinelli (Amsterdam: Institute of Network Cultures, 2007), 1–3.

18. See Karen Boyle, "Introduction: Everyday Pornography," in *Everyday Pornography*, ed. Karen Boyle (London: Routledge, 2010), 1–13.

19. Sara Ahmed, "Imaginary Prohibitions: Some Preliminary Remarks on the Founding Gesture of 'New Materialism,'" *European Journal of Women's Studies* 15, no. 1 (2008): 30.

20. As soon as Routledge publicized the plan to launch its new peer review journal, *Porn Studies*, in the summer of 2013, a petition was launched for either cancelling the journal or changing its name to Pro-Porn Studies. According to the petition, quickly signed by hundreds of scholars and activists, the editorial board is pro-porn and bound to be partial in its editorial choices and review policies. This occurred before any review work had been done, and with no attention to how the members of the editorial board identify themselves. The anecdote is telling of how the compulsive binary nature of the anti- and pro-porn debate obstructs scholarly dialogue—and indeed research—on pornography beyond simplified, even cartoonish, labeling.

21. See Don Kulick, "Four Hundred Thousand Swedish Perverts," *GLQ: A Journal of Lesbian and Gay Studies* 11, no. 2 (2005): 205–35; Paasonen, "Healthy Sex and Pop Porn."

22. Jane Arthurs, *Television and Sexuality: Regulation and the Politics of Taste* (Berkshire, UK: Open University Press, 2004), 43.

23. Susanna Paasonen, *Carnal Resonance: Affect and Online Pornography* (Cambridge, MA: MIT Press, 2011), 115–41, 153–64.

24. Schaschek, *Pornography and Seriality.*

25. See Susanna Paasonen, "Labors of Love: Netporn, Web 2.0, and the Meanings of Amateurism," *New Media and Society* 12, no. 8 (2010): 1297–312; Paasonen, *Carnal Resonance.*

26. See Feona Attwood, "No Money Shot? Commerce, Pornography and New Sex Taste Cultures," *Sexualities* 10, no. 4 (2007): 441–56; Shoshana Magnet, "Feminist Sexualities, Race and the Internet: An Investigation of Suicidegirls.com," *New Media & Society* 9, no. 4 (2007): 577–96.

27. Simon Hardy, "The New Pornographies: Representation or Reality?" in *Mainstreaming Sex: The Sexualization of Western Culture*, ed. Feona Attwood (London: I. B. Tauris, 2009), 3–18; Paasonen, "Labors of Love."

28. See for example Susanna Paasonen, "Homespun: Finnporn and the Meanings of the Local," in *Hard to Swallow: Hard-Core Pornography on Screen*, ed. Darren Kerr and Claire Hines (New York: Wallflower Press, 2012), 177–93.

29. Wendy Hui Kyong Chun, *Control and Freedom: Power and Paranoia in the Age of Fiber Optics* (Cambridge, MA: MIT Press, 2006), 106.

30. David Bennett, "Pornography-Dot-Com: Eroticising Privacy on the Internet." *Review of Education/Pedagogy/Cultural Studies* 23, no. 4 (2001): 384; Mark Dery, "Paradise Lust: Pornotopia Meets the Culture Wars," in *C'lick Me: A Netporn Studies Reader*, ed. Katrien Jacobs, Marije Janssen, and Matteo Pasquinelli (Amsterdam: Institute of Network Cultures, 2007), 125–48.

31. Paasonen, *Carnal Resonance,* 71–72, 78–88.

32. See Alexa ratings for top 500 sites: http://www.alexa.com/topsites .

33. Linda Williams, *Hard Core: Power, Pleasure, and the "Frenzy of the Visible"* (Berkeley: University of California Press, 1989), 48–49.

34. Williams, *Screening Sex*, 128.

35. Richard Dyer, *The Culture of Queers* (London: Routledge, 2002), 142.

Chapter Two

Pornography Makes the Man

The Impact of Pornography as a Component of Gender and Sexual Socialization

Matthew B. Ezzell

In the spring of 2013 I taught a course on the sociology of gender at James Madison University. As a class, we were discussing media and gender socialization, and, not surprisingly, the topic of pornography came up. I mentioned to the class that I was interested in studying male pornography *refusers*—men who make a conscious choice, for any reason, not to consume pornography. Without pause, one of the men in the class blurted out, "Good luck finding them!" The class laughed.

The man's joke and the ensuing laughter reflect existing patterns of pornography consumption among young men in the United States. Put simply, the overwhelming majority of college age males are active consumers.[1] In my own research with an international team of scholars from the fields of communication studies, psychology, and sociology, in fact, we found that 89.1 percent of young men in the United States are active consumers. Of that group, 58.7 percent consume pornography weekly and 13.2 percent engage in daily consumption, mostly (97.4 percent) via the Internet and almost exclusively (99.5 percent) for free. Further, in a shift from previous research[2] we found that almost half of our respondents (48.7 percent) had exposure to pornography prior to the age of thirteen. In this context, although men may choose to consume pornography for any number of reasons (entertainment, escape, release, revenge), it is clear that pornography is something more than fantasy. It is, instead, real: the men and women used in its production are real, the money traded in global commerce around it is real, the consumers are real, and the impact that it has on those consumers—and on others in consumers' lives—is real. At the most basic level, pornography is now a core component of boys' and young men's gender and sexual socialization. How can we make sense of it?

SEX, GENDER, PATRIARCHY, AND MANHOOD

One of the first questions asked of a pregnant woman is "Are you having a boy or a girl?" Many expectant parents who have not "found out" the anticipated biological sex of the fetus have faced frustration and, sometimes, anger from friends and family who wonder how they will buy a gift for the baby shower. Such routine interactions highlight the centrality of sex and gender as organizing principles of social life, the belief in two-and-only-two discrete sexes, our cultural conflation of biological sex and cultural gendered identities, and the gendering processes that begin before a fetus has left the womb.

To clarify terms often confused in dominant cultural discourse, when we refer to "sex" we are typically referring to body markers/signs that we label "female" and "male." And, as noted, only two options are generally put forward. But that is not all that occurs biologically in the human condition. Biologist Anne Fausto-Sterling, in fact, argues that biological sex is not a clear-cut and natural distinction in the human species, but a continuum of difference: "While male and female stand on the extreme ends of a biological continuum, there are many bodies . . . that evidently mix together anatomical components conventionally attributed to both males and females."[3] Sex, in the way we typically think of it, is not a given. And yet we have created a two-sex system that is enforced culturally and politically, and it is so deeply woven into the fabric of our social world as to appear natural and inborn. It is neither. We must uphold it through rituals of daily interaction, many of which are taken for granted. My student's joke in class, for example, can be read as an interactional display of "manliness," a way to place himself, as a "man" in this system, in the category of pornography "user" and to also reaffirm pornography consumption as a normative component of masculine signification.

My student's comment highlights one of the ways that we perform the gendered "cultural conceits"[4] of masculinity and femininity—expectations, norms, and values associated with "being a man" or "being a woman"—that are laid on top of the cultural construction of a male/female dichotomy. Importantly, gender is not something that we *are* but something that we *do*.[5] In that sense, our gendered identities must be achieved and maintained. It is important to note, further, that gender is not a category of difference but a category of *inequality*. To signify a gendered identity is to claim status within an economy of power. "Being a man" carries more cultural weight than "being a woman." Because they are culturally constructed, the hegemonic ideals of masculinity and femininity shift across time and place, but within the gendered economy of power masculinity is necessarily about dominance, and femininity is necessarily subordinated in relation to it.[6]

We live in a patriarchy. Sociologist Allan G. Johnson argues that social systems are patriarchal to the extent that they are male-dominated, male-identified, and male-centered.[7] This means that under patriarchy men tend to be in positions of power and authority, what is seen as normative and valuable tends to be associated with men and masculinity, and the cultural focus of attention tends to be on men and the things that men do. This does not mean that every male in our society has equal access to the use of power over women or feels powerful in his life. Many men do not feel powerful, in fact, and many feel like failures *as men* because the cultural mandates of masculinity are impossible to fully attain. This can be particularly difficult terrain for boys to navigate. Violence prevention educator Paul Kivel summarizes the constellation of meanings associated with modern patriarchal masculinity as follows: "Be tough, be aggressive, don't back down, don't make mistakes, be in control, take charge, have lots of [heterosexual] sex, have money, be responsible, don't show any feelings, and don't cry."[8] Although these messages are both impossible to fulfill and personally unhealthy, boys often internalize them, as they come early and often. And the stakes are high as the bounds of gender presentation and performance are policed in subtle and overt ways, up to and including acts of physical and sexual violence.

Because patriarchal masculine ideals are impossible to fully achieve and because of intersections of systems of privilege and oppression, many boys and men cannot reap what sociologist R.W. Connell calls the full "patriarchal dividend"—the advantages typically conferred on males in a patriarchal society.[9] When men's access to patriarchal advantages is threatened in some way, or when their claim to a masculine self is discredited, they may resort to displays of compensatory masculinity.[10] That is, in an effort to make up for their lack of access to the highest benefits and privileges of men in a patriarchal context, they may perform exaggerated "manhood acts"—acts that signify a masculine self and are "aimed at claiming privilege, eliciting deference, and resisting exploitation."[11] Men perform compensatory manhood acts in many social settings. Some men with physical disabilities, for example, may center their masculine identities on the control they exert over others occupationally, while others may (over)emphasize their physical strength, athleticism, or sexual prowess.[12] As one man with physical disabilities put it: "I've overcompensated by trying to please my [sexual] partner and leave little room to allow my partner to please me. . . . Some of my greatest pleasure is exhausting my partner while having sex."[13] This example highlights the importance of (hetero)sexual prowess as a signifying act of manhood under modern constructions of patriarchal masculinity. And within that fact we can glimpse one of the functions of pornography under patriar-chy—it is both a means through which boys and young men are socialized to understand what it means to "be a man" sexually and, through its consump-tion, a signifying manhood act, a means through which boys and young men enact an identity as a man.

PORN MAKES THE MAN

Pornography exposure for young boys today is, as noted, nearly ubiquitous. In the absence of comprehensive sex and sexuality education in the schools and in the absence of comprehensive and timely discussions about sex be-tween parents and their children, pornography and other forms of sexualized media function as the primary source of adolescents' sex education.[14] For example, in our study my colleagues and I found that although 89.1 percent of men are active pornography consumers, only 31.4 percent agreed or strongly agreed that sex education at school was helpful to them in learning about sex, and only 24.6 percent agreed or strongly agreed that sex education at home was helpful. In this context, pornography serves as a powerful source of information about sex, gender, and sexuality that is not mitigated by alternate forms of sex education. What is the content of this education?

The overwhelming bulk of modern pornography is created by and for heterosexual men. Of course, women and other populations of men also consume pornography, but these groups have been under-researched and the driving force of the industry, in terms of sales and production, remains fo-cused on heterosexual men.[15] The content of pornographic media varies from still images in magazines and websites to videos and films available on the Internet or on DVDs. Still images are produced across a wide continuum: glossy and "pretty" images of women by themselves in a range of poses and engaged in a range of activities (standing in a field, bathing, penetrating themselves, etc.) to images of women with other people engaged in a range of activities (various sex acts, bondage, etc.). Despite the wide availability of "tamer" fare, the driving force of the industry is increasingly "harsher" mate-rial that is more explicitly degrading, aggressive, and violent. For example, in content analysis of industry-identified top-selling videos, psychologist Ana J. Bridges and her colleagues found that over 88 percent of scenes involve acts of physical aggression (e.g., spanking, gagging, hair pulling, choking, and slapping)—overwhelmingly against women—while over 48 percent involve verbal aggression, principally name calling (e.g., "bitch" or "slut").[16] This highlights the ways that the mainstream pornography industry is phallocratic—it typifies male power and dominance.

Exhibiting such a phallocratic orientation, Bridges and her colleagues found that in the 88 percent of pornographic scenes involving overt physical aggression, over 95 percent of those aggressed against responded with neutrality or pleasure.[17] Mainstream pornography, thus, constructs a particular representation of masculinity tied to sexualized aggression and a representation of femininity tied to sexual subordination and (desired) victimization. These representations are expressions of the hegemonic ideals of masculinity and femininity under modern patriarchy and, given the early age of first exposure and high rate of consumption among boys and young men, they can be particularly powerful in shaping boys and young men's sense of self and others.

As noted above, in our research my colleagues and I found that almost half of our respondents had been exposed to pornography prior to the age of thirteen. Research shows that a majority (70 percent) of these early exposures are unintentional.[18] Whether it is intentional or not, however, research also demonstrates that children's reactions to early exposure to sexualized media are commonly negative: disgust, shock, embarrassment, anger, fear, and/or sadness.[19] Such early exposure may be to harsh or "extreme" material, and the children may not have the cognitive skills or resources to critically engage it. As an example, in 2012 I spoke with a small group of high school–aged boys (fifteen to sixteen years old) about pornography and sexuality. The group of boys did not know one another, but they had all seen the same pornographic material because of the popularity of peer-to-peer file-sharing networks and the common practice of sharing material via e-mail and/or text messages with friends.[20] Although they had seen the same material and shared it with other friends, none of the boys had actually talked about what they had seen with those friends or shared their feelings in response to it. In our discussion, they described explicit acts of violence, bondage, scat-fetishism (material centered around a sexualized focus on feces), and bestiality, and they had no idea what to do with what they had seen. They had encountered depictions of interactions that they could not imagine enjoying themselves. But, because the women in the material had all responded with pleasure, the boys were scared and perplexed. They asked, "Is that what girls actually want?" "How could they like that?" "Are girls going to expect me to do that to them?"

Despite the common experience of early negative reactions to pornography, the majority (89.1 percent in my research) of boys and young men go on to engage in active consumption. And regardless of the fact that boys and young men may not purposefully seek out displays of sexualized violence and aggression against women when they first become consumers, interview data with consumers and content analysis of online forums suggest that exposure to "harsher" content is difficult to avoid[21] and that many men's consumption follows a pattern of desensitization and escalation such that they actively look for more extreme material over time.[22] So, boys and young men on the whole experience early exposure to pornography, go on to become regular and active consumers in large numbers, and tend to seek out more extreme material the longer they consume. Why and how is this important?

MEDIA MATTER[23]

What we consume on the page or the screen has implications for life off of it. The majority of social science research on pornography has focused on its effects, particularly on consumers' attitudes and behaviors. However, debates are ongoing regarding the usefulness of effects research.[24] Experimental research, for example, may give us clues about the ways in which consumers interact with media, but it has limitations. For example, answers to questions about attitudes toward women do not necessarily speak to the enactment of any particular behaviors. Experiments also do not replicate the conditions of consuming pornography as part of a daily or weekly practice over the course of years. Further, experimental studies do not replicate the ways that boys and men use pornographic material to facilitate masturbation.[25]

Addressing some of these concerns, more recent research has begun to question the ways that media translate into perceptions of reality, attitudes, and behavior. This line of research springs out of "cognitive scripts" theory, which posits that media influence attitudes and behavior by providing a heuristic model outlining "what should or should not be happening, how people should or should not behave in response to what is or is not happening and what the outcomes of a particular course of action should be."[26] Building off of communications scholar and psychologist L. Rowell Huesmann's work on information processing, in addition to social cognitive theory,[27] cultivation analysis,[28] uses and gratifications theory,[29] media dependency theory,[30] and priming theory,[31] communications scholar Paul Wright developed a sexual script acquisition, activation, application ($_3$AM) model of sexual socialization that explains how exposure to media can impact behavior.[32] Put simply, the $_3$AM model argues that media shape our worldview by creating a readily accessible heuristic model (i.e., a script) for decision making. This approach addresses some of the criticisms of previous effects research as it provides a model for the links between attitudes and behaviors, theorizes the impact of media consumption over time, and includes analyses of the context and experience of media consumption on the potential impact of that media.

Sociologists John Gagnon and William Simon in 1973 first theorized the "sexual script" as a core component of sexual socialization that could provide a worldview that guides and shapes sexual decision making.[33] This conception of the sexual script is similar to symbolic interactionist understandings of social life.[34] Using the dramaturgical metaphor of social life as theater, symbolic interactionists theorize that social life is played out by social actors presenting selves and enacting roles on social stages in front of various audiences. Scripts, in this conception, provide the guidelines for lines of action in a given social context. Put simply, and in regard to sexual behavior, scripts "tell us how to behave sexually."[35]

According to Huesmann and as applied to pornography by Wright in his $_3$AM model, these sexual scripts must first be acquired (capture the attention of the consumer) and activated (called to mind by the consumer in context) before they are applied (used to guide decision making). All three steps can be moderated by other factors, including *audience* factors (e.g., gender, age, motivations, existing sexual scripts, moral standards, media dependency, apathy, forethought), *content* factors (e.g., arousal value, salience, prevalence, rewards and punishments), *accessibility* factors (e.g., context, frequency and duration of exposure, vividness), as well as *situational* factors (e.g., sexual arousal, script-situation correspondence). Given the increased anonymity, accessibility, and affordability of online pornography, the barriers to acquisition are low. The prevalence and salience of pornographic sexual scripts, in fact, make them almost impossible to avoid. More frequent use and consumption patterns that develop over the course of years, particularly when consumption involves cognitive and/or enactive rehearsal (i.e., masturbation to orgasm), increases the likelihood of activation. Once the pornographic sexual script is acquired and activated, particularly in the absence of meaningful and alternative sexual scripts, it can be applied in real-world contexts.

In these ways, the $_3$AM model breaks down the effects process into three components—the impact of media on acquisition of sexual scripts, the impact of media on the activation of sexual scripts, and the impact of media on the application of sexual scripts. Springing out of this model, and based on his review of accumulated studies that address sexual behavior, Wright concludes that sexualized media "almost certainly exert a causal influence on youths' sexual behavior."[36] To put this in other terms, the earlier boys and men are exposed to pornography and the more they consume and the longer that consumption takes place, in a context lacking effective or meaningful alternative scripts for gender and sexuality, the more likely pornography will directly shape the attitudes and behaviors of those boys and men.

In what ways can pornography shape the experiences and behaviors of boys and men? Some researchers have found positive[37] or neutral[38] effects. For example, in its function as a primary form of sex education for young people, pornography *can* provide information about the human body and sexual practices, thus increasing a sense of sexual competence and decreasing a sense of sexual shame.[39] But other research suggests that the impact of pornography can be negative. In a thorough review of existing literature, for example, sociologist Michael Flood notes that pornography consumption can shift boys' and men's sexual practices and expectations, harm female partners' sense of intimacy, encourage sexualized and sexually objectifying understandings of girls and women, and intensify boys' and young men's acceptance of and participation in sexual violence.[40] As an example, Neil Malamuth, Tamara Addison, and Mary Koss found that boys and men who are predisposed to violence (i.e., boys and men who are impulsive, hostile to women, and promiscuous) may seek out violent pornography which, in turn, may increase their likelihood of engaging in sexually aggressive and controlling behavior.[41] Other studies have found that boys and men who habitually consume pornography are more likely to describe women in sexual terms; to view women in stereotypical ways; to hold attitudes supportive of violence against women, and/or to engage in acts of violence against women;[42] that pornography consumption is associated with having multiple sexual partners; paying for sex;[43] and having lower levels of commitment in romantic relationships and higher likelihoods of infidelity;[44] and that consumers of paraphilic pornography (i.e., BDSM, fetishism, bestiality, and/or violent/coercive pornography) are more likely to experience diminished overall sexual satisfaction due to suppressed empathy for their sexual partners.[45]

Interviews with consumers speak in concert with the empirical studies mentioned above. Based on a nationally representative poll and in-depth interviews, U.S. journalist Pamela Paul documented a range of self-identified personal effects of pornography consumption.[46] Although some respondents highlighted positive effects, many men spoke to negative effects as well, including habituation and desensitization; an increased tendency to objectify women in and outside of pornography; pushing sexual partners to try positions/practices seen in pornography; pressuring women to have sex; experiencing sex with partners as boring; dependence on pornography to facilitate masturbation; dependence on mental images of pornography to maintain erections during sex with a partner; and feelings of depression/lack of control. Echoing Paul's work, therapists Wendy and Larry Maltz argue that pornography consumption can negatively shape some users' sexual desires and practices, deaden libido and ability to perform sexually, and compromise users' ability to connect emotionally and sexually with partners.[47]

My colleagues and I found empirical support for these arguments. For example, we found that the more pornography a man watches, the more likely he is to prefer and rely on pornography in order to obtain and maintain sexual excitement and the more likely he is to bring pornography into sexual relationships with a partner. In other words, we found that the more pornography a man consumes, the more likely he is to prefer pornography to sex with a partner, the more likely he is to conjure images of pornography during sex with a partner in order to maintain excitement, and the more likely he is to replicate sex acts seen in pornography during sex with a partner. Further, we found that the more pornography a man watches, the less likely he is to enjoy sexually intimate behaviors (e.g., kissing and cuddling), the more likely he is to experience sexual anxiety (e.g., concerns over sexual performance and penis size), and the more likely he is to sexually objectify women in public. In short, pornography provides men a sexual script that shapes the ways they view and enact their sexual selves, and the more pornography a man consumes, the more he comes to depend on it for that enactment.

THE MALE CONSUMER, THE MALE CONSUMED

When men depend on pornography to obtain and maintain sexual excitement, even with a partner, and when men's pornography consumption pushes them toward derivative, nonrelational, and less intimate sexual practices, we can see pornography not as sexual liberation but as sexual limitation. At the same time, the pornography industry and the consumption of pornographic materials reflect and represent hegemonic ideals of masculinity and male dominance. In this way, we can see that, for men, pornography offers a *collective* gain (beliefs in/enactment of male dominance) but exacts an *individual* cost (decreased empathy and intimacy, dependence, anxiety).

Men's choices to consume pornography, as sociologist Jennifer A. Johnson points out, do not occur in a vacuum.[48] Instead, they are exercised within the context of intersecting systems of inequality, namely patriarchy and capitalism. Under the modern system of global corporate capitalism, many men are exploited (by other men) at work at the same time that male dominance is maintained within the larger gender order. And even middle- and upper-class men often experience a gulf between their socialized sense of entitlement to sexual and material power and their own lived realities.[49] This demonstrates what Johnson terms the "male paradox of power" in which many men personally *feel* powerless (or, *less* powerful than they feel entitled to feel) at the same time that men are privileged *as a class*.[50] The consumption of pornography, in this context, functions as a compensatory manhood act because it allows men across the economic spectrum micro-access to the performance of the hegemonic masculine ideal. A man may feel frustrated by the distance between his sense of masculine entitlement to the patriarchal dividend—an entitlement which is acquired, in part, through the consumption of pornography to begin with—and the realities of life under global corporate capitalism. But the consumption of pornography also allows him a means through which to signify male dominance over women. As an example, sociologist Michael Kimmel points out that the sexual mandate of hegemonic masculinity is unattainable, but many young men feel entitled to sex and frustrated by women's perceived control of access to it.[51] Consuming pornography offers a salve, a way to enact masculinity and "correct" the perceived challenge to male dominance across the board. Consider the words of one college-aged man:

My friends and I share a membership [to a paid pornographic website] so we can watch it together. It's like they get all these girls who are like 19 or 20 and they're just walking around town, going to the mall . . . and then these guys offer 'em some money and they like are naked and sucking and fucking these guys they don't even know, and loving it, for like a couple of hundred bucks. Un-fucking-believable. We're all like "oh, bang that bitch!" and "fuck that little ho." And they're like college girls! It's like so cool. Why aren't they like that here in Amherst?[52]

The consumption of such material enables the men to express male dominance, to enact identities *as men*, and to bond as men through their joint consumption of an objectified, commoditized, and degraded female body. As Kimmel notes, in the face of the perceived challenge to the men's conditioned sense of sexual entitlement, "watching these girls' sexual humiliation is a way to level the playing field just a little bit."[53]

MORE THAN A MIND-SET

The impact of pornography goes beyond conditioned attitudes and dependence. It affects real-world social interaction. As my colleagues and I found, the more men consume pornography, the more likely they are to ask their partners to watch pornography with them, the more likely they are to try sex acts viewed in pornography, and the more likely they are to sexually objectify women in public. As I argued in the opening to this chapter, pornography is more than fantasy. It is real. It is implicated in real-world interactions between people. This is true for consensual sexual relationships in addition to instances of men's violence against women.

Mainstream pornography reflects a patriarchal construction of masculinity tied to sexual aggression and dominance, but it is not the only reflection of that construction. Indeed, reflections of patriarchal masculinity saturate our cultural landscape. Yet, the media system, as I argued above, is particularly powerful as a mechanism of gender and sexual socialization because of its pervasive reach, because it is rarely mediated by effective alternative scripts, and because it is pleasurable in form. Pornography, while pervasive and more mainstreamed than ever, is not *the* cause of inequality or sexualized aggression. If pornography were eradicated today there would still be men's violence against women tomorrow. It is more apt to consider pornography and other forms of sexualized media as *enabling conditions* for real-world acts of misogyny and sexual violence.[54] In a world in which popular forms of entertainment and de facto sex education center on male dominance and sexualized depictions of violence and aggression by men against women, and in which the underlying ideology of male dominance and the sexual narratives that reflect it are pervasive and normative, it is more likely that women will be systematically targeted for acts of sexualized aggression by men. Media, in this sense, both reflect and shape social reality. In other words, although media systems emerge in the context of already existing social realities and, thus, reflect those realities, they also function as agents of socialization which act back on, and shape, those realities.

One of the ways that pornography is implicated in real-world examples of men's violence against women can be seen through interviews with survivors of that violence. Some perpetrators use pornography to choreograph their abuse and others use the abuse as an opportunity to make their own pornography. For example, over 22 percent of the women in Martin Schwartz and Walter DeKeseredy's research on sexual assault in Canada reported being upset by a partner's attempts to imitate pornography in either consensual or nonconsensual contexts.[55] Of the women in Raquel Kennedy Bergen and Kathleen Bogle's survey of survivors seeking services from rape crisis centers who knew that their abuser consumed pornography, 40 percent said that the pornography was part of the abuse, with 12 percent of the total sample indicating that pornography was imitated during the abuse.[56] And finally, Diana Russell found that 32 percent of the respondents from a random sample of women in the San Francisco area who reported experiences of wife rape had been asked/forced to pose for pornography as a component of their abuse.[57] Not every man who consumes pornography will enact such violence, and not every woman who experiences men's violence can link her experiences directly to pornography in these ways, but as Bergen and Bogle conclude, it is clear that "pornography plays a role in the sexual violence experienced by some women."[58]

Even when the links are not so immediately direct, we can see the traces of pornographic ideologies surrounding gender, sex, and violence in other examples of sexual interaction between men and women including explicit acts of men's violence. The Steubenville High School rape case is one such example.[59] In August 2012, boys fondled, urinated on, and raped an unconscious sixteen-year-old girl at a series of parties over a six-hour period. The perpetrators and other people at the party took pictures of these assaults and posted the images and comments about the girl and the assaults on Twitter, Facebook, and in text messages. The dismissal of the assault of an unconscious girl and the victim blaming that occurred in the moments of the assault and over the days, weeks, and months that followed was staggering in its callousness.[60] Two of the boys were ultimately found guilty of raping the girl, but victim blaming persisted and public sympathy was often expressed not for the victim—who received death threats following the verdict[61]—but for the boys who raped her. CNN correspondent Poppy Harlow, for example, reflected that it was, "difficult, even for an outsider like [her], to watch what happened as these two young men that had such promising futures, star football players, very good students, literally watched as they believed their lives fell apart."[62]

One of the aspects of this story that stands out is not that it happened, but that it received national and international attention. How many other stories of drug-facilitated and filmed sexual assaults take place that never receive such public scrutiny? In 1988 journalist Robin Warshaw reported that although one in four women had had experiences that met the legal definition of rape, only 5 percent of them had reported those experiences to the police.[63] Women reported that they did not come forward for a range of reasons, including having a relationship with the assailant, having had prior consensual sexual interaction with the assailant, embarrassment over the details of the assault (self-blame), fear of being blamed by others, and fear of not being believed. The Steubenville case may well not have resulted in police reports either, had the assault not been photographed and shared through social media. Regardless, such instances of men's violence against women, whether or not they receive public scrutiny, are all too common.

The sad truth is that rape is not an aberration of social norms. As journalism and communications scholar Robert Jensen puts it, "Rape is illegal, but the sexual ethic that underlies rape is woven into the fabric of the culture."[64] He goes on:

> In the contemporary United States, men generally are trained in a variety of ways to view sex as the acquisition of pleasure by the taking of women. Sex is a sphere in which men are trained to see themselves as naturally dominant and women as naturally passive. Women are objectified and women's sexuality is turned into a commodity that can be bought and sold. Sex becomes sexy because men are dominant and women are subordinate.[65]

One of the mechanisms through which men are trained to view sex in these ways is the consumption of pornography, not every now and again but habitually and over the course of years. Consuming pornography delivers the sexual script of patriarchy in which men's sexual aggression is normalized and celebrated. And although we cannot know for certain whether the assailants in the case mentioned above were active consumers, it is telling that in the process of assaulting the victim they documented the abuse with photographs and videos, essentially making their own pornography as a component of the abuse. It is also telling that the boys posted evidence of these crimes on social media outlets, displaying a gross misunderstanding of what constitutes the legal crime of rape, a desensitization to the realities of men's violence against women and the humanity of the girl they assaulted, and a normative understanding of men's violence as an act of manhood under patriarchy.

The assailants in these acts of violence seemingly saw nothing wrong with what they had done, at least during and immediately after the assaults. It was not until photos of the assault began spreading through social media that Trent Mays, one of the assailants, began trying to orchestrate a cover-up.[66] Robin Warshaw's work further highlighted that although one in twelve men admitted to engaging in behaviors that meet the legal definition of rape, 84 percent of those men said that what they did was *"definitely* not rape."[67] How can we make sense of this?

The normalization of rape in our culture and the failure of many men (and women) to "see" it clearly may relate back to the patriarchal and phallocratic sexual scripts that saturate our cultural landscape and which predominate in pornography. When boys acquire, activate, and apply sexual scripts centered on aggressive and predatory masculinity and subordinated and victimized femininity, men's violence against women can become the norm, the expected pattern of sexual interaction. Recall that Ana Bridges and her colleagues found that 95 percent of those aggressed against in top-selling pornographic videos responded with neutrality or pleasure. Such "consensual depiction of aggression," they argue, runs the risk of "rendering true aggression against women invisible."[68] In this context, a "no" stated directly or indirectly may not be heard as "no" and consent may be assumed a priori. In the pornographic sexual script, men are conditioned to *get* sex and to do things *to* women—as opposed to *with* them—and not to identify and reassess enthusiastic and active consent across the evolving and negotiated process of sexual interaction.[69]

The pornographic sexual script that men are socialized to apply with women is also visible in the phenomenon sometimes referred to as "gray rape," a sexual encounter between a man and a woman which does not clearly meet the legal threshold for rape but which nonetheless is a violation of the woman's desires and personal boundaries.[70] It could refer to an interaction that was not overtly physically violent, a situation in which a woman says no but the man refuses to stop pestering her until he wears her down, or some other context that does not fit the dominant cultural narrative of "assault." Journalist and blogger Meghan Murphy put it this way:

> It's muddy, yes. But we all know (or should know), that it isn't ok. It's what happens to women. It's a run of the mill experience for many of us in this culture. It's not something easily categorized as either "rape" or "consensual." As many of us know all too well, there's much more middle ground. And that "middle ground" is often disturbingly comparable to legal rape; but sometimes more difficult to talk about or sort out in one's mind.[71]

This is more than "bad sex." It is a violation of personal space, corporal integrity, and the moral authority to determine what happens to and with your body. That it does not necessarily meet the legal threshold for rape or sexual assault does not lessen the violation:

We know when there is not consent and yet we can't call it rape in a legal sense. These experiences leave us vulnerable to being silenced, blamed, and disbelieved. They leave us feeling unsure of ourselves. We ask ourselves what happened — Was it rape? Was it "borderline assault"? Was it just a bad experience that most women probably have? Should we have said "no" more clearly? Loudly? Firmly?

Certainly it's something more than just a "bad experience" or "bad sex." And yes, it's muddy, *but only because we live in a rape culture, where the lines between consensual, nonconsensual, and legal rape are horribly blurred.*[72]

Pornography is part of the process in which those lines are blurred. It is not the only part, to be sure, but it is a core component of the gender and sexual socialization through which boys and young men learn to see and experience themselves as men. It is part of how they learn to enact their manhood along patriarchal lines. And it is part of the way that men's violence against women becomes normalized, commoditized, celebrated, and rendered invisible by its very ubiquity.

NOTES

I would like to thank Chyng F. Sun, Ana J. Bridges, and Jennifer A. Johnson, and my colleagues in an interdisciplinary, international research project that addresses pornography consumption and attitudes and behaviors, for their work together and for their support in writing this chapter. Particular thanks go to Jennifer A. Johnson, with whom I drafted a previous version of one section of this chapter. Finally, I would like to thank Robert Jensen for his support, guidance, and example, and the editors of this anthology for their insightful comments and their commitment to creating space for these discussions.

1. See Jason S. Carroll, Laura M. Padilla-Walker, Larry J. Nelson, Chad D. Olson, Carolyn McNamara Barry, and Stephanie D. Madsen, "Generation XXX: Pornography Acceptance and Use among Emerging Adults," *Journal of Adolescent Research* 23 (2008): 6–30; Chyng F. Sun, Ana J. Bridges, Jennifer A. Johnson, and Matthew B. Ezzell, "Pornography and the Male Sexual Script: An Analysis of Consumption and Sexual Relations," Archives of Sexual Behavior (forthcoming at the time of printing).

2. See for example Chiara Sabina, Janis Wolak, and David Finkelhor, "The Nature and Dynamics of Internet Pornography Exposure for Youth," *CyberPscyhology and Behavior* 11 (2008): 691–93, who found that only 14.4 percent of their respondents had exposure to pornography prior to age thirteen.

3. Anne Fausto-Sterling, *Sexing the Body: Gender Politics and the Construction of Sexuality* (New York: Basic Books, 2000), 31.

4. Fausto-Sterling, *Sexing the Body,* 31.

5. See Candace West and Don H. Zimmerman, "Doing Gender," *Gender & Society* 1 (1987): 125–51; Candace West and Sarah Fenstermaker, "Doing Difference," *Gender & Society* 9 (1995): 8–37.

6. See the chapter by Robert Jensen in this anthology for more discussion of these ideas.

7. Allan G. Johnson, *The Gender Knot: Unraveling Our Patriarchal Legacy* (Philadelphia: Temple University Press, 2005).

8. Paul Kivel, "Boys Will Be Men: Guiding Your Sons from Boyhood to Manhood," Paul Kivel: Educator, Activist & Writer, 2006,http://www.paulkivel.com/component/jdownloads/finish/1/37/0?Itemid=31(accessed 27 Jul. 2013).

9. See R. W. Connell, *Gender and Power* (Palo Alto, CA: Stanford University Press, 1987); and R. W. Connell, *Masculinities* (Berkeley: University of California Press, 1995).

10. James D. Babl, "Compensatory Masculine Responding as a Function of Sex Role," *Journal of Consulting and Clinical Psychology* 47 (1979): 252–57.

11. Douglas Schrock and Michael Schwalbe, "Men, Masculinity, and Manhood Acts," *Annual Review of Sociology* 35 (2009): 281.

12. Thomas J. Gerschick and Adam Stephen Miller, "Coming to Terms: Masculinity and Physical Disability," in *Men's Health and Illness: Gender, Power, and the Body*, ed. Donald Sabo and David Frederick Gordon (London: Sage, 1995), 183–204.

13. Gerschick and Miller, "Coming to Terms," 194.

14. See Michael J. Sutton, Jane D. Brown, Karen M. Wilson, and Jonathan D. Klein, "Shaking the Tree of Knowledge for Forbidden Fruit: Where Adolescents Learn about Sexuality and Contraception," in *Sexual Teens, Sexual Media: Investigating Media's Influence on Adolescent Sexuality*, ed. Jane D. Brown, Jeanne R. Steele, and Kim Walsh-Childers (Mahway, NJ: Lawrence Erlbaum Associates, 2002), 25–55; Jane D. Brown, Kelly Ladin L'Engle, Carol J. Pardun, Guang Guo, Kristin Kenneavy, and Christine Jackson, "Sexy Media Matter: Exposure to Sexual Content in Music, Movies, Television, and Magazines Predicts Black and White Adolescents' Sexual Behavior," *Pediatrics* 117 (2006): 1018–27.

15. For some notable exceptions to the lack of research on populations outside of heterosexual men, see Bridget J. Crawford, "Gay Does Not Necessarily Mean Good: A Critique of Jeffrey Sherman's 'Love Speech: The Social Utility of Pornography,'" *American University Journal of Gender, Social Policy and the Law* 5 (1996): 9–20; Scott J. Duggan and Donald R. McCreary, "Body Image, Eating Disorders, and the Drive for Muscularity in Gay and Heterosexual Men: The Influence of Media Images," *Eclectic Views on Gay Male Pornography: Pornucopia*, ed. Todd G. Morrison (Binghamton, NY: Harrington Park Press, 2004), 45–58; Richard Fung, "Looking for My Penis: The Eroticized Asian in Gay Video Porn," *How Do I Look? Queer Film and Video*, ed. Bad Object-Choices (Seattle: Bay Press, 1991), 145–68; Christopher Kendall, *Gay Male Pornography: An Issue of Sex Discrimination* (Vancouver: UBC Press, 2004); Jeffrey G. Sherman, "Love Speech: The Social Utility of Pornography," *Stanford Law Review* 47 (1995): 661–705; Nguyen Tan Hoang, "The Resurrection of Brandon Lee: The Making of a Gay Asian American Porn Star," in *Porn Studies*, ed. Linda Williams (Durham, NC: Duke University Press, 2004), 223–70; Bente Træen, Toril Sorheim Nilsen, and Hein Stigum, "Use of Pornography in Traditional Media and on the Internet in Norway," *Journal of Sex Research* 43 (2006): 245–54.

16. Ana J. Bridges, Robert Wosnitzer, Erica Scharrer, Chyng Sun, and Rachael Liberman, "Aggression and Sexual Behavior in Best-Selling Pornography Videos: A Content Analysis Update," *Violence Against Women* 16 (2010): 1065–85. Although "harsh" material has arguably always been available within the modern pornography industry, even industry insiders point out that the mainstream industry has grown "harsher" over time. Actor/producer Max Hardcore noted that, although in the 1980s and early 1990s a "hot" scene ended with a man ejaculating onto a woman's body, by the 2000s "almost every women [was] . . . into getting throat-fucked and ass-gaped" (see http://business.avn.com/articles/video/Max-Hardcore-Spreading-The-Love-23363.html [accessed 13 Jul. 2012]). And producer Mitchell Spinelli reflects that "girls" in the industry today are "younger," "nastier," and "harder" than they were in the 1970s, and noted that to stay relevant in the changing industry he "reinvented" his company to reflect an "aggressive, hardcore, in your face, ass-to-mouth take no prisoners" attitude (see http://www.lukeisback.com/stars/stars/mitchell_spinelli.htm [accessed 13 Jul. 2012]).

17. Bridges, et al., "Aggression and Sexual Behavior."

18. Janis Wolak, Kimberly Mitchell, and David Finkelhor, "Online Victimization of Youth: Five Years Later," *National Center for Missing and Exploited Children*, http://www.missingkids.com/en_US/publications/NC167.pdf (accessed 13 Jul. 2012).

19. Patricia M. Greenfield, "Inadvertent Exposure to Pornography on the Internet: Implications of Peer-to-Peer File-Sharing Networks for Child Development and Families," *Journal of Applied Developmental Psychology* 25 (2004): 741–50.

20. See Greenfield, "Inadvertent Exposure to Pornography."

21. See Michael Flood, "Exposure to Pornography Among Youth in Australia," *Journal of Sociology* 43 (2007): 45–60; Jennifer A. Johnson, "To Catch a Curious Clicker: A Social Network Analysis of the Online Pornography Industry," in *Everyday Pornography,* ed. Karen Boyle (New York: Routledge, 2010), 147–63; Rebecca Whisnant, "From Jekyll to Hyde: The Grooming of Male Pornography Consumers," in *Everyday Pornography*, ed. Karen Boyle (New York: Routledge, 2010), 114–33.

22. See Pamela Paul, *Pornified: How Pornography Is Transforming Our Lives, Our Relationships, and Our Families* (New York: Macmillan, 2005); Jensen, *Getting Off: Pornography and the End of Masculinity* (Boston: South End Press, 2007); Larry Maltz and Wendy Maltz, *The Porn Trap: The Essential Guide to Overcoming Problems Caused by Pornography* (New York: HarperCollins, 2008).

23. An earlier version of components of this section was codrafted with Jennifer A. Johnson.

24. See Karen Boyle, "The Pornography Debates: Beyond Cause and Effect," *Women's Studies International Forum* 23 (2000): 187–95; Robert Jensen, "Pornography and Sexual Violence," VAWNet Applied Research Forum, National Online Resource Center on Violence Against Women, July 2004, http://new.vawnet.org/Assoc_Files_VAWnet/AR_PornAndSV.pdf (accessed 18 Jul. 2012); Dick Thornburgh and Herbert S. Lin (eds.), *Youth, Pornography, and the Internet* (Washington, DC: National Academy Press, 2004).

25. Jensen, *Getting Off*.

26. L. Rowell Huesmann, "Psychological Processes Promoting the Relation between Exposure to Media Violence and Aggressive Behavior by the Viewer," *Journal of Social Issues* 42 (1986): 348.

27. Albert Bandura, "Social Cognitive Theory: An Agentic Perspective," *Annual Review of Psychology* 52 (2001): 1–26.

28. George Gerbner, Larry Gross, Michael Morgan, and Nancy Signorielli, "Growing Up With Television: The Cultivation Perspective," *Media Effects: Advances in Theory and Research*, ed. Jennings Bryant and Dolf Zillmann (Hillsdale, NJ: Lawrence Erlbaum Associates, 1994), 17–42.

29. Alan M. Rubin, "The Uses-and-Gratifications Perspective of Media Effects," *Media Effects: Advances in Theory and Research*, 2nd ed., ed. Jennings Bryant and Dolf Zillmann (Mahwah, NJ: Lawrence Erlbaum Associates, 2002), 525–48.

30. Alan M. Rubin and Sven Windahl, "The Uses and Dependency Model of Mass Communication," *Critical Studies in Mass Communication* 3 (1986): 184–99.

31. Leonard Berkowitz and K. H. Rogers, "A Priming Effect Analysis of Media Influences," *Perspectives on Media Effects, *ed. Jennings Bryant and Dolf Zillmann (Hillsdale, NJ: Lawrence Erlbaum Associates, 1986), 57–81.

32. Paul Wright, "Mass Media Effects on Youth Sexual Behavior: Assessing the Claim for Causality," *Communication Yearbook* 35 (2011)*,* 343–86.

33. John H. Gagnon and William Simon, *Sexual Conduct: The Social Sources of Human Sexuality* (Piscataway, NJ: Aldine Transaction, 1973).

34. See Kenneth Burke, *A Grammar of Motives and a Rhetoric of Motives* (Cleveland: World Publishing Co., 1962); Erving Goffman, *The Presentation of Self in Everyday Life* (New York: Doubleday, 1959); and Stanford M. Lyman and Marvin B. Scott, *A Sociology of the Absurd* (New York: Appleton-Century-Crofts, 1970).

35. Viktor Gecas and Roger Libby, "Sexual Behavior as Symbolic Interaction," *Journal of Sex Research* 12 (1976): 37.

36. Paul Wright, "Mass Media Effects on Youth Sexual Behavior," 373.

37. See Michael Kimmel, "Introduction: Guilty Pleasures—Pornography in Men's Lives," *Men Confront Pornography*, ed. Michael Kimmel (New York: Crown, 1990), 1–22; Alan McKee, "'Saying You've Been at Dad's Porn Book is Part of Growing up': Youth, Pornography, and Education," *Metro* 155 (2007): 118–22.

38. See Sheila Garos, James K. Beggan, Annette Kluck, and Amanda Easton, "Sexism and Pornography Use: Toward Explaining Past (Null) Results," *Journal of Psychology and Human Sexuality* 16 (2004): 69–96; Marie-Thérèse Luder, Isabelle Pittet, André Berchtold, Christina Akré, Pierre-André Michaud, and Joan-Carles Surís, "Associations between Online Pornogra-

phy and Sexual Behavior Among Adolescents: Myth or Reality?" *Archives of Sexual Behavior* 40 (2011): 1027–35.

39. See Jane D. Brown, et al., "Sexy Media Matter"; Aletha C. Huston, Ellen Wartella, and Edward Donnerstein, *Measuring the Effects of Sexual Content in the Media* (Menlo Park, CA: Henry J. Kaiser Family Foundation, 1998); Thomas Johansson and Nils Hammarén, "Hegemonic Masculinity and Pornography: Young People's Attitudes Toward and Relations to Pornography," *Journal of Men's Studies* 15 (2007): 57–70; Scott MacDonald, "Confessions of a Feminist Porn Watcher," *Men Confront Pornography*, ed. Michael Kimmel (New York: Crown, 1990), 34–42; Alan McKee, Katherine Albury, and Catherine Lumby, *The Porn Report* (Melbourne: Melbourne University Press, 2008).

40. Michael Flood, "Young Men Using Pornography," *Everyday Pornography*, ed. Karen Boyle (New York: Routledge, 2010), 166–76.

41. Neil Malamuth, Tamara Addison, and Mary Koss, "Pornography and Sexual Aggression: Are There Reliable Effects and Can We Understand Them?" *Annual Review of Sex Research* 11 (2000): 26–91.

42. See American Psychological Association (APA), *Report of the APA Task Force on the Sexualization of Girls* (Washington, DC: APA, 2007); Silvia Bonino, Silvia Ciairano, Emanuela Rabaglietti, and Elena Cattelino, "Use of Pornography and Self-Reported Engagement in Sexual Violence among Adolescents," *European Journal of Developmental Psychology* 3 (2006): 265–88; Ryan Joseph Burns, "Male Internet Pornography Consumers and the Attitudes Toward Men and Women," PhD diss., University of Oklahoma, 2001; James Check, "Teenage Training: The Effects of Pornography on Adolescent Males," in *The Price We Pay: The Case Against Racist Speech, Hate Propaganda, and Pornography*, ed. Laura Lederer and Richard Delgado (New York: Hill and Wang, 1995), 89–91; Deborah E. S. Frable, Anne E. Johnson, and Hildy Kellman, "Seeing Masculine Men, Sexy Women, and Gender Differences: Exposure to Pornography and Cognitive Constructions of Gender," *Journal of Personality* 65 (1997): 311–55; Gert Hald, Neil Malamuth, and Carlin Yuen, "Pornography and Attitudes Supporting Violence Against Women: Revisiting the Relationship in Nonexperimental Studies," *Aggressive Behavior* 36 (2010): 14–20.

43. Paul J. Wright and Ashley K. Randall, "Internet Pornography Exposure and Risky Sexual Behavior among Adult Males in the United States," *Computers and Human Behavior* 28, no. 4 (July 2002): 1410–16.

44. Nathaniel M. Lambert, Sesen Negash, Tyler F. Stillman, Spencer B. Olmstead, and Frank D. Fincham, "A Love that Doesn't Last: Pornography Consumption and Weakened Commitment to One's Romantic Partner," *Journal of Social and Clinical Psychology* 31 (2012): 410–38.

45. Aleksandar Štulhofer, Vesna Buško, and Ivan Landripet, "Pornography, Sexual Socialization, and Satisfaction among Young Men," *Archives of Sexual Behavior* 39 (2010): 168–78.

46. Paul, *Pornified*.

47. Maltz and Maltz, *The Porn Trap*; see also Gail Dines, *Pornland: How Porn Has Hijacked Our Sexuality* (Boston: Beacon Press, 2010); Elisabet Häggström-Nordin, Jonas Sandberg, Ulf Hanson, and Tanja Tydén, "'It's Everywhere': Young Swedish People's Thoughts and Reflections about Pornography," *Scandinavian Journal of Caring Sciences* 20 (2006): 386–93; Jensen, *Getting Off*; and Michael Kimmel, *Guyland: The Perilous World Where Boys Become Men* (New York: HarperCollins, 2008), 185–89.

48. Johnson, "To Catch a Curious Clicker."

49. See, for example, Kimmel, *Guyland*.

50. Johnson, "To Catch a Curious Clicker," 151.

51. Kimmel, *Guyland*.

52. Kimmel, *Guyland*, 182.

53. Kimmel, *Guyland*, 83.

54. See Michael Schwalbe, *The Sociologically Examined Life: Pieces of the Conversation*, 3rd ed. (New York: McGraw-Hill, 2005); and Denis McQuail, *Mass Communication Theory*, 6th ed. (Thousand Oaks, CA: Sage, 2010).

55. Martin D. Schwartz and Walter S. DeKeseredy, *Sexual Assault on the College Campus: The Role of Male Peer Support* (Thousand Oaks, CA: Sage, 1997).

56. Raquel Kennedy Bergen and Kathleen Bogle, "Exploring the Connection between Pornography and Sexual Violence," *Violence and Victims* 15 (2000): 227–34; see also Dines, *Pornland*, 95–98.

57. Diana E. H. Russell, "Pornography and Rape: A Causal Model," *Political Psychology* 9 (1988): 41–73.

58. Bergen and Bogle, "Exploring the Connection," 232.

59. The Steubenville High School rape case received widespread media coverage. For a review of some of that coverage and the underlying story, see http://www.theatlanticwire.com/topics/steubenville-rape/ (accessed 24 Jul. 2013).

60. See http://www.xojane.com/issues/steubenville-rape-verdict-alexandra-goddard;http://www.mobilebroadcastnews.com/NewsRoom/Don-Carpenter/Text-Messages-led-convictions-Steubenville-Rape-Trial; and http://www.huffingtonpost.com/2013/05/02/steubenville-rape-teen-girls-guilty-threats-twitter_n_3204301.html (all websites accessed 24 Jul. 2013) for examples.

61. Adam Clark Estes, "Police Aren't Treating Threats against the Steubenville Rape Victim Lightly," *Atlantic Wire*, March 18, 2013, http://www.theatlanticwire.com/national/2013/03/police-arent-treating-threats-against-steubenville-rape-victim-lightly/63262/ (accessed 24 Jul. 2013).

62. Adam Clark Estes, "CNN's Not the Only One Peddling Sympathy for the Steubenville Rapists." *Atlantic Wire*, March 17, 2013, para 2, http://www.theatlanticwire.com/national/2013/03/cnns-not-only-one-peddling-sympathy-steubenville-rapists/63204/ (accessed 24 Jul. 2013).

63. Robin Warshaw, *I Never Called It Rape* (New York, HarperPerennial, 1994).

64. Robert Jensen, "Men's Pleasure, Women's Pain: A Dangerous Sexual Ethic is Woven into the Cultural Fabric," *Fredericksburg Free Lance–Star*, September 1, 2002, para. 11,http://uts.cc.utexas.edu/~rjensen/freelance/rapeisnormal.htm (accessed 24 Jul. 2013).

65. Robert Jensen, "Men's Pleasure, Women's Pain," para 9.

66. Torsten Ove, "Teen's Texts Tell of Cover-Up in Steubenville Rape Trial," *Pittsburgh Post–Gazette*, March 15, 2013, http://www.post-gazette.com/stories/local/region/teens-texts-tell-of-rape-cover-up-in-steubenville-trial-679402/ (accessed 24 Jul. 2013).

67. Warshaw, *I Never Called It Rape*, 90, emphasis in original.

68. Bridges, et al., "Aggression and Sexual Behavior," 1080.

69. For further discussion of this idea see Jennifer Hornsby's chapter in this volume.

70. See Laura Sessions Stepp, "A New Kind of Date Rape," *Cosmopolitan*, September 2007, http://www.cosmopolitan.com/sex-love/tips-moves/new-kind-of-date-rape?click=main_sr (accessed 24 Jul. 2013); Sewell Chan, "'Gray Rape': A New Form of Date Rape?" *New York Times*, October 15, 2007, http://cityroom.blogs.nytimes.com/2007/10/15/gray-rape-a-new-form-of-date-rape/?_r=0 (accessed 24 Jul. 2013).

71. Meghan Murphy, "On 'Gray Rape,' Girls, and Sex in a Rape Culture," Rabble.ca, March 15, 2013, para. 6, http://rabble.ca/blogs/bloggers/feminist-current/2013/03/'gray-rape'-girls-and-sex-rape-culture (accessed 24 Jul. 2013).

72. Murphy, "On 'Gray Rape,'" paras. 27–28, emphasis added.

Chapter Three

Truth Claims about Porn

When Dogma and Data Collide

Shira Tarrant

Full disclosure: What I am about to say takes on many sacred cows and directly questions the work of several gifted feminist scholars. These scholars are respected members of activist-intellectual communities. Several are friends and mentors, and one was my doctoral advisor. Writing this piece means ruffling feathers and potentially creating conflict among those I like and respect. *Frankly*, I wonder, *is pornography important enough to risk this?*

The answer is yes. The reason to write about this topic is that pornography is at the nexus of pleasure, danger, freedom, and subjugation. The battle for gender justice is, of necessity, "a struggle also for freedom of expression, as a precursor to self-definition, visibility, and the other privileges that accompany social citizenship."[1] The arguments that pornography invokes matter a great deal in regard to liberty, justice, agency, self-definition, choice—and, thus they also matter for social citizenship. Pornography is a lightning rod for these issues, each of which is central to political theory, gender justice, and a free society. That is why pornography matters. And that is why I am writing about the collision of dogma and data in the current iteration of the sex wars. I anticipate the possibility of being misquoted in the service of dogma. I hope, though, that I will be quoted accurately in the spirit of open dialogue. And, with that said, I begin.

***

Anti-pornography feminists want to prevent harm to women. This is an important political objective. In pursuing this goal, anti-porn feminists turn to women's lived experience (and that of their male allies) as proof of the problem. They also rely on some degree of quantitative research. The intent is noble; the problem is twofold: First, this anti-porn strategy includes a selective use of both standpoint theory and second, the resulting truth claims are not entirely supported by empirical data. Preventing harm is fundamental for promoting a flourishing democratic society with maximum liberty for its members. But dogma-driven politics threatens to undermine these very same goals.

This chapter focuses on the arguments used by Stop Porn Culture (SPC), a feminist anti-pornography group based at Wheelock College in Massachusetts. SPC is arguably the most visible feminist anti-pornography organization currently working in the United States, with impact in Australia, the United Kingdom, and elsewhere around the globe. Spearheaded by professors Gail Dines and Robert Jensen, filmmaker Chyng Sun, and other affiliated scholars, members of Stop Porn Culture are regularly quoted by international media for their opposition to pornography. As part of an organized effort to shut down pornography, members of SPC actively appear in left-leaning and general-interest media such as the *Guardian*, *Time* magazine, *Al Jazeera*, and the *New York Post*.

SPC is certainly not the only feminist group opposing porn. It is, however, representative of a resurgent radical feminism (known online as RadFem) that opposes male domination and control over women by prioritizing "women's exploitation, degradation and torture within . . . pornography."[2] This perspective is valuable, but flawed. SPC is unwilling to acknowledge the counterhegemonic possibilities in feminist and queer porn, unable to consider the possibility of improving rather than eradicating porn, and rejects the possibility of neutral or even positive uses of sexually explicit material. The resulting feminist tension is not a new problem,[3] but one with renewed concern given swift changes in media technology, intractable stereotypes of sexuality and gender in all sorts of pop culture, and the unproductive infighting centered around the issue of pornography that continues to threaten feminist cohesion and political success.

Composed of self-described anti-porn radical feminists, SPC is a well-intentioned group that is concerned about the damaging effects of pornography. Unfortunately, this anti-porn narrative 1) is founded on a problematic use of feminist standpoint theory, 2) ignores counterevidence in the quantitative and qualitative data, and 3) contributes to a hostile climate that undermines its very goals. The problems raised by SPC strategies take on pointed urgency given the seriousness of gender-based issues and the need for progressive change.

FEMINIST STANDPOINT THEORY AND
TRUTH CLAIMS ABOUT PORN

Any effective political theory must describe the social, cultural, and economic problems at hand and provide solutions for change. An effective *feminist* political theory grapples with the ways in which gender subjugation intersects, overlaps, shapes—and is shaped by—various other forms of identities and oppressions. Scholars grappling with feminist standpoint theory, such as Sandra Harding, Nancy Hartsock, or Patricia Hill Collins, explain that certain sociopolitical positions are occupied by women, and by other groups lacking social and economic privilege. These subjugated positions, which include an unequal sexual division of labor, experiences of violence, and reproduction, can become vantage sites of epistemic privilege. These vantage sites are important politicized starting points for exploring questions about those who are marginalized. These vantage points are also crucial for unraveling the epistemic assumptions of those who, by virtue of social and political privilege, occupy the positions of oppressors.

As Hartsock explains, standpoint is not merely bias or opinion. Rather, feminist standpoint is an interested position in the sense of being engaged and politically aware.[4] Feminist standpoint theory specifically focuses on the political aspects of human experience and, as such, highlights a feminist standpoint, rather than a women's standpoint. In other words, feminist standpoint theory is informed by politics, not our ovaries or our emotions.

But clearly this is tricky. While feminist standpoint theory is not just the result of experience, it is still based on experience. And this is a slippery slope. Science is expected to be value neutral, but when science is done in the context of neoliberal kyriarchy, it rarely meets this standard. As feminist philosopher Sandra Harding explains, "standpoint approaches use the differences between a dominant group's values and interests and those of subordinate groups to provide research that is for the subordinate group—that answers the kinds of questions they want answered." Standpoint theory questions why even the best research practices "so often [end] up making sexist, racist, heteronormative, classist or abled claims."[5] As we will see, however, the distinction between questioning truth claims and replacing them with truth claims of one's own is easily blurred.

So what does this mean for anti-pornography feminism? Anti-porn arguments grounded in standpoint theory mean applying a politicized perspective that is derived from intersectional experiences of gender, race, sexuality, and class. So far, so good. The resulting core argument is that:

    a. If pornography is produced by white males (or their patriarchal stand-ins) who are members of the socially privileged class,

b. And the socially oppressed class has access to knowledge about social relations that is unavailable to the privileged class,
c. Then women, queer and transgender individuals, people of color, and other socially marginalized groups experience and understand pornography's oppression, whereas pornographers are unable to understand this oppression. Therefore,
d. Pornography is oppressive.[6]

What's more, the logic that SPC relies on adds a Marxist-infused anti-capitalist critique of liberalism, arguing that all porn harms all women, and that using porn harms all men. The Marxist-infused spin results in the argument that porn is oppressive because:

a. White men (or their stand-ins) profit from the use of women's bodies, who in return get low wages and take on potential physical risk to their bodies, and that porn turns women's bodies into commodities for exchange and thus produces a fundamental alienation of subject and body, which is inherently oppressive from the Marxist view; and
b. Pornography conditions men and women (and girls and boys) to expect and experience sex as eroticized dominance and eroticized degradation, solidifying political relations in sexual roles, and race relations, therefore obscuring the reality of porn's damage and locking women (and other bottoms, for lack of a better word) into this economy of desire that is built on their dominance but with no way to see it as dominance.[7]

The logic of this argument looks like this:

a. If treating bodies as commodities is oppressive; and
b. If representing sexual activity as inherently a matter of domination and submission is oppressive; and
c. If pornography treats bodies as commodities and represents sexual activity as inherently a matter of domination and submission, then
d. Pornography is oppressive.

This SPC/RadFem anti-porn logic is based on experience and truth claims. Although marginalized perspectives may contribute important insight,[8] the interpretations of these experiences are mutable and contestable.[9] In her article "Knowers, Knowing, Known"—an early argument about feminist epistemology, truth claims, and the politics of knowledge—Mary Hawkesworth points out that objections to feminist standpoint "create profound skepticism about the ability of any particular group of women to 'know' what is in the interest of all women."[10]

SPC's core logic relies on experience as the basis for how pornography's role in women's domination is interpreted and understood. The issue regarding women's "experience" lies in assuming that images of dominance or staged degradation in porn is equivalent to actual oppression; it assumes that erotic domination is equivalent to pain; that this pain is specifically a form of suffering; and that what one sees as degrading is a universal fact, rather than perspectival. This view also assumes that pain = harm to women and that pain and pleasure are mutually exclusive, and thus denies some women's claims to pleasure because, they (the moralizers) think, pain = harm = suffering, therefore how could that "pain" be pleasurable? Therein lies the resulting argument among (some) anti-porn radical feminists that "your experience is invalid" or some similar version of that.[11]

In this iteration, feminist anti-porn logic does not (and refuses to) account for the politicized perspectives of those women, queer and transgender individuals, people of color, and the workers in porn, who do not experience pornography as oppression. This perspective fails to distinguish among the myriad genres of porn, some of which fall along a continuum of misogyny and racism, and some of which do not. The SPC argument is that porn oppresses simply because the producers and the subjects of porn have different views of reality, or different standpoints. This is not a sufficient argument and furthermore, it quickly devolves into a contentious debate founded far more on dogmatic presuppositions than on data.

Being a member of a marginalized or oppressed group means living every day with discrimination, stigma, danger, and the threat of—or actual—violence. It also means less access to the goods, power, and resources society offers. These are the compelling sociopolitical problems with which feminism is concerned. And yet we must have theories that can account for the politicized experience and vantage points of those who may be subjugated in certain regards and who also do not experience pornography as always oppressive or as entirely sexist. It is not enough for anti-porn feminists to disregard statements such as those by porn performer Sinnamon Love who, when asked, "Is there racism in porn?" replied: "It exists no more in porn than in other industries," adding that it is crucial to promote anti-racist sexuality in the broader culture at large.[12]

As feminist legal scholar Mari Matsuda writes, "those who have experienced discrimination speak with a special voice to which we should listen."[13] And, given that pornography is a valence issue for good reason, of *course* we should listen. But arguing against pornography from the premise of standpoint theory means that SPC anti-porn feminism does not listen to a diversity of experiences, but instead claims to know which experience is the correct experience, and which experience is allegedly duped by the patriarchy. In a feminist debate about *Fifty Shades of Grey* and a call to burn copies of the book,[14] journalist and cultural critic Katha Pollitt comments, "Obviously this book strikes millions of women as fun and exciting. Why not try to figure out why? For example, ask the women who read it! It's always surprising to me that the 'trust women' mantra disappears when women do something the truster doesn't approve of. Then, it's 'women are brainwashed.'"[15]

Ironically, feminist standpoint theory helps reveal social oppression by questioning the presuppositions of the hegemonic "knowers." Yet, in this instance, feminist standpoint theory generates truth claims of its own. Rather than seriously considering the legitimacy of opinions by women who like porn, or who work in the industry, or the standpoint claims of queer or feminist porn producers, the accusation made by anti-porn activists is that women have been duped and that even feminist pornographers are victims of patriarchal and kyriarchal subjugation. This pick-and-choose perspective is not logically or politically sound. While there are legitimate reasons for concern about the harms of pornography, using definitions of harm that amount to "I know it when I see it" or "pornography is harmful because I feel like it is" undermines the very efforts of those who are concerned enough to mobilize against pornography. As political theorist Judith Grant writes in the summary to her article, "I Feel Therefore I Am: A Critique of Female Experience as the Basis for a Feminist Epistemology," "many feminist theorists have advanced the epistemological proposition that women know what they know via their 'experiences.' Using 'experience' as the basis for a feminist epistemology has conceptual and practical problems: it invites and perpetuates the use of a stereotypical Female thus fostering essentialist theories which romanticize women and feminine attributes. Moreover, it is difficult to operationalize as the experiences of women vary dramatically across time and cultures, classes, races, etc."[16]

Experience *qua* woman is not a sufficient foundation for a feminist political theory. And yet feminist standpoint theory explains that the social underclass experience this subjugation, and thus have a window into this lived knowledge that those at the center of privilege cannot access. Grant addresses this logical conundrum, explaining that "if experience is to be used as the basis for feminist epistemology it must be refined":

> When forced to choose between rational interpretation and intuition most of western political thought has chosen the former, and with good reason. A theory which rejects reason and also wants to be democratic is highly problematic. Without reason, analogy, axiom, and assertion can pass for argument. And assertion can only be refuted with other assertions. Thus, such theories risk devolving into authoritarian non-theories more akin to religions.[17]

Anti-pornography feminists are concerned with preventing harm toward women. This is a serious issue. Yet, the political and theoretical risks of a dogma-driven strategy are also serious: First, using truth claims to underscore contemporary anti-porn argument is at odds with the principles of feminist standpoint theory upon which SPC-type perspectives rely. Where feminist standpoint theory requires critical analysis regarding power, truth claims, and unexamined presuppositions, the RadFem/SPC anti-porn arguments rely heavily on their own truth claims regarding what constitutes healthy sexuality and progressive gender politics, rather than critically examining the concepts underscoring their position. This creates a philosophical dilemma of a Pyrrhic sort where the harms (e.g., creating damaging conflict within feminism and among anti-sexist allies; imposing standards upon others; silencing competing perspectives, which lies at the foundation of democracy and free speech) threaten to outweigh the good (e.g., preventing harm to women). As Judith Grant writes, "feminism cannot simultaneously be the lens through which experiences are interpreted, and also find its grounding in those experiences. That is, the feminist interpretive lens cannot be grounded on women's point of view. . . . To ground feminism in women's experiences and then to look to feminism to interpret those experiences is a tautology. To the extent that feminist standpoint theory accepts this tautology, it cannot accomplish what it sets out to do." Stated somewhat differently, a theory cannot be tested on the same data used to build that theory.[18]

Second, using truth claims that are not well supported by empirical data in promoting a political agenda impedes a clear understanding of pornography's political effects. Like the problems of standpoint, this direction, too, (unintentionally) undermines anti-porn efforts to protect women from harm. This is precisely where dogma and data collide. Dogma-driven activism obstructs both individual liberty and collective gender justice by normalizing discourse around sexual freedom and marginalizing perspectives that are inconsistent with its doctrine. This strategy flattens out crucial concepts of agency and choice, both central to feminist theory and concerns about pornography.

Sexual politics are at the center of public debate and pornography is at the center of these political issues concerning media, legislation, objectification, slut shaming, sex work, and sexual assault. Across the ideological spectrum are shared concerns about choice, consent, harm reduction, sexual liberation, sexual safety, sexual health, preventing sexual violence, and eradicating sexual objectification. And although feminist scholars, activists, and writers are at the forefront of policy and public awareness, there is often intra-feminist disagreement about the data and desired goals. The stakes are serious when a movement with common concerns about human well-being arrives at such stalemate and contentious debate about pornography. In their attempt to obliterate pornography, anti-porn feminists create a dangerous climate for best understanding sexual agency and sexual consent. Whether we personally like porn or not—and based on the figures, many people like it[19]—we would be smart to figure out strategies for dealing constructively with the impact of this media genre instead of trying to silence it or shut it down.

Anti-porn feminists are motivated by fears that mainstream pop culture is increasingly pornographic, and that the porn industry "produces hardcore material that is both more overtly cruel toward women and more widely accepted than ever."[20] To its detriment, however, the strategies of Stop Porn Culture include emotionally manipulative arguments intended to invoke outrage while preemptively thwarting opportunities to talk about differing perspectives on pornography.[21] This censors open dialogue, preventing intellectually honest debate about a subject where we need it the most. The feminist anti-porn position is that allowing alternative points of view from pro-pornography feminists or sex workers "would be akin to allowing the KKK to come and speak at an anti-racist conference."[22] This is a great leap of logic to equate racist hate groups with feminists. There is a serious difference between providing a platform for the KKK and supporting good-faith dialogue among feminists who disagree about pornography. As feminist pornography scholar Constance Penley points out, history provides a wealth of examples of how pornography was used "to challenge absolutist political authority and church doctrine" and has been linked to "avant-garde revolutionary art, populist struggles, [and] countercultural impulses."[23] As with so much of pop culture and mainstream media, it is not hard to find racism, sexism, and imperialist exploitation. Yet it stands to reason that within porn—as with all forms of pop culture such as TV, music, or movies—it is possible to find genres that are nonracist, nonsexist, nontransphobic, and life-affirming.

DEBATING THE DATA

If feminist standpoint theory is a flawed starting place for arguing against pornography, the research does not quickly clear this up: the data regarding pornography is fraught with disagreement. From the figures on revenue and use rates to considerations about its impact on users, nobody quite agrees on what is going on. Some data—such as demographic figures about who is using porn and how much money is earned—is simply hard to ascertain. Research about whether porn causes harm, so-called porn addiction, levels of violence in porn, and the impact this has on men's perceptions of women is contentious. For every finding of harm and pornography's negative effects, for instance, there is another study that directly contradicts this. At best, the research results are inconclusive. A new report from Middlesex University London explains that, despite widespread fears about the effects of online porn on young people, a causal relationship cannot be established between exposure to sexually explicit material and engaging in so-called risky behaviors (e.g., unprotected sex, use of alcohol or drugs in sex, and having sex at younger ages). "The majority of the research," the authors explain, "find a cross-sectional and/or correlational" relationship.[24] And, as we know, correlation is not the same as causation.

The London-based research team further explains that viewing violent imagery "can affect children and young people's attitudes and behaviours, which may subsequently affect their attitudes towards sexual relationships and behaviours within them." It is possible to extrapolate or infer what these effects may include, but significantly, the researchers note that the actual "evidence is inconsistent." The format through which young viewers are exposed to sexualized media is certainly important, but the emerging evidence about the issues remains contradictory.[25]

In terms of revenue and consumer payments, it is frequently reported that every second, people spend $3,000 on Internet porn.[26] It is also reported that there are an estimated 370 million Internet porn sites, and that industry revenues surpass earnings by Microsoft, Google, Amazon, eBay, Yahoo, Apple, and Netflix combined.[27] As SPC porn expert Gail Dines notes, finding reliable data on the porn industry is almost impossible. The statistics on viewership and revenue are therefore approximate at best. Although it is unclear whether these figures are accurate, they are the most often repeated. The most quoted statistics come from Internet Filter, Dines reports, even though she remains unsure about the accuracy of these figures.[28]

Even with this ambiguity, some data is more carefully collected than others and some research approached with more methodological rigor. Professors Caroline Heldman and Lisa Wade, for example, report that female sexual objectification undermines men's perceptions of women's competence. Female *self*-objectification, they argue, is linked to problems with cognitive development, sexual satisfaction, and grade point averages. This aspect of Heldman and Wade's research about media and internalized messages about gender and sexuality is more nuanced than other studies setting out to prove that porn causes violence against women. And this framework may also be more promising: Heldman and Wade, both of whom oppose pornography, are able to suggest ways of understanding possible media harms. This strategy can lead to media literacy solutions and feminist education about gender and objectification, without demanding censorship.[29]

In a culture permeated with men's violence against women, there is good reason to consider the violent effect porn may have on men who view it. But when it comes to the data, there is perennial debate. On the one hand, a five-person team led by Ana Bridges found high levels of aggression and degradation in popular porn videos.[30] Assuming the variables are well-defined (and I argue they are not),[31] what does aggression in porn mean in regard to violence against women? Meta-analysis from experimental studies of porn effects concludes that a connection between consumption of pornography and sexual aggression *"was especially true if the pornography was violent, and if the viewer was a man already considered at risk of offending in this regard.*"[32] What this study means is that violent pornography is not the unicausal variable it is claimed to be by SPC.

Research by Alan McKee on links between pornography and sexual aggression makes the case that the dominant academic focus on the damage pornography does is an artifact of the standard methods used in conducting this research. In McKee's view, researchers studying the effects of porn depend on dubious methods of sampling and data gathering. The connection made between exposure to pornography and increases in misogyny and aggression depend on a number of contingencies: being able to expose large numbers of people to pornography that they had not selected under uncomfortable conditions (surrounded by strangers) that prohibited normal reactions (i.e., masturbation). McKee reasons that the structure of the experiments, not the porn, is what upsets people: being asked to watch porn you did not choose, in lab-type settings, among strangers and without being able to masturbate privately, is enough to make anyone angry. Media studies expert Andy Ruddock explains that standard experiments of the effects of pornography tend "to be administered time and time again to particular sorts of samples (such as students and prisoners—both captive audiences), and the reasons for doubting the validity of effects research were clear. All that effects research had really discovered was that exposure to pornography *in experiments* makes people angry."[33]

Despite somewhat alarming claims that young boys' first exposure to porn is at age eleven,[34] research by Michele Ybarra of Internet Solutions for Kids in Irvine, California, and Kimberly Mitchell of the Crimes Against Children Research Center at the University of New Hampshire finds that "the vast majority (87%) of youth who report looking for sexual images online are 14 years of age or older, when it is developmentally appropriate to be sexually curious."[35]

So many questions remain about pornography's effects on viewers, and the quantitative jury is still out. Is sexual content in movies (if not porn) related to sexual risk taking among teens and young adults? Social psychologist and sex columnist Justin Lehmiller finds that "media exposure is only one small piece of the puzzle and there are likely many other factors that contribute to adolescent sexual behavior . . . even if we can blame the media, we can only blame it a little."[36]

Does watching pornography promote sexist standards among its male viewers? University of Montreal professor Simon Louis Lajeunesse reports that his test subjects say they support gender equality. "Pornography hasn't changed their perception of women or their relationship which they all want as harmonious and fulfilling as possible. Those who could not live out their fantasy in real life with their partner simply set aside the fantasy. The fantasy is broken in the real world and men don't want their partner to look like a porn star," says Lajeunesse.[37]

Writing for the *American Journal of Sexuality Education*, researchers Mary Ann Watson and Randyl D. Smith argue that, based on their review of the literature, there may be positive uses of porn in educational, medical, and clinical settings. "Not surprisingly," they write, "the sheer scope and variety of pornographic materials have led to heightened concern about the damaging effects of pornography on society. . . . Unfortunately, this anti-porn narrative may create a hostile climate that undermines the value of [sexually explicit material] in certain settings."[38]

But this chapter is not about proving which data set is comprehensive or which researchers have discovered "The Truth" about porn but, rather, that presuppositions impact the kinds of data that appeal to us in the first place. If our starting place is dogma-driven, then the research we conduct and find appealing will likely fall in line with this agenda. British porn scholars Clarissa Smith and Feona Attwood explain, "Antiporn feminism has proved incredibly resistant to the academic practices of theory and evidence, preferring to counter opposition with appeals to emotional truths. More than ever it relies on 'testimony,' though whose testimony counts is still a problem—those who testify to porn's pleasures or sense of liberation don't count in the same way as those who present themselves as addicts, victims, or rescuers."[39] In their own words, Stop Porn Culture's FAQ web page states "it's true that 'scientific proof' establishing a direct connection between pornography use and rape doesn't exist."[40] Yet this has not stopped anti-porn feminists from proceeding as if this scientific proof exists. Their general strategy instead relies on an urgency "more akin to a prophetic calling than philosophy."[41] As Martha Nussbaum explains, prophets (as opposed to philosophers and presumably social scientists) "believe that the urgency and magnitude of the evils they see admit of no delay, no calm and patient dialogue. . . . To prophets, philosophical patience looks like collaboration with evil."[42]

This urgency without data may be a good strategy in terms of constructing persuasive rhetoric to prove a point. But this is not good science. It is not intellectually honest, it is ultimately an untenable approach to gender justice, and unfounded or manipulated data leads us down the wrong path to solutions.

Highlighting how dogma can serve as a cover for insufficient methodological rigor, sociologist and sex-industry expert Ronald Weitzer notes that SPC-affiliated feminist porn critics "are quite skeptical of empirical research; they claim to know what porn is about, thus obviating the need for solid data on its content or effects." Weitzer argues that many of the prolific anti-porn feminist authors ignore basic academic standards, using evidence that is "typically anecdotal, including: (1) quotations from some men and women who have viewed porn; (2) descriptions of some porn websites; (3) and accounts of selected scenes in pornographic videos. The grandiose claims about porn are not based on a systematic and rigorous review of porn websites or scenes, yet the critics claim that their conclusions are indeed based on typical material."[43]

Robert Jensen, for instance, expressly dismisses empirical research, preferring not to be "paralyzed by the limitations of social science,"[44] relying instead on his personal testimonials about porn. Regarding the issue of evidence, philosopher Lori Watson boldly proclaims that "no amount of empirical data alone will settle the question as to how best to define and understand pornography."[45] Similarly, Karen Boyle writes that "it is difficult to imagine how one could be 'objective' about this, and Gail Dines maintains that easily accessible porn images are all too representative of what is out there on the Internet and in mass-produced movies."[46]

Yet, "with so much porn available today on the Internet and elsewhere, how could anyone know that what they have observed is representative of the universe?" Weitzer asks. "Dines' construction of selective evidence is especially troubling. She quotes verbatim blocs of three to four sentences from students who spoke to her after a lecture, statements bracketed by quotation marks, without indicating how these statements were recorded. How can readers have confidence in the veracity of these statements? Is Dines somehow able to remember verbatim student statements consisting of multiple sentences at a time?"[47]

Could it be that at least some of Dines's "evidence" is selective? Returning to the issue of standpoint theory and truth claims, it is plausible that at least some of the cherry-picked data is filtered through the lens of dogma and ideological presuppositions.

WHAT IS AT STAKE IN THE SEX WARS?

The sex wars involve unproductive stalemates, intractable theoretical problems, internal feminist political divisions, interpersonal animosity—and frankly, an enormous amount of intellectual and political energy that is better used fighting the problems of sexism and kyriarchy, not each other.

These problems include sexism, racism, gendered violence, persistent wage disparities, and the vast underrepresentation of women in global positions of power. We continue to live in a culture where rape is smothered in victim blaming. We have an online culture that promotes and perpetuates violence against women.[48] Even something as seemingly innocuous as the revelation that the person behind the Facebook-popular "I Fucking Love Science" is a woman resulted in a slew of online comments both objectifying and sexually demeaning the author/creator.

Much of contemporary gender and sexual bias is obvious, like the fact that Congress remains overwhelmingly male. Reproductive rights are under siege, there is persistent violence against transgender and queer people, and there is a digital climate that is overtly hostile toward women. But masculine privilege also flies under the radar: "Institutional practices and ideological beliefs about masculine superiority seem so normal or natural that we have learned not to notice when a man's opinion is taken more seriously than a woman's."[49] Given the shared goals and foundational perspectives regarding reproductive justice, sexual assault, and objectification, it is curious that pornography, sex work, hookups, and other related topics result in such divergent—and frequently contentious—conclusions within feminist circles. Truth claims that impact the ongoing feminist sex wars are a case in point.

Entering the fray of the sex wars easily means risking the ire of anti-porn feminists who presume that if you are not with them, you are against them and ipso facto promoting a pro-porn agenda. This misses the point.

Also missing the point are so-called pro-sex perspectives that privilege autonomy, agency, and pleasure, also underscored with truth claims, and without adequately accounting for the critical insight feminist analysis brings to bear. As psychologist Michael Bader writes, "Porn is not harmless. But neither is it an important cause of sexual violence or misogyny. Partisans on both sides of this debate have littered their arguments with distortions, hyperbole, and cheap rhetorical tricks."[50] We have to wade through a lot of rubbish to get to the truth.

CONCLUSION

Like any media genre, pornography both shapes and reflects assumptions about straight masculinity, female sexuality, expectations of beauty, how women are treated—particularly women of color—and the sexual pleasure and safety of all. Mainstream porn often reenacts bias about gender, race, and power. In this sense, porn is no different than Disney films, advertising, reruns of *Two and a Half Men*, and the sports section of the local paper. But because porn is explicitly focused on sex instead of infused with sex-power innuendo, porn can blur the line of consent by making nonconsensual domination sexy. That does not necessarily make it wrong, but it does create more compelling reasons for understanding what we are seeing and creating cultural climates that foster more discussion. The answer is not to shut down pornography. The answer is not silence or repression. Abstinence movements have a terrible track record.

The answer to the porn conundrum is not to eradicate pornography because "Just Say No" just does not work. It does not work for drugs, it is ineffective in terms of sexual abstinence, and it does not work for pornography, either. Even the American Academy of Pediatrics—an organization certainly not known for its radical politics—explains that abstinence-only education is a waste of time, especially "when the media have become such an important source of information" about sexual activity. Since pornography is one aspect of media, it holds that promoting porn abstinence is also an unwise strategy.[51]

Dogma-driven arguments to "stop porn culture" discourage robust dialogue, ignore potentially important data, and inadvertently promote sexual shame. Shame-based arguments are ineffective, disempowering, and harmful. Instead of encouraging silence and creating further taboo, critical media literacy, increased access to information, and greater conversation about gender, race, power, and consent promote sexual pleasure and productive solutions to sexual harm. In the 1970s educators, researchers, policymakers, and health professionals started talking out loud about drugs and addiction. The HIV and the AIDS epidemic transformed the word "condom" from one uttered in private to common vocabulary on billboards and public service announcements. The Stop Porn strategy promotes its own perspective while silencing opposing viewpoints. This form of censorship is counterproductive to resolving political and sexual concerns about safety, pleasure, liberty, and well-being.

In her essay on the politics of Stop Porn Culture's anti-pornography slideshow, author Jennifer Maher describes the visual tactic as a "'pedagogy of conversion' that draws on affect in a way not wholly dissimilar to how pornography as a genre is argued (by these very same presenters) to work upon its spectators."[52] These manipulative techniques silence conversations about sexual arousal. Where there is silencing, there is shame.

Clearly, there is need for more dialogue about pornography without the sex-shaming dynamics induced by feminist anti-porn politics. Natasha Walter, author of *Living Doll*, is critical of how feminist rhetoric is co-opted to sell male fantasies of female self-objectification as empowering. But she also notably writes "that the right to be sexual without fear of shame is 'essential for women's freedom.'"[53]

Even if it is true, as Stop Porn Culture asserts, that "pornography is a factor in shaping the attitude and behaviors in *some* men who use it and that it is a factor in *some* men's sexual aggression,"[54] this indicates a need for rational dialogue and more complete information. For instance, who are these "some men" to which Stop Porn Culture refers? Neil Malamuth, Tamara Addison, and Mary Koss suggest that there are reliable associations between "frequent pornography use and sexually aggressive behaviors . . . [and] the way relatively aggressive men interpret and react to the same pornography may differ from that of nonaggressive men."[55] These are not "some men," but *specific* men who exhibit particular constellations of habits and traits.

Yet by rigidly opposing pornography—and by using dubious data and loose definitions to do so[56]—the dominant feminist anti-porn cohort creates an us-versus-them dichotomy, pitting potential political allies against each other and wringing important nuance from the dialogues. Given pornography's ubiquitous presence in our media landscape, this strategy serves nobody well. In addition, in pursuing this crucial political concern, anti-porn feminists invoke truth claims about sexuality that are not supported by empirical data. While preventing harm is fundamental for a flourishing democratic society with maximum liberty for its members, dogma-driven ideology threatens to undermine these goals.

A far more constructive approach is informing our political perspectives with data-driven research, supporting open dialogue about contentious violence issues, and promoting porn literacy as a part of a broader media education agenda. In this way, we encourage informed conversation about pleasure and consent, while avoiding unproductive stalemates when it comes to the politics of porn. Porn literacy is a strategy to lift us out of the sex-war stalemate. It means taking the best of feminist political perspectives and bringing this information into the mainstream. It means understanding the difference between coercion and consent, and reaching across the aisle in solidarity rather than with hostility.

We can do better than misdirected outrage.

NOTES

1. Whitney Strub, "Queer Smut, Queer Rights," in *New Views on Pornography: Sexuality, Politics, and the Law*, ed. Lynn Comella and Shira Tarrant (Santa Barbara, CA: Praeger, forthcoming).

2. Radfem 2013: Resurgence of Women's Liberation. http://radfem2013.moonfruit.com/#/about/4572228606 (accessed 17 Jul. 2013).

3. For a review of the feminist pornography debates, see Carolyn Bronstein, *Battling Pornography: The American Feminist Anti-Pornography Movement, 1976–1986* (New York: Cambridge University Press, 2011).

4. Nancy C. M. Hartsock, "The Feminist Standpoint: Developing the Ground for a Specifically Feminist Historical Materialism," in *Discovering Reality: Feminist Perspectives on Epistemology, Metaphysics, Methodology, and Philosophy of Science*, ed. Sandra Harding and Merrill B. Hintikka (Boston: D. Reidel, 1983), 283–310.

5. Nina Flores, "Beyond the 'Secularism Tic'—An Interview with Feminist Philosopher Sandra Harding," *Ms. Magazine Blog*, July 19, 2013, http://msmagazine.com/blog/2013/07/19/beyond-the-secularism-tick-an-interview-with-feminist-philosopher-sandra-harding (accessed 8 Aug. 2013).

6. It is worth noting this similar line of argumentation:

a. If pornography is produced by white males (or their patriarchal stand-ins) who are members of the socially privileged class,
b. And this pornography establishes a patriarchal (and kyriarchal) narrative about objectification and silencing,
c. And this narrative is taken as authoritative and reproduces cultural demands, then
d. Pornography is oppressive.

7. Marjorie Jolles, personal correspondence, June 25, 2013.

8. bell hooks, *Feminist Theory: From Margin to Center* (Boston: South End Press, 2000).

9. Mary E. Hawkesworth, "Knowers, Knowing, Known: Feminist Theory and Claims of Truth," *Signs* 14, no. 3 (Spring 1989): 533–57.

10. Hawkesworth, "Knowers, Knowing, Known." Hawkesworth was definitely not talking about pornography in this article, but the questions she raises about feminist truth claims and the politics of knowledge are applicable here.

11. This argument owes a great deal to Marjorie Jolles, personal correspondence, June 25, 2013.

12. Sinnamon Love, "A Question of Feminism," in *The Feminist Porn Book: The Politics of Producing Pleasure*, ed. Tristan Taormino, Celine Parreñas Shimizu, Constance Penley, and Mireille Miller-Young (New York: Feminist Press, 2013), 101 and 104.

13. Mari Matsuda, "Looking to the Bottom: Critical Legal Studies and Reparations," *Harvard Civil Rights-Civil Liberties Law Review* 22 (1987) : 324.

14. Alison Flood, "Fifty Shades of Grey Condemned as 'Manual for Sexual Torture,'" *Guardian*, August 24, 2012, http://www.guardian.co.uk/books/2012/aug/24/fifty-shades-grey-domestic-violence-campaigners (accessed 8 Aug. 2013).

15. Katha Pollitt, e-mail post to wmst-L@Listserv.umd.edu, August 27, 2012, 12:24 a.m.

16. Judith Grant, "I Feel Therefore I Am: A Critique of Female Experience as the Basis for a Feminist Epistemology," *Women & Politics* 7, no. 3 (1987): 99.

17. Grant, "I Feel Therefore I Am," 113.

18. See Judith Grant, *Fundamental Feminism: Contesting the Core Concepts of Feminist Theory* (New York: Routledge, 1993), 101.

19. According to Nielsen/NetRatings, about one in three visitors to adult websites was female, with nearly 13 million American women viewing Internet porn at least once each month during the first three months of 2007. Violet Blue, "Are More Women Okay With Watching Porn?" *CNN Living*, July 24, 2009, http://www.cnn.com/2009/LIVING/personal/07/24/o.women.watching.porn/index.html?_s=PM:LIVING (accessed 13 Aug. 2013). Nielsen reports that more than 25 percent of Internet users accessed an adult website in January 2010, for about 6 percent of all U.S. Internet hits. This puts the adult category in eighth place, with social networking sites in first. It is worth noting, however, that when tracking first started in 2004, adult sites got the most page hits on the Internet and this first-place status has been dislodged. See "Thanks for Making the Internet Hot," *All Things Considered*, March 7, 2010, http://www.npr.org/templates/story/story.php?storyId=124419606 (accessed 13 Aug. 2013).

20. "What Is a Porn Culture?" Stop Porn Culture, http://stoppornculture.org/index.php/about-the-issue/definition-of-pornography (accessed 17 Jul. 2013).

21. For more on the issue of emotional manipulation and anti-porn political strategies, see Clarissa Smith and Feona Attwood, "Emotional Truths and Thrilling Slide Shows: The Resurgence of Antiporn Feminism," in *The Feminist Porn Book: The Politics of Producing Pleasure*, ed. Tristan Taormino, Celine Parreñas Shimizu, Constance Penley, and Mireille Miller-Young (New York: Feminist Press, 2013), 41–57. Also see Chris Boulton, "Porn and Me(n): Sexual Morality, Objectification, and Religion at the Wheelock Anti-Pornography Conference," *Communication Review* 11 (2008): 247–73.

22. Jennifer Maher, "Arguing with an Orgasm: The Politics and Pedagogy of the Anti-Pornography Slideshow," in *Sexing the Look in Popular Visual Culture*, ed. Kathy Justice Gentile (Newcastle upon Tyne: Cambridge Scholars Publishing, 2010), 86.

23. Constance Penley, "'A Feminist Teaching Pornography? That's Like Scopes Teaching Evolution!'" in *The Feminist Porn Book: The Politics of Producing Pleasure*, ed. Tristan Taormino, Celine Parreñas Shimizu, Constance Penley, and Mireille Miller-Young (New York: Feminist Press, 2013), 187.

24. Miranda A. H. Horvath, Llian Alys, Kristina Massey, Afroditi Pina, Mia Scally, and Joanna R. Adler, "'Basically . . . Porn Is Everywhere': A Rapid Evidence Assessment on the Effects that Access and Exposure to Pornography Has on Children and Young People" (London: Office of the Children's Commissioner/Middlesex University, 2013), 7.

25. Horvath, et al., "'Basically . . . Porn Is Everywhere,'" 9.

26. "Internet Pornography Statistics," Top Ten Reviews, http://internet-filter-review.toptenreviews.com/internet-pornography-statistics.html (accessed 17 Jul. 2013); "The Stats on Internet Pornography," State of Search, http://www.stateofsearch.com/statistics-on-internet-porn-still-a-major-industry/ (accessed 17 Jul. 2013).

27. "Porn Sites Get More Visitors Each Month than Netflix, Amazon and Twitter Combined," *Huffington Post*, May 4, 2013, http://www.huffingtonpost.com/2013/05/03/internet-porn-stats_n_3187682.html (accessed 17 Jul. 2013).

28. Gail Dines, e-mail post to wmst-L@Listserv.umd.edu, February 29, 2012, 3:32 p.m.

29. Caroline Heldman and Lisa Wade, "A Call for a Twenty-First Century 'Sex Wars,'" paper presented at the annual meeting of the Western Political Science Association, California, March 28, 2013. Philosopher Jacob Held writes that research indicates "the negative results often attributed to hard-core pornography, such as sexist attitudes, lack of understanding or empathy for women's interests, objectification, silence via disablement resulting from objectification, etc., are more reasonably attributable to sexualized media as a whole" rather than to pornography. "It is not just the pornographer's world, it is the sexist's world, and that is why [mainstream] pornographers have a voice and place within it," Held explains. These conditions thus require attention to sexist cultural contexts beyond porn production. See Jacob M. Held, "Pornography as Symptom: Refocusing the Anti-Pornography Debate on Pornification and Sexualization," *Issues in Contemporary Philosophy* 20 (Spring 2013): 15–27.

30. Ana J. Bridges, Robert Wosnitzer, Erica Sharrer, Chyng Sun, and Rachael Liberman, "Aggression and Sexual Behavior in Best-Selling Pornography Videos: A Content Analysis Update," *Violence Against Women* 16 (October 2010): 1065–85.

31. The variables that are coded as violent by Ana Bridges's research team (e.g., spanking or hair pulling) may not be seen as violent to some. It is entirely possible that there are intervening variables regarding the depictions of women in pornography and concerns about women's well-being.

32. Andy Ruddock, "Pornography and Effects Studies: What Does the Research Actually Say?" in *New Views on Pornography: Sexuality, Politics, and the Law*, eds. Lynn Comella and Shira Tarrant (Santa Barbara, CA: Praeger, forthcoming). Italics added.

33. Ruddock, "Pornography and Effects Studies."

34. "Facts and Figures," Stop Porn Culture, http://stoppornculture.org/index.php/facts-and-resources/facts-and-figures (accessed 17 Jul. 2013).

35. Michele L. Ybarra and Kimberly Mitchell, "Exposure to Internet Pornography among Children and Adolescents: A National Survey," *Cyberpsychology & Behavior* 8, no. 5 (2005): 473–86, http://unh.edu/ccrc/pdf/jvq/CV76.pdf (accessed 17 Jul. 2013). This data does not account for unwanted exposure to pornography among teens. See Janis Wolak, Kimberly Mitchell, and David Finkelhor,"Unwanted and Wanted Exposure to Online Pornography in a National Sample of Youth Internet Users," *Pediatrics* 119 no. 2 (February 1 , 2007): 247–57 , http://pediatrics.org/cgi/doi/10.1542/peds (accessed 17 Jul. 2013).

36. Justin J. Lehmiller, "Is Sexual Content in Movies Related to Sexual Risk Taking?" *Psychology of Human Sexuality*, April 17, 2013, http://www.lehmiller.com/blog/2013/4/17/is-sexual-content-in-movies-related-to-sexual-risk-taking.html (accessed 17 Jul. 2013).

37. "Are the Effects of Pornography Negligible?" University of Montreal press release, December 1, 2009, http://www.eurekalert.org/pub_releases/2009-12/uom-ate120109.php (accessed 17 Jul. 2013).

38. Mary Ann Watson and Randyl D. Smith, "Positive Porn: Educational, Medical, and Clinical Uses," *American Journal of Sexuality Education* 7, no. 2 (2012): 123.

39. Smith and Attwood, "Emotional Truths and Thrilling Slide Shows," 54.

40. "Talk Back: FAQ and a Q&A," Stop Porn Culture, http://stoppornculture.org/index.php/about-the-issue/faqs#12 (accessed 17 Jul. 2013).

41. Jacob M. Held, "Pornography as Symptom: Refocusing the Anti-Pornography Debate on Pornification and Sexualization." *Issues in Contemporary Philosophy* 20 (Spring 2013): 15.

42. Martha Nussbaum, *Sex and Social Justice* (New York: Oxford University Press, 1999), 241–42.

43. Ronald Weitzer, "Pornography: Popular Claims vs. the Evidence," in *New Views on Pornography: Sexuality, Politics, and the Law*, ed. Lynn Comella and Shira Tarrant (Santa Barbara, CA: Praeger, forthcoming).

44. Robert Jensen, "Introduction" and "The Pain of Pornography," in *Pornography: The Production and Consumption of Inequality*, ed. Gail Dines, Robert Jensen, and Ann Russo (New York: Routledge, 1997), 5.

45. Lori Watson, "A Reply to Weitzer," *Violence against Women* 18 (2012): 502–5, 504. Quoted in Weitzer, "Pornography: Popular Claims vs. the Evidence."

46. Quoted in Weitzer, "Pornography: Popular Claims vs. the Evidence."

47. Ronald Weitzer, "Pornography: Popular Claims vs. the Evidence."

48. One such instance was the violent backlash against blogger and cultural critic Anita Sarkeesian. When Sarkeesian launched an addition to her *Feminist Frequency* online video series that focused specifically on gender tropes in gaming culture, Sarkeesian became the focus of organized attacks by hackers and trolls. This hate campaign included an online game that was created called "Beat Up Anita Sarkeesian," an interactive experience that needs no explanation.

49. Shira Tarrant, *Men and Feminism* (Berkeley, CA: Seal Press, 2009), 89.

50. Michael Bader. "Is Pornography Really Harmful?" *AlterNet*, November 7, 2007. http://www.alternet.org/sex/67144/?page=1 (accessed 17 Jul. 2013) .

51. The Council on Communications and the Media, "Policy Statement: Sexuality, Contraception, and the Media," *Pediatrics*, August 30, 2010, http://pediatrics.aappublications.org/cgi/reprint/peds.2010-1544v1 (accessed 13 Jul. 2013).

52. Maher, "Arguing with an Orgasm," 86.

53. Jessica Valenti, "Living Dolls: The Return of Sexism by Natasha Walter," *Observer*, January 31, 2010, http://www.guardian.co.uk/books/2010/jan/31/living-dolls-natasha-walter (accessed 17 Jul. 2013).

54. "Talk Back: FAQ and a Q&A," Stop Porn Culture. Italics added.

55. Neil M. Malamuth, Tamara Addison, and Mary Koss, "Pornography and Sexual Aggression: Are There Reliable Effects and Can We Understand Them?" *Annual Review of Sex Research* 11 (2000): 26.

56. On the issue of spurious data, see Shira Tarrant, "Review of *Pornland: How Porn Has Hijacked Our Sexuality* by Gail Dines." *Bitch* 48 (Fall 2010); Shira Tarrant, "Porn: Pleasure or Profit? *Ms.* Interviews Gail Dines, Part II." *Ms. Magazine Blog*, July 7, 2010, http://msmagazine.com/blog/blog/2010/07/07/porn-pleasure-or-profit-ms-interviews-gail-dines-part-ii/ (accessed 13 Jul. 2013).

Chapter Four

Pornographic and Pornified

*Feminist and Ecological Understandings of
Sexually Explicit Media*

Robert Jensen

Is contemporary mass-marketed pornography consistent with the political principles and moral values necessary to achieve just and sustainable human communities?

More specifically: (1) Is contemporary mass-marketed pornography—which has grown steadily more overtly cruel and degrading to women, at the same time that it has grown more mainstream and accepted—likely to bolster our efforts to build a society based on gender justice? (2) Is the normalizing of mass-mediated sexuality more generally likely to contribute to our efforts to build stable communities?

More bluntly: Can a pornography-saturated society be safe and healthy?

My answer—building on the feminist critique of men's sexual exploitation of women that emerged more than three decades ago, understood within an ecological framework—is a clear "no." In those decades, sexually explicit material has become increasingly pornographic, confirming the insights and explanatory power of that feminist critique. At the same time, U.S. society has become more pornified, which should lead to a deeper ecological critique of our hypermediated world.

Paradoxically, that feminist critique has lost ground in the public conversation, and the culture seems largely uninterested in what lessons we can learn from that deeper critique of an image-saturated culture. After twenty-five years of research, writing, and organizing on this subject—during which I have talked to a lot of people about pornography—I believe the reason for this is simple: We are afraid of looking honestly at the proliferation of increasingly extreme sexually explicit material. What we learn by facing our pornographic/pornified culture—not just about sexual behavior, but about how we understand ourselves as part of the larger living world—is how patriarchal values are woven into the most intimate spaces of everyday life, and how a mass-mediated reality delivered through high-technology gadgets has alienated us from ourselves, each other, and our environment.

Starting from this critical feminist perspective we can, and should, work collectively to sketch the outlines of a sexual ethic that is consistent with social justice and ecological sustainability. This concept of a sexual ethic is rooted not in repressive attempts to narrowly define and arbitrarily impose on people a set of rules, but to open up a discussion that, at its core, is about what it means to be human in healthy and sustainable communities. I start with definitions of the terms politics and power, morality and ethics, sex and gender.

DEFINITIONS

In the contemporary United States, mention of "politics" or the "political" points most people toward electoral politics and the policies that those who are elected write into law. Those aspects of politics are important, but I will use these terms to describe other struggles over the distribution of power and wealth. Feminist politics focuses on resistance at multiple levels to patriarchy, a social system based on the assertion that males and females were created or evolved differently for different purposes, with men taking their rightful place on top. Electing candidates and passing laws can be part of a feminist political strategy, but the radical feminism in which I am rooted sees electoral and legislative campaigns not as ends—not as ways to try to perfect a basically healthy system—but as a means to highlight the problem of patriarchy and focus attention on the need to transform a fundamentally unjust system.

Similarly, discussion of "morality" and "ethics" often is reduced to specific rules for behavior that can be imposed on others. Some believe those rules should be codified into law, while others argue that "you can't legislate morality," but in each case "moral" is defined as rules. In this essay, I will use the terms to describe the complex ways people collectively struggle with the fundamental question: "What does it mean to be human?" In all areas of life we construct ethics—an ethic about images, a food ethic, an ethic of friendship—that shape our lives, including our political lives.

So, politics is more than the work of professional politicians, ethics is more than imposing arbitrary rules, and all political ideas have moral underpinnings. While the product of politics is law, the political process should be seen more expansively. While the product of ethical inquiry is a judgment of right and wrong, moral discourse should be seen more expansively. And politics and ethics cannot be separated. How we answer questions about what it means to be human obviously will affect how we shape the systems that distribute power and wealth.

On varying uses of "sex" and "gender": There are three categories of biological sex identity—male, female, and intersexed.[1] The vast majority of humans are born with distinctly male or female reproductive systems, sexual characteristics, and/or chromosomal structure, and there is some segment (the percentage in this category would depend on what degree of ambiguity marks the category) born with reproductive or sexual anatomy that does not fit the definitions of female or male.[2] These categories are biological—based on the material reality of who can potentially reproduce with whom—and exist independently of any particular cultural understanding of them. That is what typically is called "sex."

Beyond the category of "sex" (the biological differences between males and females), is "gender" (the nonbiological meaning societies create out of sex differences). Gender plays out in a variety of ways, including gender roles (assigning males and females to different social, political, or economic roles); gender norms (expecting males and females to comply with different norms of behavior and appearance); gendered traits and virtues (assuming that males and females will be psychologically or morally different from each other); gender identity (a person's internal sense of gender—of masculinity, femininity, or something in between—which may not be how others perceive the person); and gender symbolism (using gender in the description of animals, inanimate objects, or ideas).[3]

How should we understand the connection between sex and gender? Given that reproduction is not a trivial matter, the biological differences between male and female humans are not trivial, and it is plausible that these physical differences could conceivably give rise to significant intellectual, emotional, and moral differences between males and females. However, for all the recent advances in biology and neuroscience, we still know relatively little about how the basic biological differences influence those capacities, though in contemporary culture we routinely assume that the effects are greater than have been established. Some even assert that male and female humans are so different that we may as well be from different planets—the "Men Are from Mars, Women Are from Venus" phenomenon.[4] Male and female humans are much more similar than different,[5] but in patriarchal societies based on gendered power, focus on the differences is used to rationalize disparities in power.

So, while sex categories are part of any human society, the pernicious effects of patriarchal gender politics can, and should, be challenged.

RADICAL FEMINISM: SEX AND POWER IN PATRIARCHY

While we have limited understanding of what the differences in male and female biology mean for intellectual, emotional, and moral differences, there is no evidence that any of those differences are relevant in determining the political status of men and women. Whatever the differences in opinion (between feminists and nonfeminists, and among different styles of feminism) about the distinctions between males and females, this much is uncontroversial in the contemporary United States: Men and women should be equal citizens.

The denial of that status to women is a product of patriarchy, whether grounded in God or evolution. Both theological and secular arguments for patriarchy assert that the differences are essentially immutable, an odd claim given that patriarchy is a relatively recent phenomenon in human history. The development of patriarchy is tied to the domestication of animals and agriculture, when the communal and cooperative ethic of gatherer-hunter societies was replaced with ideas of private ownership and patrimony that led to men controlling women's reproduction and claiming ownership of women.[6] In the 200,000-year history of the modern human, patriarchy is less than 10,000 years old.

My analysis and arguments are rooted in a radical feminist critique of patriarchy. By feminist, I mean an analysis of the ways in which women are oppressed as a class—the ways in which men as a class hold more power, and how those differences in power systematically disadvantage women in the public and private spheres. Gender oppression plays out in different ways depending on social location; men's oppression of women is in connection with other systems of oppression—heterosexism, racism, class privilege, and histories of colonial and postcolonial domination.

By radical feminist, I mean the analysis of the ways that in this patriarchal system in which we live, one of the key sites of this oppression—one key method of domination—is sexuality. Two of the most well-known radical feminists have been central to the feminist critique of pornography—the writer Andrea Dworkin,[7] and Catharine MacKinnon, a lawyer and law professor.[8] The radical feminist philosophy that has shaped my thinking is most clearly articulated by Marilyn Frye.[9]

I also understand radical feminism not just as a way of critiquing men's domination of women, but as a way to understand systems of power and oppression more generally. Hierarchies of any kind are inconsistent with human flourishing unless a compelling argument can be made that the hierarchy is necessary to help those with less power in the system, a test that can rarely be met. Feminism is not the only way into a broader critique of the many types of oppression, of course, but it is one important way, and was for me the first route into such a framework.

Each system of power and oppression is unique in its own way, but there are common features. Most people's philosophical and theological systems are rooted in basic concepts of justice, equality, and the inherent dignity of all people. Most of us endorse values that—if we took them seriously— should lead to a rejection of the violence, exploitation, and oppression that defines the modern world. If only a small percentage of people in any given society are truly sociopaths—incapable of empathy, those who enjoy cruel and oppressive behavior—then a radical analysis should make sense to lots of people.

But it is not that easy, because of the rewards when we are willing to subordinate our stated principles in service of oppressive systems. Feminism helped me understand the complex process, which tends to work like this:

- The systems and structures in which we live are hierarchical.
- Hierarchical systems and structures deliver to those in the dominant class certain privileges, pleasures, and material benefits, and some limited number of people in subordinated classes will be allowed access to those same rewards.
- People are typically hesitant to give up privileges, pleasures, and benefits that make us feel good.
- But, those benefits clearly come at the expense of the vast majority of those in the subordinated classes.
- Given the widespread acceptance of basic notions of equality and human rights, the existence of hierarchy has to be justified in some way other than crass self-interest.
- One of the most persuasive arguments for systems of domination and subordination is that they are "natural" and therefore inevitable, immutable, just the way things are.

So, oppressive systems work hard to make it appear that the hierarchies—and the disparity in power and resources that flow from hierarchies—are natural and, therefore, beyond modification. If men are naturally smarter and stronger than women, then patriarchy is inevitable and justifiable. If white people are naturally smarter and more virtuous than people of color, then white supremacy is inevitable and justifiable. If rich people are naturally smarter and harder working than poor people, then economic injustice is inevitable and justifiable. And, if human beings have special status in the universe, justified either on theological or biological grounds, then humans' right to extract whatever we like from the rest of the living world is inevitable and justifiable.

For unjust hierarchies, maintaining this belief in naturalness is essential to rationalizing the illegitimate authority that is exercised in them. Not surprisingly, people in the dominant class exercising that power gravitate easily to

such a view. And because of their power to control key storytelling institutions (especially education and mass communication), those in the dominant
class can fashion a story about the world that leads some portion of the
people in the subordinated class to internalize the ideology.

At the core of patriarchal ideology is the naturalizing of male dominance.
Any politics aimed at a more just and sustainable world must include a
rejection of patriarchy.

THE PORNOGRAPHY DEBATE, THEN AND NOW

When I was born in 1958, the cultural conversation on pornography took
place largely within a framework of moral assertions. The obscenity law
regulating sexual material was typically defended as necessary because such
uses of sex were immoral, while defenders of pornography argued that individuals should be free to use such material because there was no harm to
others and the state should not make moral decisions for people. The anti-
pornography view was articulated mostly by conservative and religious people; liberals and secular people dominated the defense of pornography.

In the 1970s, a vibrant feminist movement challenged men's violence
against women, pointing out that male dominance produced a rape culture
that formally criminalized but routinely excused that violence.[10] Feminist
critics also began to explore the cultural support for that violence, analyzing
mass media—the dominant form of storytelling in modern culture—and
highlighting misogynistic images in advertising and entertainment that eroticize domination and subordination. That included a feminist critique of pornography, focused not on subjective sexual mores but on the harm to women
used in pornography and against whom pornography is used.[11]

This analysis was controversial not only in the dominant culture but also
within feminism, leading to what became known as the "porn wars" or the
"sex wars" in the early 1980s. Three major positions within feminism have
emerged from this struggle: (1) anti-pornography feminists, who typically
identify as radical feminists; (2) anti-censorship feminists who are critical of
misogynistic pornography but reject the legal approach radical feminists proposed; and (3) a pro-pornography group that valorizes pornography as a
discourse which subverts traditional gender norms and has liberatory potential for women's sexuality.

Activist groups such as Women Against Pornography in New York used
slideshows and tours of pornography districts to educate and protest, and
there was a flurry of this kind of activism in the late 1970s and early 1980s.
But radical feminists did not face organized opposition from other feminists
until Dworkin and MacKinnon developed a civil-rights ordinance that rejected criminal obscenity law and allowed women to pursue damages against

pornography producers and consumers.[12] Passed in 1983 by the Minneapolis City Council but vetoed by the mayor, it was passed and signed into law in Indianapolis in 1984 but rejected on constitutional grounds in the federal courts.[13] Efforts to pass the law in other jurisdictions continued into the 1990s, failing at the legislative and judicial levels.

By the mid-1990s, the feminist critique of pornography had been pushed out of the public discussion, and the normalizing and mainstreaming of pornography was underway. Journalists began writing routinely about pornography as an ordinary business that raised no particular moral or political concerns.[14] These stories sometimes mentioned opposition to the industry, but simply as one aspect of doing business that pornographers had to cope with—pornography was becoming a relatively uncontroversial part of contemporary culture.

The feminist anti-pornography movement languished in the United States until the late 2000s with the formation of Stop Porn Culture.[15] This attempt to restart that movement in the face of increasingly intense misogyny in pornography that is increasingly mainstream has had some limited success in the United Kingdom and Scandinavia, but is still marginal in the United States.

A FEMINIST CRITIQUE OF PORNOGRAPHY

The feminist critique argues that pornography (used colloquially, to describe the genre of sexually explicit mass media) is routinely pornographic (used in a feminist sense, to describe sexualizing the social subordination of women).

A discussion of the ideology of pornography requires a sketch of the industry. The two main categories in today's pornographic movie industry (whether distributed as a traditional movie on DVD or in various forms online) are "features" and "wall-to-wall/gonzo." Features resemble a Hollywood movie, with plot and characters. Wall-to-wall movies are all-sex productions with no pretense of narrative or dialogue. Many of these movies are shot gonzo style, in which performers acknowledge the camera and often speak directly to the audience. In addition, there are specialty titles—movies that feature sadomasochism and bondage, fetish material, transsexuals—that fill niche markets. Heterosexual material dominates the industry, with a thriving gay male pornography market and a smaller lesbian pornography market. While inexpensive digital technology has made it easy for ordinary people to make and share online their own pornography, much of this noncommercial material mimics the industry.

The majority of hard-core movies include oral, vaginal, and anal sex, almost always ending with ejaculation on the woman. A 1993 study of pornographic heterosexual videotapes found that the tapes typically presented a world in which women were younger, more sexually active, and more expressive than men; women were frequently depicted in subordinate positions (e.g., kneeling down in front of a partner); and sexual contact was usually between strangers.[16] A more recent content analysis of fifty best-selling adult videos revealed a similar pattern of inequality and violence. Nearly half of the 304 scenes analyzed contained verbal aggression (for example, name calling or verbal threats), while over 88 percent showed physical aggression (including hair pulling, open-hand slapping or spanking, choking, and whipping). Seventy percent of aggressive acts were perpetrated by men, and 87 percent of acts were committed against women. Fewer than 5 percent of the aggressive acts provoked a negative response from the target, such as requests to stop. This pornographic "reality" was further highlighted by the relative infrequency of more positive behaviors (verbal compliments, embracing, kissing, or laughter), portrayed in fewer than 10 percent of the scenes.[17]

As pornography depicting conventional sexual acts has become routine, gonzo producers have pushed the limits of social norms and women's bodies with painful and body-punishing pornsex.[18] Multiple-penetration scenes (a woman being penetrated by more than one man at the same time, such as in a vaginal-anal "double penetration"), gagging (forcing a penis down a woman's throat deeply and roughly enough to make her gag), and ATM (ass-to-mouth, in which a man penetrates a woman anally and then places his penis in her mouth or the mouth of another woman) are found throughout the gonzo genre.

Nearly every scene ends with the "cum shot" or "money shot"—male ejaculation into a woman's mouth or on her face or body. As one pornography director put it, "it's like a dog marking its territory."[19] Another veteran pornographic director and actor put it more bluntly: "I'd like to really show what I believe the men want to see: violence against women . . . [but] the most violent we can get is the cum shot in the face. Men get off behind that, because they get even with the women they can't have."[20]

Combining such quantitative studies with qualitative analyses using more interpretive methods, the main messages of pornographic films can be summarized as:

1. All women always want sex from men;
2. Women like all the sexual acts that men perform or demand, and
3. Any woman who does not at first realize this can be persuaded by force. Such force is rarely necessary, however, for most of the women in pornography are the "nymphomaniacs" of men's fantasies. Women are the sexual objects, whose job it is to fulfill male desire.[21]

There are thousands of films produced each year in the United States, with considerable variation in style and quality of production. But the vast majority of commercially produced sexually explicit films share an ideology that can be summarized as:

1. We all must be sexual all the time; sex must be hot; hot sex requires inequality, and
2. Men are naturally dominant; women are naturally submissive; therefore
3. Pornography portrays men and women in their "natural" roles free from constraints imposed by repressive social norms, leading to a simple conclusion:
4. Women are whores.[22]

No matter what a woman's role or status, all women are for sex at the discretion of men. Men's desires define women's value to men and define women's essence: women not only owe it to men to service them sexually, but also owe it to themselves. Women can find their authentic selves only by embracing this status as whores. Pornography erases the good girl/bad girl framework; all women are "bad," created that way for men to use sexually. In the pornographic world, women are allowed to fill a variety of professional and social roles, as long as they recognize that they are made women by not allowing those roles to impede their core function as whores, as beings who exist to provide sexual pleasure to men.

To summarize the feminist critique—understanding pornography as sexual material that helps maintain the sexual subordination of women—Dworkin writes, "In the subordination of women, inequality itself is sexualized: made into the experience of sexual pleasure, essential to sexual desire. Pornography is the material means of sexualizing inequality; and that is why pornography is a central practice in the subordination of women."[23] Dworkin identified what we might call "the elements of the pornographic," the ways in which that subordination is enacted. Not all pornography includes all these elements, but all these elements are present throughout contemporary pornography:

1. Objectification: when "a human being, through social means, is made less than human, turned into a thing or commodity, bought and sold."
2. Hierarchy: a question of power, with "a group on top (men) and a group on the bottom (women)."
3. Submission: when acts of obedience and compliance become necessary for survival, members of oppressed groups learn to anticipate the orders and desires of those who have power over them, and their

compliance is then used by the dominant group to justify its dominance.
4. Violence: when it becomes "systematic, endemic enough to be unremarkable and normative, usually taken as an implicit right of the one committing the violence."[24]

PORNOGRAPHY AND GENDER EQUALITY

A commitment to gender equality means treating women as full citizens in the political sphere and being skeptical of any claims that human nature justifies unequal treatment in any other arena. This commitment to equality requires a relentless critique of patriarchy and a rejection of any policy or practice that reinforces male dominance, including in the realm of sexual activity. The feminist claim that "the personal is political" is not a retreat into narcissism, but a call to examine how what has traditionally been considered private and beyond politics, such as intimate relationships, are structured by politics—in this case, particularly gender politics.

Like any complex system, patriarchy is not monolithic. In some patriarchal societies, women's sexuality is kept out of public view to ensure the ability of specific men (fathers, husbands) to control specific women (daughters, wives). In other societies, women's sexuality is commodified for mass consumption and wider use. In the contemporary United States, people are quick to label more "traditional" societies as patriarchal and regressive, but consider the practices of more "modern" societies as a sign of women's liberation. But the two systems are flip sides of the same patriarchal coin: The common assumption is that women's sexuality should be available to men on men's terms.

In the version of patriarchy dominant in the United States, pornography, prostitution, and stripping—what I call the sexual-exploitation industries— are a routine part of contemporary culture. Even though some aspects are criminalized and other aspects regulated, the vast majority of men have some experience with at least one of these industries that allow men to rent women's bodies for sex, which at its most brutal involves the actual buying and selling of women and children.[25]

Whatever one's view of the role of intimacy and sexuality in human society, it is difficult to imagine achieving gender equality when members of one group (women) can routinely be rented to members of another group (men) for sexual pleasure. Supporters of the sexual-exploitation industries focus on the right of women to choose to participate in these activities. While individual choice is an essential component of any modern democratic system, people choose within parameters set by society. To claim that freedom is simply the ability of an individual to choose, abstracted from the reality of a society and its values/norms/practices, and that such a thin conception of freedom defines political equality—is simplistic, obscuring the realities of power.

A system in which one group of people can rent—even buy and sell—the bodies of members of another group undermines equality by reinforcing the inherently lesser status of the "object" that can be used in that way. Under conditions of real equality, it is hard to imagine that such a practice would exist. The sexual-exploitation industries in patriarchy are inconsistent with, and impediments to, gender equality, and any society claiming to be democratic must work to achieve gender equality.

AN ECOLOGICAL CRITIQUE OF PORNOGRAPHY

I use the term ecological not to contrast "dirty" pornography with other forms of sex that are "pure," nor merely to label pornography as a form of cultural pollution. Ecology is the study of interactions among organisms and their environment; an ecological approach directs our attention to the effects of human practices on the larger living world, recognizing that our understanding of ourselves shapes the way we act in the world and affects the world. We should always evaluate all human practices ecologically.

An ecological analysis is not an alternative to a feminist analysis, but a companion. The feminist critique not only points out that much of pornography is pornographic, in the sense that it reflects and reinforces patriarchy's domination/subordination dynamic, but also highlights how pop culture more generally is pornified.[26] Thinking ecologically about how sexually explicit material of all kinds has become normalized provides a case study of the consequences when mediated reality overwhelms nonmediated experience.

First, note the use of the terms "mediated" and "nonmediated" rather than "mediated" and "real." The dominant contemporary vehicles for storytelling—television, film, video, online, digital—are all real. They are tangible, existing in the world, not in our imaginations. But while stories told through these technologies are as real as stories told face-to-face or storytelling in print, not all forms of storytelling in all arenas have the same effect on how we humans understand ourselves in the world.

When asked to reflect on the potential effects—positive and negative—of different storytelling media, many people deflect the question by pointing out that people have been afraid that every new communication technology would degrade human communication and yet we have adapted successfully to all those new technologies. Skeptics warned, for example, that the telephone would undermine the quality of conversation. The same concern has been raised about the rise of texting, with many bemoaning the loss of depth in "conversations" typed on a smartphone.

Humans certainly adapt to the new technologies, but is that always a mark of progress? Telephone conversations and texting are routine, but are they the equivalent of face-to-face conversations? When we want to deliver serious news, for example, we often bypass more convenient opportunities to telephone and wait to talk in person, because we recognize that a face-to-face conversation is a richer experience. People sometimes will text to avoid having an unpleasant conversation. Does this practice foster interpersonal relationships that contribute to a healthy culture?

This does not mean that every new human practice is inferior to existing practices, only that we shouldn't assume that every new practice is superior to what came before. It is also important to realize that the effects of technology are not easily quantified and not always evident in the moment; our experience of technology—how it makes us feel, how it changes us, over time—is not a footnote to "real" data but is often the most important data. Equally crucial is realizing that the people most immersed in a practice do not have an unchallengeable understanding of the practice; insight comes not only from those within a practice, but from those who stand outside.

All these ways of knowing are crucial to examining the pornifying of culture, the way in which sexually explicit images—whether overtly misogynistic or not—are increasingly taken as an acceptable, even an essential, part of pop culture. This is most evident in the call for what is variously called "ethical," "feminist," or "egalitarian" pornography—sexually explicit material that attempts to avoid the domination/subordination dynamic of commercial pornography.[27] Whether practitioners of these styles achieve their goal is debatable, but equally important is the impetus for the project, the unstated assumption that sexually explicit material is necessary and/or desirable, and hence we must find a way to produce pornography with politics we can endorse.

The feminist critique raises a painful question: Why do so many men routinely use images of women being sexually degraded as a masturbation aid, and why do so many women accept that as unavoidable? What does the acceptance of misogynistic pornography say about the enduring strength of patriarchy? The ecological approach asks an equally challenging question: Why do so many men and women believe that explicit movies are essential to being sexual? What does the normalizing of pornography say about the larger culture? Has the saturation of the culture with sexual images so crippled our imaginations that many people feel dependent on movies with graphic sex? Is this need for pornography an impediment to, rather than a way to foster, healthy sexual relationships?

The ecological approach focuses on the healthfulness and sustainability of human practices. This approach differs from the moralism of conservative critiques—rather than imposing hard-and-fast rules to shore up existing power structures, our focus should be on the construction of an ethic that can help us build a sustainable culture that is part of a sustainable world.

At the heart of the crises that threaten the health of the ecosphere[28] is a human disconnection from the nonhuman world. The high-energy/high-technology world creates myriad ways that take us away from the nonhuman world. We flip a switch to create the comfort of heating and cooling without much awareness of the ecological destruction associated with that energy consumption. We click on sexually explicit images to create sexual arousal without much awareness in the moment of the disconnection required for that pleasure consumption.

This is not an argument that pornography use leads directly to ecological destruction. Rather, it is an attempt to explore how the trappings of a high-energy/high-technology society can make us less aware of the kind of biological beings we are in the ecosystems on which we depend for life. As we become more creatures of technology rather than biology, we drift away from the understanding that our actions affect the rest of the living world. As a general rule, any technology that fosters that split is potentially harmful, especially when that split comes with something as central to human life as sexual activity. If we can so easily treat sex as nothing more than an act of pleasure acquisition that can be accomplished through a screen, in what other ways are we disconnected that have become equally routine?

Consider nature shows on television. From one perspective, in an increasingly urban and developed world with fewer wild spaces, nature shows help educate people about the nonhuman world. But what kind of understanding does that mediated experience provide? While such shows impart information, allowing us to "see" things with which we have no direct experience, what do we really know at the end of the program? Critics have pointed out that the direct experience of the nonhuman world typically is far slower than the pace of a professionally edited television show, that direct learning about the nonhuman world requires cultivating a patient style of observation that is exploded by film, television, and the digital world.[29] Nature shows, in this sense, are distinctly unnatural.

The same analysis applies to sexual activity. Just as a nature show provides an intense experience of animals in the wild, for example, sexually explicit material can quickly provide an intense sexual experience. But is that the best way to experience sex? Do those mediated experiences erode our capacity to connect to each other sexually? Is it possible that sex and intimacy are realms of human experience that do not translate well to routine, explicit representations in mass media?

There is wide variation in the human species, of course, and there need not be a single answer for everyone. But the questions matter. Has our world become so mediated that we assume every human experience needs to be on the screen? Is the power of sexuality diminished when rendered explicitly in film and video? Human beings have long used their creative capacities to create music, literature, and art with sexual themes; exploring the mystery of sexual desire enriches our lives. But that does not mean that we must pursue the most graphic, sexually explicit material in every medium, or that graphic, sexually explicit movies are natural or inevitable.

PORNOGRAPHY AND ECOLOGICAL SUSTAINABILITY

Again, to critique sexually explicit material in an ecological context is not to suggest that if not but for pornography, and mass media more generally, humans would be in a sustainable relationship with the larger living world. Instead, just as the pornographic nature of so much sexually explicit material both reflects and reinforces the unjust patriarchal system, the pornified nature of society reflects and reinforces an unsustainable relationship of humans to the larger living work that is inherent in a high-energy/high-technology system. In both realms, pornography is not *the* problem, but is part of a larger set of problems.

To work through this, we can begin with a simple question: What is sex for? Of all of the ways in which people might possibly understand and use sexuality in their lives, which are most consistent with sustainable human flourishing? At various times and places, especially within certain religious traditions, an answer to the question "what is sex for?" has been imposed on people in ways that are not just arbitrary and constraining, but sometimes stunningly inhumane. But because society has answered a question badly in the past does not mean we must avoid the question.

Sex is, of course, central to reproduction, but sex also just as clearly plays a role in human life far beyond reproduction. The variety of ways societies across time and place have made sense of this question indicates that there likely is no single answer for all times and places. Even within one individual's life, sex can play a different role at different times. As young people, sex may be primarily about exploring ourselves and our limits as we mature, while as adults the most important function of sex may be to foster the intimacy that enriches a primary relationship. In general, we can think of sex as a form of communication, a way we learn not only about others but about ourselves. We can collectively try to understand which conceptions of sex are most healthful without claiming definitive knowledge or the right to impose subjective judgments on others.

An analogy to food is helpful. Just as we recognize that sex is more than the acquisition of pleasure, eating is more than just the acquisition of calories. In linking a food politics with a food aesthetics and ethics, Wendell Berry argues that how we eat is not a trivial matter but central to the quality and sustainability of our culture:

Like industrial sex, industrial eating has become a degraded, poor, and paltry thing. Our kitchens and other eating places more and more resemble filling stations, as our homes more and more resemble motels. "Life is not very interesting," we seem to have decided. "Let its satisfactions be minimal, perfunctory, and fast." We hurry through our meals to go to work and hurry through our work in order to "recreate" ourselves in the evenings and on weekends and vacations. And then we hurry, with the greatest possible speed and noise and violence, through our recreation—for what? To eat the billionth hamburger at some fast-food joint hellbent on increasing the "quality" of our life? And all this is carried out in a remarkable obliviousness to the causes and effects, the possibilities and the purposes, of the life of the body in this world.[30]

Berry's description of "industrial eating," as he suggests, is also an accurate account of pornography, a kind of "industrial sex." Eating processed fast food is a fundamentally different experience than eating food to which one has a more direct connection. Not everyone need be a farmer or accomplished chef to attend to those connections. Processed fast food creates distance between us and the living world, and the same is true of processed fast sex. In both cases, people's reflexive response often is, "Maybe, but I like it." There is no doubt that fast food and fast sex are efficient at producing a certain type of pleasure, but this analysis asks us to step back and reflect on what is lost in the normalizing of those forms of pleasure.

A SEXUAL ETHIC FOR JUSTICE AND SUSTAINABILITY: WHAT DOES IT MEAN TO BE HUMAN?

The task of constructing a sexual ethic should not be seen as simply about writing rules, legal or moralistic. We can realize that there is a moral dimension to all human activity—all political, economic, and social policies are based on some notion of what it means to be human. A deeper, richer conversation about that question is needed in contemporary U.S. society on every issue, including pornography.

The conservative critique of pornography typically grows out of repressive patriarchal traditions, which means that group's rejection of pornography is not part of a larger project of gender justice. The liberal embrace of pornography offers a superficial endorsement of gender equality while contributing to the entrenchment of patriarchy through the sexualizing of inequality. And both the conservative and liberal perspectives fail to wrestle with the complex questions about the effects of mass-mediated storytelling in the realm of sexuality and intimacy.

A sexual ethic for justice and sustainability would reject the hierarchy of patriarchy and hierarchy more generally, recognizing that systems of domination and subordination are inherently abusive. That does not mean that intimacy and sex are risk-free; opening up to powerful feelings during sex means risking rejection and disappointment and facing our complex emotional lives. Attempts to make this human interaction free of any risk would almost certainly render human interaction meaningless. But when there is no common understanding of what role sex has in our lives, people are much more likely to get hurt much more often, not just psychologically but physically. And in patriarchy, those injuries will be endured mostly by women and children. The conversation about a sexual ethic is not a restriction of anyone's freedom, but a part of the quest for a more expansive freedom for all.

A sexual ethic for justice and sustainability also would question contemporary society's uncritical embrace and celebration of the technologizing of all human activity. That doesn't mean that all mediated storytelling with sexual themes is inherently negative, only that we need to consider not only the pleasures that come with technology but the deeper implications of them. We need not romanticize a mythical golden age to recognize that what we call progress does not always enhance the quality of our lives.

A sexual ethic for justice and sustainability should advance what feminist Carter Heyward calls the struggle to be in "right relation" to each other. Although Heyward is a theologian, her analysis has little to do with conventional notions of God and the divine, and instead seeks a deeper understanding of how we forge healthy connections in an unhealthy world. She suggests that the state of being in right relation allows us to feel, and act on, our courage, compassion, anger, forgiveness, healing, and faith. When we struggle to achieve right relation, we move away from alienation toward mutuality.[31] Again, this call for mutuality is not an attempt to tame the power of sexual desire, but instead an attempt to help us escape the domination/subordination dynamic and the disconnection that is so pervasive in modern life. Heyward makes it clear that this is always a struggle:

> Nonalienated sexual lovemaking brings pleasure and delight. It also brings sadness. It brings memories and reminders. It brings feelings of loss and grief and of longing to hold onto an intimacy we cannot finally have, because relational mutuality, the essence of erotic love, is not possessive. The erotic opens us, changes us, and moves us in becoming ever more fully ourselves in relation.[32]

What role would pornography play in our attempt to achieve this? The answers may vary for different people, but an honest assessment begins with these questions: Do sexually explicit images cut us off from each other and from ourselves? Does pornography inhibit our ability to be fully alive sexually? If sex with another person requires vulnerability, does the use of sexually explicit images help us move toward others or retreat from them?

Ironically, critics of pornography are often accused of being prudish and fearful. But it seems to me that a deeper fear underlies the culture's embrace of pornography, a fear of that pervasive emptiness of modern life. James Baldwin, one of the twentieth century's most fearless writers, understood that the retreat from vulnerability is a fatal liability:

> I think the inability to love is the central problem, because the inability masks a certain terror, and that terror is the terror of being touched. And, if you can't be touched, you can't be changed. And, if you can't be changed, you can't be alive.[33]

NOTES

1. This is the definition used by the Intersex Society of North America: "'Intersex' is a general term used for a variety of conditions in which a person is born with a reproductive or sexual anatomy that doesn't seem to fit the typical definitions of female or male. For example, a person might be born appearing to be female on the outside, but having mostly male-typical anatomy on the inside. Or a person may be born with genitals that seem to be in between the usual male and female types—for example, a girl may be born with a noticeably large clitoris, or lacking a vaginal opening, or a boy may be born with a notably small penis, or with a scrotum that is divided so that it has formed more like labia. Or a person may be born with mosaic genetics, so that some of her cells have XX chromosomes and some of them have XY." See Intersex Society of North America, http://www.isna.org/faq/what_is_intersex (accessed 19 May 2014).

2. One prominent researcher reports that the best estimate of the percentage of people born intersexed is 1.7 percent. See Anne Fausto-Sterling, "The Five Sexes, Revisited," *Sciences* 40:3 (July/August 2000): 20.

3. "Feminist Epistemology and Philosophy of Science," August 9, 2000, Stanford Encyclopedia of Philosophy, http://plato.stanford.edu/entries/feminism-epistemology/ (accessed 19 May 2014).

4. John Gray, *Men Are from Mars, Women Are from Venus* (New York: HarperCollins, 1992).

5. Janet Shibley Hyde, "The Gender Similarity Hypothesis," *American Psychologist* 60, no. 6 (September 2005): 581–92.

6. Gerda Lerner, *The Creation of Patriarchy* (New York: Oxford University Press, 1986).

7. Andrea Dworkin, *Pornography: Men Possessing Women* (New York: Perigee, 1979; (reprint edition Dutton, 1989).

8. Catharine A. MacKinnon, *Feminism Unmodified: Discourses on Life and Law* (Cambridge, MA: Harvard University Press, 1987).

9. Marilyn Frye, *The Politics of Reality: Essays in Feminist Theory* (Freedom, CA: Crossing Press, 1983) and *Willful Virgin* (Freedom, CA: Crossing Press, 1992).

10. Emilie Buchwald, Pamela Fletcher, and Martha Roth, eds., *Transforming a Rape Culture*, 2nd ed. (Minneapolis: Milkweed Editions, 2005).

11. Andrea Dworkin and Catharine A. MacKinnon, *Pornography and Civil Rights: A New Day for Women's Equality* (Minneapolis: Organizing Against Pornography, 1988).

12. Catharine A. MacKinnon and Andrea Dworkin, *In Harm's Way: The Pornography Civil Rights Hearings* (Cambridge, MA: Harvard University Press, 1997).

13. *American Booksellers Association, Inc. v. William H. Hudnut*. Ordinance judged invalid, 598 F.Supp. 1316 (S.D. Indiana, 1984). Judgment affirmed, 771 F.2d 323 (7th Cir. 1985). Judgment affirmed, 106 S. Ct. 1172 (1986), and petition for rehearing denied, 106 S. Ct. 1664 (1986).

14. Timothy Egan, "Wall Street Meets Pornography," *New York Times*, October 23, 2000, http://www.nytimes.com/2000/10/23/technology/23PORN.html?ex=1157083200&en=608f80ea0b539eb0&ei=5070 (accessed 19 May 2014).

15. http://stoppornculture.org/. I was one of the founders of the group and cocreator of an educational slideshow.

16. Hans-Bernd Brosius, James B. Weaver III, and Joachim F. Staab, "Exploring the Social and Sexual 'Reality' of Contemporary Pornography," *Journal of Sex Research* 30, no. 2 (1993): 161–70.

17. Ana J. Bridges, Robert Wosnitzer, Erica Scharrer, Chyng Sun, and Rachael Liberman, "Aggression and Sexual Behavior in Best-Selling Pornography Videos: A Content Analysis Update," *Violence against Women* 16, no. 10 (October 2010): 1065–85.

18. Gail Dines, *Pornland: How Porn Has Hijacked Our Sexuality* (Boston: Beacon Press, 2010).

19. Chyng Sun and Miguel Picker, *The Price of Pleasure: Pornography, Sexuality, and Relationships* (Northampton, MA: Media Education Foundation, 2008).

20. Robert J. Stoller and I. S. Levine, *Coming Attractions: The Making of an X-Rated Video* (New Haven: Yale University Press, 1993), 22.

21. Robert Jensen, *Getting Off: Pornography and the End of Masculinity* (Boston: South End Press, 2007).

22. Robert Jensen, "Pornography as Propaganda," in Gerald Sussman, ed., *The Propaganda Society: Promotional Culture and Politics in Global Context* (New York: Peter Lang, 2011), 159–74.

23. Andrea Dworkin, *Letters from a War Zone: Writings 1976–1987* (London: Secker & Warburg, 1988/Chicago: Lawrence Hill Books, 1993), 264–65.

24. Dworkin, *Letters from a War Zone*, 266–67.

25. Rebecca Whisnant and Christine Stark, eds., *Not For Sale: Feminists Resisting Prostitution and Pornography* (North Melbourne, Australia: Spinifex Press, 2004).

26. I borrow the term from, but use it differently than does Pamela Paul in her book, *Pornified: How Pornography Is Transforming Our Lives, Our Relationships, and Our Families* (New York: Times Books, 2005).

27. Tristan Taormino, Constance Penley, Celine Parreñas Shimizu, and Mireille Miller-Young, eds., *The Feminist Porn Book: The Politics of Producing Pleasure* (New York: Feminist Press, 2013).

28. Bill McKibben, *Eaarth: Making Life on a Tough New Planet* (New York: Times Books/Henry Holt, 2010).

29. Bill McKibben, *The Age of Missing Information* (New York: Plume, 1992).

30. Wendell Berry, "The Pleasures of Eating," in Wendell Berry, *What Are People For?* (San Francisco: North Point Press, 1990), 147.

31. Carter Heyward, *Touching Our Strength: The Erotic as Power and the Love of God* (San Francisco: Harper & Row, 1989), 139.

32. Heyward, *Touching Our Strength*, 124.

33. James Baldwin, from an interview in *The Advocate*, excerpted in *Utne Reader*, July/August 2002, 100.

Part II

The Politics of Pornography

Chapter Five

The Problem with the Problem of Pornography

Subordination, Sexualization, and Speech

Jacob M. Held

When one surveys the literature on pornography, what becomes clear is the striking bipolarity of the discourse. On one side are the First Amendment proponents who want to protect all speech and so argue against any form of regulating the production, distribution, or consumption of pornographic material.[1] In this group also fall those who see porn as negligible in impact or a positive good in terms of sexual education, self-exploration, and empowerment.[2] This side of the debate is often reluctant to consider or recognize any ill effects of pornography. On the other side are the classic anti-porn feminists who demonize the former and claim that pornography is discrimination, that it leads to or encourages sexual violence, and that anyone who argues otherwise is themselves complicit in the evils of pornography.[3] Martha Nussbaum sees this approach as more akin to a prophetic calling than philosophy: "prophets . . . believe that the urgency and magnitude of the evils they see admit of no delay, no calm and patient dialogue."[4] However, recent trends in the literature demand that we revisit the classic debate and perhaps re-conceptualize the problem itself.

If the problem with pornography is what it does, that is, that it is discrimination as averred by Catharine MacKinnon and others, then the problem with pornography is the problem of sexualization. All media that depict sexuality in such a way as to demean, degrade, or otherwise categorize as inferior one class, all media that objectify women, are in this regard as detrimental as hard-core pornography, if not more so since mainstream media is more acceptable and pervasive than hard-core porn. Although some authors like

MacKinnon may be sympathetic to casting a wider net, the solutions they offer are aimed exclusively at hard-core porn so that they are ineffectual, and were their proposals broadened to include all relevant sexualizing media, disastrous to freedom of expression. If one is determined to combat the ill effects of pornography, then porn is a symptom of a broader cultural phenomenon: oversexualized media. If porn is taken as the primary target, it becomes a red herring. Focusing on sexualization highlights that the solutions proffered by anti-pornography theorists and activists are misguided. A new approach is needed if we are to effectively and prudentially deal with a real concern, overly sexualized media and its impact on culture. In this regard, if the problem is one of a culturally prevalent and problematic sexualization of girls and women, then the response must be proportionate. If the problem originates when young children are acculturated to accept inappropriate or even harmful stereotypes of gender and sexuality, then our response ought to aim at these formative moments.

SEXUALIZATION

Recent work focusing on sexualization highlights "pornification," how porn sensibilities infiltrate all aspects of culture, often focusing specifically on the problem of the oversexualization of girls and young women.[5] In this regard, many of the issues that have motivated the discourse on pornography seem to indicate that a shift is needed from the classic debate regarding free speech and discrimination, as exemplified through the work of Andrea Dworkin (1946–2005) and Catharine MacKinnon, to encompass a much broader phenomenon, "pornification."[6] The influence porn culture has on mainstream media is sometimes referred to as "pornification,"[7] as culture becoming "porned"[8] or "pornified,"[9] or simply denoted as "raunch culture."[10] This influence is taken as part of the trend in culture to sexualize childhood, specifically the childhood of young girls. Sexualization occurs when "a person's value comes only from his or her sexual appeal or behavior . . . a person is held to a standard that equates physical attractiveness . . . with being sexy; a person is sexually objectified . . . [and/or] sexuality is inappropriately imposed upon a person." Examples of sexualization may include the inappropriate imposition of sexuality on young girls through "adultifying" children and "youthifying" adult women in advertising, to children's fashion where thongs are marketed to tweens (girls ages seven to teen years).

This trend of sexualization was the focus of a recent report by the American Psychological Association (APA). In 2007, the APA reported what has been suspected and anecdotally confirmed for some time. The sexualization of girls in our culture negatively impacts them in several ways. The definitive effects of sexualization are unclear; however, preliminary data indicates the effects are far-ranging and far from negligible. Self-objectification, that is, treating oneself as a commodity, a sexual object to be assessed and ultimately consumed, can lead to a fragmentation of one's consciousness and to difficulty concentrating and so lowering performance on tests and in other academic pursuits, perhaps leading many young women to not pursue these endeavors since they subsequently find them unfulfilling or difficult.[11] Focusing on one's body image and imposed expectations, often unachievable or downright harmful if met, can lead to feelings of shame, anxiety, and self-disgust.[12] One would suspect that this mentality would lead to myriad problems beyond those catalogued, such as eating disorders, low self-esteem, and depression or depressed mood.[13] These effects have been noted by several authors.[14]

Girls surely bear the brunt of sexualization, but the effects are felt throughout culture. The effects of sexualization can negatively impact boys and men through setting up unrealistic or harmful expectations about masculinity, sexual relationships, and female sexuality, resulting most notably in a lack of empathy for women. Such dispositions can harm not only men's capacity to form meaningful relationships, but promote and reinforce sexism through the acceptance of sexual harassment and the dismissal of women's issues as legitimate.[15]

What these studies emphasize is that one of the foundational concerns about pornography, that it foments an atmosphere hostile to women and women's interests, is not unique to pornography. In fact, given the prevalence and content of contemporary sexualized media, mainstream media outlets are greater purveyors of harmful or demeaning gender stereotypes than is hard-core pornography. Although "pornification" emphasizes the way in which porn has infiltrated mainstream culture, to see it as a one-way relationship is infelicitous. Trends in porn surely do shape attitudes of consumers, but are also responsive to market demand.[16] It is a feedback loop, so holding one or the other to be primarily responsible is to narrowly focus one's attention. It is this narrow focus that limits the value of the classic anti-pornography position.

THE CLASSIC CONTENTION: PORN IS DISCRIMINATION

One classic and still influential position against porn is Catharine MacKinnon and Andrea Dworkin's basic claim that pornography "eroticizes hierarchy, it sexualizes inequality. . . . It institutionalizes the sexuality of male supremacy, fusing the eroticization of dominance and submission with the social construction of male and female."[17] As a practice, MacKinnon and Dworkin contend, pornography reinforces a hierarchy of inequality and perpetuates a culture that excuses and rationalizes sexual aggression and male dominance. Insofar as the discourse of pornography sets and maintains expectations, it creates a narrative about what women are and how they fit into society. Insofar as these expectations are adopted and reified through our subsequent decisions and interactions, they create a reality of gender inequality. Andrea Dworkin reiterates that what is at stake is the very status of women as a class. She claims, "Pornography is the material means of sexualizing inequality; and that is why pornography is a *central practice* in the subordination of women."[18] The problem is fundamentally one of recognition, or more accurately, misrecognition. Pornography as a tool facilitates and reinforces the misrecognition of women through their objectification and degradation, which when taken as authoritative constructs a social position for them that is debilitating.

Rae Langton's recent work focuses on a MacKinnon-style claim emphasizing porn's impact on women's speech acts. Langton claims that pornography silences women insofar as it disables the illocutionary effectiveness of certain of women's speech acts, thus limiting their capacity to function as equals in society. Working from J. L. Austin's speech act theory, Langton offers an account of how words do things, one notable instance being illocutionary statements in which words effect a change in the world. A good example is a priest declaring a couple married. In that declaration it is so. Illocutionary statements of this sort only function in a socially constructed world of symbols if felicity conditions are met, that is, if the authority exists to utter such an illocution and it is taken up in the right context, namely, the utterance is recognized by the addressee in its original intention and the authority of the speaker is recognized and respected such that the speaker's intention is given credence and is thus effectual. One is only able to perform an illocutionary act if one has the authority to perform such an act and the addressee recognizes and respects that authority. But some utterances are infelicitous; they fail to accomplish what they were meant to. Silence is the result of having the felicity conditions of one's otherwise functional illocutionary utterances removed, such that one is disabled from effecting with one's words what one otherwise might have been able to effect. This can occur for two reasons: first, the intention of the speaker may be misinterpreted such that the illocutionary act attempting to be effectuated is misconstrued; second, the intention of the speaker can be clear and clearly understood, but the addressee may fail to recognize or respect the speaker's authority to make such an illocution. One can be silenced because their utterances go unheard since the intention is lost, or they go unheeded since the authority of the speaker is denied. The idea that pornography is discriminatory is tied to the idea that pornography limits women's capabilities through various forms of disablement.[19]

Consider, along with Mary Kate McGowan, the example of sexual refusal. She contends women are often the victims of sexual assault and violence because their refusal is misrecognized. Their refusal of the other's sexual advance is not taken up, thus her act of negation is disabled. This disablement can be accounted for in the two ways indicated above. First, one could claim that given the dominant narrative in pornography, when the text wherein women utter "No" but mean "Yes" is taken as authoritative, uptake is denied to women's sexual refusals. That is, the intention behind a woman's refusal is misconstrued since the addressee has been acculturated to interpret women's refusals as coded messages to be more persistent.

But the problem is not solely one of uptake. It is not simply that the intention of the female speaker is misinterpreted. The problem is that these illocutions fail often because women are not recognized to have the authority to refuse the sexual advances of men. McGowan, borrowing from Austin as well, notes that some authoritative speech acts "set the boundaries of permissibility through 'the exercising of powers.'"[20] These speech acts are denoted "exercitives." Sexual refusal is a form of exercitive in which a woman is not authorizing sexual access to her body, thus exercising her right to be sovereign over her body. When this capacity is denied, it is not that the addressee misunderstands her intention when she refuses his sexual advances; it is that he does not recognize her authority to exercise this type of control over her body. A historical example of this would be the contention that wives could not be "raped" by their husbands since they were as wives marital property, a belief and practice still all too common.[21] If for MacKinnon porn discriminates through the sexualization of power, here it silences by reinforcing the narrative in which women never refuse and in fact lack the ability to do so. If porn is able to delineate the scope of exercitives by dictating who is and who is not able to make these kinds of claims, it can silence women through illocutionary disablement. Insofar as it sets the discourse, it effectively denies women their capacity to do fundamental things with words, thus limiting their ability and capability to function in the society facilitating their subordination. The harm caused by this kind of disablement is one that directly impacts a woman's capacity to function as an equal. Drawing an analogy between this understanding of pornography and sexual harassment is instructive.

Sexual harassment, in the form of hostile environment harassment, occurs whenever a coworker's conduct becomes severe or pervasive enough to create an environment that affects one's performance or otherwise creates a hostile working environment.[22] The analogy between pornography and hostile environment harassment is straightforward. In the case of pornography, society becomes a hostile environment insofar as women are demeaned as a class and lowered in social position through prevalent, consistent, and severe objectification. The existence of pornography thus creates a hostile environment for women insofar as it promulgates and reinforces an authoritative text that degrades women, thus denying them the capacity to exercise basic rights such as control over their own bodies and sexual refusal. Pornography, if we accept and extrapolate the analogy, harasses women. Treating pornography as discrimination is similar to extending the sexual harassment model of discrimination outward to the public arena, and this analogy also helps explain previous measures that opponents of pornography have advocated as correctives.

CLASSIC RESPONSES TO PORNOGRAPHY

In 1983, MacKinnon and Dworkin drafted an amendment to the Minneapolis Civil Rights ordinance that would construe pornography as discrimination. Pornography was defined as:

> The graphic *sexually explicit* subordination of women, whether in pictures or in words, that also includes one or more of the following: (1) women are presented as sexual objects who enjoy pain or humiliation; or (2) women are presented as sexual objects who experience sexual pleasure in being raped; or (3) women are presented as sexual objects tied up or cut up or mutilated or bruised or physically hurt, or as dismembered or truncated or fragmented or severed into body parts; or (4) women are presented as being penetrated by objects or animals; or (5) women are presented in scenarios of degradation, injury, abasement, torture, shown as filthy or inferior, bleeding, bruised, or hurt in a context that makes these conditions sexual; or (6) women are presented as sexual objects for domination, conquest, violation, exploitation, possession, or use, or through postures or positions of servility or submission or display.[23]

When this ordinance was adopted by the city of Indianapolis it was quickly challenged and struck down as unconstitutional. But how pornography is defined in this ordinance is illuminating. Porn is usually defined as sexually explicit material, the express intent of which is to arouse the viewer, or a variation on that theme. Occasionally it is conflated with obscenity, in which case it is defined according the Supreme Court's standards in *Miller* where a work is obscene when "the average person, applying contemporary standards" would deem that the work taken as a whole appeals to prurient interests, depicts sex in a patently offensive way, and lacks serious literary, artistic, scientific, or political value.[24] Although MacKinnon's definition keeps the standard reference to sexual explicitness, there is no reference to arousal or consumer response, nor is there any reference to community standards, redeeming value, or offense. The defining characteristic for MacKinnon is subordination. But then one wonders why such works need to be also sexually explicit. If presenting women in subordinate roles is what matters, then why must the presentations also be sexual, or even sexually explicit?

Wendy McElroy notes that this is not a definition, but a conclusion.[25] As with obscenity laws in general, the most problematic element of this law is the use of evaluative criteria. Consider the definition of pornography as "the graphic sexually explicit subordination of women." This criterion is fraught with the same interpretative problems from which previous obscenity laws suffered. Who determines if a representation is "subordinating?" Whether or not a depiction represents an inappropriate power relation is very much open to debate, aside from the contentious claim itself that presenting such relationships is itself discriminatory. One's conclusion regarding these matters will ultimately rest on one's view of sexuality and interpersonal relationships. To illustrate the problem this standard raises, consider MacKinnon and Dworkin's own views on the matter. Dworkin once claimed, "It's very hard to look at a picture of a woman's body and not see it with the perception that her body is being exploited."[26] It is not a stretch to conclude that the definition above, if interpreted in light of Dworkin's own perceptions of female sexuality, would determine all sexually explicit, and perhaps all, depictions of women to present them as subordinate and so pornographic. Likewise, "MacKinnon has condemned pornography specifically because it shows that women 'desire to be fucked.' . . . MacKinnon also echoes Dworkin's thesis that women who believe they voluntarily engage in, and enjoy, heterosexual sex are victims of 'false consciousness.'"[27] What this definition illustrates is not what porn is, but how the anti-porn activists view sexuality. "Such descriptions are normative, or biased. They embody the viewer's reactions, and their desire to condemn pornography."[28] But sex can have many meanings beyond what one viewer or critic may ascribe. MacKinnon's definition is motivated by a desire to promote, or rather prohibit, a particular view of sexuality.

The problem with normatively loaded definitions is highlighted again in the case of trying to distinguish pornography from erotica. Gloria Steinem recommends understanding erotica as "mutually pleasurable" or sexual expression among equals, whereas pornography is "violence, dominance, and conquest."[29] Porn is about domination and objectification; erotica is about mutuality. And what is the point of the distinction: to vindicate erotica while condemning pornography. If the purpose was not to condemn porn it would be hard to find a reason to make the distinction at all. Both erotica and pornography may contain explicit sex, both may arouse. They seem to be identical except that some find the presentation of sex and sexuality in porn abhorrent whereas the sex in erotica is acceptable. This distinction is only relevant if the point of classification is to implicitly evaluate, and in this case condemn, what is being classified.

These definitions, therefore, begin from a political position. The position is laudable; it is about equality and nondiscrimination. It sees pornography as complicit and a major actor in fomenting discrimination against women.

However, since the definition is aimed at depictions of women that do foment discrimination, its focus on sexually explicit material is infelicitous since contemporary research indicates that mainstream media is as effective or more so in contributing to a misogynistic culture. Thus, the political position that motivates this definition and attacks pornography is more relevant to sexualized media in general and therefore should focus its efforts on a broader swath of culture, namely, media that portray women in subordinate roles that demean and degrade them. This is the approach Canada recently took.

In 1992 the Supreme Court of Canada in *R. v. Butler* interpreted Canadian anti-obscenity laws to apply to "degrading" and "dehumanizing" depictions of women. Degrading and dehumanizing materials were deemed to fail the community standards test and the moral corruption implicit therein was acknowledged to have a detrimental effect on society, in this case, a discriminatory effect on women. As one author notes, "Obscenity in Canada is now about gender equity."[30] In this case, the Canadian court decided to remove protections to speech when they functioned in a way that discriminated against women as well as other minority groups, following a logic similar to analogous hate speech laws found in the United Kingdom, such as the Public Order Act of 1936, Race Relations Acts of 1965 and 1976, and the Public Order Act of 1986.[31] These laws restrict speech and make it prosecutable when (depending on the particular act) its intent is to incite racial hatred or it has the effect of causing animus resulting in demonstrable harm. Pornography, it can be argued, is equally as harmful and functions as incitement to sexual hatred.[32] But when sexual speech becomes actionable under laws due to its purported impact on gender equity or the public discourse on women, then it ought to no longer be merely hard-core pornography that is singled out. The degrading and demeaning messages associated with pornography are prevalent in mainstream media. If sexual explicitness is not a necessary condition of a work being degrading or demeaning, then critics of pornography need to either expand their target or admit that they single out porn not because it is a more significant issue or threat, but because it is expedient. This narrow focus on pornography is what needs to be reevaluated as the discourse moves forward. To focus only on sexually explicit material is to focus too narrowly. Yet casting a wider net would make a significant portion of arguably redeemable and valuable speech actionable. This is the crux of the problem with a legal remedy, whether it is civil or criminal.

Whether it is hate crime–style legislation in Britain, anti-obscenity laws in Canada, or MacKinnon-style civil rights ordinances, there are major flaws with these approaches. First, with respect to U.S. law, are these measures constitutional?[33] Second, would they have the effect they aim at, or would they result in foreseeable harms to legitimate social interests while producing no substantial benefit? Finally, can the scope of these laws be focused narrowly enough as to avoid a general chilling effect on speech, or over prosecution and the persecution of unpopular forms of expression?

In practice these laws have failed to answer any of the above questions adequately. They have been implemented selectively and capriciously and fail to have the intended effect. Although MacKinnon lauded *R. v. Butler*, its application has been less than cause for celebration. The LGBTIQ community has been hit particularly hard, as the cases of lesbian booksellers Little Sisters and Glad Day attest.[34] Approaching the matter as a civil rather than a criminal matter may help. As Ann Scales (1952–2012) notes, the civil approach places the "first interpretative moves in the hands of the victims of pornography."[35] Catharine Itzin is also supportive of the civil approach, arguing that the best approach is to "make incitement to sexual hatred and violence illegal and . . . enable women who could prove they were injured by pornography to sue and seek compensation."[36] This again prosecutes pornography or sexual speech in a manner similar to sexual harassment. Only now we have the problem of determining who the harasser is. Is it all pornography, or only some? Is it sexually explicit materials or all sexualized materials? Who is to be held accountable? Surely, these are not insurmountable issues, but they may be significant enough to question the prudence of this approach. And the problem of application remains. Can judges consistently apply vague, normative standards on gender-appropriate language, art, or performances?[37] The notion that porn is a significant source of gender inequity, and so targeting it legally would be constructive, is at question. Pornography is symptomatic of a deeper problem.

Pornography objectifies women, and objects cannot speak; their words are misconstrued or fall on deafened ears. Langton discusses this in terms of solipsisms, realms in which women fail to be recognized as full people. In the context above, women are not recognized as capable of asserting certain things, and performing certain actions through speech because their language environment has become hostile. Their phrases cannot be taken up and so they are disabled in the sense that they cannot do the same things with words as others. The silence that Langton is concerned about, and the discrimination that MacKinnon militates against, is the result of a dominant narrative, one that sexualizes women, objectifies them, and thereby diminishes their position in society. This kind of discourse arguably does silence them by both interfering with uptake and denying them their authority to exercise control over their sexual destinies, as McGowan so eloquently makes the case. However, pornography is not the sole culprit. Pornography is but one aspect of a discourse that objectifies women and perpetuates the solipsisms of which Langton is critical. The discourse that demeans and degrades women is the discourse that sexualizes them, where their value is found in their sexual attractiveness and they are reduced to sexual objects. This discourse is everywhere from Bratz dolls and Barbie to Girls Gone Wild, from hard-core porn to beauty pageants and competitive cheerleading. Women's lowered social status and their subsequent silence is a result of a narrative that reduces them to sexual objects, and this narrative is ubiquitous in the media. It is easy to attack pornography. It is easy to attack because it is the ugly side of sexualization, but simply because it is politically opportune does not make it an expedient or even valuable target. Pornography does not exercise the kind of power or authority that Langton maintains it does, it does not wield that kind of power over our discourse. Any argument made on behalf of Langton, MacKinnon, or other anti-porn activists should more accurately be turned on media writ large, and then their solutions fail as either too narrowly directed—or if properly directed too sweeping—thus chilling legitimate speech dealing in sexual themes.

The problem with pornography has always been phrased in terms of the problem with the impact of pornography. This impact can be measured in terms of silence and illocutionary disablement or sexual harassment and diminished capacities. However, these ill effects are not the result of pornography alone. Pornography is simply the most explicit purveyor of the objectifying messages that result in these harms when taken as authoritative in our discourses on sexuality and gender. Yet, porn is by no means the most prevalent force promoting this image of women.

The problem with a MacKinnon-style position is that it presumes pornography to be the authoritative narrative on sex and sexuality, that porn is a necessary or at least significant component in the propagation of a discriminatory attitude toward women. The concern is expressed in terms of the message of porn, that is, its degrading, humiliating, and demeaning content. Hard-core porn does not have a monopoly on this content. A recent study reinforces the contention that it is the portrayal of women, not the sex, that is impactful on viewers' attitudes. Christopher Ferguson states, "Although sexual and violent content tends to get a lot of attention, I was surprised by how little impact such content had on attitudes toward women. Instead it seems to be portrayals of women themselves, positive or negative that have the most impact, irrespective of objectionable content. In focusing so much on violence and sex, we may have been focusing on the wrong things."[38] Focusing on sexualized media seems a more effective direction to take. Sexualization focuses on the impact on young girls, and highlights how toys, cartoons, and fashion are much more potent cultural forces in this regard.[39] It may be politically expedient to attack porn since it will find few supporters aside from the usual First Amendment proponents. It may be an obvious target; it is seedy, dirty, and lacks any obvious meritorious properties. But focusing on it will do nothing to ameliorate the concerns on which anti-porn activists are focused. So the legal remedies are predicated on insufferably vague laws prone to abuses. In addition, if the problem with porn is the problem of sexualization and objectification, then the rationale that would allow us to take legal action against pornography, however so defined, would equally legitimate actions against all aspects of sexualizing media. Such laws would afford the courts the ability to regulate speech based on the appropriateness of the message, which violates the rubric that the court's assessment must remain value neutral.[40] In addition, such vague, open-ended statutes would violate the legal principle of fair warning, leaving people open to prosecution for offenses that they could not have reasonably known ahead of time were against the law. This concern was raised myriad times by Justice William O. Douglas, most vociferously in *Ginsberg v. New York*, 390 U.S. 629 (1968).

Pornography is a symptom of a culture that devalues women. It would not survive nor thrive were it not the case that men are acculturated from a young age to commodify and consume women, and women acculturated to sell themselves as sexual commodities. Even if pornography were miraculously destroyed, there would still be objectifying and demeaning discourses that seek to put women "in their place." In the 1940s there were adventure magazines that depicted women being captured and sexually abused by Nazis, and pin-ups depicting big-breasted, curvaceous women in slinky, see-through outfits.[41] In the 1980s and 1990s, even outside of hard-core pornography, mainstream rock, heavy metal, and rap music was defined by misogyny.[42] Objectifying and demeaning women is not a new phenomenon, and it is not the sole intellectual property of the hard-core porn industry.

FOCUSING ON SEXUALIZATION

When the American Psychological Association published its report on the sexualization of young girls it made several recommendations as to how one might combat the problem of sexualization. The APA recommended comprehensive sexual education programs that educate age-appropriate children about healthy expressions of sexuality. The association recommended providing courses and resources to help young children and adults develop media literacy skills so that they can interpret the images they are inundated with and have greater control over how these images are processed and internalized. Similar recommendations have been made by others.[43] These efforts seek to make sexualization visible for what it is: an inappropriate co-opting of sexuality. Malcolm Parks seems to believe this type of approach will prove effective, claiming "Positive depictions of women challenge negative stereotypes even when the content includes sexuality and violence . . . viewers often process popular media portrayals in more subtle ways than critics . . . give them credit for."[44] Once sexualization is brought into the light, and once girls themselves—as well as parents, teachers, and others—have the means to decipher and reject these messages, the consumer as informed is put in greater control. But all those involved, especially parents, need to be aware of how they buy into and are complicit in the sexualization of our youth.[45] As one scholar notes, "The more we learn how to 'decode' porn media, the better situated we are to know the difference [between fantasy and reality, yes and no, coercion and consent]. The more willing we are to teach age-appropriate media literacy to children and young adults, the better able they are to navigate the sexually mediated world we live in."[46] Producers also share some responsibility. When it comes to producing media, positive depictions of women ought to be more visible and negative ones limited, if not in scope then at least in terms of accessibility to young people who lack the critical skills necessary to unpack and assess these media messages. Combatting sexualization is about reappropriating the discourse on sexuality. Legal remedies are on a whole infelicitous, although regulation warrants consideration, such as regulating how we market to children, children's programming in general, when we allow questionable content to be broadcast, and producer responsibility for content.[47] Yet educational measures may have a more significant and desirable impact by allowing an informed populace to curb demand through informed consumption.

In early 2010 Representative Tammy Baldwin (D) of Wisconsin introduced H.R. 4925, the Healthy Media for Youth Act. In September of 2010 S. 3852, the Healthy Media for Youth Act was introduced in the Senate and sponsored by Senator Kay Hagan (D) of North Carolina; it unfortunately, yet predictably, died in committee. These acts sought to create panels to advise the media on how to portray women more positively and provide funds to both research the effect of sexualized media on young girls as well as promote media literacy to school-age children. They sought to promote positive images of women and female sexuality and advise industry actors on how they might better assist in promoting the goals of the APA Task Force. These acts were thus aimed at sexualized media in general, approaching the issue from the perspectives of both the consumer and producer. Such measures seek to minimize the negative impacts of sexualized media by focusing on the significant purveyors of degrading or demeaning portrayals of women and girls through implementable mechanisms that are proportionate to the problem. As such they avoid the key pitfalls of traditional anti-porn measures. First, they focus on the root of the problem, which is not primarily material of a sexually explicit nature, but sexualized media. As such these measures are not too narrowly focused. In addition, they approach the issue not as one of prohibition but of regulation alongside education, thus offering solutions respectful of free expression while holding accountable consumers and producers. Finally, they are practicable.

Recently, activists and scholars such as Gail Dines have begun advocating grassroots-style activism.[48] She promotes her cause through her website, stoppornculture.org. The APA, in the appendix to its report, lists myriad websites and programs that can be utilized in similar ways. Robert Jensen makes an appeal to individuals to educate their children properly. As parents he advises us to raise boys to be empathetic and compassionate, and raise daughters to be strong, independent, and self-possessed. He writes: "At the moment, it is the pornographers' world. They are the ones telling the most influential stories about gender and power and sex. But that victory is just for the moment, if we can face ourselves and then build a movement that challenges them."[49] But, it is not truly the pornographers' world, it is the sexists' world, and that is why pornographers have a voice and place within it. It is Disney, Marvel, and Mattel's world. A world of sexualized prepubescent girls, and this is the world we must reclaim, not simply from Larry Flynt or Wicked Productions, Playboy or Jenna Jameson, but from mainstream media. We do need to take back control of our stories, the stories of sexuality, mutuality, and compassion. But stories compete in a marketplace of ideas. We must tell more compelling stories and educate consumers, thus removing the demand for objectifying, sexualizing media. Yet in so doing we need to avoid the pitfalls of so much of the anti-pornography discourse. We need to not demonize sex and alternative sexualities while promoting independence and self-determination. Too often the anti-porn position looks anti-sex. It attacks pornography for presenting sex in a way it finds demeaning, but others may find enjoyable and rewarding. Instead, this position needs to be seen in line with its true intent, as pro-sex. The fact that people oppose the images in pornography or sexualized media should be because they view sex as an important element of our lives, a foundational way in which we are and in which we engage with each other.[50] But as a foundational element of our lives and a free expression of desire, we cannot a priori reject as demeaning and degrading sex acts some may interpret as violent, misogynistic, or otherwise untoward expressions of sexuality, but others find fulfilling. Rough sex such as choking or slapping can be mutually fulfilling. Bondage can be a legitimate expression of one's sexuality. Thus we need a more comprehensive, more engaged discourse on pornography. Not one about regulation and limitation, but one about understanding and empowerment. Given the important role sex and sexuality play in our lives, from questions about personal identity, gender, and politics to interpersonal relationships, we need to have a fruitful dialogue on this topic.

In considering how we as a society ought to deal with pornography, Pamela Paul dismisses the classic legal approaches as illiberal, promoting free speech and markets so that informed, mature adults can choose for themselves. She focuses not on supply but demand. Paul states, "If demand didn't exist, the product would not sell—and would disappear. There may be fault distributed across the board in the production of pornography, but the most consequential players are the men eager and willing to pay for it."[51] And as Justice Louis Brandeis (1856–1941) once noted, "If there be time to expose through discussion the falsehood and fallacies, to avert the evil by the processes of education, the remedy to be applied is more speech, not enforced silence."[52]

Too often in this debate, pornography is demonized and along with it alternative sexualities. But sex is not itself bad, and neither are alternative sexualities that push the boundaries of acceptable sex and allow for sexual exploration beyond the safe and comfortable conventions of conventional morality. Our sexuality is how we express ourselves to others. It is how we express our desires to our partners. In this regard, to classify some as obscene, unworthy of depiction, inherently misogynistic merely because they affront conventional morality is to delimit for a portion of the populace how they are allowed to express their sexualities and so how they are allowed to develop their interpersonal relationships. In this regard, the classic anti-porn position has lost sight of its original goal: women's equality.

Demonizing alternative sexualities, or even violent and grotesque sexualities, does not promote women's equality. In fact, it limits expression. The real culprit, as argued above, isn't hard-core pornography, but mainstream depictions of women wherein they are presented as subordinate to men. But to prohibit or limit this arena of speech would be impossible, and if possible, undesirable. We cannot police the minds of consumers, but we can educate them. There will always be undesirable speech; it cannot be eliminated. But likewise, there can always be a response—our response.

Ultimately, what recent research demonstrates is that the negative results often attributed to hard-core pornography, such as sexist attitudes, lack of understanding or empathy for women's interests, objectification, or silence via disablement resulting from objectification, are more reasonably attributable to sexualized media as a whole. Insofar as one is concerned with objectification through media representations of women as submissive, demeaned, and so forth, pornography is an infelicitous target and is merely symptomatic of an oversexualized discourse. The solution to this problem is not the prohibition or litigation of one narrow aspect of this phenomenon, hard-core pornography, but the regulation, in conjunction with efforts to educate consumers of the producers of sexualized media, especially producers who aim their products at children and young adults.

NOTES

An earlier version of this paper appears as "Pornography as Symptom: Refocusing the Anti-Pornography Debate on Pornification and Sexualization," *Philosophy in the Contemporary World* 20, no. 1 (Spring 2013): 15–27.

1. For discussions of these issues see Nadine Strossen, *Defending Pornography: Free Speech, Sex, and the Fight for Women's Rights* (New York: New York University Press, 2000); Ronald Dworkin, *Freedom's Law: The Moral Reading of the American Constitution* (Cambridge, MA: Harvard University Press, 1996); Wendy McElroy, *XXX: A Woman's Right to Pornography* (New York: St. Martin's Press, 1995).

2. See McElroy, *XXX*; Alan Soble, *Pornography, Sex and Feminism* (Amherst, NY: Prometheus Books, 2002).

3. See Catharine MacKinnon, *Only Words* (Cambridge, MA: Harvard University Press, 1996); Andrea Dworkin, "Power," in *The Problem of Pornography*, ed. Susan Dwyer (Belmont, CA: Wadsworth Publishing Company, 1995), 48–52; Rae Langton, *Sexual Solipsism: Philosophical Essays on Pornography and Objectification* (Oxford: Oxford University Press, 2009).

4. Martha C. Nussbaum, *Sex and Social Justice* (New York: Oxford University Press, 1999), 241.

5. M. Gigi Durham, *The Lolita Effect: The Media Sexualization of Young Girls and What We Can Do about It* (New York: Overlook Press, 2008); Diane E. Levin and Jean Kilbourne, *So Sexy, So Soon: The New Sexualized Childhood and What Parents Can Do to Protect Their Kids* (New York: Ballantine Books, 2009); Patrice A. Oppliger, *Girls Gone Skank: The Sexualization of Girls in American Culture* (Jefferson, NC: McFarland and Company, Inc., 2008).

6. American Psychological Association (APA), Task Force on the Sexualization of Girls, Report of the APA Task Force on the Sexualization of Girls (Washington, DC: APA, 2007), 2.

7. Susanna Paasonen, et al., *Pornification: Sex and Sexuality in Media Culture* (Oxford: Berg, 2007).

8. Carmine Sarracino and Kevin M. Scott, *The Porning of America: The Rise of Porn Culture, What It Means, and Where We Go from Here* (Boston: Beacon Press, 2008).

9. Pamela Paul, *Pornified: How Pornography Is Damaging Our Lives, Our Relationships, and Our Families* (New York: Henry Holt and Company, 2005).

10. Ariel Levy, *Female Chauvinist Pigs: Women and the Rise of Raunch Culture* (New York: Free Press, 2005).

11. (APA), Task Force on the Sexualization of Girls, *Report of the APA Task Force on the Sexualization of Girls* (Washington, DC: APA, 2007), 22.

12. APA, *Report of the APA Task Force*, 23.

13. APA, *Report of the APA Task Force*, 24.

14. Gail Dines, *Pornland: How Porn Has Hijacked Our Sexuality* (Boston: Beacon Press, 2010); Levin and Kilbourne, *So Sexy, So Soon*.

15. APA, *Report of the APA Task Force*, 29–35. For further discussion of this issue see Matthew Ezzell's chapter in this volume.

16. For further discussion of this relationship see Susanna Paasonen's chapter in this volume.

17. Catharine A. MacKinnon, "Frances Biddle's Sister: Pornography, Civil Rights, and Speech," in *The Problem of Pornography*, ed. Susan Dwyer (Belmont, CA.: Wadsworth Publishing Company, 1995), 59–60.

18. Andrea Dworkin, "Against the Male Flood," in *Feminism and Pornography*, ed. Drucilla Cornell (Oxford: Oxford University Press, 2007), 30.

19. Langton, *Sexual Solipsism*, especially chapters 1 and 3. For a more detailed discussion of Langton and these ideas, see Jennifer Hornsby's chapter in this volume.

20. Mary Kate McGowan, "Debate: On Silencing and Sexual Refusal," *Journal of Political Philosophy* 17, no. 4 (2009): 489.

21. See Diana Russell, *Rape in Marriage* (New York: Macmillan, 1982).

22. See "Facts About Sexual Harassment," U.S. Equal Employment Opportunity Commission, http://www.eeoc.gov/eeoc/publications/fs-sex.cfm (accessed 25 Nov. 2012).

23. *American Booksellers Association, Inc. v. William H. Hudnut, Mayor, City of Indianapolis*, 771 F.2d 323, 324 (7th Cir. 1985), 324.

24. *Miller v. California*, 413 U.S. 15 (1973)

25. McElroy, *XXX*, 46–48.

26. Andrea Dworkin, "Where Do We Stand on Pornography?" *Ms.*, January/February 1994, cited in Strossen, *Defending Pornography*, 23.

27. Strossen, *Defending Pornography*, 211.

28. McElroy, *XXX*, 43.

29. Gloria Steinem, "Erotica and Pornography: A Clear and Present Difference," in *The Problem of Pornography*, ed. Susan Dwyer (Belmont, CA.: Wadsworth Publishing Company, 1995), 31.

30. Ann Scales, "Avoiding Constitutional Depression: Bad Attitudes and the Fate of *Butler*," in *Feminism and Pornography*, ed. Drucilla Cornell (Oxford: Oxford University Press, 2007), 324.

31. Susan M. Easton, *The Problem of Pornography: Regulation and the Right to Free Speech* (New York: Routledge, 1994).

32. Catherine Itzin, "Pornography and Civil Liberties: Freedom, Harm, and Human Rights," in *Pornography: Women, Violence, and Civil Liberties*, ed. Catharine Itzin (Oxford: Oxford University Press, 1992), 585.

33. Strossen, *Defending Pornography*, chapters 2 and 3.

34. Strossen, *Defending Pornography*, 232–34; Scales, "Avoiding Constitutional Depression," 326.

35. Scales, "Avoiding Constitutional Depression," 326.

36. Itzin, "Pornography and Civil Liberties," 580.

37. For a presentation of this argument see Jacob M. Held, "One Man's Trash Is Another Man's Pleasure: Obscenity, Pornography, and the Law," in *Porn, Philosophy for Everyone: How to Think with Kink*, ed. Dave Monroe (Malden, MA: Wiley-Blackwell, 2012), 119–29.

38. Science Daily, "Strong Female Portrayals Eliminate Negative Effects of Violent Media," http://www.sciencedaily.com/releases/2012/08/120830065813.htm (accessed 31 Aug. 2012).

39. Jennifer Smith and Mindi Wisman, "What Are We Doing to Girls? The Early Sexualization Phenomenon and How Communities Are Responding." Charlotte, VT: New England Network for Child, Youth and Family Services, 2011.

40. Strossen, *Defending Pornography*, 55.

41. See Sarracino and Scott, *The Porning of America*.

42. Kimberle Crenshaw, "The 2 Live Crew Controversy," in *Feminism and Pornography*, ed. Drucilla Cornell (Oxford: Oxford University Press, 2007), 218.

43. Smith and Wisman, "What Are We Doing to Girls?"; Robert Jensen, *Getting Off: Pornography and the End of Masculinity* (Boston: South End Press, 2007); Dines, *Pornland*.

44. Science Daily, "Strong Female Portrayals."

45. Smith and Wisman, "What Are We Doing to Girls?" 7.

46. Shira Tarrant, "Pornography 101: Why College Kids Need Porn Literacy Training," http://www.alternet.org/story/148129/pornography-101%3A-why-college-kids-need-porn-literacy-training (accessed 5 Jan. 2012).

47. Smith and Wisman, "What Are We Doing to Girls?" 33–36; Levin and Kilbourne, *So Sexy, So Soon*, 36–37.

48. Dines, *Pornland*, 163.

49. Jensen, *Getting Off*, 184.

50. For more on this issue see Robert Jensen's chapter in this volume.

51. Paul, *Pornified*, 265.

52. Justice Louis Brandeis, *Whitney v. California*, 724 U.S. 357, 377 (1927).

Chapter Six

"The Price We Pay"?

Pornography and Harm

Susan J. Brison

Defenders of civil liberties have typically held, with J. S. Mill, that govern-ments may justifiably exercise power over individuals, against their will, only to prevent harm to others.[1] Until the 1970s, liberals and libertarians assumed that since producers and consumers of pornography clearly didn't harm anyone else, the only reasons their opponents had for regulating por-nography were that they considered it harmful to the producers or consumers, they thought it an offensive nuisance, and they objected on moral or religious grounds to certain private sexual pleasures of others. None of these reasons was taken to provide grounds for regulating pornography, however, because (1) individuals are considered to be the best judges of what is in their own interest (and, in any case, they cannot be harmed by something to which they consent); (2) what is merely offensive may be avoided (with the help of plain brown wrappers and zoning restrictions); and (3) the private sexual activities, of consenting adults anyway, are no one else's, certainly not the state's, business.

In the 1970s, however, the nature of the pornography debate changed as feminists argued that what is wrong with pornography is not that it morally defiles its producers and consumers, nor that it is offensive or sinful, but rather that it is a species of hate literature as well as a particularly insidious method of sexist socialization. Susan Brownmiller was one of the first to take this stance by proclaiming that "[p]ornography is the undiluted essence of anti-female propaganda."[2] In this view, pornography (of the violent degrad-ing variety) harms women by sexualizing misogynistic violence. According to Catharine MacKinnon, "[p]ornography sexualizes rape, battery, sexual

harassment, prostitution, and child sexual abuse; it thereby celebrates, promotes, authorizes, and legitimizes them."[3]

The claim that women are harmed by pornography has changed the nature
of the pornography debate, which is, for the most part, no longer a debate
between liberals who subscribe to Mill's harm principle and legal moralists
who hold that the state can legitimately legislate against so-called "morals
offenses" that do not harm any nonconsenting adults. Rather, the main academic debates now take place among those who subscribe to Mill's harm
principle, but disagree about what its implications are for the legal regulation
of pornography. Some theorists hold that violent degrading pornography
does not harm anyone and, thus, cannot justifiably be legally regulated, socially stigmatized, or morally condemned. Others maintain that, although
harmful to women, it cannot justifiably be regulated by either the civil or the
criminal law since that would cause even greater harms and/or violate the
legal rights of pornography producers and consumers, but that, nevertheless,
private individuals should do what they can (through social pressure, educational campaigns, boycotts, etc.) to put an end to it. Still others claim that
such pornography harms women by violating their civil right to be free from
sex discrimination and should for that reason be addressed by the law (as
well as by other means), just as other forms of sex discrimination are. But
others argue that restricting such pornography violates the moral rights of
pornography producers and consumers and, thus, restrictions are morally
impermissible. In this chapter, I will argue that there is no moral right to such
pornography.

WHAT IS PORNOGRAPHY?

First, however, I need to articulate what is at issue, but this is hard to do,
given various obstacles to describing the material in question accurately. (I
have encountered the same problem in writing about sexual violence.) There
is too much at stake to be put off writing about issues of urgent import to
women because of squeamishness or fear of academic impropriety—but how
can one write about this particular issue without reproducing the violent
degrading pornography itself? (Recall the labeling of Anita Hill as "a little
nutty and a little slutty" because she repeated, in public, the sexually demeaning language that Clarence Thomas had allegedly uttered to her in private.) However, if one doesn't write graphically about the content of violent
degrading pornography, one risks being viewed as either crazy (she must be
imagining things!) or too prudish to talk frankly about sex. And what tone
should one adopt—one of scholarly detachment or of outrage? There is a
double bind here, similar to that faced by rape victims on the witness stand: if
they appear calm and rational enough for their testimony to be credible, that

may be taken as evidence that they cannot have been raped. But if they are emotional and out of control enough to appear traumatized, then their testimony is not considered reliable.

Any critic of violent degrading pornography risks being viewed not only as prudish (especially if the critic is a woman), but also as meddling in others' "private" business, since we tend not to see the harm in pornography—harm which is often made invisible and considered unspeakable. But "we" didn't used to see the harm in depriving women and minorities of their civil rights. And "we" didn't used to see the harm in distributing postcards depicting and celebrating lynchings. More recently, "we" didn't see the harm in marital or "date" rape, spousal battering, or sexual harassment.

Even now, as Richard Delgado and Jean Stefancic point out, "members of the empowered group may simply announce to the disaffected that they do not see their problem, that they have looked for evidence of harm but cannot find it. Later generations may well marvel, 'how could they have been so blind?' But paradigms change slowly. In the meantime, one may describe oneself as a cautious and principled social scientist interested only in the truth. And one's opponent, by a neat reversal, becomes an intolerant zealot willing to trample on the liberties of others without good cause."[4]

A further problem arises in critically analyzing violent degrading pornography—deriving from precisely those harmful aspects of it being critiqued— which is that descriptions of it and quotations from it can themselves be degrading, or even retraumatizing, especially for women who have been victimized by sexual violence. But one thing that is clear is that feminist critics of such pornography are *not* criticizing it on the grounds that it is erotic, or sexually arousing, or that it constitutes "obscenity," defined by the Court as "works which, taken as a whole, appeal to the prurient interest in sex, which portray sexual conduct in a patently offensive way, and which, taken as a whole, do not have serious literary, artistic, political, or scientific value."[5]

Those who work on this issue—and have familiarized themselves with the real world of the pornography industry—know all too well that pornography is not merely offensive. In contrast, here is how some of them define "pornography": "the graphic sexually explicit subordination of women through pictures or words that also includes women dehumanized as sexual objects, things, or commodities; enjoying pain or humiliation or rape; being tied up, cut up, mutilated, bruised, or physically hurt; in postures of sexual submission, servility or display; reduced to body parts, penetrated by objects or animals, or presented in scenarios of degradation, injury, torture; shown as filthy or inferior; bleeding, bruised, or hurt in a context that makes these conditions sexual."[6]

I define "pornography," for the purposes of this chapter, as violent degrading misogynistic hate speech (where "speech" includes words, pictures, films, etc.). Of course, what is commonly referred to as "pornography" is a much broader category, but I am focusing on only this subcategory. I will argue that, if pornography (the subcategory I've just defined) unjustly harms women (as there is reason to suppose it does), then there is no moral right to produce, sell, or consume it. (I will not here be arguing for or against its legal restriction. If there is no moral right to pornography, then any purported legal right to pornography must be grounded in something else. There may well be other reasons to defend a legal right to pornography, and, in any case, no position on that issue is dictated by my arguments against the alleged moral right.)

PORNOGRAPHY AND HARM

I cannot hope to adequately portray the harm inflicted on girls and women in the production of pornography (for the reasons given above), but there is plenty of research documenting them. One of the most powerful forms of evidence for such harms is the first-person testimony of "participants" in pornography.[7] A not uncommon scenario in which a girl becomes trapped in the pornography industry is described by Evelina Giobbe in her testimony to the U.S. Attorney General's Commission on Pornography. After running away from home at age thirteen and being raped her first night on the streets, Giobbe was befriended by a man who seemed initially kind and concerned, but who, after taking nude photographs of her, sold her to a pimp who raped and battered her, threatening her life and those of her family until she "agreed" to work as a prostitute for him. Her "customers" knew she was an adolescent and sexually inexperienced. "So," she testified, "they showed me pornography to teach me and ignored my tears and they positioned my body like the women in the pictures, and used me." She tried on many occasions to escape, but, as a teenager with no resources, cut off from friends and family, who believed she was a criminal, she was an easy mark for her pimp: "He would drag me down streets, out of restaurants, even into taxis, all the while beating me while I protested, crying and begging passersby for help. No one wanted to get involved."[8] She was later sold to another pimp who "was a pornographer and the most brutal of all." According to her testimony, he recruited other girls and women into pornography by advertising for models. "When a woman answered his ad, he'd offer to put her portfolio together for free, be her agent, and make her a 'star.' He'd then use magazines like *Playboy* to convince her to pose for 'soft-core' porn. He'd then engage her in a love affair and smooth talk her into prostitution. 'Just long enough,' he would say, 'to get enough money to finance your career as a model.' If sweet talk didn't work, violence and blackmail did. She became one of us."[9]

Giobbe escaped the pornography industry by chance, after "destroy[ing] herself with heroin" and becoming "no longer usable." She considers herself one of the lucky ones—"a rare survivor."[10] And this was *before* the AIDS epidemic.

According to a 2004 article in the *Sunday New York Times Magazine*, pornography—of an increasingly violent sort—has played an important role in the global sex trafficking of girls and women who, lured by promises of employment (for example, as nannies or waitresses), end up trapped in foreign countries, with no money, no legal papers, no family or friends, and no ability to speak the local language. U.S. Immigrations and Customs Enforcement (ICE) agents at the Cyber Crimes Center in Fairfax, Virginia, are "tracking a clear spike in the demand for harder-core pornography on the Internet. 'We've become desensitized by the soft stuff; now we need a harder and harder hit,' says ICE Special Agent Perry Woo."[11] With ICE agents, the author of this article looked up a website purporting to offer sex slaves for sale: "There were streams of Web pages of thumbnail images of young girls of every ethnicity in obvious distress, bound, gagged, contorted. The agents in the room pointed out probable injuries from torture. 'With new Internet technology,' Woo said, 'pornography is becoming more pervasive. With Web cams we're seeing more live molestation of children.'"[12]

It is not enough to say that the participants in pornography consent, *even* in the case of adult women who apparently do, given the road many have been led (or dragged) down—since childhood in some cases—to get to that point. Genuine autonomous consent requires the ability to critically evaluate and choose from a range of significant and worthwhile options. Even if all the participants genuinely consented to their use in the pornography industry, however, we would need to consider how pornography influences how *other* nonconsenting women are viewed and treated. Compare the (thankfully imaginary) scenario in which there existed "slave clubs" where some black men or women consented to be brutalized and degraded for the pleasure of their white customers. Suppose the black "performers" determined that, given the options, it was in their best interest to make money in this way. Their financial gain—imagine that they are highly paid—more than compensates for the social harm to them as individuals of being subjected to a (let's say) slightly increased risk (resulting from the prevalence of such clubs) of being degraded and brutalized outside their workplace. Some of them even enjoy the work, having a level of ironic detachment that enables them to view their customers as pathetic or contemptible. Some, who don't actually enjoy their work, don't suffer distress, since they manage to dissociate during it. Others are distressed by it, but they have determined that the financial benefit outweighs the psychic and physical pain. For those black men or women who did not work in the clubs, however, there would be nothing that compensated for their slightly increased risk of being degraded and brutalized as a result of it. They would be better off if the clubs did not exist. The work the black "performers" in the clubs did would make it harder for other black men and women to live their lives free of fear.

The harms pornography causes to nonparticipants in its production—often called "indirect" or "diffuse" harms, which makes them sound less real and less serious than they actually are—include (1) harms to those who have pornography forced on them, (2) increased or reinforced discrimination against—and sexual abuse of—girls and women, (3) harms to boys and men whose attitudes toward women and whose sexual desires are influenced by pornography, and (4) harms to those who have already been victimized by sexual violence. The first three categories of harm have been amply documented.[13] That the proliferation of pornography leads to attitudinal changes in men, which, in turn, lead to harmful behavior, should not be surprising, especially given the high rates of exposure of preteen and teenage boys. On the contrary, as Frederick Schauer testified at the Pornography Civil Rights Hearing in Boston in 1992, it is "a constant source of astonishment that a society that so easily and correctly accepts the possibility that a cute drawing of a camel can have such an effect on the number of people who take up smoking, has such difficulty accepting the proposition that endorsing images of rape or other forms of sexual violence can have an effect on the number of people who take up rape."[14]

One might object, though, that pornography is merely a symptom (of a misogynistic, patriarchal society), not a cause.[15] Even if this were the case, however, that would not mean that we should not be concerned about it. The fact that there are so few female legislators in the United States at the federal level is a symptom, not a cause, of patriarchy. But this does not mean that we should not do anything about the political status quo. In any case, pornography is more than a mere symptom: it fosters and perpetuates the sexist attitudes that are essential for its enjoyment, even if it does not create them.

It should be noted here that the fact that the *point* of pornography (from the standpoint of the producers) is to make money by giving pleasure does not mean that it cannot also be harmfully degrading. On the contrary, it is pleasurable (and profitable) *precisely because* it is degrading to others. And it is reasonable to expect a spillover effect in the public domain, since its enjoyment requires the adoption of certain attitudes. In fact, although it may be difficult to see the process of dehumanization at work when girls and women are routinely portrayed as being worthy of degradation, torture, and even death, empirical studies have shown that exposure to such portrayals increases the likelihood that people will take actual sexual violence less seriously—and even consider it to be justified in some cases.[16]

There is another connection between the dehumanization of girls and women in pornography and their brutalization in rape, battering, forced prostitution, and sexual murder, which is that, in a society where women are victimized in these ways at an alarming rate, it shows a callous disregard for the actual victims to have depictions of sexual violence bought and sold as entertainment. For a short while, after 9/11, we empathized so much with the victims of the terrorist attacks that films of similarly horrifying attacks were withdrawn because they were no longer considered entertaining. But victims of sexual violence are given so little respect that many of us see nothing wrong with being entertained by depictions of what they have had to endure.

If we take seriously the harm of pornography, then we want to know what to do about it. Should the government intervene by regulating it? The standard debate over pornography has framed it as a free speech issue. The drafters of an anti-pornography ordinance adopted by the city of Indianapolis argued that pornography constitutes a violation of the civil rights of women. In response to those who asserted that the First Amendment protected pornography, they argued that pornography violated the First Amendment rights of women (by "silencing" them—depriving them of credibility and making "no" appear to mean "yes" in rape scenarios), as well as their Fourteenth Amendment rights to equal protection. In his opinion in *American Booksellers Association v. Hudnut*, which ruled unconstitutional the Indianapolis anti-pornography ordinance, Judge Frank Easterbrook acknowledged that pornography harms women in very significant and concrete ways:

> Depictions of subordination tend to perpetuate subordination. The subordinate status of women in turn leads to affront and lower pay at work, insult and injury at home, battery and rape on the streets. In the language of the legislature, "[p]ornography is central in creating and maintaining sex as a basis of discrimination. Pornography is a systematic practice of exploitation and subordination based on sex which differentially harms women. The bigotry and contempt it produces, with the acts of aggression it fosters, harm women's opportunities for equality and rights [of all kinds]" Indianapolis Code §16-1(a) (2). Yet this simply demonstrates the power of pornography as speech.[17]

Easterbrook seems to take the harms of pornography seriously, but he then goes on to talk about its "unhappy effects" which he considers to be the result of "mental intermediation." He assumes that speech has no (or merely negligible) effects that are not under the conscious control of the audience, although this assumption is undermined not only by the widely acknowledged power of advertising, but also by recent work in cognitive neuroscience on the prevalence of unconscious imitation in human beings.[18] It might be argued, though, that if we consider the producers of pornography to be even partially responsible for the violence perpetrated by some of its consumers, then we must consider the perpetrators *not* to be responsible or to be less than fully responsible for their crimes. But this does not follow. Even if the perpetrators are considered to be 100 percent responsible, some responsibility can still be attributed to the pornographers. (In fact, two or more people can each be 100 percent responsible for the same crime, as in the case of multiple snipers who simultaneously fire many shots, fatally wounding their victim.)

The courts have, for now, decided that even if serious harm to women results from it, pornography is, qua speech, protected (except for that material which also meets the legal definition of obscenity). That is, there is currently a *legal* right to it, falling under the right to free speech. But *should* there be?

A MORAL RIGHT TO PORNOGRAPHY?

Of course we value freedom of speech. But how should we value it? What should we do when speech is genuinely harmful? Traditionally, in the United States, the constitutionally protected right to free speech is held to be of such high importance that it trumps just about everything else. For example, in the *Hudnut* case discussed above, it was acknowledged that the pornography producers' and consumers' legal right to free speech was in conflict with women's right to equal protection, but it was asserted (without argumentation) that the free speech right had priority. Acceptance of this claim without requiring a defense of it, however, amounts to adopting a kind of free speech fundamentalism. But to see how untenable such a view is, suppose that uttering the words "you're dead" caused everyone within earshot (but the speaker) to fall down dead. Would anyone seriously say that such speech deserved legal protection? Granted, the harms of pornography are less obvious and less severe, but there is sufficient evidence for these harms for it to be reasonable to require an argument for why the legal right to pornography should take priority over others' legal rights not to be subjected to such harms.

If we reject free speech fundamentalism, the question of whether pornography should be legally restricted becomes much more complicated. My aim in this chapter is not to articulate or defend a position on this question; rather, I aim to undermine the view that there is a moral right to pornography that undergirds a legal right to it.

In "The Right to Get Turned On: Pornography, Autonomy, Equality," Andrew Altman shifts the debate over pornography in a promising way by arguing that there is a *moral* right to (even violent misogynistic) pornography, falling, not under a moral right to free speech, but, rather, under a moral right to sexual autonomy (that also covers the right to use contraceptives and the right to homosexual sex).[19] In this view, which Altman dubs "liberal sexual morality," whatever harms resulting from pornography are just the price we pay for the right to sexual autonomy. Sexuality is an important, arguably central, aspect of a flourishing human life. Sexual expression is one of the primary ways we define ourselves and our relations to others, and a healthy society should value and celebrate it. But what does it add to these claims to say that we have a moral *right* to sexual autonomy? And, if we do have such a right, does it include a right to produce, distribute, and consume pornography (defined, as above, as violent degrading misogynistic hate speech)?

Although philosophers disagree about the nature of rights (and indeed even about whether such things exist at all), most hold that to say that someone, x, has a moral right to do something, y, means that others are under a duty not to interfere with x's doing y. (Of course, x's right is limited by others' rights, as expressed by the saying "your right to swing your arm ends at my face.") But beyond this, there is little agreement. Some hold that rights are natural, inalienable, God-given. Others hold that rights talk is just a shorthand for talk about those interests that are especially important to us (for example, because protecting them tends to increase our welfare). Some hold that we have positive rights, just by virtue of being human, such that other people are under an obligation to provide us with whatever we need to exercise those rights. (If there is a positive right to education, for example, then society has an obligation to provide free public education for all.) Others hold that we have only negative rights (unless individuals *grant* us positive rights by, for example, making promises to assist us) that require only that other people not interfere with our exercising those rights. (The right to privacy, if taken to be simply a right to be left alone, is an example of a negative right.)

On any account, the concept of a right is diffuse. To say that x has a moral right to do y does not, by itself, say very much, unless we specify what others are required to do (or to refrain from doing) in order not to violate that right. There is a wide range of different responses to x's doing y, given that x has a right to do y—from complete acceptance (or perhaps even positive support) to something just short of physical restraint or intervention. Where is the alleged right to pornography located on this spectrum of moral assessment?

Altman considers the right to pornography and the right to sexual orientation to have the same foundation in a right to sexual autonomy. What should our (society's) attitude be toward the exercising of that right? Should we tolerate it, that is, have no laws against it, while allowing private individuals to lobby against it or to try to dissuade people from it? Or should we actively embrace it? Assimilating the right to pornography with the right to sexual orientation muddies the waters here. Presumably, according to liberal sexual morality, the right to sexual orientation requires more than mere tolerance. It requires society's complete acceptance (and, I would argue, positive support, given that prejudice and violence against gays and lesbians persists in our society). It is wrong to hold that gays and lesbians have "bad characters" or to try to get them to "reform."

The right to pornography, however, does not lie on the same end of the spectrum, since Altman claims that getting off on pornography is a sign of a bad character. Some feminists and liberals who defend a legal right to pornography also hold that all sorts of private pressures—protests, boycotts, educational campaigns—should be brought to bear on the pornographers. Altman's position is that there is not just a legal right, but also a *moral* right to pornography, even if there is something bad about exercising it. There are persuasive reasons for holding that we have legal rights to do some things that are morally wrong, in cases in which enforcement would be impossible or would involve gross violations of privacy. But Altman seems to hold that we have a *moral* right to do some things that are morally wrong. What does this mean? It cannot mean that people have a right to do things that are wrong in that they harm others. It might mean that people have the right to do things that other people consider wrong (but that are not harmful to others), that is, people have the right to do harmless things that other people morally disapprove of. However, if the behavior, for example engaging in homosexual sex, is not unjustly harming others, then liberals who subscribe to Mill's harm principle have no grounds for considering it to be wrong.

So where should the right to pornography be located on the spectrum of moral assessment? There is no one answer to this question. We need to look at particular cases. Suppose I have a twenty-one-year-old son—I'm assuming minors have no right to pornography—who is a heavy consumer of pornography (of the kind I've been talking about). What does his (alleged) right to pornography entail? Given my opposition to pornography, presumably I would not be under an obligation to positively support his pornography habit by buying it for him. But would I have to pretend that I'm not aware of it? Would I be under a duty not to try to dissuade him from viewing pornography? Would his sister be under a duty not to throw the magazines out when she saw them in common areas of the house? Would it be wrong for his buddies to try to talk him out of it? Would his teachers have a duty to refrain from arguing against it? Would it be wrong for his neighbors to boycott the local convenience store that sold it? Would his girlfriend (or boyfriend) who became convinced it was ruining their relationship be under a moral duty not to rip it out of his hands? If the answer to each of the above questions is "no," which I think it is, then it's not clear what, if anything, his right entitles him to.[20] What is clear is that, if a right to pornography exists, it is quite unlike a right to engage in homosexual sex or to use contraceptives, and is located at the opposite end of the spectrum of moral assessment.

Perhaps there is, nevertheless, something special about sexual arousal ("getting turned on") that gives it special moral status. But Altman has not said what makes sexual arousal different (in a morally significant way) from other forms of arousal, for example, that of racial animus. It makes sense to say that there is a right to be turned on—not a special right, but, rather, one falling under a general right to liberty, but this general right to liberty is delimited by the harm principle. There is no general right to have pleasurable feelings (of any sort, sexual or otherwise) that override others' rights not to be harmed. There is no moral right to achieve a feeling of comfort by unjustly discriminating against homosexuals on the grounds that associating with them makes you uncomfortable. Likewise, there is no moral right to achieve a feeling of superiority (no matter how pleasurable such a feeling might be) by discriminating against those of a different race. And it doesn't matter how central to one's self-definition the feeling in question might be. For parents, the satisfaction of ensuring the good upbringing and education of one's children is of paramount importance, and yet this degree of importance does not give racist parents the right to racially segregated housing or schools.

It might be argued that sexual arousal is special in that it is a bodily pleasure and, thus, more natural, possibly even immutable. Even if this were so, it would not follow that one has a right to achieve it by any means necessary. To take an example of another kind of "bodily" pleasure, suppose that there are gustatory pleasures that can be achieved only in immoral ways (for example, by eating live monkey brains—which some people used to do—or organs or flesh "donated" by (or purchased from) living human beings, or food that has been stolen from people on the verge of starvation). That there is a (general) right to enjoy eating what one chooses to eat—it would be (in general) wrong, for example, for me to force you to eat, or not to eat, something—does not mean that one has a right to eat whatever gives one pleasure.

But it is not the case that what people find sexually arousing is a simple biological fact about them, a given, something immutable. People can be conditioned to be aroused by any number of things. (In one study, men were conditioned to be aroused by a picture of a woman's boot.)[21] Emotions, especially ones with strong physiological components, such as sexual arousal, *feel* natural. They don't seem to be socially constructed, because we don't (at the time) consciously choose them: they just *are*. But emotions are, at least to some extent, learned reactions to things. There are gender differences in emotional reactions; for example, men tend to get angry in some situations in which women tend to feel, not angry, but hurt. But this does not mean that such differences are *natural*.

Given the wide variety of sexual fantasies and fetishes we know about, it's conceivable that just about *anything* could be a turn-on for someone—looking at photos of dead, naked bodies piled in mass graves in Nazi death camps, for example, or looking at photos of lynched black men. According to liberal sexual morality, the only reason for supposing that there might not be a moral right to make a profit from and get off on such "pornography" would be that the photographed people are posthumously harmed by it (given that they did not consent to their images being used in this way). But suppose

they had consented. Or suppose, more plausibly, that the images were com-
puter-generated—completely realistic-looking, but not images *of* actual individuals. Liberal sexual morality would have to allow (some) people to make
money by others getting turned on by these images. Not only that, but given
that sexual desires are malleable, the pornographer also has a right to make
money by acculturating others to be turned on by such images. (In other
words, the pornographer has a right to turn the world into a place where
people get turned on by such images.) And, if our attitude toward this is
grounded in the right to sexual autonomy, it should be similar to our attitude
toward homosexuality: we shouldn't merely tolerate it, we should come to
accept and support it.

   While conceding that there are limits to the right to sexual autonomy—it
is constrained by the harm principle—Altman assumes (as most liberals do)
that one cannot be harmed by something to which one consents. I argued
earlier that the way many models get lured into the pornography industry
should make us at least question the extent to which they are consenting to
what is being done to them. But suppose they do consent. Does that mean
that we must tolerate the production and use of whatever pornography results? Unfortunately, one doesn't have to construct a thought experiment to
test our intuitions about this. According to the *New York Times*, Armin
Meiwes, "[a] German computer technician who killed and ate a willing victim he found through the Internet," was recently convicted of manslaughter.
His "victim," Bernd-Jürgen Brandes, had "responded to an Internet posting
by Mr. Meiwes seeking someone willing to be 'slaughtered.'" "'Both were
looking for the ultimate kick,' the judge said." It was "an evening of sexual
role-playing and violence, much of it videotaped by Mr. Meiwes," enough to
convince the court that the "victim" consented.[22] Does the right to sexual
autonomy include the rights to produce, sell, and get turned on by the video-
tape of this "slaughter"—a real-life instance of a snuff film? If we cannot
prove that there is a causal connection between the film and harm to others,
the answer, according to liberal sexual morality, is "yes."

   Altman claims that "even if a causal connection between violent pornography and sexual violence were clearly established, it would still be insufficient to conclude that, in contemporary society, the production, distribution
and viewing of violent pornography lay beyond the limits of an adult's right
to sexual autonomy" because *other* media—he cites slasher films—arguably
"cause at least some amount of violence against women, sexual and otherwise. However it is not reasonable to hold that adults have no right to produce, distribute and view such movies."[23] Why, if one has established that,
say, slasher films are harmful, we must hold that adults have a right to them
is not explained. But even if we agree that adults have the right to produce/
consume nonpornographic media even if it is as harmful as pornography, it
does not follow that adults have the right to produce/consume pornography.

To assume that it does would be like arguing against prohibiting driving while talking on cell phones on the grounds that this is not the *only* thing (or even the main thing) contributing to automobile accidents.

Altman accepts that "it is reasonable to hold that the existence of . . . pornography makes it more difficult for women to live their lives as the sexual equals of men, i.e., more difficult relative to a society which was ruled by a liberal sexual morality and had fewer women, or none at all, who were willing to engage in humiliating conduct as part of the production of pornographic materials,"[24] but he notes that women are better off in a society with liberal sexual morality than in a society with traditional sexual morality (for example, Saudi Arabia). I agree, but surely these are not the only two possibilities. I would advocate the alternative of a progressive sexual morality. What might that look like? We don't even know. Even our most deep-seated assumptions about sexuality may turn out to be mistaken. We used to view rape as motivated purely by lust (or, in wartime, by a desire to humiliate enemy men) and battering as a way of showing spousal love. Some of us still do. Gradually, however, we are breaking the link between sexuality and violence. Perhaps some day we'll have reached the point where sexual violence is no longer arousing, where it makes no sense to talk of killing and being killed as the "ultimate" sexual "kick."

According to liberal sexual morality, the harms of pornography are the price we pay for having the right to sexual autonomy in other areas, for example, the right to have sex outside of marriage (including homosexual sex) and the right to use contraceptives. But this view (of the right to sexual autonomy as an all-or-nothing package) is formed in response to legal moralism, and makes sense only if one considers all these rights to be rights to do harmless things that some people nevertheless morally condemn. In such cases, proponents of liberal sexual morality say: "If you don't like it, don't look at it (or hear about it or think about it)." This is a satisfactory response only if the behavior in question isn't harming anyone. But as our views about what constitutes harm have changed, our views of what is our business have also changed. Just as we no longer look the other way in response to marital or "date" rape, domestic violence, and sexual harassment, we should no longer accept pornography's harms as the price we pay for sexual autonomy.

NOTES

This paper is a revised version of "'The Price We Pay'? Pornography and Harm," in *Contemporary Debates in Applied Ethics*, ed. Andrew I. Cohen and Christopher Heath Wellman (Oxford: Blackwell, 2005), 236–50; revised and printed in *Ethics in Practice: An Anthology,* ed. Hugh La Follette (Hoboken, NJ: Wiley, 2008). I'm grateful to Ann Bumpus, Christopher Wellman, and Thomas Trezise for helpful discussions of many issues in this chapter, and to Margaret Little for invaluable comments on earlier drafts. I'd also like to thank Tien-Tien Jong for expert assistance in revising this piece for the present volume.

1. John Stuart Mill, *On Liberty* (Indianapolis: Hackett Publishing Co., 1978). Mill considered his harm principle to apply equally to governmental regulation and to "the moral coercion of public opinion." The harm principle states that "the only purpose for which power can be rightfully exercised over any member of a civilized community, against his will, is to prevent harm to others" (9). Mill does not specify what counts as harm. Following Joel Feinberg, I consider it to be a wrongful setback to one's significant interests. See Joel Feinberg, *The Moral Limits of the Criminal Law, Vol. 1: Harm to Others* (New York: Oxford University Press, 1984).

2. Susan Brownmiller, *Against Our Will: Men, Women and Rape* (New York: Bantam Books, 1975), 443.

3. Catharine MacKinnon, *Feminism Unmodified: Discourses on Life and Law* (Cambridge, MA.: Harvard University Press, 1987), 171.

4. Richard Delgado and Jean Stefancic, *Must We Defend Nazis? Hate Speech, Pornography, and the New First Amendment* (New York: New York University Press, 1997), 37.

5. *Miller v. California*, 413 U.S. 15, 24 (1973).

6. This is the definition used in the anti-pornography ordinance drafted by Andrea Dworkin and Catharine MacKinnon, passed by the city of Indianapolis, but ruled unconstitutional by the 7th Circuit Court of Appeals. MacKinnon, *Feminism Unmodified*, 176.

7. Those who are interested in reading more about this are referred to *Attorney General's Commission on Pornography, Final Report* (Washington, DC: U.S. Department of Justice, 1986); Catherine Itzen, ed., *Pornography: Women, Violence and Civil Liberties* (New York: Oxford University Press, 1992); Laura Lederer, ed, *Take Back the Night: Women on Pornography* (New York: William Morrow and Co., 1980); Laura J. Lederer and Richard Delgado, eds., *The Price We Pay: The Case against Racist Speech, Hate Propaganda, and Pornography* (New York: Hill and Wang, 1995); MacKinnon, *Feminism Unmodified*; Catharine A. MacKinnon, *Only Words* (Cambridge, MA: Harvard University Press, 1993); Catharine A. MacKinnon and Andrea Dworkin, eds., *In Harm's Way: The Pornography Civil Rights Hearings* (Cambridge, MA.: Harvard University Press, 1997); Diana E. H. Russell, ed., *Making Violence Sexy: Feminist Views on Pornography* (Buckingham, UK: Open University Press, 1993).

8. Quoted in Russell, *Making Violence Sexy*, 38.

9. Russell, *Making Violence Sexy*, 39.

10. Russell, *Making Violence Sexy*, 39–40.

11. Peter Landesman, "The Girls Next Door." *Sunday New York Times Magazine*, January 25, 2004, 72.

12. Landesman, "The Girls Next Door," 74.

13. See the Attorney General's Commission on Pornography; Itzen, *Pornography*; Lederer, *Take Back the Night*; Lederer and Delgado, *The Price We Pay*; MacKinnon, *Feminism Unmodified*; MacKinnon, *Only Words*; MacKinnon and Dworkin, *In Harm's Way*; Russell, *Making Violence Sexy*.

14. Cited in MacKinnon and Dworkin, *In Harm's Way*, 396.

15. For a discussion of this issue see Jacob Held's chapter in this volume.

16. See MacKinnon and Dworkin, *In Harm's Way*, 46–60; Lederer and Delgado, *The Price We Pay*, 61–112; Russell, *Making Violence Sexy*, 113–213.

17. *American Booksellers Association, Inc. v. Hudnut*, 771 F.2d 323 (7th Cir. 1985), 329. This view cannot consistently be held, however, by liberals and feminists who support laws against sex or race discrimination and segregation in schools, workplaces, and even private clubs. One does not hear the argument that if segregation harms minorities' opportunities for equal rights, this simply demonstrates the power of freedom of association, which is also protected by the First Amendment.

18. The recent research discussed in Susan L. Hurley, "Imitation, Media Violence, and Freedom of Speech," *Philosophical Studies* 17/1–2 (January 2004): 165–218, suggests that the imitation of others' behavior, including others' violent acts, is not a consciously mediated process, under the autonomous control of the viewers/imitators.

19. Andrew Altman, "The Right to Get Turned On: Pornography, Autonomy, Equality," in *Contemporary Debates in Applied Ethics*, ed. Andrew I. Cohen and Christopher Heath Wellman (Oxford: Blackwell, 2005), 223–35. Since some theorists ground the right to free speech in

a right to autonomy, however, there may not be such a sharp distinction between these two approaches. See Susan J. Brison, "The Autonomy Defense of Free Speech," *Ethics* 108 (1998): 312–39.

20. I also mean for the above thought experiment to illustrate the fact that the nature of the duty one has with respect to the holder of the alleged moral right to pornography depends on one's relationship to the right holder. Presumably a neighbor would be under a duty not to snatch pornography out of the right holder's hands. But if someone *else*, the right holder's lover, say, is under no such duty, then it's not clear what the right amounts to.

21. Russell, *Making Violence Sexy*, 129.

22. Mark Landler, "German Court Convicts Internet Cannibal of Manslaughter," *New York Times*, January 31, 2004, A3.

23. Altman, "The Right to Get Turned On," 228–29.

24. Altman, "The Right to Get Turned On," 233.

Chapter Seven

Heidegger, Feminism, and Pornography

Natalie Nenadic

My assumption is that thought itself arises out of incidents of living experience and must remain bound to them as the only guide posts by which to take its bearings. —Hannah Arendt

In the 1980s and early 1990s, a series of legal initiatives took place in the United States aimed at having pornography recognized as a form of sex discrimination against women.[1] This policy response was a practical effect and culmination of an historic breakthrough in our understanding of pornography. This new understanding now centered on pornography's role in affecting women's social inequality and challenged a governing view that pornography is mainly neutral, sexually explicit material that moreover is sexually liberating.

This alternate understanding emanated from feminism's response to the harmful consequences to women of pornography's new and rapid encroachment in the public and private spheres of late modern democratic society in the 1970s onward, when pornography became more "democratically" available than ever before. Pornographic movie theaters and outlets mushroomed in urban environments, which were soon zoned to low-income and racially segregated parts of cities, and an expanding variety of magazines were now widely available and stashed in households across the country. Aiming to understand how "pornography works in everyday life,"[2] that is, how it is usually experienced, especially by those most deleteriously impacted by it, feminism gathered the findings of immediate sources of inquiry that for the first time centered on survivor accounts and included research in areas such as the social sciences, work by health professionals and social workers, and the results of simply mapping the content of the vast majority of readily available pornography. This "bottom-up" procedure revealed pornography as a medium in which sexually explicit content is overwhelmingly about showing and endorsing sexual means of harming people, mainly women, and conditioning consumers' arousal to cues that present women as sexually vulnerable and violable, for instance, enjoying pain, humiliation, rape, being tied up, cut up, mutilated, bruised, being sexually submissive, or reduced to their sexual body parts; in sum, some form of male dominance and female subordination.[3] This nascent alternate understanding was followed by these high-profile civil rights legal initiatives to which it gave rise. Out of this groundswell, this new understanding was able to break the surface for the first time in the wider social consciousness and to make a small, but noticeable, dent in the increasingly popular and hardened position that pornography's new proliferation is mainly about the expansion of sexual freedom.

I claim that we may express this breakthrough in our understanding philosophically in terms of Martin Heidegger's phenomenology and fundamental ontology, concepts he significantly treats in his magnum opus *Being and Time* (1927)[4] and whose first incarnations we find in his early lecture courses (1919–1925).[5] For Heidegger, philosophy's task is to retrieve a previously unconsidered or unknown dimension of the human condition and to situate that new understanding within an existing philosophical discourse that is part of an historical tradition, a task for which that tradition is both a hindrance and a resource. Phenomenology is the method by which the inquirer draws out that usually concealed dimension of the human condition from the concrete, everyday way that it is experienced. And fundamental ontology is a wider, more encompassing notion of being or what philosophy considers real about the world than the reductive, absolutely certain, and definitive determinations of philosophy's ontological tradition from Descartes onward, determinations that are assumed to exhaust the reality of the respective domain at issue. Fundamental ontology instead assumes that our determinations about the world, while secure, cannot be exhaustive as the world is too complex to be simplified in this way; something always escapes our conceptual grasp. Accordingly, fundamental ontology encompasses dimensions of the world that escape or do not quite fit traditional ontology's definitive claims, claims that thereby conceal these dimensions, which may demand phenomenological treatment that may yield new, more adequate understanding of the domain in question.

Feminism's world-involved, multidisciplinary inquiry into pornography's human fallout, which yielded a new and sounder understanding of pornography and its recent proliferation than the conventional view that it is neutral, sexually explicit material that reflects the expansion of sexual freedom, may be considered precisely such a phenomenological procedure that inhabits a more fundamental ontological ground of experiences than the prevailing understanding. Furthermore, I want to suggest a distinctive role for philosophy in this larger multidisciplinary effort. Just as Heidegger does vis-à-vis his own project, I claim that we may cast feminism's phenomenological findings in terms of a criticism of traditional ontology. But, in this case, that traditional ontology concerns a gendered notion of freedom on which the prevailing view of pornography rests, wherein men are assumed to experience freedom through treating women in the ways that pornography presents, and women through enjoying it. This gendered freedom, whose beginnings and earliest forms go back to the Enlightenment, conceals and harms entire dimensions of the human condition.

HEIDEGGER, FUNDAMENTAL ONTOLOGY, AND PHENOMENOLOGY[6]

To show how we may thus philosophically express these immediate, theoretical, and legal developments that culminated in this breakthrough in our understanding of pornography, I begin by introducing the relevant aspects of Heidegger's thought. *Being and Time* is his major criticism of the Cartesian and neo-Cartesian assumptions that have governed and, on this view, limited philosophy in the modern era and especially in his time. On this traditional approach, philosophy's knower is in some manner detached from the world, and what he or she knows about it is what fits the form of absolute certainty, in determinations that are thus said to exhaust what is essential or real about the domain at issue and are therefore definitive. Whatever eludes this kind of conceptual grasp is not considered real and, so, is not philosophically significant. In mastering more and more of the world in this way, this knower is considered progressively freer, in a freedom that, for Heidegger, is problematic. For in its aftermath, we recognize less of the world outside our absolute command, recognition that he considers essential for triggering a fundamental questioning of how we understand ourselves and the world, meaning our freedom to choose some other paths, which is freedom in his sense.

In contrast, Heidegger posits a wider notion of being or what philosophy considers real, which he calls "fundamental ontology."[7] It refers to that more basic ground of experience from which our concepts about the world are drawn and that is always "more" than what they can capture, however much they do tell us. Summarizing what fundamental ontology encompasses, he states: "Above all, what I experience really exists."[8] This ground reflects the world's complexity and ampleness, that "excess" that always shadows our knowledge of the world. Positively valorizing such everyday experience as philosophy's life source and main point, Heidegger considers it something philosophy must continue to grapple with, because human existence is in continuous renewal: "there is always more work to be done; there are always further dimensions of human experience that can be explored."[9] In a traditional ontological approach, however, this ground to which philosophy, according to Heidegger, always returns does not exist.[10] Fundamental ontology's epistemological stance, in contrast, exhibits a certain humility vis-à-vis the world's richness, which cannot be *fully* expressed by our concepts yet remains the regenerating source of continued inquiry and new, more objective understanding.

As Heidegger specifies elsewhere, this basic gap between the world and our concepts about the world is even wider concerning knowledge of the humanistic or social realm. For this realm is more variable and fluctuating than, for instance, domains of the inanimate object world or of nature, about which the natural and physical sciences discern laws or patterns, which are accordingly more stable and enduring. That is, how we can know a given domain—the specifics of the ways we concretely grapple with it and the extent of the fit between the concept we thus elicit and the part of the world that it conveys—"springs from [the] objects of our investigation." Method, in other words, is determined by the content.[11] Accordingly, our concepts about the social realm must remain more open to and vigilant about new, previously unconsidered, or overlooked worldly phenomena, developments, and contexts, in light of which a given concept might need to be tweaked, expanded, amended, or even discarded if it is to remain as illuminating as possible and therefore relevant. As Heidegger states this point, "[humanistic science] must necessarily be inexact just in order to remain rigorous. . . . The inexactitude of the historical humanistic sciences is not a deficiency, but is only the fulfillment of a demand essential to this type of research."[12]

This recognition of the greater "inexactitude" attending knowledge of this realm reflects respect for the kind of domain we are dealing with, namely one whose "matter" is in some sense wider, more changing, and more unwieldy than that of other domains of inquiry. This means that it is harder to gain a secure handle on this "matter," and when we do, we must remain more "on our toes" regarding phenomena that escape that conceptual grasp so as to be able to continue refining our understanding in light of them. This recognition is the reason that Heidegger adds "that the projecting and security of the object-sphere of the historical sciences is not only of another kind, but is much more difficult of execution than is the achieving of rigor in the exact sciences."[13] That is also why, especially about these humanistic areas, we cannot impose an absolute, ostensibly exhaustive and final determination upon them, which does not mean that we cannot have very stable determinations or that they must degenerate to relativism, only that they must be more modest, which allows them to maintain an opening or "eye" to the world.[14]

Such absolutism, Heidegger suggests, is less about understanding the area and more about unburdening the inquirer of the difficult and ongoing task of having continuously to rethink that understanding or to remain open to pursuing new and further lines of inquiry in relation to it. This posture, he claims, relinquishes continued philosophizing and tends instead towards complacency, which is "the bankruptcy of philosophy (*Bankrott der Philosophie*)."[15] He remarks on this postures's escape from the difficulties and complexity of life experience, which he claims undermines philosophy because life as it is concretely experienced is for him precisely "'the main point of philosophy.'"[16] "To be sure, it is most comfortable to place oneself outside of the world and outside of life directly into the land of the blessed and the absolute. I just do not understand why one philosophizes at all, when one is already 'that far along.'"[17] As Karsten Harries suggests, this posture is about the dream of a "philosophy to end all philosophy," one that gives us the final word to end all such inquiry.[18] Or, as Richard Rorty elaborates, it would achieve "'complete clarity'—that is, is an unproblematic grasp of the way things really are, one which will give philosophy perpetual peace."[19]

Accordingly, fundamental ontology contains the findings of traditional ontology, though recognizing them as only a sliver of what that area is about, *and* contains the multitude of our dynamic, interconnected involvements with things and with others in the world. Its epistemological stance assumes a knower who is situated in and affected by the world. Heidegger scholar Scott Campbell summarizes the difference between this traditional approach and the one to which Heidegger is trying to redirect philosophy and thereby also remind us that our situatedness in the world is the ground from which philosophy has always emanated, whether it has explicitly recognized that or not. Campbell writes:

> In contrast to philosophy's tendency toward theoretical detachment, Heidegger wanted to develop a kind of philosophizing that would try to understand life and language from the experience of being an active participant in life and language. This means that philosophical activity investigates the experience of life as it is lived and the experience of language as it is spoken. . . . [He] demand[ed] that living and speaking become thematic for philosophical inquiry.[20]

The knower who inhabits this stance is more cultivated to notice and treat, as real, phenomena that may reveal themselves in the space of that "inexactitude" between an established concept of an area of the world and what escapes it, instead of dismissing such phenomena outright as is more typical of the stance of traditional ontology.

For Heidegger, thinking happens precisely in such worldly spaces. It is provoked by a disturbance lurking in the shadows of what we think we so surely know about the area and consider beyond question, a disturbance that now more palpably resists that powerful interpretation. Against the latter, this anomaly reveals itself like a faintly pinging S.O.S., summoning the inquirer's attention and solicitude. It gives her deeper pause, becoming, as Heidegger variously describes it, a source of increasingly heightened "disquiet," "distress," "urgency," or "anxiety"[21] about that settled understanding and, at the same time, about herself as she is thus placed in a position to have to decide what to do about that disturbance—to pursue its implications, which throws her off her usual course, or to damp it down. This disturbance may indicate something amiss about our usual ways of making sense of that area but that has not yet been said and that now more evidently demands creative and radical questioning and possibly articulation as new, more adequate understanding.[22]

This circumstance lands the inquirer at something of an existential and ethical crossroads as the heightened disposition of "anxiety" to some extent indicates. She is confronted with a difficult and unenviable choice. She must decide whether to risk, especially professionally, going off the established track and "going it alone" to pursue what is likely a long, arduous journey towards the *possibility* of original thinking, but for which there is no guarantee that this pursuit will lead anywhere and where indeed many such pursuits are not too fruitful, or whether to conduct the relatively easier and more standard work that Heidegger refers to as "collecting information" according to a governing interpretive framework. That framework may reflect the original thinking of a past philosopher, thinking that responded to pressing issues of that time but whose limitations are now appreciated in light of newly uncovered experiences or circumstances.[23] Moreover, in the rare case that this path does lead somewhere, it will require the much more difficult and time-consuming work of charting new theoretical or philosophical terrain, which even then will not immediately be more widely intelligible precisely because it is original.

A "phenomenon" is Heidegger's technical term in *Being and Time* for such provocations to thinking that reveal themselves within our everyday experiences in the world, precisely in these places of "inexactitude," through some such barely discernible disturbance that now more evidently protrudes through our usual interpretation of the area. As he summarizes, "a 'phenomenon' in a distinctive sense . . . is something that proximally and for the most part does not show itself at all: it is something that lies *hidden*, in contrast to that which proximally and for the most part does show itself," namely what we already so thoroughly know or think we know about the domain in question.[24] In his earlier writings, Heidegger refers to concealed dimensions of human experience that barely flicker through an assumed understanding as "relucent" within that interpretation. In a decisive moment of insight, what is "relucent" becomes for some reason more luminous and profoundly and unavoidably troubling to the inquirer, affecting her in such a manner that the problematic nature of continuing to go along with how things are usually interpreted becomes much clearer. A radical questioning of these ways sets in, and the inquirer may then pursue a countermovement against this flow. This countermovement goes down to the immediacy of life where an aspect of the human condition in need of retrieval has thus been revealing itself and in light of which she may need to interpret life and to live it in some other way.[25]

A "phenomenon" often pertains to something nearby, which precisely because it is so familiar we continue overlooking it in terms of its being possibly in need of radical questioning and of new understanding. In his essay, "The Word of Nietzsche," Heidegger refers to this proximate source of theoretical discovery: "What is given to thinking to think is . . . something lying near, that which lies nearest, which, because it is only this, we have therefore constantly already passed over."[26] In other words, because it is close, we tend not to give it a second thought as we consider it already thoroughly known. We have a common sense about it, so we assume it a least likely place to discover something new and, so, least in need of investigation. But, as such, it is for Heidegger precisely where one might contemplate investigating by returning to that ground of experiences that underlies that understanding yet is out of view when that understanding becomes rigidified.[27]

In *Being and Time*, Heidegger makes this point in relation to the text's project of questioning the subject of traditional ontology, namely a detached and disembodied, thinking being, which Heidegger, in contrast, treats as first and foremost a worldly being. Although our closest, most basic ways of existing are through our multitudinous dynamic involvements in the world, this domain, he says, remains "ontologically . . . farthest."[28] He means that it is not philosophically mapped in a way that acknowledges it to exist and considers it philosophically significant, philosophy's life source. The posture of traditional ontology passes over this domain and moreover actively conceals it through its epistemological absolutism, a domain however that summoned Heidegger's attention and gave him pause about traditional ontology's assumptions and project, which he expressed philosophically, among other ways, as fundamental ontology, one of his breakthroughs.

A given "phenomenon" may have remained mainly hidden for a variety of reasons. For instance, it may pertain to something that has not yet broken the surface to some sustained measure of wider intelligibility and, so, remains "*undiscovered*" in this sense; the usually hidden, systematic harms of pornography that feminism of the nineteen seventies and nineteen eighties brought to much wider visibility may be considered such a "phenomenon." Or perhaps a "phenomenon's" implications were once discovered but then, for some reason, became "*buried over*," and maybe they are now newly appreciated as in need of excavation and resuscitation;[29] this feminist understanding of pornography that, earlier, broke the surface and has since been effectively reburied in the aftermath of the explosion of Internet-age pornography may be considered a "phenomenon" in this particular Heideggerian sense. A "phenomenon" may be hidden in an especially egregious manner through a kind of cover-up that may "become complete."[30] In this case, the experiences at issue are so deeply buried out of sight that they have now become disguised as something else, as when an ontological determination claims already to account for them, supplanting another, more adequate understanding and thus misrepresenting them.

Here, Heidegger says that a "semblance"[31] or "disguise" has come so effectively to stand in for phenomena as to pass off as their essence or being. The more effectively and seamlessly it stands in for phenomena and, in this manner, shuts them out, the more convincingly that determination is seen as their essence. He describes this frustrating predicament tersely and, it seems, a bit sarcastically: "Yet so much semblance, so much 'Being'" ("Wieviel Schein jedoch, soviel 'Sein'").[32] Such concealment through "disguising" is, he says, especially dangerous. It misleads in a manner that becomes stubbornly entrenched,[33] as here phenomena are especially effectively disappeared. Not only are they not registered, but worse still they are actively interpreted as something else, in a determination then cast as absolute and therefore closed to further questioning. In this outcome, all traces that this disappearing process has occurred are lost as this disguise-determination now dons the form of self-evidence and lucidity. Whatever one might perhaps have sensed as not quite right or not entirely right about the "disguise" has been most effectively dispatched from view, as historical traces of how this situation came about have disappeared.

"Phenomenology" in Heidegger's sense, then, denotes the move of letting oneself get pulled off course, and hence taking the risk, concertedly to follow and tend to a "phenomenon," namely this seemingly "strange" dimension of some area of our concrete worldly involvements that is thought already to be understood, a dimension usually hidden in any of a variety of ways. Phenomenology refers to the work of grappling with what a "phenomenon" is indicating, that is, of digging around in this "black hole" off the grid of official intelligibility and struggling with this dimension of human experience so as to excavate and hold it in a manner that more widely communicates what one discovers there. Thus, even more fundamentally, phenomenology's procedure consists of concrete relations with others in which one is listening to, speaking, and discussing with them in one's effort to name, express, and thematize what is latent in a "phenomenon." Such relations, Heidegger claims, reflect *logos* in its original, actual, worldly sense, which he retrieves from Aristotle's philosophy, before the notion of *logos* subsequently became rigidified over the history of philosophy to signify reason or understanding that is detached from the world.[34] In other words, groping our way towards stabilizing new understanding is born of such actual interaction and communication with others.

More specifically, a "phenomenon's" disclosure of a usually concealed dimension of lived experience reflects an intensified moment of one's everyday involvements in the world, a moment in which the inquirer is struck by a heightened anxiety reflecting appreciation of the phenomenon's disclosure. And hence, according to (the early) Heidegger, he or she is also possessed by a need to communicate and converse about it so as to make sense of this new predicament. As he remarks, "When we experience uncanniness, we start to speak." We search out conversation because at this decisive moment one is ready to engage in a discussion about the area of human experience at issue and thus about who one is. Authentic listening to and speaking with others begins in this perturbing recognition of a concealed aspect of human existence (at least concealed to oneself) that demands externalization through articulation and communication, which is the basis of forming new understanding or concepts about our world.[35] It is the ground or "conceptuality of our [established] concept[s]," which then "gives to us [other] directions in which [one] can question the world and [oneself]."[36]

We may summarize in very typical Heideggerian language this "bottom-up" procedure of theoretical discovery emanating from attentive listening to, speaking, and discussing with others in the world. The inquirer draws the "phenomenon" out of *concealment* to *unconcealment*, in an undertaking that may yield fundamentally new understanding that shakes the ground beneath the governing ponderous framework for interpreting that area of human life.[37] Phenomenology in Heidegger's sense is furthermore the method he posits for holding that understanding in a manner that is not absolute. It grasps dimensions of human experience without closing the resulting concept from the world, instead maintaining the concept's continued relationality in the world. Phenomenology is Heidegger's way of trying to fashion, as Campbell describes, a kind of "nonobjectifying objectivity," that is, a manner of approaching and knowing life as it is concretely lived without, however, taking the vitality out of it in the way that an *absolutist* scientific objectification does.[38]

This work of phenomenologically eliciting new understanding latent in a "phenomenon" that inhabits this wider worldly ground encompassed by fundamental ontology may result in what Heidegger calls a "crisis in concepts." The term describes major conceptual shifts in the sciences, including humanistic sciences, shifts that may be considered their philosophical moments and, within philosophy per se, its most philosophical moment;[39] and the term is also relevant to characterizing smaller conceptual shifts.[40] A "crisis in concepts" in this larger sense is the beginning of something that is like what the philosopher of science, Thomas Kuhn, would later call "paradigm shifts"[41] and the biophysicist and philosopher of science, Evelyn Fox Keller, would refer to as poetic or philosophical moments in science.[42] Heidegger describes such a moment:

> [T]he real "movement" . . . takes place when . . . basic concepts undergo a
> more or less radical revision which is transparent to itself. The level which a
> science has reached is determined by how far it is *capable* of a crisis in its
> basic concepts. In such immanent crises the very relationship between posi-
> tively investigative inquiry and those things themselves that are under interro-
> gation comes to a point where it begins to totter. [43]

Heidegger suggests that "thinking" or what he refers to here as "the real 'movement'" in our understanding of a domain occurs when the shortcomings of a governing conceptual framework about it become especially evident, first to the thinking inquirer(s) and, through them, eventually to the discipline and then to the profession once they have had time to catch up. A "phenomenon" now presses up against and resists more obtrusively and "noisily" the governing conceptual grid that it shadows—especially upon being phenomenologically treated—and a crack starts to appear in that framework, making the need for another framework more undeniable. The relationship between phenomena and our taken-for-granted framework comes to a head, that is, to a point where, as Heidegger says, that framework "begins to totter." This opens a clearing for the possibility for another, more adequate understanding of the area to take root. As he describes elsewhere, a question is thereby given "fruitful unrest and movement,"[44] with the result that "research [of the area may now be placed] . . . on new foundations."[45] For Heidegger, thinking is most rigorous the closer one comes to thus pushing a concept to its break point, which constitutes the "real progress" within the domain of inquiry.[46]

FEMINISM AND PORNOGRAPHY

Catharine MacKinnon, a leading feminist theorist on pornography and a pioneer of the civil rights legal initiatives to address it, summarizes some of the effects of feminism's response to pornography's new proliferation. In her introduction to the edited volume of these legal hearings of the 1980s and early 1990s, she refers to the concrete and multifaceted developments that came together in such a way that shook the ground under the prevailing understanding of pornography, which considers it to be mainly neutral, sexually explicit material that moreover reflects and is a phenomenon of sexual liberation. Such assumptions pervade a variety of disciplines and everyday life, so that this "earthquake" had actual and potential repercussions across a wide range of areas, pushing those assumptions closer to a break point. She states about this development, whose Heideggerian undertones we may now better appreciate:

[T]he exposure of pornography's harms has moved the ground under social theory across a wide range of issues. . . . The place of sex in speech, including literature and art . . . has been thrown open to reconsideration, historically and in the present. The implications of . . . the relation between the way people are imaged and imagined to the ways they are treated . . . are being rethought. The buying and selling of human flesh in the form of pornography has given scholarship on slavery a new dimension. . . . . The cultural legitimation of sexual force, including permission for and exoneration of rape and transformation of sexual abuse into sexual pleasure and identity, is being newly interrogated. New human rights theories are being built to respond to the human rights violations unearthed. As events that have been hidden come to light, the formerly unseen appears to determine more and more of the seen. The repercussions for theory, the requisite changes in thinking on all levels of society, have only begun to be felt.[47]

Here MacKinnon synthesizes some of the threads of this world-involved and multidisciplinary undertaking that we may, to a significant degree, consider phenomenological in Heidegger's sense and as indicating a needed casting in Heideggerian terms. For various avenues of inquiry have converged on a "phenomenon," namely a usually concealed dimension of human experience that shadows the dominant understanding of that area but through which the "phenomenon" nevertheless somehow faintly "flickers" or is "relucent." In this case, the "phenomenon" pertains to the widespread and sex-specific harms associated with pornography and thus to its role in women's social inequality. These lines of inquiry have, in their respective disciplinary domains and ways, elicited what is latent in the "phenomenon." They have phenomenologically drawn it out of concealment to precipitate a radical questioning of governing interpretations of pornography, questioning that is even more pointed and potent when these threads are rigorously theoretically gathered, as in MacKinnon's work. Because these concrete and conceptual developments happened to be followed by an unprecedented practical policy initiative with its public hearings and discussion, that questioning and resulting alternate understanding of pornography was able to break the surface for the first time in a more sustained way.

We may cast this bottom-up conceptual development and practical response in further philosophical terms, this time Hegelian ones, even though Hegel's metaphysical determinations about concrete human sociality are notoriously absolutist and are therefore a target of Heidegger's criticism of metaphysics. Hegel considers philosophy's task, from his era onward, to be mainly about discerning a new, previously unknown shape of human oppression in a world-involved way, thereby helping to bring it to world awareness; however, he does so in a manner that evinces what he considers the a priori law of the progress of freedom across history, freedom moreover that is gendered or ontologically distinguished by sex. The new understanding emerging from this convergence of multidisciplinary and practical developments concerning pornography reflects the breakthrough of this previously "unknown" shape of oppression to a wider human consciousness.

According to Heidegger, phenomenology in his sense describes how major shifts in our understanding occur, whether in philosophy or in other areas of inquiry,[48] with the latter evident here in the multifaceted feminist and other responses to pornography and summarized to some extent by MacKinnon. In all of these instances, the inquirer tends to the complexity, richness, and difficulties of life as it is concretely lived, and from there she elicits and articulates a usually concealed dimension of it to render it more intelligible. Here especially this process of radical questioning and retrieval emanates from listening to and from speaking and discussing with others in the world, in particular attentive listening to survivor testimony. In this context of heightened "distress" or "anxiety" between the interlocutors, one tries to give voice to this area of experience, which survivors especially need to externalize and are freer to do so when their experiences are considered *real*.

For Heidegger, these two aspects, namely tending to this area of experience and phenomenologically drawing it out through careful listening and discussion, reflect respectively the ground and method by which "all the academic disciplines as well as . . . all modes of life" are revitalized.[49] The more absolute and closed off to the world a given disciplinary understanding becomes, the more necessary it is to reinstate and reanimate that area's original direct rapport with the world.[50] As is the case with philosophy as Heidegger understands it, in these other areas too the most significant strides occur out of their confrontation with life as it is concretely lived.[51] What he considers the "real progress" or "real 'movement'" within a discipline, including philosophy, takes place precisely when this confrontation is such that it yields a crack in a governing understanding, and a major rethinking of how we make sense of some part of that area.[52]

According to Heidegger, the different fields of the humanities are "layers of manifestation (*Bekundungsschichten*)" of life experience,[53] especially when they converge on a "phenomenon" and draw out of unconcealment something usually hidden about an area of human existence thought already to be well understood and therefore beyond need of questioning. As such, these fields provide a significant part of the "matter" or the prephilosophical insights with which philosophy must grapple as part of its own distinctive way of entering the problem at issue and drawing out, in its own terms, what is latent in the "phenomenon." Philosophy is organically connected to these fields and is inextricable from them. That is, their layers of manifestation contribute to making the "phenomenon" more luminous and noticeable to the philosopher about something nearby and usually overlooked, but now more clearly and perturbingly summoning response.

The philosopher, consciously planted in the world, gathers insights from these more immediate areas of inquiry that are, so to speak, "first on the scene" of the "phenomenon" and are expressing what it indicates from their own angles and reflecting varying levels of theoretical rigor. The philosopher pulls them together in a way that more perspicuously thematizes this previously unconsidered or less-addressed dimension of the human condition, and situates that new understanding as an original contribution to an existing philosophical discourse. More specifically, Heidegger suggests that philosophy's vocation today has something to do with phenomenologically retrieving a concealed dimension of the human condition from the concrete, everyday living, listening, and speaking with others and situating it in relation to philosophy's history, just as he situates his own project in relation to the philosophies of Descartes, Aristotle, and others.[54] Here, history is appreciated as both a resource for this contemporary philosophical undertaking as well as a source of problematic assumptions passed down through time and now more evidently in need of dismantling. That new understanding, at the very least, compels us to question and perhaps also to amend in some way the inherited and governing conceptual frameworks through which we interpret the domain at issue.[55]

Hegel, who likewise considers philosophy organically connected to and inextricable from other areas of humanistic inquiry and practical developments in the world, also describes philosophy's relation to them in a way that is illuminating to our topic of the multidisciplinary and practical responses to pornography's harms. On his view, philosophy's task is to capture such insights and developments of its era as "higher-order" thought. The philosopher, he says, is "*a child of his own time* [and] thus philosophy, too, *is its own time comprehended in thoughts.*"[56] He further specifies that philosophy necessarily comes on the scene *after* there have already been some such stirrings about the issue in other, more immediate disciplines and through practical developments in the world,[57] which have begun bringing some awareness of it to the fore.

Accordingly, he compares philosophy and its timing to the owl of Minerva, the owl being the sacred bird of Minerva, which is the Roman name for Athena, the deity of wisdom or of philosophy. He says that "the owl of Minerva begins its flight only with the onset of dusk."[58] In other words, philosophy arrives on the scene at the end of the day, so to speak, when such worldly and extraphilosophical developments have already, to some extent, occurred. These areas are beginning to reveal their respective bits of a new major philosophical understanding that needs to be charted, bits that to philosophy however still appear as murky, unintelligible fragments that are not so philosophically relevant.

For both Hegel and Heidegger, philosophy's specific intervention here is to discern a clearer, more encompassing pattern in these assorted, yet inherently connected, historical-humanistic phenomena about a usually concealed aspect of the human condition and that for Hegel pertains specifically to unearthing a "new" shape of oppression. The philosopher unifies more luminously these scattered flickers that dot the landscape of a given time, emitted by these other disciplinary areas, in a task to be embarked upon when the sun is beginning to set on that time. As Hegel famously elaborates: "As the *thought* of the world, it appears only at a time when actuality has gone through its formative process and attained its completed state. . . . When philosophy paints its grey in grey, a shape of life has grown old, and it cannot be rejuvenated, but only recognized, by the grey in grey of philosophy."[59] From such direct and multidisciplinary involvement with historical-humanistic phenomena, the philosopher can then significantly contribute to pulling out of philosophical obscurity the dimension of reality that these are indicating and thereby help bring it into the fold of what philosophy henceforth legitimately grapples with.

I propose a particular role for philosophy in this multifaceted revelation of pornography's harms, which shook the ground under conventional interpretations of pornography as neutral, harmless, sexually explicit material that is liberating. This role—which reflects one possible philosophical intervention here among others—centers on an idea of freedom that is distinguished by sex, on which these interpretations rest. That is, a way phenomenologically to elicit new *philosophical* understanding from these multidisciplinary "layers of manifestation" of the "phenomenon" of pornography's sex-specific harms is to show the gendered freedom that is centrally operative within modern pornography and that functions to conceal its harms and thus to facilitate them. For instance, the findings of these other disciplines show that the overwhelming content of mainstream pornography is about presenting, in an endorsing way, women as sexually vulnerable and violable through, for example, enjoying pain, rape, being tied up, cut up, mutilated, bruised, and being sexually submissive. The harms here include, among others, what is done to women and girls in the making of pornography and how it influences its consumers to see and treat women. However, these harms are significantly concealed through pornography's presentation of this content as in fact naturally *liberating* for women, while to treat women as such is presented as men's sexual liberation.

In its earliest forms, positing a notion of freedom that is ontologically differentiated by sex goes back to the beginnings of political modernity. For my present purposes, though, I bracket these earlier manifestations, noting only that the Enlightenment's "universal" freedom (*Liberté, Egalité, Fraternité*) considered men naturally to experience it in the public sphere, with its legal guarantees of equality, and women to experience it in man's private sphere, outside the reach of those guarantees, in an arrangement that also concealed systematic sex-specific harms. This gendered freedom evolved over the modern era such that the sexual abuses, mainly of women and girls, associated with today's pornographic culture and society are concealed as a gendered sexual liberation.

A philosophical-phenomenological treatment of these harms, including their revelation through other disciplines and developments in the world, inhabits, as they do, a more fundamental ontological ground that contains and treats as real the experiences of abuse that the prevailing understanding covers up. This move in other words goes down to the "conceptuality" or worldly ground underlying that understanding. Such investigation follows Heidegger in his project of redirecting philosophical inquiry to concrete everyday experience so as to retrieve usually concealed dimensions of it and therefore of the human condition, which he considers the main point of philosophy. But pornography's concealment and facilitation of abuses occurs not only through the fact that conventional interpretations of pornography reflect categories and assumptions about humanity that are considered fixed and absolute, which shuts down inquiry at the edges of that understanding. Rather, this cover-up occurs furthermore through "disguising" those experiences through the ontological understanding that stands in for them and casts them as reflecting women's different essence or being in which they express and experience freedom differently from men. This ontology interprets these experiences as not really hurtful but in fact liberating.

The philosophical role that I suggest here, accordingly, goes beyond the most basic Heideggerian move of somehow retrieving and holding these experiences that are not usually on philosophy's radar[60] from out of a wider domain of human existence than allowed by the governing and absolute interpretations. That is, there is more to a neo-Heideggerian role in this issue than generally inhabiting that space of human experience to which Heidegger opens philosophy through his criticism of traditional ontology and his positing of fundamental ontology. As he does in his own specific project, especially in *Being and Time*, I too furthermore suggest that this grounded treatment of pornography must critically confront a *particular* trajectory of traditional ontology. In this case, the traditional ontology at issue is within the history of *political* philosophy, especially the modern era, and has distinguished freedom by sex. I thereby follow Heidegger further by situating philosophical treatment of a contemporary challenge within philosophy's history, which is both an obstacle and a resource for that task.

Such consideration of pornography incorporates insights from the other, more immediate areas of inquiry and developments in the world. They shook the ground under the prevailing common sense about pornography and also prephilosophically indicated a crisis within philosophy about modernity's notion of freedom. A significant contribution of late modern continental philosophy, especially Heidegger's, is its diagnosis of the ambivalence of modernity and its freedom. The modern subject's absolute freedom to master the world undermines existential freedom, which is the freedom to re-think and choose one's existence and is precipitated by some unexpected and disorienting aspect of the world that escapes our grasp but that this absolute posture shuts out. Contrary to governing narratives of the modern era as being about the unambiguous progress of freedom, such late modern philosophical critique claims that there has also been a dark side to this freedom. More systematic treatment of pornography along the philosophical lines that I suggest unearths and maps a powerful and altogether new strand of such critique as an original contribution to this late modern philosophical tradition. Appreciating the advancements that the modern era has brought for women, this treatment also delineates and confronts a destructive or nihilistic side of it, which is most prominently evinced today through the pornographic culture of our Internet age.

***

Heidegger's thought is a significant resource for philosophically illuminating the harms, especially to women and girls, of pornography's new proliferation in late modern democratic society and culture. His criticism of traditional ontology and recognition of a more fundamental ontology places treatment of this contemporary ethical crisis squarely within philosophy's purview because he considers investigation of lived experience that retrieves hidden dimensions of the human condition to be philosophy's main point. His work allows for a phenomenological interpretation of feminism's multi-faceted response to this development, which radically questioned conventional interpretations of pornography that consider it neutral, sexually-explicit material that is liberating, and of the organic connection of these extra-philosophical discoveries to philosophy. Finally, his critique is instructive for how to situate retrieval of the experiences of pornography's sex-specific harms within philosophy's history, specifically as part of a criticism of a parallel strand of traditional ontology, in this case, one that distinguishes freedom by sex and that in its contemporary incarnation obscures and facilitates sex-specific abuses associated with pornography. This parallel critique in turn indicates a nihilistic dimension of modernity that has yet to be philosophically charted.

These multidisciplinary developments of the late nineteen seventies to the early nineteen nineties made the first notable dent in the wider consciousness concerning a governing understanding of pornography. They gained for feminism at least a seat at the table of discussion about pornography. Since then, in the wake of the Internet Revolution, we have been confronted with a huge and entirely new dimension of this problem. Through the power of Internet-age technology and its mushrooming array of digital gadgets, pornography's message of a gendered sexual liberation that obscures and promotes widespread abuses has achieved unprecedented ubiquity and reach into our lives.

It is now simultaneously entrenched and concealed as such like never before. In addition, pornography's content has become even more violent and degrading of women as pornography's consumers, increasingly desensitized to earlier content, are attracted to deeper ways of humiliating women, ways that nevertheless continue being cast as liberating *for women*. Against the force of this technological "tsunami," feminism's resistance to pornography has now become hardly audible, certainly more muted than in earlier decades, whose work is, today, barely known to have even taken place. The previously "undiscovered" "phenomenon" of pornography's harms that earlier feminism retrieved has now become a "phenomenon" in the sense that Heidegger describes as something that was once discovered but has now become reburied. It has become stubbornly entrenched and in need of re-excavation.

Perhaps Hegel's insights about the process by which a "new" shape of oppression comes to wider awareness is, to some extent, relevant here. This path, he notes, is a terribly long and painstaking one that often meanders.[61] Some awareness of that oppression might break the surface now and again and here and there, only to be followed by resubmersion. This movement evinces a tempo that is something along the lines of "one step forward, two steps back." And this rhythm continues until some monumentally significant confluence of forces and events results in that recognition taking hold in a way that becomes secured as a new common sense, such as occurred for him in recent history concerning slavery, whose systematic harms have been effectively concealed for ages. Hegel's modern optimism, of which the late modern philosophical tradition is dubious, however assumed that such ultimate breakthrough to awareness was *inevitable* because it was part of an absolute law or logic governing human sociality.

The philosophical task today of charting a nihilistic dimension of modernity that includes treatment of pornography's sex-specific harms in our Internet age will also benefit from Heidegger's philosophy. Again, it will require grappling with this "phenomenon" as it is now concretely lived, that is, getting as close as possible to how it is experienced in everyday life, for which the findings of more immediate areas of inquiry are key. Furthermore, it could use the resource of Heidegger's reflections on technology.[62] They analyze the unique difficulties that the power and overwhelming reach of modern technology pose to even noticing the existence of a "phenomenon" beyond the way that technology creates and shapes our understanding of the world. In our case, pornography's merger with digital technology so powerfully shapes social reality, including by mainstreaming pornography, that the possibility of noticing the "phenomenon" of pornography's wide-ranging harms and of other forms of sociality by which to make choices about one's existence are arguably becoming more remote now than ever before.

NOTES

This paper is part of a larger, more systematic Heideggerian (and Hegelian) treatment of pornography on which I have been working for many years, including throughout graduate school. However, I had to set it aside to address the emergency of the Bosnian genocide, in particular naming and conceptualizing, with Asja Armanda, what was then the "unknown" crime of "genocidal sexual atrocities" and helping to bring it to world recognition, including through enlisting Catharine MacKinnon in this effort and coinitiating with her a landmark lawsuit that pioneered its recognition under international law. I have now returned to my earlier work on Heidegger, pornography, and technology. I presented this unpublished research in a graduate seminar at the University of Kentucky in spring 2010, to which I also brought resources from Hannah Arendt's work, especially her reflections on "thoughtlessness," technological genocide, and "banal" evil in *Eichmann in Jerusalem: A Report on the Banality of Evil*, thus merging my feminist philosophical work on genocide with my feminist philosophical work on pornography. Through the generous support of a 2013–2014 American Association of University Women Fellowship, I can now consolidate my research and writings on pornography. This paper has benefited from discussion generated at the annual meeting of the Comparative and Continental Philosophy Circle in Santa Barbara (March 20–23, 2013), a venue to which I am generally grateful for its support of this larger project. In this regard, I am especially thankful to David Jones. An earlier version of this paper also benefited from presentation at the American Political Science Association Annual Meeting in Chicago (August 29–September 1, 2013) and at Kennesaw State University, Georgia, November 8, 2012. Thank you to Daniel Dahlstrom for the opportunity to review Scott Campbell's excellent book, *The Early Heidegger's Philosophy of Life: Facticity, Being, and Language*, in Gatherings: The Heidegger Circle Annual (2014), which has significantly enriched this paper.

1. These proceedings, testimony, and analysis are gathered in Catharine A. MacKinnon and Andrea Dworkin, eds., *In Harm's Way: The Pornography Civil Rights Hearings* (Cambridge, MA: Harvard University Press, 1997).

2. Catharine A. MacKinnon, "The Roar on the Other Side of Silence," Introduction to *In Harm's Way: The Pornography Civil Rights Proceedings*, ed. Catharine A. MacKinnon and Andrea Dworkin (Cambridge, MA: Harvard University Press, 1998), 23.

3. MacKinnon and Dworkin, *In Harm's Way*, 428–29; cf. Christopher N. Kendall, *Gay Male Pornography: An Issue of Sex Discrimination* (Vancouver: University of British Columbia Press, 2004). I also discuss some of these points in Natalie Nenadic, "Review of *Art and Pornography: Philosophical Essays*," *Notre Dame Philosophical Reviews*, 2014.01.18.

4. Martin Heidegger, *Being and Time*, trans. John Macquarrie and Edward Robinson (New York: Harper & Row, 1962, 2008).

5. Scott M. Campbell, *The Early Heidegger's Philosophy of Life: Facticity, Being, and Language* (New York: Fordham University Press, 2012).

6. I have addressed some of these concepts in earlier form in Natalie Nenadic, "Heidegger, Arendt, and *Eichmann in Jerusalem*," *Journal of Comparative and Continental Philosophy* 5, no. 1 (2013): 36–48.

7. Heidegger, *Being and Time*, 34.

8. Cited in Campbell, *The Early Heidegger's Philosophy of Life*, 40; Martin Heidegger, *Grundprobleme der Phänomenologie* (winter semester, 1919–1920), ed. Hans-Helmuth Gander, Vol. 58 of *Gesamtausgabe*, 1992, 103. I hereafter cite this as "G 58" followed by the page number. Although at this stage, Heidegger does not yet use the term "fundamental ontology," he is nevertheless trying, in various ways, to express that ground.

9. Campbell, *The Early Heidegger's Philosophy of Life*, 113.

10. Cf. Campbell, *The Early Heidegger's Philosophy of Life*, 39–40.

11. Campbell, *The Early Heidegger's Philosophy of Life*, 26, 229.

12. Martin Heidegger, "Age of the World Picture," in Heidegger, *The Question Concerning Technology and Other Essays*, trans. William Lovitt (New York: Harper Torchbooks, 1977), 120. See also his expression of this point in his early work: "[indeterminacy] is not a deficiency in method, rather it ensures the free and ever new means of getting at factical life in its temporal, forward development; this is an indeterminacy which does not blur its object, but

rather secures for it the possibility of being genuinely encountered and indicated without ever being predetermined." Cited in Campbell, *The Early Heidegger's Philosophy of Life*, 70; Martin Heidegger, *Phänomenologische Interpretationen zu Aristoteles: Einführung in die phänomenologische Forschung* (winter semester, 1921–1922), ed. Walter Bröker and Kate Bröcker-Oltmanns (1985, 1994), 175; Vol. 61 of *Gesamtausgabe*, trans. Richard Rojcewicz as *Phenomenological Interpretations of Aristotle: Initiation into Phenomenological Research* (Bloomington: Indiana University Press, 2001), 131–32. I henceforth refer to this volume as "G 61" and indicate the page number from the German first followed by a slash and then the page number from the English translation.

13. Heidegger, "Age of the World Picture," 120.

14. On a related point, see Robert Scharff's Heideggerian critique of postmodernism: "What Postmodernists Don't Get," 1997, http://www.focusing.org/postmod.htm (accessed 4 Jan. 2014).

15. Cited in Campbell, *The Early Heidegger's Philosophy of Life*, 66; from Heidegger, G 61: 89/67.

16. Campbell, *The Early Heidegger's Philosophy of Life*; G 61: 99/74.

17. Campbell, *The Early Heidegger's Philosophy of Life*; G 61: 99/75.

18. Karsten Harries, "Philosophy in Search of Itself," in *What Is Philosophy?*, ed. C. P. Ragland and Sarah Heidt (New Haven, CT: Yale University Press, 2001), 62.

19. Richard Rorty, "Analytic Philosophy and Conversational Philosophy," in *A House Divided: Comparing Analytic and Continental Philosophy*, ed. C. G. Prado (Amherst, NY: Humanity Books, 2003), 25.

20. Campbell, *The Early Heidegger's Philosophy of Life*, 2.

21. Cf. Campbell, *The Early Heidegger's Philosophy of Life*, 7.

22. Campbell, *The Early Heidegger's Philosophy of Life*, 117, 95.

23. Heidegger, *Being and Time*, 77.

24. Heidegger, *Being and Time*, 59.

25. Campbell, *The Early Heidegger's Philosophy of Life*, 95.

26. Martin Heidegger, "The Word of Nietzsche," in Heidegger, *The Question Concerning Technology and Other Essays*, 111.

27. Cf. Campbell, *The Early Heidegger's Philosophy of Life*, 127, 89.

28. Heidegger, *Being and Time*, 36.

29. Heidegger, *Being and Time*, 60, italics in the original.

30. Heidegger, *Being and Time*.

31. Heidegger, *Being and Time*, see also 30.

32. Heidegger, *Being and Time*.

33. Heidegger, *Being and Time*.

34. In his earlier writings Heidegger is more explicit and detailed about the role of attentive listening and speaking with others in the phenomenological process of retrieving and holding a usually concealed dimension of the human condition, that is, in the process of concept formation. See, for example, Campbell, *The Early Heidegger's Philosophy of Life*, part IV, "The Language of Life."

35. Cited in Campbell, *The Early Heidegger's Philosophy of Life*, 172–73, see also 164; Martin Heidegger, *Grundbegriffe der aristotelischen Philosophie*, ed. Mark Michalski, Vol. 18 of *Gesamtausgabe*, 261, trans. Robert D. Metcalf and Mark B. Tanzer as *Basic Concepts of Aristotelian Philosophy* (Bloomington: Indiana University Press, 2009), 175. I hereafter cite this as "G 18" followed first by the German page number and then the page number in the English translation.

36. Campbell, *The Early Heidegger's Philosophy of Life*, 176; G 18: 269/183.

37. Heidegger, *Being and Time*, 49–50.

38. Campbell, *The Early Heidegger's Philosophy of Life*, 36. In his early efforts to put forth a new approach to conceptuality that can hold a concept without closing it to the world, Heidegger uses the term "formal indication." It provides philosophical analysis that "lets the object under investigation *be*" (Campbell, 70–71, 48, 76, italics in the original); see also Daniel O. Dahlstrom, "Heidegger's Method: Philosophical Concepts as Formal Indications," *Review of Metaphysics* 47, no. 4 (1994): 775–95.

39. Heidegger, *Being and Time*, 29; see also Harries, "Philosophy in Search of Itself," 62.

40. Heidegger, *Being and Time*, 29–31.

41. Thomas Kuhn, *The Structure of Scientific Revolutions*, 2nd ed. (Chicago: University of Chicago Press, 1970); see also Richard Polt, *Heidegger: An Introduction* (Ithaca, NY: Cornell University Press, 1999), 33.

42. Evelyn Fox Keller, *Reflections on Gender and Science* (New Haven, CT: Yale University Press, 1985).

43. Heidegger, *Being and Time*, 29, italics in the original.

44. Martin Heidegger, *What Is Philosophy?*, trans. Jean T. Wilde and William Kluback (Lanham, MD: Rowman & Littlefield, 2003), 59.

45. Heidegger, *Being and Time*, 29.

46. Heidegger, *Being and Time*, 29–31.

47. MacKinnon, "The Roar on the Other Side of Silence," 16–17, italics added.

48. On the development of this Heideggerian idea vis-à-vis philosophical moments or conceptual breakthroughs in the area of law, see Nenadic, "Heidegger, Arendt, and *Eichmann in Jerusalem*," and Natalie Nenadic, "Genocide and Sexual Atrocities: Hannah Arendt's *Eichmann in Jerusalem* and Karadzic in New York," *Philosophical Topics* 39, no. 2 (2011): 117–44.

49. Campbell, *The Early Heidegger's Philosophy of Life*, 46, 232.

50. Campbell, *The Early Heidegger's Philosophy of Life*, 127.

51. Campbell, *The Early Heidegger's Philosophy of Life*, 67. This basic Heideggerian point that major new developments in philosophy and in other disciplines occur out of their confrontation with life as it is concretely lived is also how MacKinnon refers to law. This point is vintage MacKinnon, found throughout her works, but has yet to be connected to Heidegger's philosophy. See, for example, Catharine A. MacKinnon, "'Freedom from Unreal Loyalties': On Fidelity in Constitutional Interpretation," in Catharine A. MacKinnon, *Women's Lives, Men's Laws* (Cambridge, MA: Harvard University Press, 2005), 65–71. Explicitly referring to a "bottom-up" procedure, she states that "[l]egal change comes from life, not from the brow of moral readers [detached from the world]" (68, 67); see also, Catharine A. MacKinnon, "Rape, Genocide, and Women's Human Rights," *Harvard Women's Law Journal* 17 (1994): 5–16.

52. Heidegger, *Being and Time*, 29–31.

53. Campbell, *The Early Heidegger's Philosophy of Life*, 232; G 58: 54–55.

54. Cf. Heidegger, *What is Philosophy?*

55. Cf. Heidegger, *What is Philosophy?*

56. G. W. F. Hegel, *Elements of the Philosophy of Right*, ed. Allen W. Wood and trans. H. B. Nisbet (New York: Cambridge University Press, 1991), 21, italics in the original.

57. Cf. Shlomo Avineri, *Hegel's Theory of the Modern State* (Cambridge: Cambridge University Press, 1974).

58. Hegel, *Elements of the Philosophy of Right*, 23.

59. Hegel, *Elements of the Philosophy of Right*, 23, italics in the original.

60. The leading philosophy that has begun seriously grappling with this dimension of human experience is in the analytic tradition, especially in the philosophy of language. This work may be considered, in some sense, phenomenological even as it does not explicitly situate itself as such because it tends not to be technically versed in Heideggerian phenomenology. With some exceptions, this very important work usually does not connect its investigation to issues and topics in the history of philosophy. Cf. Rae Langton, *Sexual Solipsism: Philosophical Essays on Pornography and Objectification* (New York: Oxford University Press, 2009); Ishani Maitra and Mary Kate McGowen, eds., *Speech and Harm: Controversies Over Free Speech* (Oxford: Oxford University Press, 2012); Rebecca Whisnant, "Confronting Pornography: Some Conceptual Basics," in *Not For Sale: Feminists Resisting Prostitution and Pornography*, ed. Christine Stark and Rebecca Whisnant (North Melbourne: Spinifex Press, 2004); Lori Watson, "Pornography," *Philosophy Compass* 5/7 (2010): 535–50.

61. Cf. G. W. F. Hegel, *Lectures on the Philosophy of World History: Introduction*, trans. H. B. Nisbet (Cambridge: Cambridge University Press, 1975); G. W. F. Hegel, *Phenomenology of Spirit*, trans. A. V. Miller (New York: Oxford University Press, 1977).

62. Heidegger, *The Question Concerning Technology and Other Essays*; Martin Heidegger, *Bremen and Freiburg Lectures: Insight into that Which Is and Basic Principles of Thinking*, trans. Andrew Mitchell (Bloomington: Indiana University Press, 2012).

Part III

Pornography and Speech

Chapter Eight

Pornography and "Speech"

Jennifer Hornsby

This chapter starts with extracts from a symposium on Rae Langton's *Sexual Solipsism: Philosophical Essays on Pornography and Objectification*. The extracts are taken from my contribution and Langton's "Replies" in that symposium. ¹ They are followed here by my "Afterword."

SUBORDINATION, SILENCING, AND TWO IDEAS OF ILLOCUTION, BY JENNIFER HORNSBY

Extract 1

As I see it, two normative principles inform Rae Langton's treatment of the subject of pornography. There is a political principle: that a right to equality is fundamental, being the wellspring for rights to liberty. And there is an ethical one: that there is something wrong about treating a person as a thing. So unexceptionable does each of the principles seem to many (although the first is foreign to libertarian thinking) that they could appear to provide a slender basis for demonstrating the evil role pornography at present plays in human life. It might be thought that if pornography is evil, that is because it has harmful effects, or because it is intelligible that some find it obnoxious. But such considerations are beside the point for Langton. Of course she knows something about pornography's harmful effects, and that some people are repelled by it. But these things don't matter to her argument. Her argument concerns what pornography does. It subordinates and silences women. And we are to understand what pornography does making use of the idea of an illocutionary act.

My suggestion in what follows will be that we do well to distinguish between two rather different conceptions of illocutionary act if we are concerned with what pornography does. I don't mean to say that Langton conflates the two. The suggestion is meant to provide clarification. . . . (The territory of the illocutionary is contested, as are proposals for making demarcations within it. In urging the importance of a certain distinction for particular purposes, I don't pretend to resolve the various disputes that there may be about these things.)

Extract 2

There is surely an idea of *speech* according to which most pornography, even if only because most of it uses images rather than words, is not "speech." (Pornographic films may be scripted, of course; but those who claim that pornography's protection is justified on free speech grounds don't address their claims to the speech of the fictional characters in pornographic films.) If the word "speech" in the First Amendment of the U.S. Constitution meant what it is ordinarily taken to mean, then *prima facie* the amendment wouldn't begin to establish pornographers' right to make and sell the material they do. It might be said that "speech" in the context of the amendment has to be understood broadly, so that it means "speech and expression," and that pornography is *expression* in the relevant sense. But that seems wrong when "expression" is understood in context—by reference to the other categories that the amendment explicitly covers, "of speech or of the press; or the right of the people peaceably to assemble, and to petition the Government for a redress of grievances." The First Amendment looks as if it were meant to serve to curb state power specifically as this needs to be curbed in the service of genuine democracy in which people can hold different views, and can let their views be known individually or collectively. It is surely doubtful whether in order to play such a role, it needs to accord a license to anyone to publish and distribute pornographic material. Even if pornography were "expression" in some sense, someone innocently reading the First Amendment *de novo* might well doubt that pornography falls within its remit.

I shall come back to "expression." But for the time being, none of this actually matters to the argument of Langton or of anyone else who might think that it could be a question in law whether pornography's producers should be free to carry on as they do without restriction or fear of penalty. The reason why it doesn't matter is that the First Amendment has been so interpreted in the courts (which, to judge by their pronouncements in this connection, have been served by libertarian judges) that pornography has come to be speech *de jure*. One has to reckon pornography speech, then, if one wants to contribute to any actual live debate about it and to be heard in the United States. . . . But notice now that Langton has a further reason to take pornography to be speech, beyond the history of its handling in U.S. courts. Illocutionary acts are a sort of speech act. So even if pornographic images and films are not speech in any ordinary sense, they could seem to need to be considered such, given the way their operation is to be understood.

Whatever category pornography might be supposed to fall into, one might be interested in whether there is some idea of illocution that has a place in elucidating speech-in-the-ordinary-sense. And one may think that there is. One may think of linguistic communication as a rational, human practice characterized by a certain sort of effortless meeting of minds—effortless inasmuch as by using a few words, you can, and very often do, get across to someone exactly the message you intend without needing to draw on any special capacities on their part to divine your intention. If you are the speaker, then all that you require, on the part of the person you address, in order for you to succeed in saying something to them, is what J. L. Austin called "uptake."[2] Uptake constitutes fulfillment of your intention to have said something to them; and there will have been uptake if linguistic communication has taken place in the way it ordinarily does.[3] An illocutionary act might be thought of as one whose work is done through uptake. Call the illocutionary acts got from this conception of how ordinary speech works "communicative," so that performance of communicative acts is distinctive of, even if not confined to, the use of language. On this understanding of them, all of Austin's long list of examples of illocutionary acts can be thought of as communicative: all are acts brought off (provided certain conditions are met) by virtue of a speaker's securing uptake. It is true that the case I have treated—of *saying to another*—is far from being a paradigmatic illocutionary act for Austin. Austin's special interest was in examples where, thanks to conventional arrangements, performance of an illocutionary act ensures not merely that a speaker has done something communicative but has effected how things stand: two people may be married, for example, or a ship may have a name, given only a certain piece of speech. The idea of performativity which shows up in such examples, and which triggered Austin's special interest, is of great importance in Langton's account, where it is connected with the objectification of women. Still, I think that Austin failed to realize that his own conception of an illocutionary act embraces the simple case I have treated as well as his own, no doubt more interesting, examples.[4] At any rate, an idea of a communicative illocutionary act might be based in things Austin says, however he is best interpreted.

It is possible now to see connections between illocution and such defenses of free speech as might seem to be enshrined in the First Amendment but for the courts' interpretation of "speech." If freedom of speech is freedom to engage in communicative activity, then a free speech regime would apparently be one in which democracy can flourish. It will be a regime, arguably, in which the people are sovereign; in which anyone can answer back, so that nonviolent methods of resolving conflicts are likely to be sought; in which tolerance is promoted; in which _____.You may fill in the blank here with anything you think might belong in some argument that people should be accorded a right to free *speech*, which is not a general right to liberty.

Now pornographic material is not a medium for *communicative* acts. And this is not merely because it is not intuitively speech. When pornography is in question, three features of communicative illocution are missing. In the first place, no message can be isolated as what's communicated on occasion. Second, even insofar as some sort of message may be conveyed, whether on some occasion or cumulatively, it cannot be identified as something which its producer intended to convey. Thirdly, and relatedly, even insofar as some sort of message may be conveyed, it is not itself a content of an awareness that the consumer shares with the producer. These features help explain why the process by which pornography alters minds may best be thought of as a sort of conditioning, and thus a process which may be gradual, and which isn't to be understood by reference to the rational nature of those engaging in it.

One can now see why pornography should not be thought to belong in a category of expression any more than it belongs in a category of speech. A person who *expresses* herself intentionally reveals her mind in some aspect. But this is not something that pornographers do *qua* producers of pornography. A look at the industry helps to make this clear. At conferences of the pornography industry, such matters are discussed as (a) how to make yet more violent and degrading images of women, and (b) how to react to pornography being bought by younger men and boys.[5] New products may be required, the conference participants think, in view of (a) men's becoming desensitized, and thus being in the market for new and harsher material, and (b) an expansion of their potential audience. What a pornographer produces, then, depends upon how he thinks he may maximize his profits in the climate his predecessors have created, and not upon which of his ideas he might wish to get across. If the category of "expression" had seemed apt for pornography, that could only be because it uses expressive means, not because pornographers express their ideas. Of course pornographers are likely to share in the view of women that they help to impose upon others, but they don't produce pornography in order that they should express that view.

At this point, pornography might seem to be so far from ordinary speech as to make it appear doubtful whether it can be treated by speech act theory at all. But in fact there is another idea in Austin which ensures there can be a conception of illocutionary acts which extends the class beyond the communicative ones. There can be a conception of *forceful* acts. In the case of communicative acts, "uptake" on a hearer's part is constituted by awareness of what the speaker is up to in speaking—awareness, to use Austin's terminology again, of the *force* of the utterance, where the speaker intends the utterance to have that force. But material can have force in the relevant sense without its being conferred by a speaker's intention. Its having the force it does—subordinating women, as it might be—can be a matter simply of audience reactions to it. (Compare: when a piece of [literal] speech has the force of warning that the ice is thin, say, the audience's hearing it is a matter simply of their being so warned.)

A speech-act-theoretic notion of illocution, albeit not a communicative one, is crucial here. Illocutionary acts are done *in* speaking: the force is integral to the act of speaking. Perlocutionary acts, by contrast, are done by virtue of speaking having effects in its turn. When pornography is seen to have the force of subordinating women, women being subordinated is not conceived as a sort of spin-off from pornography, as merely an effect of its consumption: it is something achieved *in* its consumption. By invoking an Austinian notion of illocutionary act, Langton can show pornography to *be* (rather than to result in) the subordination of women. (The account of course needs the sort of further spelling out and defense which Langton gives it.)

When the idea of a *forceful* illocutionary act is recognized and acknowledged to be broader than that of a *communicative* illocutionary act, one may want to distinguish between pornography's role as subordinator and as silencer. Viewed as a subordinator of women, pornography is seen as doing something illocutionary. But viewed as a silencer of women, pornography might be seen as doing something *perlocutionary*: one of its effects is that women are incapacitated as speakers. Indeed one might think that pornography silences at least in part *because* it subordinates. But even if silencing itself is to be treated as perlocutionary, the notion of illocution is still needed in characterizing it. For a person being silenced is a matter of her being illocutionarily disabled. And the point to notice now is that the disablement in question is disablement specifically in *communicative* illocutionary acts. So we need to invoke the narrower communicative conception of illocution, as well as the conception upon which Langton relies, if we are to elaborate the claim that pornography subordinates women *and* silences them.

Extract 3

If I've quarrelled with anything in Langton in the above, it is the starkness of the dilemma that she posed in her response to Leslie Green. Here she said: "Either pornography is not speech, in which case a free speech principle does not protect it; or pornography is speech, in which case speech act theory can help us understand it." [6] I want to say that pornography is *not* speech, even though the theory of speech acts provides resources for understanding it. I think that if we refuse to call pornography speech, we are better placed to see the damage it does. I have said something about how a conception of communicative acts might yield an idea of *speech-and-expression*, the value of the freedom of which can be independent of whatever value might be placed on freedom generally. It seems to me important to allow for such value if we want to keep a general (nonegalitarian) libertarianism at bay in thinking about pornography, and again if we want to have cognizance of the real injury done by silencing.

In responding to Ronald Dworkin, Langton says that Dworkin assimilated an argument from equality to a moralistic one, and thereby absolved himself from actually addressing the argument of those feminists he had purported to reply to. I agree. But I think there is a prior point. Very certainly the feminist argument from equality actually makes no appeal to a moralistic consideration—that pornography may disgust and offend. But why should Dworkin have thought that someone who introduces a moralistic consideration makes an actual mistake? Well, Dworkin defends pornography because he thinks that no one should be prevented from expressing their opinions on the grounds that others don't like those opinions. And he speaks in favor of a moral climate in which anyone's opinion should be capable of reception as well as expression: "We retain our dignity, as individuals," he says, "only by insisting that no one . . . has the right to withhold opinion from us on the ground that we are not fit to hear and consider it." Evidently Dworkin's own argument relies upon treating pornography's producers as expressing their opinions, and its consumers as receiving opinions which are up for their consideration. But in that case, Dworkin places pornography in a communicative category in which it doesn't belong. It is no wonder that he should lose sight of the argument from equality. Dworkin wants us to think that pornographers have a right to noninterference in their money-making activities, and he encourages us to think this through the ploy of misconceiving those activities. It is true of course that pornographers may be of the opinion that women are servile sexual objects; this may even be something they are "minded to say." But the opinion is neither expressed by its producers, nor heard and considered by its consumers when material is the medium of a conditioning process by which women come to be treated as sexual objects.

The concept of freedom of speech and expression that Dworkin defends cannot serve his argument for pornographers' rights. Something from Dworkin might be added, then, to the defenses of free speech that I gestured towards above. And there is a further defense which might also be added. I mean now the one which Langton introduces when she considers John Stuart Mill's "Argument from Truth."

Langton points out that Mill's argument is really an argument from *knowledge.* Mill thinks that free speech is conducive to the spread and increase of knowledge, and that "knowledge is part and parcel of well-being for humankind." When curbs on free speech are taken, as Mill takes them, to be barriers to freedom of expression of *knowledge,* we may come to see women's illocutionary disablement as ensuring that women are less effective participants in the transmission of knowledge, and relatively powerless members of a free speech community. And we might treat such disablement and powerlessness as among pornography's effects. The idea of women as silenced has been treated in the specific context of what pornography does, so that it is easy to focus on certain special examples of it: the familiar example is of the woman to whom a man makes sexual advances and whose "*No*" is not recognized for the refusal it is intended to be. But being unable to do what one wants using language can be much more widespread than such examples suggest. And when the epistemic dimension of speech is recognized, the idea of silencing may take on a new dimension.

We surely need to allow for matters of degree here. One can be regarded as more or less capable of knowing things, thus more or less credible, and more or less worth making enquiries of. So a person may be more or less silenced. But when silencing is thought of as pornography's perlocutionary effect, there is no need to think of it as an all or nothing matter. Indeed when silencing is taken as an effect of the use of pornography (rather than, as with subordination, constitutive of its use), it is possible to see it as one contributory factor to a certain system of disadvantage.

RESPONSE, BY RAE LANGTON

The focus of Hornsby's . . . attention is my development of a feminist argument that pornography is speech that subordinates and silences women. The concern is not simply with material that is sexually explicit and arousing—pornography in the vernacular sense—but with a subset of this material that arguably harms women, depicting women "dehumanized as sexual objects, things or commodities; enjoying pain or humiliation or rape; being tied up, cut up, mutilated, bruised, or physically hurt . . . shown as filthy or inferior; bleeding, bruised or hurt in a context which makes these conditions sexual," to borrow the words of a famous feminist definition, drafted by Catharine MacKinnon and Andrea Dworkin.[7] I began with a hunch: if courts said pornography is speech, then speech act theory might shed light on it.

J. L. Austin was interested in the way saying something can be, in itself, *doing* something: how the utterance of certain words in certain conditions might be, in itself, the performance of something, and not simply the production of certain effects: "I do," said during a marriage ceremony; "you're fired!," said by an employer. Feminists too have been interested in the way sayings can be doings: how the production of certain words and images might be the performance of something—subordination—as well as cause something as its effect. An investigation looked promising. Feminists who said pornography *is* the "graphic, sexually explicit subordination of women in pictures or words" might be right, for the same reason Austin was right in thinking an utterance of "I do" (in the right context) *is* marrying. Suppose "blacks are not permitted to vote" is uttered by an apartheid legislator, on a particular occasion, in a particular context.[8] Such an illocution might be subordination—it would *enact* subordination—as well as (perhaps) causing it. It might be, in Austin's terms, a "verdictive" that ranks a group as inferior, as well as an "exercitive" that deprives a group of powers and rights, and legitimates discrimination against them. If pornography turned out to be relevantly comparable to this sort of speech, then it might be an illocutionary act of subordination too—or so I argued.

Hornsby's essay . . . raises questions about whether pornography is speech at all. . . . [Her] perspective grounds her conclusions about pornography, with which I am broadly in sympathy: the communicative speech of women needs protecting, when it is silenced by pornography; and pornography itself does not need protecting, because it is not communicative.

Communication is the central point of speech, according to Hornsby. Her response in this symposium is backed by her own important and influential work on speech act theory, in which linguistic communication is seen "as a rational, human practice characterized by a certain sort of effortless meeting of minds," where a speaker manages to say something to someone, simply through being recognized as doing so—simply through, as Austin put it, "uptake" on the part of the hearer. While Hornsby admits that Austin initially focused on ceremonial examples, such as marriage and christening, in which convention has an important role to play in enabling a saying to be a certain sort of doing, nonetheless the simple case of communication—the case of saying something to someone—should still, in her view, be regarded as the central case of illocution. And it is the central case for political philosophy too, she thinks, and on this I agree. Freedom of speech is not freedom to make meaningful noises or marks, but freedom to engage in communicative activity: so illocution is central not only to speech act theory, but to the goals of free speech, such as the flourishing of democracy, the promotion of tolerance, and the achievement of knowledge.

Pornography itself is not communicative illocution, according to Hornsby: instead of speakers intending to reveal their minds to hearers, there are producers intending to maximize their profits. Pornography is not even expression, she thinks. Even if producers have certain views about women, they are not producing pornography in order to express that view, but in order to make money. And since pornography is not communicative illocution, it is not the sort of speech that a plausible theory of free speech would protect.

What then becomes of the claim I defended, that pornography is an illocution that subordinates women? I said that Hornsby is tempted to deny this, because she has argued in the past that pornography is not illocution at all— since it is not communicative. In Hornsby's distinctive vision of illocution, communication has always been at the center.[9] In Hornsby's past work on pornography and speech act theory, she has argued, not that pornography is *subordinating* speech, but that it is *not speech*. The significance of speech act theory for Hornsby is that it enables us to see the special way in which women are *silenced*, prevented from performing communicative illocutions, through "illocutionary disablement," as I called it. "No," when said by someone intending to refuse sex, sometimes might not get to count as a refusal. But speech act theory can't help us understand what kind of illocution pornography itself might be, since pornography isn't communicative, hence isn't illocution—or so she has been inclined to argue. . . . For Hornsby, the central case [of illocution] is that "effortless meeting of minds" that occurs in ordinary communication, where a hearer recognizes what a speaker is trying to do.

AFTERWORD, BY JENNIFER HORNSBY

I shall say something more about the argument that I attempted in suggesting that pornography does not belong in a certain category of communicative speech in the third section below. In section 2, I want also to introduce a new concern about pornography, namely its use by children. I mean to show that there is a properly feminist issue here. But I shall begin with something about how the stage was set when Langton first wrote on the subject of pornography, and about how things have changed.

1

Nancy Bauer has described "Langton and Hornsby" as part of "a movement within analytic feminist philosophy of the last decade whose aim is to show how Austin's work might be deployed to bring pornography out from under the protective wing of free speech law." [10] I can convey my own view of the relevant history by entering three reservations about this description.

In the first place, if "free speech law" here means law in pursuance of the First Amendment of the U.S. Constitution, and if the aim of the "movement" were as Bauer says, then it would have been an aim in vain. For in American courts, pornography would seem to have come to be free speech de jure (as I put it above). But of course it is possible to be concerned about what pornography may do without having it as an objective to bring about changes in any country's law. Secondly, it isn't clear that there has been a *movement* within analytic feminist philosophy deploying Austin's work. Certainly a group of women, all analytic philosophers, have brought philosophy of language, some of it taking off from Austin, to bear on debates about pornography and about hate speech. [11] But the members of that group have not confined themselves to Austin's work, and they have not all spoken with the single voice that "movement" would suggest. Thirdly, it isn't clear that the names of Langton and Hornsby should so readily be conjoined in this context. Some of Langton's work has used speech act theoretic notions to give substance to some specific claims about pornography; she has also written extensively on objectification. My own much smaller contribution (always from the east side of the Atlantic) has been within a general debate about freedom of speech, in which issues about pornography and hate speech may be raised.

Nevertheless the impression that a group of feminist philosophers have been concerned with American "free speech law" is understandable, for our work in this area surely took its inspiration from Catharine MacKinnon, who is a lawyer as well as an activist and a scholar. MacKinnon's book, *Only Words*,[12] was a response to pornography as a real-world phenomenon, affecting real men and women, and it contested legal judgements that had been based on rights provided by the U.S. Constitution. MacKinnon's argument was that pornography had been afforded the protection of speech only as a consequence of the courts simply ignoring the Constitution's Fourteenth Amendment, which established a concern with citizens' *equality*.

MacKinnon drew attention to a judgment made in an Appeals Court in 1985, which comes close to saying that the fact that pornography does harm in creating and sustaining the inequality of the sexes ensures that it must be protected. The passage MacKinnon quoted from the judgment has been much requoted over the years. I reproduce just a small portion of it now, with some of the sentences enumerated for purposes of reference. Here then is Judge Easterbrook writing for the Court:

> (1) The bigotry and contempt [pornography] produces, with the acts of aggression it fosters, harm women's opportunities for equality and rights [of all kinds]. Yet (2) this simply demonstrates the power of pornography as speech. (3) All of [pornography's] unhappy effects depend on mental intermediation. Pornography affects how people see the world, their fellows, and social relations.[13]

MacKinnon's argument used (1) as premise. Some of Langton's work takes off from (2): she explores how pornography, considered as speech, works its power. My own concern relates to (3). Here we find Easterbrook's reason for treating pornography as speech: its effects depend upon mental intermediation. In my final section, I consider how *mental intermediation* is to be understood if it can serve to mark out that which a right to freedom of speech and expression guarantees.

Easterbrook was ruling on Dworkin and MacKinnon's definition of "pornography," from which Langton quotes above. Their definition was evidently designed to cover material extant and in use more than thirty years ago when pornography was mostly bought in shops; but with some adjustments, it might be used to capture some material now extant—now that the Internet has made film showing a woman physically and verbally abused readily available.[14] At any rate some of the same kinds of depiction of women that MacKinnon includes in the scope of pornography are found in what many mean by "porn" nowadays. In film on present-day websites, women are certainly depicted as "dehumanized as sexual objects, enjoying pain or humiliation or rape." The top website found with a simple search for the single word "porn" immediately offers choices within it under the heads of such tags as *slut, gagging, dp, humiliation, domination, slave, slapped, degradation, choke, used, brutal, shame, choking, vicious, violated, destroyed, puking.*[15] A customer can take his pick, although any particular choice of material will perforce combine many of these themes. The customer also has "access to total degradation," but for that he does have to pay. (He has no need to pay for rape scenes, however: these are accessible on five of the top ten sites that may be found using the two words "free porn.")[16]

Let me use the word "porn" then, as I think MacKinnon and Langton have both used "pornography," so that it would cover the material picked out by Dworkin and MacKinnon's definition when that is updated to include the new kinds of violation of a woman that have come to be shown in readily accessible websites. On such an understanding of porn, explicit description or display of sexual organs or activity is not *eo ipso* porn. Plenty of pornography, as some may understand that, does not qualify as porn: it is not my concern, and perhaps has never been the concern of so-called "anti-porn feminists." Dworkin and MacKinnon wanted to define certain material by reference to what it does, and then to say what sorts of material may be included as being such as to do that.[17]

However exactly one might want to circumscribe the material of concern (which I am calling porn), if it is to be understood in the speech act terms in which Langton wants to understand it, isolating it as a category will not be achieved by saying simply that it is material meeting such-and-such conditions. The reason is that a speech act, in the paradigm case at least, involves not only an utterance (here "material"), but also a speaker, a hearer, *and a context.* Langton notes this, and says that "we need to think of concrete utterances in specific contexts" (see her n.7 below). But is this really how we need to think? I suggest not.

The remoteness of an arbitrary consumer of porn from an arbitrary producer makes it difficult to know quite what "a specific context of utterance" might mean in this case. But however "context of utterance" might be understood, an attempt to define porn by reference to *concrete utterances* would seem to lose sight of its *cumulative* effects. The question of how pornography affects how people see the world, their fellows, and social relations (to steal some words from Easterbrook) is surely a macro-social question—a question that invites one to consider porn's possible part in the creation or perpetuation of a gender system infused with inequality and/or violence. One can understand why MacKinnon should have called pornography a *practice*, rather than have thought of it as any set of utterances.[18] When she called it "masturbation material," she sidestepped the question about the context in which pornography is consumed by paying heed to how the sorts of depictions of women that concerned her were actually typically used.

Another way to avoid treating porn as material contained in individual acts in specific contexts is to follow Leslie Green, who introduced the verb "pornographize" having application to producing, distributing, or using certain material.[19] Green's approach makes it possible to take the step of thinking of porn as material belonging in an institution in which the players pornographize—an institution which in its turn might be defined in terms of an industry and its market. (In order to see a market at work, one needs to realize that paid-for material is got from websites co-owned by those that deliver free porn, and that money is made through advertisers from supplying the free material.) "Porn," then, will be the material made and supplied in that market. And the production and consumption of new and harsher material by pornographizers will reveal the market to be one in which demand is created by supply. (One has here an example of what J. K. Galbraith called the "dependence effect," by which "wants depend on the process by which they are satisfied.")[20]

However exactly "porn" is understood, for the purposes of present debate, the word will apply to certain material currently produced and consumed by actual people. That means that when speech act terms are introduced, the material will be cast in the role of agent, as that which *does* something—as a speaker does this or that other thing with words on this or that other occasion. The terms and distinctions of speech act theory can then be applied. But now, when porn is said to do something—to subordinate women, say, or to silence them—it may be seen as an agent within a certain market-driven institution. Whereas what a speaker does using some particular sentence on occasion depends upon a context that she shares with a hearer and that affects the sentence's interpretation, the context of porn can now be only the social world wherein pornographizers do what they do *qua* pornographizers.

Still, something like an idea of "context of utterance" may be needed in a treatment of porn that takes it to do such things as a speaker may do. For the material may be viewed by others than those who belong in the market base of the pornographizers who produce and distribute the material. Consider a ten-year-old boy who views porn quite unaware of its intended deployment, and who is not (yet) caught up in what MacKinnon calls the practice. Perhaps he comes upon the material accidentally. Or perhaps he seeks it out, thinking that he can learn from it what sex is all about. Either way, he will be affected by it differently from an adult man. And what porn *does* when viewed by this boy will be different from what it routinely and cumulatively does.

2

This brings me to children's use of Internet porn more generally, not by ten-year-olds necessarily, but by children whose first and continued understandings of sex may be informed by watching vicious (etc.) film of women humiliated (etc.). Concerns about this are new: free streaming pornography sites are only a few years old, and only relatively recently have many children made a habit of never being without their smartphones. In recent months, the media in the United Kingdom have reported specifically on Internet pornography specifically as it is watched by teenagers and young children—by boys in the main. The question of late has not been a familiar sounding one: "Is pornography protected from censorship by virtue of our right to free speech?"; the question has been "How might children be protected from pornography?"

The UK media's attention to this question results from the publication of the Children's Commissioner for England's report, "The Effect that Access and Exposure to Pornography Has on Children and Young People."[21] The report draws from work by groups of academics who reviewed 41,000 pieces of research between them. "Gender differences emerged as a continuous and highly pertinent theme." Boys access pornography more than girls, and do so more frequently, and they generally view pornography more positively, girls generally reporting that it is unwelcome. There are effects of access on beliefs: "pornography is linked to unrealistic attitudes about sex, to beliefs that women are sex objects, and to less progressive gender role attitudes." And there are effects on behavior and expectations: "too often girls feel they have no alternative but to submit to boys' demands, regardless of their own wishes," and "too many boys believe that they have an absolute entitlement to sex at any time . . . in any way."[22]

The release of the documentary film *In Real Life*[23] has led to further media coverage. The film contains interviews with two fifteen-year-old boys, and it is not possible to know the extent to which they might be representative of British teenagers. Nevertheless these boys give one a sense of how children's use of Internet pornography might impinge on existing mores. One tells the interviewer that his use of porn has "ruined the whole sense of love." Another tells of the problems of finding girls attractive in the manner of the women who are portrayed in the pornography that he and his friends all watch. And he explains that a girl who does submit to a boy's demands is forthwith branded a slag. "That's the thing that kills me," he says, "seeing those amazing girls with such nice personalities, and seeing that guys have already gone and done that to them." Evidently the double standard lives on. If anything has changed, it is the image of a girl's defilement: her seeming to be worthy of vilification can be traced to the misogyny of present-day pornographic fantasy.

The UK newspapers ask, "Is Internet porn causing harm to our children?" By and large they answer *Yes*, with the prime minister adding his voice, deploring "the corrosion of childhood." As the debate has been conducted, any harm specifically to girls would seem to be a matter merely of their female sensitivity: girls are more likely than boys to express disgust when they encounter pornography. Well, I think that any feminist will want to frame the question differently from the newspapers.

When the so-called porn wars raged in the late 1970s and 1980s, the issue was a gendered one. Disagreement between feminists concerned, very roughly, whether pornography was or was not to women's detriment. Was sexuality a site of sex discrimination, and pornography's production and consumption harmful to women and sustaining of sexual inequality? Or was men's and/or women's viewing of pornography liberating for women, and any anti-pornography opinion at the service of a moralistic political right wing? Such debate would seem to have been forgotten. But children's viewing of Internet material surely raises some of the old questions in a new version. Need one be moralistic to think that girls who are deprived of their right to sexual autonomy when they might first have exercised it are casualties of porn? Need one be illiberal to think that boys' viewing of porn may impact adversely their notions of gender and sexuality? Many are confident that it makes no difference to *adult* men's attitudes to women whether or not they regularly view film of women being cruelly humiliated and verbally abused. It seems harder to be confident that the attitudes of children who still have everything to find out about sex and sexuality will not be affected by porn. Perhaps one can do no more than speculate whether it might be to the detriment of women that a generation of boys come of age having violent sexual imagery as their learning experience. But if one does so speculate, then one's worry will not be about the corrosion of *childhood*. The worry now, if ignorant children are apt to learn what some of them come to believe, is that porn plays a role in sustaining some of the norms that it depicts.[24]

The evidence suggests that boys who view readily available porn acquire certain sexist stereotypes. It is possible to think that those same stereotypes are *reinforced* when adult men view the same material. The idea that pornography has some of the power of the self-fulfilling speech acts known as performatives then comes to seem rather plausible. In finding it plausible, one has no need to treat porn, or any particular instance of its production or distribution or consumption, as itself an act of speech.

3

I have wanted to put it into question whether pornography is speech, meaning by pornography that which I've here been calling porn, and meaning by "speech" that which a correct understanding of the *right* to free speech provides reasons for protecting. I want now to bring Easterbrook's idea that pornography works through "mental intermediation" into relation with a suggestion I made in the symposium. The suggestion was that although we might think of porn as communicative in its way—so that the content of what the producers produce impinges in some way upon the consumers—still it is not communicative speech of a sort that brings it under the head of a right to free speech. (Justifications of a right to free speech may justify the protection of more than is straightforwardly communicative. But we shall see that what is at issue in the case of porn is exactly how it works as communicator.)

Easterbrook gave no reason for declaring that pornography is speech, save that its effects were wrought through mental intermediation. His reason for thinking that this is how porn works was its effects on people's view of the world, of other people, and of social relations. Unless pornography affects the mental states of those who use it, it could hardly be responsible for producing contempt, fostering aggression, and harming women's opportunities for equality. That pornography has the power it does is not in question. The question is why the power that it has should be thought to be the power of speech.

Bauer spoke of "the legal sense of the word speech."[25] Presumably she meant the sense that has accrued to "speech" in jurisdictions of the United States. But one can be in a position to appreciate the point and value of people's being accorded a right to free speech without one's understanding being framed by American courts. A right to free speech is upheld in the European Convention on Human Rights, which happens not to contain the word "speech" (its Article 10 has: "Everyone has the right to freedom of expression"). And such a right is granted in the United Nations Declaration of Human Rights. In the context of that declaration, the right is accorded to "all members of the human family" by virtue of their "inherent dignity" and of their "being endowed with reason and conscience." In this context, speech would seem to be characteristic specifically of human beings, by virtue of their humanity. There is a connection here with the idea I introduced of a rational, human practice.

If the distinction I made between two different ways in which a message can be received is a viable one, then two species of "mental intermediation" must be distinguished. One species would be that which I took to go hand in hand with illocution, the other that which I denied that pornography involves. In seeing what can be at issue here, it might help to think about how animal communication is different from the distinctively human sort. When a house sparrow emits a noise to indicate the arrival of a hawk, all the house sparrows in hearing distance hide themselves. Fear of danger is communicated, no doubt, so that there is mental intermediation in some sense. But birds lack the faculty of reason: they react instinctively to the squawks they hear from fellow birds. My idea was that a specifically human faculty is engaged when there is the sort of meeting of minds that may characterize the speech to which everyone has a right. When there is such mental intermediation, a recipient of speech is not simply a passive recipient of a message: she is someone with capacities of judgment and understanding, who can make up her own mind. These capacities are brought into play when one person understands another: they are exercised in receiving speech. (A recipient of speech also has capacities to speak herself, so that she can answer back to speech when circumstances are right.)[26]

When Easterbrook spoke of pornography as working through mental intermediation, he relied only on the fact that producers and consumers of pornography alike have minds, and that the minds of consumers may be altered in ways predictable from the content of the material produced by producers.[27] Easterbrook simply assumed that someone at the receiving end of pornography is engaged with the material as an audience of speech would be engaged. And by setting aside questions about what confers a right to free speech, Easterbrook had no need to consider whether pornography's producers and consumers stand to one another in the sort of reciprocal/interactive relation that human beings stand to one another when they are participants in illocutionary acts. (Of course I don't say that pornographizers are much like sparrow hawks. The example of bird communication is meant only to draw attention, by way of its absence, to something present in human communication when there is "uptake" in Austin's sense on the part of the hearer.)[28]

In questioning whether pornography is speech, I have no need to take issue directly either with MacKinnon or with Langton. MacKinnon argued that pornography (as she defined it) did not merit protection by the U.S. Constitution as a whole.[29] And Langton treated pornography as speech because some U.S. courts had declared it to be so.[30] It is possible then to think of both MacKinnon and Langton conceding that pornography is speech simply for the sake of argument—MacKinnon for the purpose of speaking to the harms it does, Langton for the purpose of using speech act theory to illuminate the manner in which it does those harms.

Much has changed in the thirty years since Dworkin and MacKinnon wrote their anti-pornography ordinances, and questioning the legal status of porn may have come to be futile. Now that porn has a global distribution, questions about its possible regulation by this state or that seem bound to be academic. But perhaps it is still worth knowing what pornography does, and worth considering how it does it. "Free speech" has come to be a rallying cry, used by those who have no interest in the question of what belongs under the head of speech, and who take it that once something has been declared to be speech, social and political considerations have no bearing on it. Perhaps then it is worth guarding against the thought that insofar as pornography does harms to women, it does so in the service of the greater good of free speech.

Even if there is nothing to be done about porn, there may be a point in *not* conceding that pornography is speech.

NOTES

1. The extracts are reprinted with permission from Hart Publishing, Oxford, having been published originally, along with papers by other symposiasts, in *Jurisprudence* 2, no. 2 (2011). Langton's book, *Sexual Solipsism*, was published by Oxford University Press in 2009.

2. J. L. Austin, *How to Do Things with Words* (Oxford: Oxford University Press, 1962).

3. "*Succeeded* in saying" because your communicative purpose might have been frustrated. It can be allowed that in such a case—where, as it might be, the person you addressed literally didn't hear you—you said something to them. But still you would have fallen short of a sort of successful speaking which I believe needs to be captured in an account of language use.

4. Austin's initial concern was with examples where performativity is at the fore. I believe that his struggles to distinguish the "constative" from the "performative" might be explained by his failure to realize that the conception of speech acts he had introduced actually covered a great deal more than those examples.

5. See Gail Dines, *Pornland: How Porn Has Hijacked our Sexuality* (Boston: Beacon, 2010).

6. Langton, *Sexual Solipsism*, 101.

7. See Catharine MacKinnon, "Francis Biddle's Sister," in *Feminism Unmodified* (Cambridge, MA: Harvard University Press, 1987).

8. As Jennifer Saul has pointed out, in order to think in terms of speech acts, we need to think of concrete utterances in specific contexts; and this at the very least complicates discussion of pornography. I have ridden roughshod over this requirement; and, I regret, continue to pay it insufficient respect. See Saul, "Pornography, Speech Acts, and Context," *Proceedings of the Aristotelian Society* 106, no. 2 (2006): 61–80.

9. Jennifer Hornsby, "Illocution and its Significance," in *Foundations of Speech Act Theory*, ed. S. L. Tsohatzidis (Routledge, 1994); "Disempowered Speech," in Sally Haslanger, ed., *Philosophical Topics* 23 (1995): 127–47.

10. Bauer, "How to Do Things with Pornography," in *Reading Cavell*, ed. Alice Crary and Sanford Sheih (London and New York: Routledge, 2006), 74.

11. Members of the group include the editors of and some of the contributors to *Speech and Harm: Controversies over Free Speech*, ed. Ishani Maitra and Mary Kate McGowan (Oxford: Oxford University Press, 2012). In her foreword to that volume, MacKinnon cites much of the work that brings philosophy of language to bear on pornography.

12. Harvard University Press, 1993. The argument I'm concerned with is in chapter 3.

13. *American Booksellers Association, Inc. v. Hudnut*, 771 F.2d 323 (7th Cir. 1985).

14. It is of some interest to see how technological change has necessitated definitional changes in what is proscribed under the heading of "child pornography" by UK legislation in the last thirty years. (Of course someone with a historical interest in pornography would work with a definition very different from any that gesture toward what comes into the extension of what is nowadays known as porn.)

15. The list of tags was garnered by me, one day in July 2013, on which http://www.xvideos.com topped the list.

16. *Observer*, June 23, 2013. Access to some of the sites showing rape is prohibited in the United Kingdom, but that doesn't prevent them from being freely available de facto.

17. They defined pornography by reference to the fact (as they took it to be) of its subordinating women: "'Pornography' means the graphic sexually explicit subordination of women." The definition is in the 1983 Model Antipornography Civil Rights Ordinance published in Andrea Dworkin and Catharine MacKinnon, *Pornography and Civil Rights: A New Day for Women's Equality (*Minneapolis: Organizing Against Pornography, 1988), 138–42. Langton quotes from the part of the definition that specifies the kinds of depiction of women that pornography may include.

18. MacKinnon actually called it "a practice of sexual politics, an institution of gender inequality." *Feminism Unmodified* (Cambridge, MA: Harvard University Press, 1987), 148.

19. Leslie Green, "Pornographizing, Subordinating, and Silencing," in *Censorship and Silencing: Practices of Cultural Regulation*, ed. Robert Post (Los Angeles: Getty Publications, 1998).

20. J. K. Galbraith, *The Affluent Society* (Boston: Houghton Mifflin, 1958), 158. No doubt it is not an example of the sort Galbraith had in mind in describing the workings of corporate planning and mass advertising. When the market of the pornography industry is treated as subject to the dependence effect, pornographizing will include not only producing, distributing, and using certain material, but also some of what goes on at conferences of the industry (see above where n.5 is flagged).

21. Published 24 May 2013, http://www.childrenscommissioner.gov.uk/content/publications/content_667 (accessed 11 Jul. 2013).

22. Quotations from the report for the most part are from the section "Findings," 5.

23. Directed by Beeban Kidron, United Kingdom, 2013.

24. Langton thinks of pornography as constructing reality inasmuch as it is *authoritative* speech and can be treated as *verdictive*. She might say that pornography as viewed by young children on their phones is *exercitive* speech. See section 1 of "Pornography's Authority? Reply to Leslie Green" (98–102 in *Sexual Solipsism*) for Langton's account of how the two Austinian categories of verdictive and exercitive may be distinguished.

25. Bauer, "How to Do Things with Pornography," 75.

26. In the first paragraph of the judgment which I quote from above, Easterbrook attended to the point that the "unanswerability" of porn might be thought to count against its being speech. He said that its unanswerability could only be part of a case that porn is outside the coverage of the First Amendment if the right to free speech is justified on Mill's grounds that truth will prevail if speech is free. But one surely needn't share Mill's optimism that a free speech regime conduces to truth in order to think that speech lacks its usual point when it deprives those whom it affects of the capacity to answer back.

27. I may have an explanation of why Easterbrook introduced "mental intermediation." Dworkin and MacKinnon had proposed to treat pornography as a violation of women's civil rights and to allow women harmed by pornography to seek damages. If the Dworkin-MacKinnon ordinance had succeeded, then reparation for acts committed by consumers of pornography could have been got from pornography's producers. Thus, for example, a woman who had been abused by men in consequence of those men viewing particular material would have been able to claim damages from whoever made the material and made it available. It could then seem as if guilt were to be lain at the door of pornography's producers and distributors rather than of the porn-using abusers of women. Enter Easterbrook. In drawing attention to the fact that the material works through mental intermediation, he removed any appearance that the abusers might themselves be innocent. Well, of course if there were such an appearance, it would be right to remove it. But in fact there was no question of the ordinance serving to let abusers off the hook. It is one question what the states of mind of abusers were *qua* abusers, and another question exactly how those states were reached. If the state of mind of an abuser was reached through the consumption of pornography, then this would show that pornography alters minds, but it could hardly demonstrate that pornography is speech.

28. I note that audience "uptake" in a sense much like Austin's can belong to what is not straightforwardly communicative, but which may properly be brought under the head of speech. Given that "force," like "uptake," is a term used by Austin for something proprietary to illocutionary acts, I may have been unwise to speak of pornography as a *forceful* act. I wanted only to be clear that pornography might impact upon people's attitudes, in just such specific ways as genuinely illocutionary speech may impact.

29. In arguing that pornography does not merit *protection* as speech under the U.S. Constitution, MacKinnon had no need to address the question of whether it falls within the *coverage* of the First Amendment.

30. See the first two sentences of her "Speech Acts and Unspeakable Acts," *Philosophy and Public Affairs* 22 (1993): 305–30; reprinted in *Sexual Solipsism*, 25–63. See also what she calls her "hunch" in her "Response" above.

Chapter Nine

Pornography and the Philosophy of Language

Louise Antony

Rae Langton and Jennifer Hornsby, together with a number of other feminist philosophers, have argued that the philosophy of language has important bearing on our understanding of pornography and its effects on the well-being of women. Specifically, Langton and Hornsby have each argued that J. L. Austin's theory of speech acts can illuminate both the nature of the harm pornography does to women, and the way in which pornography contributes to the perpetuation of sexual violence. I want to argue that these applications of speech act theory are misguided—both from a philosophical point of view, and from a pragmatic, political point of view.

In the first section, I provide some background to the development of this Austinian approach to pornography, and briefly survey my objections to Langton's and Hornsby's views. In the second section, I focus on Langton's attempt to show that pornography is an *illocutionary* speech act, specifically that it is a verdictive or an exercitive speech act. In the final section, I consider a second appeal that Langton makes to Austin, and in which she is joined by Jennifer Hornsby. This is the claim that pornography silences women by disrupting uptake of their refusals.

BACKGROUND

There has been a feminist debate about pornography since the 1970s,[1] but for much of that time, the debate focused on censorship, and was framed in terms of a conflict between *rights* and *interests*: do the free speech rights of those who produce or consume pornography trump the interests of those who might be harmed by pornography? Although there was vigorous discussion among feminists about prior conceptual issues (e.g., what is the difference between "pornography" and "erotica?") and empirical issues (e.g., does consumption of pornography increase the likelihood the consumer will commit sexual assault?), the question at the end of the day was still this: are the harmful effects of pornography so great, or of such a type, as to warrant restrictions on freedom of speech?

This changed dramatically, however, in 1987, when feminist legal theorist Catharine MacKinnon published *Feminism Unmodified.* MacKinnon argued there and in subsequent works that the issue of pornography should be understood in terms of a conflict *within* the realm of rights. Pornography, she claimed, is a form of conduct, conduct that subordinates women. As such, pornography *constitutes* an active violation of women's civil rights, in exactly the same way that racial discrimination in housing or employment constitute*s* a violation of the rights of members of racial minorities.

MacKinnon's reconceptualization of pornography as an act of discrimination provided the basis for a novel approach to the regulation of pornography. In the old model, the policy debate focused on restrictions on the production, sale, and distribution of pornography; the main legal issue was whether it would be possible to craft effective measures that would not violate citizens' constitutional rights to freedom of expression and privacy. But if, as MacKinnon argued, pornography is a form of sex discrimination, such rights would not come into play. Civil law provides a general mechanism by which victims of discrimination may seek redress from those who committed the discriminatory acts, and in such cases, there is no question of the accused's defending his or her actions on the grounds that he or she was simply exercising his or her right to free speech. The First Amendment does not protect otherwise illegal acts just because they happen to involve speech.

It was this argument that had provided the basis for the model ordinance that MacKinnon had drafted together with feminist author and activist Andrea Dworkin (1946–2005), legislation that would empower women who had been harmed by pornography to sue the producers or purveyors for damages in civil court. In 1984, this legislation was adopted by the city council of Indianapolis, and was immediately challenged on the grounds that it involved an unconstitutional restriction on speech (*American Booksellers Association, Inc. v. Hudnut*). The Seventh Circuit Court found for the plaintiffs. In his majority opinion, Judge Frank Easterbrook wrote:

> The ordinance discriminates on the ground of the content of the speech. Speech treating women in the approved way—in sexual encounters "premised on equality" (MacKinnon, *supra,* at 22)—is lawful no matter how sexually explicit. Speech treating women in the disapproved way—as submissive in matters sexual or as enjoying humiliation—is unlawful no matter how significant the literary, artistic, or political qualities of the work taken as a whole.

The state may not ordain preferred viewpoints in this way. The Constitution forbids the state to declare one perspective right and silence opponents.[2]

Easterbrook's opinion makes clear that the most important element of MacKinnon's theory is the treatment of pornography as a kind of *conduct*; this is what was supposed to take pornography out of the realm of protected speech. But it is also crucial to MacKinnon's analysis that pornography be a certain *kind* of act—an act of discrimination. MacKinnon's aim was to obviate the old debates about the *effects* of pornography, as if the harmfulness of pornography lay entirely in its social consequences. MacKinnon certainly did not deny that pornography had harmful effects, but she wanted to show that, apart from the harms that pornography caused, there was a harm that pornography *constituted*.

This she could achieve if she could demonstrate that pornography *was* an act of discrimination. Discrimination is inherently harmful. A person who is denied a job because of her race has been harmed simply by virtue of having been discriminated against; she does not need to show that the discrimination has led to some further harm in order to have a legitimate grievance. Thus, MacKinnon argues, even if pornography causes harm to women, it is the harm constituted by pornography that warrants immediate legal redress.

MacKinnon's policy objective, then, made the distinction between an act's *merely causing* harm and its *constituting* harm crucial to her legal analysis. This is serious work for a philosophical distinction to do, and one may reasonably question whether the philosophy is up to the job. District Court judge Barker, in the supplement to *Booksellers v. Hudnut*, disparaged the distinction:

> It appears to be central to the defense of the Ordinance by defendants that the Court accept their premise that the City-County Council has not attempted to regulate speech, let alone protected speech. Defendants repeat throughout their briefs the incantation that their Ordinance regulates conduct, not speech. They contend (one senses with a certain sleight of hand) that the production, dissemination, and use of sexually explicit words and pictures *is* the actual subordination of women and not an expression of ideas deserving of First Amendment protection.[3]

Philosopher Rae Langton rose to MacKinnon's defense. Langton argued that MacKinnon's controversial claim that pornography *is* an act could be understood in terms of J. L. Austin's theory of speech acts.[4] In the first place, Langton says, Austin shows us that there is a whole range of actions that one can perform merely in speaking: promising is one such action, sentencing and marrying are others. There is therefore no need to deny that pornography is speech in order to assert that it is also conduct. Pornography could be a kind of speech act.[5]

If pornography is a speech act, Langton continued, then Austin's theory supplies a way of understanding MacKinnon's controversial claim that pornography constitutes and does not simply cause harm to women. The key is Austin's distinction between two kinds of actions that one can perform by means of speech: the *illocutionary* act, and the *perlocutionary* act. Both types of act have an act of speaking, or a *locutionary* act, at their heart. The illocutionary act is fully constituted by the locutionary act; it is (as Austin sometimes puts it) the act one performs *in* speaking.[6] The perlocutionary act, in contrast, depends on factors that lie outside the act of speaking; it is an act that one performs *by* speaking.

Let me offer an example that will make the distinction clear. Suppose one morning I say to my spouse, "I promise to take out the trash." Simply in saying those words (seriously, and with the knowledge that my spouse understands them), I have performed an illocutionary act: I have made a promise. Saying such words in the appropriate context is all that promising consists in—nothing more is necessary. But now it may also happen that when I say, "I promise to take out the trash," I cause my spouse to form a certain belief, namely, that the trash will (finally!) be removed. In that case, I will not just have performed an act of promising, but I will also have performed an act of *convincing*. Unlike the promising, however, the convincing was not inherent to the act of speaking itself. Convincing, unlike promising, requires that my speaking bring about certain effects: to convince someone of something, I must cause the person to change his or her mind. If I do bring about such a change, brava!—because I might have failed.

I cannot fail to promise if I say the right words in the right context. But I can surely make a promise without my spouse coming to believe that I will do the thing I promised to do. Perhaps I am quite absent-minded, and frequently forget what it is I promised to do; in that case, my spouse may doubt whether the trash will be taken out, even if he has no doubts about the sincerity—or the validity—of my promise. Since there is only a contingent connection between making a promise and engendering a belief (i.e., convincing), the making of a promise does not *constitute* the engendering of a belief, even though it may very frequently *cause* the engendering of a belief. (Other examples: I can *threaten* someone without succeeding in *frightening* him; I can *urge* someone to do something without *persuading* him to do it; and I can *lie* to someone without *deceiving* him. Frightening, persuading, and deceiving can never be other than perlocutionary effects of the speech acts that have in fact caused them.)

Getting back to Langton: Austin's distinction between illocutionary and perlocutionary acts, Langton argues, nicely illuminates MacKinnon's distinction between pornography's merely *causing* the subordination of women, and it *constituting* the subordination of women. Langton suggests that when MacKinnon says that pornography is or constitutes *subordination*, we can read her as saying that subordination is an illocutionary act, akin to promising, rather than a perlocutionary act, like convincing. Specifically, pornography is either a *verdictive* speech act—it renders an authoritative judgment that women are inferior, like the authoritative judgment of a referee—or an *exercitive* speech act—it strips women of power, in the way an act of government can strip away people's right to vote. Either way, the harm pornography does is inherent to the pornographic speech act itself, and not merely a contingent consequence of it.

I intend to raise some serious questions about whether there can be such a thing as an *illocutionary* act of subordination. But first, let me describe the second appeal that has been made to Austin on behalf of MacKinnon, by Langton and by Jennifer Hornsby.[7] This second application of speech act theory pertains to another controversial claim of MacKinnon's, namely, the claim that pornography *silences* women.[8] How might this be so? Let's first look at the pertinent aspect of Austin's theory, and then see how Langton applies it.

Speech acts, as Austin explains them, depend for their successful execution on certain *contextual* conditions being met. Not every utterance of the phrase "I promise . . ." constitutes a promise: it does not if it is uttered by an actor on a stage, or if it is pronounced by a parrot, or by a person who has no idea what it means. Conditions such as these—that the speaker be serious, and that she understand what she is saying—are general conditions[9] on the successful performance of *any* speech act. These conditions are limited, for the most part, to requirements on the speaker and her context; that is why I said earlier the illocutionary act is "fully constituted" by the locutionary act, performed in a suitable context. In saying that, however, I glossed over the fact that there is a general condition that adverts to the speaker's *audience.* In order for an utterance to constitute a speech act of any kind, there must be what Austin calls "uptake:" "An effect must be achieved on the audience if the illocutionary act is to be carried out. How should we best put it here? And how can we limit it? Generally the effect amounts to bringing about the understanding of the meaning and of the force of the locution."[10]

Langton's and Hornsby's idea is that pornography can silence women by disrupting the uptake of their speech. Consider the speech act of *refusing.* If one cannot refuse without there being uptake, then a woman cannot refuse to have intercourse with someone if her audience fails to understand that she *has* refused. And if it is a common and potent effect of pornography that men become incapable of understanding when some particular woman tries to refuse sexual congress, then pornography has disrupted the uptake of the woman's (attempted) refusal. Pornography, in this case, makes it so that the woman has *not* refused, that she has literally *said nothing*, and thus that she has been *silenced.*

According to Langton and Hornsby, there are at least two ways in which pornography can disrupt the uptake of a woman's attempted refusal.[11] First, it can inculcate false beliefs about women. (This is in line with another theme of MacKinnon's—that pornography "tells lies about women.") In this analysis, pornography promotes a view of women's sexual appetites as indiscriminate and insatiable. A man who has come to accept this view will be unable to understand that a woman is actually refusing sex. He may, for example, be disposed to interpret normal signs of refusal (such as a woman's saying "No—I refuse—get off me") as coy invitations to continue his sexual advances. Or he may have come to believe that many women "like it rough," so that this particular woman's struggles and screams are simply moves in a sexual game. Either way, pornography makes it the case that there is virtually nothing that a woman can do to convey to a man that she does not consent to having sex. She has been rendered incapable of performing the speech act of refusing.

The second way, according to Langton, that pornography might disrupt uptake of a woman's refusal is by *objectifying* women—that is, by causing men to view and to treat women as mere objects, devoid of subjectivity and will. This mechanism is very different from the first. With the first route, a man disables a woman's speech by construing all her words and actions (perversely) as a form of consent. But consent requires agency. With this second posited mechanism, the man disables a woman's speech by failing to see her as having any agency at all, by treating her as if she were a parrot, or a tape player—a thing that can make speech sounds, but can mean nothing by them.

One thing that I want to point out is that Langton's first appeal to Austin is independent of the second. Langton could be correct about the speech act status of pornography without it being the case that pornography silences women in any of the ways Langton considers. Conversely, Langton could be right about pornography silencing women, either through falsification or through objectification, without it being the case that pornography is any kind of speech act at all. The speech act analysis of silencing focuses on the conditions necessary for a *woman* to perform a certain speech act, and depends only on the failure of the *man*'s uptake. The causes of that failure of uptake are incidental to the failure itself. But even if the two analyses are independent, it might be thought that subordination and silencing are still related—that pornography achieves its subordinating effects *by* silencing women. But Langton cannot say this; to do so would undercut her argument for classifying subordination as an *illocutionary* effect of pornography. If subordination is an illocutionary act, then it must be set in place as soon as the pornographic speech act is performed, and cannot depend on further contingent developments. (Recall the difference between promising and persuading.) Hence, if it is even *possible* for a man to consume pornography

without ever attempting to have intercourse with a woman against her will—
and surely this possibility must be conceded—then silencing can be only
contingently connected with the performance of the pornographic speech act.

In what follows, I intend to show that neither of Langton's two appeals to
Austin is successful. In the next section, I argue against the claim that subordination is, or could be, an illocutionary act. I will not challenge the claim
that pornography *is* a speech act, although I agree with those of Langton's
critics who argue that it is not.[12] What I focus on instead is the question of
whether the condition of subordination is one that could be brought about by
any illocutionary act. Elsewhere, I have argued that it is not.[13] Here, I defend
my argument, and my reading of Austin, against Langton's objections. More
important, however, I show that Langton's preferred reading undermines her
defense of MacKinnon.

In the final section, I discuss Langton's treatment of silencing. Here I
concede Langton's reading of Austin,[14] but I argue that the kind of act for
which uptake is required is not the kind of act with which the law can be
concerned. If the uptake requirement is taken as seriously as Langton proposes to take it, then, I contend, the law cannot, and indeed should not,
attempt to guarantee speakers the right to perform the *speech act* of *refusal*.
What the law can and should guarantee is a person's right to *refuse*.

IS SUBORDINATION AN ILLOCUTIONARY ACT?

The key element in MacKinnon's theory, the element that is supposed to
disarm the freedom-of-speech objection to the regulation of pornography, is
her claim that pornography *constitutes*, and does not merely cause, the subordination of women. The most important aspect of Langton's charitable reconstruction of MacKinnon's theory is, accordingly, the suggestion that this
key distinction can be explicated in terms of Austin's distinction between an
illocutionary and a *perlocutionary* speech act. But a careful look at Austin's
own characterization of this distinction, together with his rationale for drawing it, makes it clear that the distinction cannot do what Langton wants it to
do in the case of pornography.

The intuitive root of Austin's distinction between illocution and perlocution is just the distinction MacKinnon needs: between "an action we do" on
the one hand, "and its consequences" on the other.[15] But Austin is pessimis-
tic that such a distinction can be drawn for actions in general. He says that if
the action is "not one of saying something but a non-conventional 'physical'
action," drawing such a line is "an intricate matter":

> [W]e can . . . class, by stages, more and more of what is initially and ordinarily
> included . . . under the name given to "our act" itself as *really* only *conse-*
> *quences*, however little remote and however naturally to be anticipated, of our

actual action in the supposed physical minimum sense, which will then trans-
pire to be the making of some movement or movements with parts of our
body.[16]

So, suppose (to use Austin's example) I kill a donkey. One might say that the
death of the donkey was not really a part of my action, but only a consequence of it—all that I *did*, really, was to shoot the donkey. But can I stop
there? The same reasoning suggests that the gun going off was really only an
effect of a yet more fundamental thing I did, namely squeezing the trigger.
But of course the trigger's displacement was itself a consequence of my
flexing my finger. If there is any end to this process at all, Austin says, it
must always be with some such "movement or movements with parts of our
body" as a finger flex.[17] Unless we are willing to accept the consequence that
the only proper actions we perform are movements of this kind, "minimal
physical actions," we will probably not find any principled criterion for
making the intuitive distinction we want.

But Austin thinks the situation is different if the action *is* "one of saying
something." In a case of saying something, there can be a principled distinction between the act and its consequences, a distinction that is often marked
linguistically:

> [*N*]*omenclature* affords us an assistance which it generally withholds in the
> case of "physical" actions. . . . We not merely do not use the notion of a
> minimum physical act (which is in any case doubtful) but we do not seem to
> have a class of names which distinguish physical acts from consequences:
> whereas with acts of saying something, the vocabulary of names for acts seems
> expressly to mark a break at a certain regular point between the act (our saying
> something) and its consequences (which are usually not the *saying* of any-
> thing), or at any rate a great many of them.[18]

Thus consider the following pairs of terms for things that we can do using
speech: "promise"/"convince;" "threaten"/"frighten"; "lie"/"deceive." The
first term in each pair signifies something that we do simply "*in saying
something;*" the second signifies something that we do only if our saying
something has certain consequences.

Austin did not go very far into the metaphysics of action, but he did say
that the reason we don't find a natural way to parse ordinary actions—to
detach a bodily movement proper, say, from its "immediate and natural
causes"—is that in these ordinary cases, the latter are *in pari materia* with the
former. Things are different in the case of acts of saying: "[W]hatever the
immediate and natural consequences of an act of saying something may be,
they are at least not normally further acts of saying. . . . So that we have here
a sort of regular natural break in the chain, which is wanting in the case of
physical actions, and which is associated with the special class of names for

illocutions."[19] These observations of Austin's connect with his stated purpose in *How to Do Things with Words*, which is to illuminate a special function of language that he feels has been neglected by his fellow philosophers. In Austin's view, philosophers had focused exclusively on the descriptive function of language, overlooking a certain *performative* function that language frequently takes on. Language can be used to say how things are, Austin allows, but it can also be used to *change* how things are. And this type of change occurs not merely as a consequence of information conveyed, but inherently, in virtue of a mere saying. When the officiant proclaims the couple before her to be "legally wed," the couple *is* married; the world has been changed. The officiant is not *describing* the couple's new status; she is *creating* it. Importantly, the creation of this new status is not a mere consequence of the officiant's pronouncement; the generation of the marital bond is inherent in the pronouncement itself.

The special kind of action that Austin wants to characterize is therefore bound up with the special kind of "effect" that the action can have, an effect that is constituted by the speech act itself. A merely descriptive use of language can have many effects: for example, my mechanic saying to me, "You need a new catalytic converter," can cause me to believe that I need an expensive repair, which can cause me to revise my vacation plans. It can also cause me to instruct the mechanic to go ahead and do what's needed. But the mechanic merely saying what he said doesn't constitute any of these things; all of these effects are contingently connected with the mechanic saying what he said. When the mechanic, however, having completed the work I ordered, says to me, "You owe me $1,500," he thereby makes it the case that I owe him that amount. My owing him that money is not a mere effect of him saying so—while I probably do form the belief that I owe him the money, the debt is there whether I acknowledge it or not. The existence of the debt is an effect, but a special kind of effect—a constitutive one—of the mechanic's speech.

There is thus a connection, for Austin, between the special kind of "doing things" with words that he wishes to isolate, and the peculiar, not-merely-causal relationship between doings of that sort and their characteristic effects. The connection, it emerges, comes through the notion of a *convention*. Thus, Austin writes that the first "necessary condition" for a use of language being performative is that "[t]here must exist an accepted conventional procedure having a certain conventional effect, that procedure to include the uttering of certain words by certain persons in certain circumstances."[20] This tells us two things at once: first, that the kind of fact that a speech act can bring into being is, of necessity, a *socially constructed* fact, and second, that the effects constitutive of a successful performative use of language are those effects *stipulated* within the convention to be the effects of a speech act of that type. Illocutionary effects are constitutively connected to the speech act that generates them, as per the founding convention. Perlocutionary effects occur simply as may be: their connection to the speech act is contingent, and their occurrence is dependent on factors outside the scope of the convention.

This suggests to me a test: to see if some particular effect of a speech act is illocutionary or perlocutionary—to see, that is, if the effect is constitutively connected or merely causally connected to the speech act in question—we should look to see if it is the kind of effect that can *only* be achieved by conventional means. So here is my main objection to Langton's view: subordination—at least the kind of subordination that Langton wants to link to pornography—fails the test. Even if pornography is a speech act, and even if it causes the subordination of women, the subordination cannot be an illocutionary effect of the pornographic speech act.

But have I read Austin correctly? Austin suggests something close to my test in the following passage:

> Certainly we can achieve the same perlocutionary sequels by non-conventional means . . . , means that are not conventional at all or not for that purpose; thus I can persuade some one by gently swinging a big stick. . . . Strictly speaking, there cannot be an illocutionary act unless the means employed are conventional, and so the means for achieving it non-verbally must be conventional.[21]

Arguably, the condition Austin is giving here is weaker than the one I am proposing. Austin appears to be leaving open that there can be effect-types such that they can be produced either by conventional or nonconventional means. Were there to be such effect-types, their instances would only be illocutionary if the conventional means were to be employed, but they could be genuinely illocutionary in those circumstances.

Langton holds that such effect-types do in fact exist, and that they are frequently implicated in those speech act types Austin calls "exercitives" and "verdictives." She writes: "[S]ome 'illocutionary effects' (if we call them that) can *only* be achieved through illocution, but they cannot be achieved by perlocutionary means—as, for example, when a judge gives sentence. However, in other cases, something can be achieved through performing an illocutionary act, *and* also by ordinary causal means."[22] She offers two examples. Here's the first:

> Suppose my team *loses the game*. One way that might happen is (primarily) illocutionary: the referee calls my shoving a foul. Another way that might happen is not illocutionary but (primarily) causal: I kick the ball between my team's own goalposts.[23]

And the second:

Suppose *women suffer economic disadvantage*. One way that might happen is illocutionary: enactment of law prevents women from owning property. Another way that might happen is simply causal: the cumulative effect of biased hiring practices means that women end up in lower paid jobs. [24]

These examples, Langton argues, show that the condition "'uniquely achievable via convention' won't do . . . to pick out an illocutionary 'effect.'" Hence, she concludes, my objection fails: "Subordination could in principle be achievable both ways: through conventional means, e.g., in apartheid legal enactment, in which case illocutionary; or non-conventionally, as the cumulative fall-out of small biased actions, in which case as a causal effect." [25]

Neither of Langton's examples, however, is apt. Both give us cases in which there is some state of affairs that can be brought via two different causal routes, one of which involves a speech act, the other of which does not. But the existence of such states of affairs is irrelevant to my test. I never denied, nor does my test require, that an illocutionary act can never have as *an* effect a condition that could be produced in other ways. Perlocutionary effects, after all, are causal consequences of illocutionary acts, and are certainly of the type that can be brought about by nonconventional means. [26] What Langton's examples *should* show, but don't, is that the effect in question, *when* produced by an illocutionary act, is an *illocutionary* effect of that illocutionary act, rather than just a downstream consequence.

The illocutionary act of enacting laws divesting women of property rights might contribute causally to the impoverishment of women (as in today's world, it certainly would), but it is not the same thing as impoverishing women. (Suppose, in some strange possible world, women hold a grossly disproportionate amount of wealth, which consists of two parts: property obtained through unjust means, but also well-earned salaries that are quite large. A revolutionary government which expropriated the women's property would not thereby impoverish them.)

In Langton's example, the referee certainly performs an illocutionary act in calling a foul. But the only illocutionary effect of that illocutionary act— the only state of affairs that the referee brings into existence simply in calling the foul—is the existence of the foul. There being a foul is not the same condition as the game being lost, any more than my having made a promise is the same condition as my having convinced my spouse. Certainly there being a foul *can* be one of the conditions that brings it about that the game is lost, but a foul on its own doesn't do it. There may be circumstances in which the foul being called, at the particular time it's called, results in the offending player's team losing the game, but those circumstances are only contingently connected to the circumstances that make the referee's speech act sufficient for the existence of the foul. [27]

However, here's a slightly different example that might have more of the structure Langton intended. Consider the verdictive speech act performed by an umpire in baseball when he yells "strike!" after a ball has been pitched. According to the rules of baseball, the umpire is authoritative with respect to the classification of pitches; if the pitch is *called* a strike by the umpire, then it *is* a strike. The umpire's call is thus a paradigm case of a verdictive speech act, and the pitch being a strike is a paradigm case of an illocutionary effect. However, the rules of baseball specify different ways for a pitch to be a strike. If the batter does not swing, then the status of the pitch is determined by the umpire's call, as explained above. But it's also the case that if the batter swings and misses, then the pitch is a strike. Swinging a bat in a path that fails to connect it with a ball is certainly not an illocutionary act—it is more like what Austin calls an "ordinary physical act." In that case, one might ask, don't we have an example of a type of condition—a pitch being a strike—that can be brought about either as the illocutionary effect of an illocutionary act (the umpire's call) or as a causal consequence of an ordinary physical act (the batter swinging and missing)?

No. Notice that the condition we are considering—a pitch being a strike—is a socially constructed condition. Outside the game of baseball, you can swing at balls with bats and miss to your heart's content, but you cannot thereby create (or earn or commit or incur) a strike. Now my test says only that to be an illocutionary effect, the effect must be of a type that can be brought about only through *conventional* means. It doesn't say that the conventional means has to be a speech act. I do not deny that an illocutionary effect could be of a kind that could be brought about by some nonillocutionary *but still conventional* means, like a gesture, or some other type of physical action. In short: it is the *conventions* of baseball that *make* swinging and missing count as a strike, just as it is the conventions of driving that make certain hand gestures count as signals, just as it is the conventions of promising that make certain utterances of "I promise . . ." count as promising. The *conventions* are what make the constitutive work possible.

In fact, I am being too concessive in allowing that the batter's swing-and-miss can constitute a strike. It is true that the rules of baseball specify that strikes are, in a sense, multiply realizable, so that there can be "called" strikes (batter doesn't swing) and "earned" strikes (batter swings and misses, or connects and fouls). However, there is also a meta-rule that says that nothing is a strike unless and until the umpire calls it one. Suppose that a batter does in fact swing, and misses the ball, but the umpire misperceives the batter's motions: he might think that the batter "checked" his swing. If the umpire, thinking this, calls the pitch a "ball," then—*abracadabra!*—it *is* a ball, the batter's swing notwithstanding.

There is, of course, room for this sort of discrepancy in the case of a called strike as well. If the umpire misperceives the placement of the pitch relative to the batter, thinking that it is inside the strike zone when in fact it is not, the pitch is still a strike if the umpire calls it a strike. It is the umpire's call, not the trajectory of the pitch, that makes a pitch a strike. True, we all understand what's meant when someone (watching a replay in slow motion, for example) says of a ball called a strike—"that wasn't a strike at all!" But all that can mean is that the ball did not in fact satisfy the conditions that the rules say *ought to guide the umpire's decision*. A decent umpire strives to make his decisions track the actual features of the pitches he is judging, and an umpire who makes too many mistakes will be fired. But it is still the case that it is the umpire saying "strike" that makes it so.

But why would the officials of baseball set things up in a way that allows for this kind of conflict, between the conditions that are supposed to obtain in order for something to be a strike, and the conditions that actually constitute something being a strike? Simple—the social demands of organized sport require there to be effective procedures for determining the moves that constitute the game. Specifying a set of objective conditions that must be satisfied isn't enough. If the conditions do not *naturally* determine a certain outcome—and objective conditions cannot *naturally* determine a socially constructed condition—then the determination of the outcome will require some kind of intervention by an intentional agent. In the typical case, the intervention is simply a matter of observation—the pitch must be *observed* to be inside or outside of the strike zone. But observations vary by observer and by perspective. With many different observations in play, there is the possibility of conflicting conclusions, and with that possibility, a need for an adjudicative procedure. One easy solution: vest authority for the adjudication in one, single observer—the umpire.

It is typical of verdictive and exercitive speech acts that they serve this sort of social function—the function of creating an effective way of adjudicating matters of fact that have, or that have been assigned, social importance. Since there is no effective procedure for the learning of empirical truths, any procedure that accomplishes the needed social function is going to be one that makes possible a conflict between the circumstances that are supposed to constitute the socially important state of affairs, and the circumstances that actually control the constitution of that state of affairs. The fact that efficacy generally requires us to vest the authority for such adjudications in one or a small number of persons only increases the likelihood of mismatch between the socially constructed condition and the objective condition the former is meant to track.

The general point becomes clearer if we consider a different example of a verdictive speech act: a jury finding a defendant "guilty." Clearly this is a speech act; but is the defendant's condition of being guilty a *conventional* effect of the jury's performing that speech act? We have an ordinary word, "guilty," that signifies a nonconventional relation (or at least a relation that entails the obtaining of some nonconventional relation). A person is guilty—in this ordinary sense—of committing a murder only if the person has killed someone.[28] Now at the time of trial, the defendant either has or has not killed someone, and it's beyond the power of the jury to alter that fact. What, then, can the jury accomplish in "finding the defendant guilty"? I contend that the jury can put the defendant into the condition of being *legally guilty*—a condition that is related to the condition of being guilty in the ordinary sense, the way a pitch that is called a strike is related to the condition of having passed through the strike zone. The condition of legal guilt is a social construction; it exists through and in virtue of the legal justice system. Legal guilt is supposed to track ordinary guilt; the jurors are supposed to exercise their conventional power to find the defendant legally guilty if and only if the evidence against the defendant is compelling. But even if the jurors follow this norm, it is possible for them to convict someone who is not guilty in the ordinary sense.

The situation is equally clear in the case of exercitive speech acts. When the judge sentences the convicted defendant, when the police officer places the suspect under arrest, when the duly designated functionary christens the ship—the conditions created by these acts of speech are all conditions ontologically dependent on the conventions that establish and define them. There may be a variety of conventions that could have been chosen to bring about the same legal conditions as being under sentence, being arrested, being named.[29] But none of these conditions could obtain without there being *some* convention or other, making it the case that certain sayings or actions constitute certain conditions.

Langton struggles a bit with the conditions brought about by the performance of verdictive speech acts. In "Pornography's Authority?"[30] she first characterizes the difference between verdictives and exercitives in terms of "direction of fit":[31]

> A verdictive is an authoritative judgment that something *is* so. An exercitive is an authoritative decision "that something *is to be so*." Both kinds of illocution require authority, but there is a difference in their direction of fit. A verdictive aims to fit the world; an exercitive aims for the world to fit the words. A verdictive purports to map a reality. ("The ball is out.") An exercitive purports to create a reality. ("You're out." "You're fired.")[32]

But Langton quickly acknowledges that this direction-of-fit characterization doesn't quite work. If verdictives merely aim to fit the world, what does the umpire accomplish in issuing his call, beyond what anyone accomplishes in simply describing the events of the game?

> When someone authoritatively says, "this is how it is," that can be a verdictive judgement [sic] that something is so, and it is then "taken as being that way":

verdictives construct part of reality, in making something *count* as thus and so. . . . If the ball is called "Out" by the umpire, it is "taken as being out," *counts* as out: the score adjusts itself to fit the umpire's words. There is something interesting here: for in this latter respect a verdictive has, so to speak, an exercitive dimension.[33]

Langton cannot have it both ways. If the condition to which the verdictive is meant to conform—the ball rolling past a certain line—is the kind of condition that cannot be brought about simply by an umpire saying it is so, then it will not be the sort of condition that the issuance of a verdictive can bring about. But if the condition *is* one that can be brought about simply by the umpire saying it is so—the ball being "out"—then that condition has to be of a different type than the one to which the verdictive aims to conform.

Distinguishing socially constructed conditions—"being a strike," "being out"—from the nonconventional factual conditions the social constructions are meant to track gives us the framework we need to explain what performative speech acts *do*. (Remember the *special* kind of doing something that Austin strove to characterize.) Once this distinction is made, it is clear that my original test holds: any effect, condition, or state of affairs that can be brought about simply by the performance of an illocutionary act, must be of a type that can only be brought about by conventional means. No authority on earth can make it the case that some ball follows some particular trajectory, *just by saying so*. Making a struck ball into a *foul*, however, is another matter; *that* the umpire can accomplish simply by declaring it to be so.

So now, what about "subordination," the condition which Langton claims can be an illocutionary effect of the pornographic speech act? It's clear that the kind of subordination Langton is interested in, and the kind MacKinnon was concerned with, is a condition that will fail my test. Subordination is not a convention-bound condition. (If it is in any sense "socially constructed," it is so only in the causal sense—it takes social interaction of some sort in order for subordination to be produced.) My test directly entails, then, that subordination is not the sort of condition that can be brought about merely by someone saying so. "Subordinating" cannot, therefore, be a kind of illocutionary act; subordination cannot be an illocutionary effect of any speech act.

But this argument may seem too quick. Aren't there, after all, forms of subordination that *do* pass my test? Consider subordination in the context of such institutions as the military, where ranks are set out by law. When a person enlists in the U.S. Army, he or she becomes a private, and thereby becomes subordinate to corporals, sergeants, lieutenants, and all the other officers up the chain of command. In the civilian world, the same thing can happen with jobs in hierarchically structured organizations. When I accepted a job as a chambermaid, I became subordinate to the supervising maid; she controlled my schedule and assigned me specific tasks while I was at work.

When I accepted an appointment as a professor at a university, I became subordinate to a department chair, a dean, a provost, and various other policy-making officers.

It's important to note, however, that in all these cases, the nature and scope of the subordination is defined and constrained by the laws or practices that partly constitute the institutions involved. A U.S. Army sergeant may order a private to scrub the latrines or to do fifty sit-ups, but he may not order a private to have sex with him. My maid-supervisor could order me to scrub the latrines, but not to do fifty sit-ups. My department chair cannot order me to do either of those things, but he can assign me eight-o'clock classes. (For the record: I'd rather scrub latrines.)

The kind of subordination we are talking about in all these cases is, I submit, a *conventional* form of subordination, akin to the socially constructed condition I earlier called "legal guilt." Conventional subordination is, I think, a condition that *can* be brought into being through the performance of a speech act. But this is not the only kind of subordination there is. Conventional subordination depends on people standing in conventionally defined relations to each other. The nonconventional form of subordination is a condition that depends on the de facto distribution of liberties, opportunities, and standing among persons; it is (to a first approximation) the condition of being *effectively treated as inferior* by others.

Unlike the relation between legal guilt and ordinary guilt, there does not in general exist—nor is there typically meant to exist—a *systematic* relation between conventional subordination and de facto subordination. I don't mean to deny that certain conventional roles also do track relations of de facto subordination. Some marriage ceremonies still involve a woman vowing to "love, honor, and obey" her husband, and the segregationist laws of the United States were designed to express and make effective the subordinating attitudes and opinions of racist whites. What I am saying is that the general point of our having such a condition as conventional subordination is not to track or enforce relations of de facto subordination. Various forms of conventional subordination serve the worthy purpose of organizing social life for the benefit of all. I am conventionally subordinate to my department chair, not because I am, or am regarded as being, a person of lesser worth than my chair. His and my hierarchical relationship exists because of a long-standing consensus about the utility of a certain way of organizing academic institutions, not because it affords a way of concretizing invidious judgments.[34]

In general, we can characterize the difference between conventional subordination and de facto subordination in this way: the first is a matter of *authority* and the second is a matter of *power*. Authority and power both have their limits, but the limits of authority are determined by the conventions that set it up. My department chair may or may not view me with respect. But whatever his personal opinion may be, his behavior toward me is governed by our contractual relationship. He is authorized to criticize and sanction me if I fail to perform my duties, but not to insult me, mock me, or physically strike me. Whether he has the power to do any of these things, however, is a different matter, and not one that a mere contract can confer.

Now there are, to be sure, forms of authority that are not tied to any particular conventions. The best example of such authority is *epistemic* authority. Epistemic authorities are individuals whose testimony on certain subjects is, if not necessarily accepted as true, at least accorded a high degree of respect. (Epistemic authorities can disagree with one another.) Now of course there are socially accepted markers of epistemic authority—diplomas, certificates, and licenses—and conventions surrounding the placement of such markers—graduations, investitures, and ordinations. But one can also become an epistemic authority in other, less ceremonious ways. A person who demonstrates a good track record in a certain area may simply come to be recognized as someone who knows—witness the rise of blogger Nate Silver as an election prognosticator. Unfortunately, though, the good track record is not necessary; it is the social recognition that actually constructs the authority, and there is nothing to guarantee that social recognition follows actual knowledge or expertise.[35]

What are the powers that attend epistemic authority? The chief power is the power to affect people's beliefs. In the cases of conventionally certified epistemic authority, there will be some delineation of the domains in which the person is to be regarded as authoritative: a license to practice medicine does not certify its bearer as an authority on gardening. These delineations are meant partly as information for the epistemic consumer—"the licensee is reliable on matters X, Y, and Z"—and partly as quality control. If a doctor fails as a medical expert, she is subject to sanctions. This, if not simple concern for her patients, will discourage the doctor from making authoritative claims outside her area of expertise. But in the cases where epistemic authority is conferred, as it were, by social acclaim, there are no boundaries. A political pundit gains epistemic authority when he gains a following, and becomes an expert in any subject on which his followers seek his opinion. This can amount to a great deal of power.

Langton contends that pornographers have epistemic authority in this sense. The creators and purveyors of pornography are regarded by many men (and boys) as experts on sex, and because they are regarded as experts, they are successful in getting their audiences to believe what they say.[36] But shaping the beliefs and attitudes of men is not the full extent of the power of the pornographers. Insofar as the members of pornography's audience are powerful—insofar as pornography exists within a patriarchal society—the consumers of pornography have the ability to shape reality itself. Expecting certain behavior from women, they can coerce women into displaying it. Women who cannot be coerced directly can be shaped indirectly, through a culture of indulgence and shaming that makes it difficult for such women to project their own views of who they are and what they want. Pornography, in this way, confers on men who make it and men who consume it, the power to "make it so by saying it is so."

I do not here want to challenge any part of this causal story.[37] What I do want to point out however, is that we have come very far from the idea that pornography is a verdictive or an exercitive *speech act*, and that the kind of "authority" that confers upon an umpire the power to make a pitch into a strike, or that gives a judge the power to sentence a person to ten years in jail, is of a piece with the kind of authority and power we have just been discussing. Even admitting that pornographers have the kind of epistemic authority that Langton claims is accorded them, the only power they have is to make consumers of pornography *believe* certain things. That is, they have the power to *convince*. But convincing is a paradigm case of *perlocution*. It is a wholly contingent matter whether some act of arguing, enjoining—or promising—has its desired effect. It is not something that can be done "in the saying;" rather it is something that is done by means of speech.

Langton does not deny that the way in which the umpire's saying "makes it so" is different from the way pornography's testimony "makes it so." But from this she simply concludes that there are two different ways "in which verdictive saying so can sometimes make it so, two ways in which verdictive speech can 'construct' reality." Drawing language from MacKinnon, Langton continues: "The first is by making it *count* as so; 'When the powerful say "this is how it is," it is *taken to be* that way.' The second is by sometimes making it, in part, really so; 'When the powerful say "this is how it is," *the world arranges itself to affirm* what the powerful say.'"[38] Here Langton has simply abandoned any distinction between authority and power. Significantly, it is *power* that MacKinnon is talking about in the passage Langton quotes. MacKinnon is pointing to a *causal* feedback loop that is vitally important to the construction and maintenance of the gender hierarchy. I positively affirm the existence of such loops, and I do not deny that pornography plays a role in their creation.[39] But that much can be established without any appeal to Austin.

I am not the first person to criticize Langton's treatment of "authority" in her discussion of pornography.[40] Green, Butler, and Bauer have all argued that pornography lacks the kind of authority it would need to enable a verdictive or exercitive act of speech. But I want to connect Langton's failure to distinguish authority from power to her failure to recognize the difference in ontological type between the socially constructed conditions that can be brought about by verdictives and exercitives from the nonconventional conditions to which such speech acts are meant to be responsive. To make this connection, I must return to the text. We'll see that what Austin has to say about authority and its role in the performance of speech acts bolsters my case against Langton's idea that de facto subordination could be a kind of illocutionary act.

In general, Austin tells us, the conventions that constitute and govern speech acts serve also to fix what he calls the "felicity conditions" for the performance of the speech act in question. Langton acknowledges this. But she neglects the fact that Austin divides these conditions into two types. The first type of conditions are those that are strictly necessary; if any of these conditions is violated, then no speech act has been performed. Conditions of the other type ("Γ-conditions") are not necessary to the speech act having been performed, but violations of these conditions render the act "unhappy" or defective.

The distinction can be illustrated nicely by the example of *promising*. In order for a person to make a promise by saying "I promise . . .", it is strictly necessary that the person understand the words that he or she is uttering; without such comprehension, no utterance of those words constitutes the making of a promise. However, it is not necessary for a person to make a promise that he or she intends to keep it; one can make an insincere promise. One is not supposed to do this; the practice of promise making only has a point if promise makers generally intend to do what they have promised to do. But the insincerity does not destroy the promise, or prevent it from having been made. If the promise is *seriously* made—that is, if the promiser knowingly follows the formula for promising, in circumstances where the promiser's audience can be expected to take a promise to have been made— then the promiser incurs the obligation distinctive to promising, whether or not he or she intends to discharge it.

The distinction between necessary felicity conditions and Γ-type felicity conditions provides a vocabulary for characterizing the cases I discussed earlier, in which a conventional condition fails to coincide with the ordinary, objective condition it is supposed to track. The obtaining of the ordinary condition, in such cases, is one of the Γ-type felicity conditions for a perfor- mance of the speech act in question. Thus, for example, it is a Γ-type felicity condition of the performance of the speech act of finding a defendant guilty that the defendant *be* guilty in the ordinary sense. But if the jury errs, and "finds guilty" an innocent person, that unlucky person, though innocent in the ordinary sense, is still *legally* guilty. The verdictive speech act has been performed, just unhappily.

In the case of exercitive and verdictive speech acts, the necessary felicity conditions will always include a specification of the authority associated with the speech acts in question. In the U.S. legal system, judges and juries are the only agents who can exercise the power of creating (what I've called) legal guilt. The prosecuting lawyer may *say* "the defendant is guilty," but he cannot mean by these words that the defendant is legally guilty—he lacks the authority to say so, and hence also the authority to make it so. The umpire in baseball is authorized to declare pitches to be balls or strikes. Although the outraged fan can scream the words "that was a strike!" he or she cannot mean by those words what the umpire can mean. She has no authority in the matter.

Authority (in connection with speech acts) involves a certain kind of power, but the power so conferred should be distinguished from power in general. An officer of the law has the power to clap a suspect in handcuffs, but so does anyone who can get their hands on a pair of handcuffs. What the officer possesses that an ordinary citizen lacks is the *authority* to handcuff.[41] It is that authority that makes a particular act of saying "you are under arrest" into an actual arrest, and it is that same authority that makes it *legitimate* for the officer to exercise the power of cuffing the suspect. It is not, however, the officer's authority that gives the power to handcuff; if he or she lacked that before, becoming an officer won't provide it. Likewise, with respect to education, anyone literate can write an "A" on an essay paper, but only an authorized teacher can assign a grade by doing that.

The distinction between authority and power is perfectly coordinate with the distinction I drew earlier, between conventional conditions and "ordinary" conditions. The power that is conferred on someone who satisfies the conventionally specified conditions for being authoritative is, essentially, the power to bring about the conventional conditions constitutively connected with the speech act type. In other words, the power conferred by the governing conventions of a speech act is the power to bring about only the *illocutionary* effects of the speech act. Insofar as there is some regular connection between those illocutionary effects and further perlocutionary effects, the authority conferred by the governing convention also confers the power to bring about these further effects. But such power as that is not inherent in the authority connected with the speech act; it is contingently connected to it. If my assigning a poor grade to a student causes the student to study harder, then my power to assign grades gives me, de facto, the power to change the work habits of my student. But if the student is indifferent to the grade, my power extends only as far as my authority does—to the generation of a conventional state of affairs.

This brings us to another important feature of Austin's account of illocution that concerns the distinction between authority and power for which I've been arguing. Austin insists that conventions are only binding upon those who willingly participate in the practices that the conventions define and govern. The constituting conventions, he says, must be "accepted." And Austin is very clear that "acceptance" in his sense has these several features pertinent to our discussion: first, it is *intentional*, second, it is *normative*, and third, it is *voluntary*.

When I say that acceptance is, for Austin, an intentional matter, I mean that it depends on the attitudes of the individuals involved, and not merely on their behavior, or the behavior of others toward them. Austin writes: "[F]or a procedure to be *accepted* involves more than for it merely to be the case that it is *in fact generally used*, even by the persons now concerned."[42] Accordingly, Austin emphasizes that the question of whether "there exists" an accepted conventional procedure of a certain sort cannot be reduced to facts about things done and said, but must involve something normative, something like endorsement: "*Above all* all must not be put into flat, factual circumstances; for this is subject to the old objection to deriving an 'ought' from an 'is.' (Being accepted is *not* a circumstance in the right sense.)"[43] Acceptance, finally, is a *voluntary* matter: "[I]t must remain open for anyone to reject any procedure . . . even one that he has already hitherto accepted."[44] It follows that the authority vested in someone by virtue of some conventional practice is "authoritative" only for those who accept the practice, and thus only for those who endorse the authority. I can throw balls around any way that I like; if I am not playing baseball (and indeed, if I am not participating in an appropriately sanctioned game), the umpire has no authority over me.[45]

Power differs from Austinian authority in every one of these respects: Power does not in general depend on anyone's intentional states (although it may, depending on what the power is a power to do). Power involves nothing essentially normative and can often be characterized completely in terms of "flat, factual circumstances." And finally, a person can have power over another with or without that person's consent or endorsement.

Langton essentially inverts the Austinian connection between authority and power. She treats power as *evidence* of authority:

> Does pornographic speech have the authority required to substantiate MacKinnon's claim [that pornography *is* subordination]? Is this crucial felicity condition satisfied? These are not really questions to be settled from the philosopher's armchair. To answer them, one needs to know about the role pornographers occupy as authoritative speakers about the facts, or supposed facts of sex.[46]

Now I'm all for getting out of the armchair (or at least for e-mailing questions to someone who does), but Langton is misidentifying the empirical issue here. It's true that I may need to learn something about prevailing conventions in order to figure out who has the authority ("which side does the prosecution sit on?") and what it is they have the authority to do ("can the prosecutor determine which evidence is admissible?"). But if I am *within* the convention—if I *accept* the convention, in Austin's sense—then the question who has authority *should be* a question I can answer from the armchair. Langton thinks that we need to determine whether pornographers are *effective* in promulgating a certain view of sex, whether they have the *power* to get people to believe them. I completely agree that this is not a matter that can be settled a priori, but it is also not a matter that has anything to do with the sort of authority that enables illocutionary acts. Finding out who is looked to for information about sex is one of the "flat, factual circumstances" that Austin explicitly denies is relevant to the question of the acceptance of a convention.

Putting this all together: the kind of subordination Langton is concerned with is clearly what I've called de facto subordination—the kind of condition that is determined by power relations and not constituted by the speech acts of conventionally authorized speakers. Subordination of this kind is therefore not a type of illocutionary act. Pornography may or may not be a speech act, but if it is, subordination can be only one of its perlocutionary effects.

But let's step back a moment. Maybe I am being too rigid in insisting that pornography fit the precise conditions that Austin articulated in defining the notion of an "illocutionary" act. Can't we expand the notion of "illocution" a bit? And thus expanded, isn't the notion aptly suggestive of the way pornography works? And finally, isn't the important point in all this *whether* pornography subordinates women? If it does, why does it matter whether it does so via illocutionary constitution or by perlocutionary causation?

Langton, in her response to me, raises all these questions. She suggests that the real difference between the two of us may be temperamental: I am a "methodological pessimist, who doubts that philosophy of language has much to offer the political theorist;"[47] Langton is more optimistic. Langton speculates, further, that this dour outlook has affected my interpretation of Austin. Because I am a glass-half-empty kind of gal, I read Austin in a blinkered way: I take the "paradigm" of an illocutionary act to be "the ceremonial performance, where a speaker enacts a move in a ritual." Langton concedes that there are such cases "in Austin" and she allows that "we are entitled to mine his work as we see fit,"[48] the implication being that there is considerably more interpretative leeway than I permit. But Langton charges that I have lost sight of the issue that is really important: according to her, I think "it doesn't matter whether pornography subordinates, or women are silenced."[49] I am disappointed by the first two charges, and wounded by the third. I care very deeply about the ways in which cultural productions shape perceptions, beliefs, and desires among both men and women. What I reject is the equivalence between the matter as Langton states it first, and the formulation she gives subsequently: "more precisely, it doesn't matter whether pornography is an illocution that subordinates, and whether women suffer illocutionary disablement."[50]

The claim that pornography is an illocutionary act of subordination was supposed to do some serious legal work; it was supposed to draw a distinction between pornography's being inherently harmful and its being only contingently harmful. If the notion of illocution is to do that work, then there must be clear criteria to apply to a case in point. It is not enough that there merely be some resemblance between some paradigm case of Austin's and the case of pornography.[51] I have argued that Austin's work does offer clear criteria for illocution, and that "subordination" does not satisfy them. If I have made a mistake there, I'll be glad to be corrected. But I see no point in loosening the notion of "illocution" just in order to make pornography fit. The loosening blurs, and thus abandons, the very distinction that MacKinnon's analysis depended upon.

The upshot: MacKinnon's attempts notwithstanding, the debate about pornography has not been transformed. We face the same issues we faced before: Does pornography harm women? How does it harm women? How can those harms be prevented? J. L. Austin has nothing to tell us about these questions, and it's a bit surprising that anyone thought he would.

SILENCING: REFUSALS VERSUS ACTS OF REFUSING

I would like to turn, finally, to the claim that pornography *silences* women. Although this claim is independent of the claim that pornography *subordinates* women, there are some connections among the issues they raise.

First, as I've already noted, the claim that pornography silences women is potentially in tension with the claim that pornography is an illocutionary act of subordination. If silencing is the means through which the subordination is accomplished, then subordination cannot be an illocutionary act. This result does not depend on my test for distinguishing (what I call) the illocutionary effects of a speech act from its other effects. It follows simply from Austin's characterization of perlocutionary effects as "what we bring about or achieve *by* saying something, such as convincing, persuading, deterring, and even, misleading or surprising."[52] Clearly, any effect of a speech that requires a mediating mechanism must be perlocutionary.

I am not, however, concerned at this point with the status of the subordinating effect of the pornographic speech act. Rather, I want to explore the implications of the claim that pornography—by whatever means—disrupts uptake of a woman's refusal, bringing to bear some of the points from the previous discussion.

"Uptake" is defined by Austin in the following way: "An effect must be achieved on the audience if the illocutionary act is to be carried out. How should we best put it here? And how can we limit it? Generally the effect amounts to bringing about the understanding of the meaning and of the force of the locution."[53] A *refusal* appears to be a kind of performative speech act; as such, it requires uptake in order for it to be successfully carried out. Normally, this is not a problem; a person says "No," her audience understands, and that's that.

According to Langton and Hornsby, however, the conditions that are created by pornography are abnormal. Pornography causes men who consume it to form certain false beliefs about women, and these beliefs render men incapable of understanding a woman's speech when she refuses sex. A man might come to believe, for example, that women often enjoy "rough" sex and so make a pretense of resistance in order to spur a potential partner on to greater and greater displays of physical force. If such a man attempts to have sex with a woman who does not want to have sex with him, he will be incapable of understanding her speech or her behavior as indicating a refusal. "No" for him will have ceased to mean no. In that case, the woman's attempt to refuse will not be understood; her act of speaking will have received no uptake. It will be as if she has said nothing; she will have been silenced.

I do not deny that such situations can and do arise. Neither do I doubt that a steady diet of certain kinds of pornography may produce in the men who follow them a seriously distorted idea about what women want, and about how they express their own needs and desires. I do not even object to analyzing such situations in term of speech acts and "uptake." But I do not think that such an analysis will prove useful in the long run.

I first want to suggest that the kind of disabling present in the example given above is an instance of a more general form of communicative failure, and one that the Austinian framework cannot characterize on its own. What we need is the notion of a linguistic *signal.* Communicative failures can arise whenever some background feature of the communicative situation removes the *informational* content of a verbal sign. That is, the failure of uptake in the cases Langton and Hornsby have in mind is actually a special case of a more general phenomenon. Consider the case of a superior—a teacher, perhaps, or an employer—who sexually propositions his subordinate. Here the problem is not with the uptake of a refusal, but rather with the significance of a person saying "yes." The problem here is not that the subordinate cannot perform the speech act of consenting. She certainly can: she can do it by uttering the words that conventionally convey consent. The problem is that her performing such an act under circumstances in which she stands to lose something by refusing makes her verbal signal *equivocal*; her utterance of "yes" fails to carry the information that signal generally carries about the state of mind of the person who has uttered it.

In one view of the relation between mind and language—a view that some call simple-minded, but that I call plausible—language serves, or can serve, to express mental states. In this view, the fact that certain words are typically used to express certain particular mental states makes it possible for a hearer to take the utterance of those words as *evidence* about what the speaker has in mind. However, there are situations in which the particulars make it impossible to tell whether the words being uttered carry the information they are normally taken to be conveying. So in my example above, of the superior propositioning the subordinate, the subordinate's "yes" could signify either the state of mind that it conventionally signifies—her unconditional willingness to accept the proposition—or it could signify merely a rational calculation that she would be harmed by saying no. Here the subordinate's problem is not that there would be no uptake of her refusal—it is that she has no means of signaling *unqualified* consent.

Let's consider, in this light, the difference between *refusing* and *performing the speech act of refusal*. Refusing, I contend, is an inner, mental act. It is something one can do all by one's self, and without making any overt sign that one has done it. Suppose that I receive a letter offering me a certain amount of money for a car that I want to sell. I can, immediately upon receipt of the letter, make up my mind to reject the offer. I can do this without speaking or writing any words, shaking my head, or doing anything else that would be observable by a second party. But in this case, the second party has a legitimate interest in knowing what I have decided. I also have an interest in letting the second party know that I don't want the deal—I don't want the second party to renew this offer, or maybe I want him to try a higher offer. It is thus in our mutual interest for me to perform the speech act of refusal—for me to employ the conventional signs for "no" in indicating to the would-be buyer that I refuse his offer.

Here, in the performance of an act of refusal, all of the Austinian conditions have a point. A refusal, as opposed to a "refusing," must be performed before an audience,[54] and it must involve some outward manifestation of my inner state. There may be conditions on the identity of the audience. It may be that I can only perform a refusal in the presence of the person who made the demand. But at the very least, I must make the refusal in the presence of someone who understands the words that I am uttering, and the speech act that I am performing by means of uttering those words. It is clear, at any rate, that my speech act will be thwarted—it will be "unhappy," as Austin would say—if my audience cannot hear me (she has turned off her hearing aid), if she cannot understand English (or my accent), or if she does not realize that I am performing the speech act of refusal (she thinks that I am merely reporting an inner state of resolution).

But once all of this is in place, we can see that there is room for the kind of distinction I drew earlier, between a socially constructed conventional condition, and a de facto condition that the former is meant to track. Refus*als* are meant to track refus*ings*—or to put things more perspicuously, conventional signs of refusal are meant to be expressive of inner states of refusing. The conventional condition of refusal exists so that we can achieve certain kinds of social effects that we could not achieve otherwise. So, for example, it is useful in the formation of contracts for there to be an overt act that stands for and can legally be taken as evidence of actual consent. There are even, in many such cases, a requirement that *uptake* be overtly signaled.

In the case of sports, the vestiture of authority in individual umpires or referees serves partly to solve a certain coordination problem: whose perspective will prevail? In those cases, there is nothing morally important about the tracking relations between the umpire's calls and the de facto conditions to which the calls are meant to conform. In the case of interpersonal interaction, the tracking relation between conventional condition and de facto condition are morally serious. If someone signs a contract under threat, and this is discovered, the contract becomes void: the actual state of voluntariness—not merely the outward sign—is a condition on the validity of the contract.

Under certain circumstances, however, the presence or absence of an outward sign is probative. If I can produce a document, signed by you, saying that you gave me your car, I may be forgiven for removing it from your driveway, even if it turns out later that (unbeknownst to me) your signature was extorted.

So now the issue is—what should the law be concerned with in the case of sexual relations? Surely the morally relevant conditions are the conditions of de facto consent or refusing. That is, what the law should aim to preserve is the right of any individual to refuse to have sex with another person. One possible approach would be to try to guarantee the ability of every individual to perform a speech act of *refusal*. But given the requirement of "uptake" this approach would be futile. The law cannot mandate that, every time I try to communicate, there will be an audience suitable for the performance of the speech act I mean to perform. A depraved audience can disrupt uptake in the way we've seen. But so can an audience who doesn't speak my language, an audience who cannot hear, or, in case I speak a signed language, by an audience who *only* hears.

A different approach would be to simply require that both (or all) parties to sexual congress de facto consent to the act in question. In that case, a person charged with sexual assault would bear the burden of demonstrating de facto consent. For these purposes, proof of overt acts that conventionally convey consent *might* be probative; they *might* provide evidence of innocence. But there also might be, as in the case of the superior who propositions his subordinate, conditions that render such conventional acts nonprobative. In that case, even if the subordinate performed the speech act of consenting, it would be the fact that the speech act *might* have been "unhappy" that would be of concern to the law.

In sum: it may be that pornography silences women by disrupting uptake of their attempted refusals. It is unclear, at best, what would follow from this in the realm of policy. A more general policy, directed at safeguarding a person's right to *refuse*, and predicated on a more general analysis of the relation between inner thoughts and outward conventional signs, would be preferable.

NOTES

Thanks to Kent Bach, Nancy Bauer, Sally Haslanger, Ishani Maitra, Rae Langton, Joseph Levine, and Georges Rey for helpful conversation or correspondence about the issues in this paper.

1. See for example Ann Garry, "Pornography and Respect for Women," *Social Theory and Practice* 4 (1978): 395–421, and Helen Longino, "Pornography, Oppression, and Freedom: A Closer Look," in *Take Back the Night*, ed. Laura Lederer (New York: William Morrow, 1980), 40–54.

2. Significantly, Easterbrook stated clearly that the court "accept[ed] the premises of [the] legislation. Depictions of subordination tend to perpetuate subordination." However, he continued, this court-accepted fact "simply demonstrates the power of pornography as speech. All of [the] unhappy effects [of pornography] depend on mental intermediation." See *American Booksellers Association, Inc. v. Hudnut*, 771 F.2d 323 (1985), Boston College website,http://www.bc.edu/bc_org/avp/cas/comm/free_speech/hudnut.html (accessed 17 Mar. 2014).

3. *American Booksellers Association, Inc. v. Hudnut*, 598 F. Supp. 1316 (1984). See Casetext.com,https://casetext.com/case/american-booksellers-ass39n-inc-v-hudnut/#.UyIA4V7e7Oo (accessed 17 Mar. 2014).

4. Rae Langton, "Speech Acts and Unspeakable Acts," *Sexual Solipsism* (Oxford: Oxford University Press, 2009), 26.

5. This move does not address all the objections that can be made to the claim that pornography is an act (see Jennifer Saul, "Pornography, Speech Acts, and Context," *Proceedings of the Aristotelian Society* 106, no. 1 [June 2006]; 229–48, for discussion), but it does establish that there is no conceptual barrier to something's being both speech and an act.

6. Provided that certain contextual conditions are satisfied. I will say more about contextual conditions shortly.

7. Langton, "Speech Acts and Unspeakable Acts"; Jennifer Hornsby, "Feminism in Philosophy of Language: Communicative Speech Acts", in *Cambridge Companion to Feminism in Philosophy*, ed. Miranda Fricker and Jennifer Hornsby (Cambridge: Cambridge University Press, 2000), 87–106. I have given a detailed critique of Hornsby's view of silencing in my "Is There a 'Feminist' Philosophy of Language?" in *Out of the Shadows*, ed. Anita Superson and Sharon Crasnow (Oxford: Oxford University Press, 2012), 245–86.

8. I'll defer, for the moment, the question of the relationship between *subordinating* and *silencing*. If subordination is accomplished *by* silencing, then subordination cannot be the *illocutionary* act-type, and that might pose a problem for the view that subordination is an illocutionary effect of pornography.

9. These conditions are one type of what Austin calls "felicity conditions." I'll explain felicity conditions in more detail in what follows.

10. J. L. Austin, *How to Do Things with Words*, 2nd edition, ed. J. O. Urmson and Marina Sbisà (Cambridge, MA: Harvard University Press, 1975), 116–17.

11. This analysis has also been articulated and defended by Jennifer Hornsby ("Speech Acts and Pornography," *Women's Philosophy Review*, no. 10 [Nov. 1993]: 38–45), Ishani Maitra ("Silencing Speech," *Canadian Journal of Philosophy*, Vol. 39, no. 2, [June 2009]: 309–38), and Caroline West (Rae Langton and Caroline West, "Scorekeeping in a Pornographic Language Game," *Australasian Journal of Philosophy* 77 [1999]: 303–19).

12. Saul, "Pornography, Speech Acts, and Context."

13. Louise Antony, "Against Langton's Illocutionary Treatment of Pornography," *Jurisprudence* 2, no. 2 (2012): 387–401.

14. Although I think a case can be made that the requirement of uptake sits ill with Austin's overall theory of speech acts.

15. Austin, *How to Do Things with Words*, 111.

16. Austin, *How to Do Things with Words*, 111–12.

17. Austin, *How to Do Things with Words*, 112.

18. Austin, *How to Do Things with Words*, 112.

19. Austin, *How to Do Things with Words*, 14.

20. Austin, *How to Do Things with Words* 14.

21. Austin, *How to Do Things with Words*, 119. See also from Lecture X: "Illocutionary acts are conventional acts: perlocutionary acts are *not* conventional" (Austin, *How to Do Things with Words*, 121, emphasis in original).

22. Rae Langton "Replies to Jurisprudence Symposium on Sexual Solipsism" (Symposium in *Jurisprudence* 2 [2011]: 379–440). Quotation from Langton's manuscript, 8.

23. Langton, "Replies" (Langton manuscript 8).

24. Langton, "Replies" (Langton manuscript 8–9; italics in original).

25. Langton, "Replies" (Langton manuscript 9).

26. For example, I might be able to convince my spouse that the garbage will be taken out by promising to take it out, but he could also become convinced simply by seeing me carrying the trash toward the door. But of course in the first case *being convinced* is simply a perlocutionary effect of my illocutionary act of promising.

27. Austin says that "the illocutionary act and even the locutionary act too involve conventions: compare them with the act of doing obeisance. It is obeisance only because it is conventional and it is done only because it is conventional. Compare also the distinction between kicking a wall and kicking a goal" (Austin, *How to Do Things with Words*, 107).

28. While it may be possible to kill someone by speaking, the death would not, even in such a case, be a *conventional* effect of the speech. Maybe I speak at such a high volume and pitch that I trigger a heart attack, so that it's the physical effects of my utterance that produce the effect. Even if the lethal mechanism involves the victim understanding what I said—maybe the heart attack comes from the shocking news I deliver—the death is a contingent and natural effect, not a conventional one.

29. I don't have a general account of the individuation conditions for socially constructed types, but I trust the intuitive idea is clear.

30. Rae Langton, "Pornography's Authority? Response to Leslie Green," *Sexual Solipsism*, 89–102.

31. This is not a notion that Austin employs, but is rather one introduced by John Searle in his development of speech act theory, as Langton acknowledges. See "Pornography's Authority?" note 10, 93–94.

32. Langton, "Pornography's Authority?" 93–94.

33. Langton, "Pornography's Authority?" 94.

34. Some people will challenge the idea that hierarchical forms of organization can *ever* serve the interests of everyone involved. They might point to such studies as the Stanford Prison Experiment as evidence that merely having people pretend to stand in a subordinating position with respect to others induces relations of de facto subordination. I do not deny that this can and does happen. I say only that it need not, particularly if deliberate safeguards are built into the institutional practice. The matter deserves a great deal more discussion, however, which I cannot provide here. But see Rebecca Hanrahan and Louise Antony, "Because I Said So: Toward a Feminist Theory of Authority," *Hypatia* 20, no. 4 (Fall 2005), 59–79, for an elaboration of the position I'm taking here.

35. See Silver's discussion of the poor success rates of economic and political pundits in his book, *The Signal and the Noise* (New York: Penguin Press, 2012).

36. Langton is clear that it is an empirical question whether this is true, and cites a large body of research that supports her claim that viewing pornography induces in men false beliefs about women and dehumanizing attitudes toward them.

37. Although I will note that this view is at odds with the view—which Langton elsewhere espouses—that women do not, as a matter of fact, have the desires that pornography attributes to them.

38. Langton, "Pornography's Authority?" 95–96 (quotations and italics in original).

39. For a compelling description of the causal efficacy of stereotypes and gender norms in producing facts that seem to confirm those stereotypes and justify those norms, see Marilyn Frye's essay, "Sexism," in her book *The Politics of Reality: Essays in Feminist Theory* (New York: Crossing Press, 1983), 17–40. And for a detailed and persuasive account of the connection between the ontology and the epistemology of social construction, see Sally Haslanger, "On Being Objective and Being Objectified," in Louise Antony and Charlotte Witt, *A Mind of*

One's Own: Feminist Essays on Reason and Objectivity (Boulder, CO: Westview Press: 1993), 209–53.

40. Leslie Green, "Pornographizing, Subordinating, Silencing," in *Censorship and Silencing: Practices of Cultural Regulation*, ed. Robert Post (Los Angeles: Getty Research Institute, 1998), 285–311; Judith Butler, *Excitable Speech: A Politics of the Performative* (New York and London: Routledge, 1997); Nancy Bauer, "Pornutopia," *n+1* 5 (Winter 2007): 63–73.

41. I am assuming, for the sake of this discussion, that there could be such a thing as a legitimate policing authority, but I fully recognize that there are serious questions about the legitimacy of police authority in many parts of the United States.

42. Austin, *How to Do Things with Words*, 29 (emphasis in original).

43. Austin, *How to Do Things with Words*, 29 (emphasis in original).

44. Austin, *How to Do Things with Words*, 29.

45. I acknowledge that it is problematic how this requirement is supposed to be met in the case of the law; when one is within the jurisdiction of a particular legal system, one must obey or face sanctions whether one regards the system as legitimate or not. However, I think the distinction between *power* and *authority* can be put to use here. Legal systems are typically—maybe necessarily—backed by systems of power. One can therefore be coerced into conforming to laws even when one does not acknowledge their legitimacy. (See discussion following.)

46. Langton, "Speech Acts and Unspeakable Acts," 44–45.

47. Langton, "Replies" (Langton manuscript 3).

48. Langton, "Replies" (Langton manuscript 6).

49. Langton, "Replies" (Langton manuscript 12).

50. Langton, "Replies" (Langton manuscript 12).

51. I do not, in fact, see how choice of "paradigm" case can make a difference. I have been unable to find in Austin a single example of an illocutionary act that fails my necessary condition, nor one that possesses the features that I argue disqualify de facto subordination as an illocutionary act.

52. Austin, *How to Do Things with Words*, 109.

53. Austin, *How to Do Things with Words*, 116–17.

54. Or by means of some document meant to be public.

Part IV

The Value of Pornography

Chapter Ten

Porn, Sex, and Liberty

A Dialogue

Nina Hartley and Jacob M. Held

The following is a dialogue constructed from interviews between Jacob M. Held and Nina Hartley, later revised and fictionalized with contributions from both Held and Hartley.

We enter the dialogue as Professor Comstock is finishing his presentation, "Pornography as Illocutionary Disablement, and Civil Suits as a Means to Enfranchise the Silent Majority," sponsored by the University of Northern Bumblecuss's Department of Political Science. Unbeknownst to Comstock, Lila Deer, a well-known porn star, thirty-year veteran of the sex industry, and sex education advocate, is in attendance. Having spoken the previous night on misconceptions of the porn industry she was interested in hearing for herself Comstock's take on the familiar academic condemnation of pornography and the sex industry. Let us listen in as Dr. Comstock finishes . . .

Comstock: . . . Catharine MacKinnon has suggested that pornographers should be liable to civil suits. Her argument is that pornography functions as de facto discrimination, and so it should be actionable as a violation of women's civil liberties. She maintains that pornography functions as the equivalent of a "Whites Only" sign. It portrays women as less than, it supports and promotes a hierarchy where women are demeaned, and this is played out throughout culture in the form of discrimination and sexual violence. Pornographers bear responsibility for their product and how it gets used, and should be liable when their products lead to actions and practices that negatively impact women. [1]

Pornography objectifies women, and objects cannot speak; their words are misconstrued or fall on deafened ears. Langton discusses this in terms of

179

solipsisms, realms in which women fail to be recognized as full people.[2] The narrative propagated by porn, that all women want all forms of sex from all men, that they never mean "no" or even lack the ability to assert control over access to their own bodies, creates an environment wherein they are not recognized as capable of asserting certain things because the discourse has either become hostile to them or interlocutors have become hostile by virtue of not recognizing their capacity to exercise control over their bodies. Porn silences women by "disabling" their speech. If it sets up a culture where men don't respect women when they say "no" or causes men to misinterpret that "no" as a coded "yes," then either it leads men to misunderstand what women say, or it leads them to believe that women don't have a right to refuse sex, that they effectively don't control access to their own bodies. Their phrases can't be taken up and so they are disabled in the sense that they can't do the same things with words as others. But with pornography the result is more deleterious, since the effects are insidious and ubiquitous. Consider the construction of gender and sexuality, as it is produced via a sexualized, or porned, culture. If one were to view the many blogs, file-sharing sites, and discussion threads throughout the Internet devoted to pornography, one would find a common theme in the discussions of the consumers. They are fans of their favorite porn starlets because they believe these women are truly into whatever activity they are filmed performing. They not only view these stars as enjoying their activity, but they view the activity as inherently enjoyable. Female sexuality is constructed around the porn fantasy. The effect of pornography stretches far beyond the simple consumer, the adult video store, or the computer screen. It constructs a reality that, once reified, sets expectations for women and men, formulates and reinforces sexualities that are ultimately destructive and foments inequality.[3] Beyond the destructive impact this has on personal relationships and self-image, social roles become ossified and demand women to occupy the role of the objectified other; they are treated accordingly, in the work place, the home, the political arena, and so on. In an increasingly pornified culture women are perpetually objectified and othered.

Deer: Dr. Comstock. Last night I spoke on my role in the adult industry at length, the misperceptions surrounding it, and these typical criticisms. It seems that these criticisms haven't much changed over the past thirty years. You're claiming what MacKinnon began with, that porn is some monolithic entity with a political agenda to disenfranchise women, or at least that it has that effect. I'd like to remind everyone here of two things. First, porn is not monolithic, it is incredibly diverse.[4] And second, porn is merely one aspect of our culture. I think the porn industry bears the brunt of the criticism because it deals with sex. Regardless, it is protected as speech.

Pornography is a media product. If women can sue pornographers for the actions of others, then we'd all be free to sue Hollywood for any insult to our sensibilities, or any publisher of a book we don't like. We could sue publishers when a lone nut, or group of nuts, commit crimes or advocate violence after reading Marx's *Das Kapital*, Hitler's *Mein Kampf*, or even *The Catcher in the Rye*. Producers of media aren't liable for the actions of a few bad actors, and if we take the alternative route we'll destroy free speech and with it the value we gain as an open society free to exchange all manner of ideas, from the acceptable to the absurd and offensive. The First Amendment applies equally to sexually explicit speech. Sex is as relevant to our lives as religion or politics, so speech about it ought to be as free, since it is as valuable. We don't censor or prosecute "offensive" or "inappropriate" political or religious speech, so we should likewise leave our hands off of sexual speech.

Anti-porn feminists claim porn portrays women negatively. But porn only portrays women as "less than" if one thinks that sex is something women do not or should not want for their own reasons. Freedom of expression protects both speech of which we approve and speech we deplore. That is the essence of First Amendment protection, a protection from which feminism has benefitted greatly. It's worth noting that in some societies that ban porn, feminist literature is also suppressed. In fact, in 1992 the Canadian Supreme Court interpreted Canadian anti-obscenity laws to apply to "degrading" and "dehumanizing" depictions of women, and although MacKinnon lauded the decision it led ironically to the seizure of Andrea Dworkin's own work at the border.[5] The answer to speech one dislikes is speech of one's own, and that can only flourish in an environment where people can express themselves without fear of legal repression. And MacKinnon and her comrades are clearly not silenced.

Comstock: But we're not just talking about speech here. The point is that porn has an impact beyond speech, it has an effect on women's lives, their very ability to function in society. It's like hate speech. It diminishes a historically disenfranchised group, fomenting further discrimination, and thus it's not simply a speech issue, but a freedom issue. Like hate speech, pornography can be argued to incite sexual hatred, sexual hate speech.[6]

Deer: Porn is not hate speech. It has no political agenda. The way it portrays both men and women is deliberately unrealistic in keeping with the general approach of all entertainment media. Anti-porn feminists are pretty big on actual hate speech themselves. I've had plenty of it hurled at me, but I don't favor legal action to make them shut up. Regardless, I'm not convinced that banning actual hate speech makes anyone safer. You can ban speech and writing all you want, but you can't ban ideas, you can't control thought.

Better to understand what motivates such ideas by having the freedom to examine it, question it, and force it to stand up to criticism. The radical feminist movement has produced many books that are full of anti-male hate speech directly encouraging readers to castrate men, hurt them, kill them, and so forth. I don't favor suppressing these ugly creations because I have faith in readers to recognize them for what they are and reject them.

Comstock: Fair enough, but we're not just talking about speech. We're talking about the impact this speech has. Porn is misogynistic speech. The argument is that it's akin to incitement to sexual hatred.

Deer: Porn is not misogynistic. It's misanthropic. It takes an equally dim view of both genders, rendering them both as cartoon characters. Why? Because it's an entertainment medium. Again, the anti-porn folk have taken the term misogyny and hijacked it so that only they get to say what it means. It's misogynistic to insist that all women in porn are victims, dupes, and pitiable. It's misogynistic to assume that we are not full human beings deserving of respect for our choices, even if you don't agree with them. To quote Sojourner Truth, "And ain't I a woman?"

Comstock: But, there is a proven impact on consumers who watch porn. They are less empathetic to women and their suffering, and they are more likely to accept the rape myth.[7] I'm not saying they are more prone to rape, but men who routinely consume porn do have an altered view of women, a view of them as "less than," as objects for male use and male pleasure, and surely this is reflected in our culture.

Deer: The culture is already dismissive of women's interests, as manifested by the flurry of anti-choice legislation in all of the "red states." Those men don't use porn as a means to dismiss women's interests. They use the Bible, and I don't see one feminist agitating for the suppression of the Bible as the main source of misogyny in the West. No, they just create a pincher movement against female sexual autonomy. From one side: the Bible-thumpers and their "reverence for life." From the other side, the anti-sex work feminists and their "concern over exploitation." Caught in the middle: women just trying to do what's right for them and their families. If we do live in such a culture, porn as a "reason" is the last influence on the block, way, way behind thousands of years of biblically inspired values and law. Porn has been widely available for about a hundred years. Women's lot in life has been dismal for thousands of years before that.

Comstock: But porn contributes significantly, and it is becoming more influential. Children are exposed at increasingly younger ages and it is shaping how we view sexuality and how we interact with each other.

Deer: All culture impacts how women are viewed. Anti-woman propaganda has been around for thousands of years, well before porn was a commonly available media product; before the early twentieth century, porn was the provenance of the educated class, which didn't trust the "lower orders" with such things, thinking it would lead to such things as mass rape. Women were routinely beaten, raped, sold, and so on, with NO legal recourse. Why? Because they were considered the property of their fathers, husbands, sons, or uncles.

Comstock: But simply noting the scope of the problem of sexism and misogyny doesn't let porn off the hook. Porn contributes to the problem, and not insignificantly. Porn as a form of popular media influences our discourse on sexuality, it creates and reinforces expectations about gender, and so on. In this way it's influential like any other form of media, from advertising to prime time television. You can't deny its impact, and given the message it sends—the degradation and humiliation of women—the impact it has is quite negative and I'd say harmful.

Deer: I don't deny the influence of media, all media. Movies are fantasy, and porn is no different. If a person has a hard time in this culture of artificially created sexual scarcity, it's not hard to understand why a man's fantasy product would include women who want to have sex easily. In the real world it's hard to get a woman to go to bed with you if you're not rich, handsome, hung like a pony, or a jerk who will prey on a woman who's drunk. Most men aren't rich, handsome, hung like a pony, or a jerk, so sex with willing partners is hard to come by. Why? Because the culture shames women who "just" want to fuck for "fun" and not "relationships." Female fantasy, aka "romance," is equally limiting to men, equally fantastical and unrealistic, equally silly and fake. In the romance genre the tall, dark, handsome, rich, experienced, sexually masterful, intelligent, capable hero happily finds contentment with monogamous marriage to a virgin. Is this realistic? Is this not a fantasy that excludes most men?

All media affects consumer's attitudes about many things. Popular media, advertising media, all have an effect. Porn consumption also can affect women's attitudes toward men: why don't you have a six-pack? Why don't you have a ten-inch penis? Why can't you last an hour before ejaculating? Much more important to how men view women is their home environment: family history, how their parents interacted, whether or not they have been abused, what they were taught at home about the roles of men and women, religious indoctrination, and so on. Most men can tell the difference between a fantasy and a human in their presence. But to your last point, the fact is, many heterosexual women do enjoy forceful sex play. Not politically correct, but there you have it.

Comstock: We're speaking at two different levels. You're talking about informed, developed mature adults interacting as autonomous individuals. In that case, yes I have to agree. Some people may enjoy forceful sex play, they may enough rough sex—slapping, choking, and so forth. But this presumes mature, autonomous adults choosing to do so among a wide range of options.

Deer: But what else should we assume? We're talking about adults, we're talking about real people who want to exercise a degree of freedom in what they consume and who they sleep with and how. Either we assume adults can make informed decisions for themselves, that they deserve freedom, or we deny them of it and end up with a nanny state spoon-feeding us appropriate literature, appropriate views and . . .

Comstock: . . . and I'm talking about the formation of ideas of sexuality, the fact that children are influenced by porn to see sexuality a certain way. In this case, if they are acculturated to view forceful sex play as enjoyable, they are likely to force that upon a partner, or expect it from them. In addition, they may view women as things, objects to be forced into submission for male pleasure. This is the problem, this is the connection between porn and a rape culture, and studies bear it out. The influence of porn hinders the development of adult sexuality; it hinders people's development as they try to become free, autonomous human beings. Culture is a limiting factor on autonomy and porn is an unacceptable one that distorts views of sexuality and creates malformed adults.

Deer: Like all other media and forms of culture, porn will have an impact, but don't exaggerate it. Porn doesn't create a rape culture. Most men can't rape. Rapists rape. They do it a lot and they have never needed porn to tell them how or why. No violent person has ever needed any outside media to compel them to harm others. Wrongdoers do wrong all on their own.

I ask anti-porn women: at what other time in history would you choose to live as a woman of your current class? With all that's still to be done for gender and sexual equality, being a woman in the West today is the apex of female agency in all of recorded history. Even royal women in the past had to deal with shit from men, and it was only worse for the majority of women who were of the serving or working class. Are these women truly saying that dirty pictures are the worst thing ever to happen to women? Worse than honor killings? Worse than bride burnings? Worse than child marriage?

Worse than being forced to carry to term a baby they don't want and can't afford because some male-controlled legislature says that life begins at conception? Really? It's a freaking privilege that they even get to have this silly conversation over porn.

Comstock: But even if it's better than it used to be, that doesn't mean one stops progressing. Before the passage of the Civil Rights Act of 1964 it would've been silly to claim, "But blacks are better off than when they were slaves. It's a privilege for them to even be able to have this silly debate about civil rights."

Deer: That analogy is so far off base. Women now are not in a similar position as blacks in the 1960s, and the cause of current discrimination and inequity may be a misogynistic culture, but as I said, one that existed before porn, and would exist if porn was eliminated.

Comstock: Yet discrimination feeds on attitudes, and attitudes towards women as crafted by or propagated in porn lead to a diminished view of women. And given the young age at which children are exposed and the influence porn wields on such young viewers, there's reason to be concerned.

Deer: Oh, yes. What of the children. We must think of the poor children, having porn thrown at them from all directions. Kids get exposed to sex, it happens. You respond not by denying that sex exists, but by educating them. As far as porn goes, I don't think it has more of an impact than the accumulated effects of all the other media to which we are exposed. Considering children, before the late nineteenth-century invention of childhood as a separate, "innocent" period, children were not protected from the world. Child labor, child prostitution, child exploitation, child abuse, exposure to social violence such as public executions, were common. The idea that children don't have an innate sexuality is false. We are born with all the anatomy we need to be sexual. Left to their own devices most children discover self-soothing through genital stimulation by the age of three. Instead of gently teaching children about privacy and letting them know WHERE to self-sooth, we freak out, punish the child for OUR discomfort, and continue the fallout of our erotophobic culture.

Comstock: Yet by promoting an unflattering, at best, view of women, porn contributes to women's inequality. Women are silenced, that is, their words aren't taken with the same seriousness or to mean the same thing as men's words. From sexual refusal to workplace harassment, porn culture diminishes the capacity of women to function, to do things in the world.

Deer: Women are free to speak, to make porn of their own, and are doing so more and more every day. The anti-porn women sure aren't "silenced." Who's silenced are my sisters and me who are sex workers, who are dismissed, diminished, and disrespected daily by those who purport to be on our side, but only if we repent of our wicked ways. As a member of a marginalized class (sex worker), I know prejudice when I see and feel it, and the anti-porn feminists are simply prejudiced, pure and simple.

Porn's not to blame for inequality. Men's disrespect of women has been embedded in culture over millennia since long before the advent of commercial porn. We've made some progress in certain parts of the world toward changing that. We can now report rape and be believed. Women can say no and have the bastard arrested if he persists. When police respond to a domestic violence call, someone will be arrested. I'm not saying things are perfect, but they're a hell of a lot better than they were when I was a child. For reference, *Roe v. Wade* was decided when I was fourteen. Most recent studies show a sharp decline in the incidence of rape in the very countries where porn is most available. I don't suggest that these things are linked in some positive way, but if porn really did produce anti-social behavior, given how much porn is around we should expect to see the statistics tilting in the opposite direction.

Comstock: So you're not concerned with the force shown in porn, the violence, and so on? You don't think it contributes to date rape, gray rape, or sexual assault?

Deer: Why do anti-porn proponents let rapists off the hook like this? "Porn made me do it" is no more effective a defense than "the devil made me do it." Case in point: When Elliot Spitzer was caught using prostitutes and ruined his career, anti-porn activist Melissa Farley came to his defense, saying in essence that it's male nature to be that way and if those icky prostitutes hadn't tempted him, he'd not have done such a thing. It was an astounding example of "throw the whore under the bus," because, you know, sex work is disgusting. She chose to defend a white, privileged man instead of a working woman, even when it came to light that Spitzer is a mean john. He'd never dream of treating a woman from his own class the way he treated these working women, but he feels fine doing so with the hired help. And now he's being rehabilitated. It's disgusting and they enable it.

Comstock: But what about the idea that porn leads to a lack of empathy? Don't avoid the issue. We live in a rape culture, and porn promotes and supports the idea that women should be and always are available to men as sex objects, that they won't say "no" or in fact lack the ability to do so.

Deer: Rape is wrong and the law knows it. If the anti-porn folk really want to help women, they'll stop harping on porn and start fighting for the more rigorous prosecution of rape. Violence against women needs to be addressed when and where it occurs, not in the abstract. Porn doesn't tell anyone rape is excusable. Porn tells them that women initiate sex when they want it. Again, blame the actor for his actions. Porn is not to blame for men being unable to tell the difference between a movie and real life. Do we watch *Fast and Furious* to learn how to drive? Do we watch James Bond movies to learn how spies do their jobs? No. We watch movies to be entertained. Blame the person who did the bad thing. On a side note, besides being disrespectful of women, anti-porn feminists are very disrespectful of men. They infantilize them by assuming that men are such mindless, idiotic, impulsive creatures that they can't be trusted to know the difference between right and wrong.

Comstock: So you're comfortable with the portrayal of women in porn? You think that if men took porn to be representative of how women are, society would be just fine?

Deer: Women express their sexuality boldly in porn as it exists, rather than as constructed in the paranoid minds of fanatics. I've seen what anti-porn feminists consider evidence of "violence" in mainstream porn, and by the criteria they've established for their so-called studies, any depiction of pene-trative intercourse qualifies. That reflects the realities of neither porn nor daily life. Porn is a mirror to culture, not an engine. A culture gets the porn it deserves, the porn that the people who grew up in a culture think is sexy is due to their conditioning. If one looks at the totality of porn and not just those aspects of it that shock and horrify, one will see a wide range of behaviors, from mild to wild. Some of the content is rough. Some is romantic. All is consensual and if porn were as influential as its enemies claim, we'd actually see greater respect for the variety of consensual sexual behavior than we do in the real world. If porn is guilty of anything in terms of content, it would be a tendency to oversimplify sex and ignore the problems that can come with it. Porn is Happyland where everyone is always in the mood. That fantasy depends on willing and eager participants engaged in mutually enjoyable activities. It's dopey sex education, but it's intended as entertainment rather than instruction. And at some point you have to trust the consumer to know the difference.

Audience Member 1: Excuse me, could I interject?

Comstock: Of course.

Audience Member 1: Ms. Deer, I appreciate what you're saying, but I think you too are coming from a privileged position. By all accounts you are a very successful business woman. Likewise, you seem to be a genuinely satisfied person. That is, you have a career you enjoy and that you have flourished in. But don't you think using your experience as representative is a bit disingenuous. If you look at most women in the porn industry, they aren't able to maintain a career in it for as long as you have. They are young when they enter and they often regret their decision later on. There is rampant drug use and abuse in the industry. So aside from the cultural impact, aren't you the least bit concerned with the nature of the industry itself, for those girls not fortunate enough to be as successful as you, Jesse Jane, or even Jenna Jameson?

Deer: I'm not surprised someone brought this up. The industry has for a long time been the subject of criticism. But I think it's important to begin not from a condemnation of sex work as somehow less than, but from the point of view of the sex industry as an industry.

That being said, your perception is incorrect. By assuming that porn in particular is more dangerous to young performers than other branches of the entertainment industry, which historically uses vulnerable people looking for approval and validation, shows an anti-sex bias. Ask any person who makes a living in the entertainment industry: STIs, drug abuse, and emotional and sexual abuse are quite prevalent just off set. Because porn is ABOUT sex, people assume that the problems in it are limited to it. Instead, it's more useful to view porn as part and parcel of the entertainment-industrial complex.

Audience Member 1: So regulation is needed?

Deer: Regulation by hostile, puritanical outside forces has not and will not do one thing to mitigate any problems in the business. We have a very good STI testing and control program in place. Since 1998 when universal testing began we've seen only two instances of on-set transmission of HIV, and those were in 2004. In the same time period Los Angeles County reported 30,000 new cases of HIV. All performers are tested every two to four weeks for HIV, chlamydia, gonorrhea, and syphilis, and the results are placed in a database accessible to producers, directors, and performers. As well, each performer asks on set to see their partner's results. If not current, the person with the outdated test is sent home. Contrary to the received "wisdom" of porn sex being somehow more dangerous than "regular" sex, we would all be better off if people having recreational sex were as careful and health-conscious as people in porn. Porn performers know their HIV status and the status of their screen partners. What percentage of the general population can say that?

Audience Member 1: But what about allegations of abuse of performers and exploitation?

Deer: Listen, there has never been a death on a porn set or from anything happening on a porn set—a claim that certainly couldn't be made by heavily regulated enterprises such as mining, agriculture, construction, forestry, fire-fighting, law enforcement, industrial food processing, or stunt work. It's worth noting that people come of age to do legal porn at eighteen, the same age at which they become eligible for military service. With new regulations permitting women in combat and the staggering statistics recently made public concerning the extent of rape and sexual abuse in the military, it would seem that the honor of serving this country in uniform is far more dangerous than having sex on a porn set.

Audience Member 1: But at eighteen . . . to make such a drastic decision as to enter the porn industry. You're so young, naïve.

Deer: . . . and joining the military? You grow up watching jingoistic displays of military might, being sold a bill of goods about money for college, travel, opportunities. . . . How is your criticism of the porn industry not also relevant to the military, aside from the fact that as a culture we laud military service and disparage sex work? It's your anti-sex bias at work, not your concern for young girls. Anti-porn feminists presuming to speak for all women will not concede that a particular woman can choose sex work of her own volition because it suits her nature, her personality, her temperament, her scheduling needs, her sexual needs, her artistic needs, or her financial needs. I've long thought that most of anti-porn feminism's harping about the brutality and degradation that the porn industry inflicts on poor innocent women stems from projections; how the anti-porn ideologues would feel if they "had" to do porn. They are judging others for a path they couldn't or wouldn't take. And no one on that path suggests that they should or would welcome their company any more than the staff at Wheelock College would welcome me as a faculty member. Not all people are suited to all jobs, and quite frequently the reason says more about the people than it says about the jobs.

And notice how these arguments always infantilize women. Because of social custom and history, young women are often thought to be meek, mild, and vulnerable. Some certainly are. As a rule, women who seek work in porn are competitive, physical, ambitious, striving, independent, hard-working, and entrepreneurial. They are much more varied than their detractors make them out to be. Conceiving of porn performers as individuals works against the demagogic narrative of all-porn-women-are-victims

Comstock: The audience member is getting at an important issue, though. You presume women in porn are self-possessed, strong individuals. But many are young as she mentions, say eighteen, nineteen. Even though it is true you can enter the military at this age, or any dangerous industry to be sure, isn't the porn industry more prone to exploiting these vulnerable women, and aren't the psychological effects significant? Does the porn industry appeal to vulnerable women, say women who've been the victims of sexual assault, and exploit that vulnerability to line the pockets of a few men?

Deer: No more so than anywhere else. Far more women who've been victims of sexual abuse don't and would never choose sex work than those who do. Up to a third of all women may have been abused as children, and the vast majority of them find other ways of coping or making a living than sex work. Whether or not the person who chooses sex work has been abused is not necessarily relevant to their choice of occupation. Not to imply that all people who choose porn are mentally or emotionally the picture of perfect health. But porn does appeal to a certain personality type. Just by choosing to be entertainers of any sort they distinguish themselves from most. All entertainers, be they clothed or unclothed, seek validation, approval, and attention, myself included. All entertainers are a little crazy. Why else put oneself on stage and risk rejection? Porn folk do not significantly differ from nonsexual performers in that respect.

The entertainment industry will take advantage of anyone who will let it. It is a gaping maw ever in need of feeding. The more outlets there are for "content," the greater the need for new, new, new. The professional porn business is much smaller than the larger industry of which it is a remote corner. This actually works to the advantage of porn performers. Porn performers who have drug problems and porn producers who take advantage quickly become known to the working community and are likely to be avoided. We share vital intelligence as much as the next group of people who work closely together, and word gets around. In any trade one encounters people hell-bent on self-destruction or predation on those around them. This population tends to be self-limiting. And if you're concerned about drug use as self-medication, consider that this country consumes more psychoactive chemicals than the rest of the world combined. Porn performers are neither more nor less representative of this statistical fact than nonperformers.

Comstock: To piggyback off of the audience member's concerns, but at eighteen they've chosen a career that has little chance of long-term success and from which there is no possibility of movement—they are trapped by the industry. Do you deny that porn performers have little alternative once tagged as porn performers?

Deer: First, often this talk comes around to the idea that women are coerced into porn, and I want to absolutely reject that notion, without equivocation. In California porn is a legal industry and there is no need to coerce anyone into it. People arrive daily looking to join the ranks of adult performers, and there's not enough work to go around. I can't speak to conditions in other countries, but we're talking about American-made porn here. Every person on set has a cell phone. The Los Angeles police would love to get a call from a frightened porn performer asking for rescue. There are witnesses on set and people talk. Abusive directors are quickly found out and no one will work for them or give them money to shoot. There is no need or motivation for legal pornographers to put themselves at risk by coercing anyone into doing anything when willing talent is readily available with a single phone call to a booking agency.

As for being "trapped," that is a different matter. The culture at large is very conflicted about sex workers in general, especially porn performers. The stigma, while less intense than in the past, is still present, making it hard to transition into a different line of work if one wishes to do so. Porn creates a gap in the resume not easily explained. Few performers enjoy the class privilege of, say, feminist college professors, and the job market is very tight regardless of gender. The job skills needed in porn are different than those required for civilian work, which doesn't mean that those who engage in it have no other skills that might suit them for a different occupation if the opportunities were made available to them. It's also fair to say, as with other entertainers, that one of the reasons people get into porn is that "regular" work doesn't interest them. But there is a viable opportunity for success, at least as much as in any other job. It depends on how one defines "success." The data show that social mobility in the United States is declining rapidly. For the first time in three generations young people cannot expect to attain a higher standard of living than their parents, regardless of the jobs they choose. Job security in the United States is more tenuous than ever, and courts are consistently on the side of business over the rights of workers. Many female porn performers do find both creative satisfaction and financial independence in their careers. Women in porn have options that the men don't have. They can feature dance, do private escorting, brand a sex toy, run a membership site, do cam shows, and charge for personal appearances.

I think the image problem sex work has is often a result of our erotophobic culture, an anti-sex bias, rather than a concern about working conditions, which if you remove the idea that having sex for money is problematic, is quite attractive. If porn performers may or may not have medical insurance, retirement accounts, own property, or enjoy other benefits once considered routine in most forms of employment, they are no different from those working as contractors or part-time employees in thousands of other industries. That's the new economy, and in no way is it unique to pornography. With all the people sleeping on the street, with all the abused children that need foster care, with all the abused spouses that need shelter, with the staggering number of inmates incarcerated for nonviolent offenses, with all the old people who can't afford their medicine, why the emphasis on the largely imaginary miseries of what amounts to less than a thousand individuals who are not asking for help or pity? Why this prurient interest in those "poor young women" who are "being taken advantage of?" Because they're naked? Because they're having sex?

Porn performers choose their profession for the same reasons anyone chooses any job: it seems like a good idea, it seems like a way to make money, it seems like fun, it fits their schedule, it suits their personality and/or needs at the moment. What better jobs these days are open to young people with high school educations? It's not like most in porn are from a class that has the option to go to medical school, law school, business school . . .

Comstock: That's exactly the point. You take a class of young women, those that don't have medical school, or college, or what have you as a real possibility, and then you hold out work in the porn industry and tell them they can make good money. When their other options are food service, or some other low skilled minimum-wage job, what do you think they're going to choose?

Deer: Yes, porn pays a lot more than food service, waiting tables, or child or elder care. For those suited to it, sex work is a pretty great job.

Comstock: But what other choice do they have? They end up in porn because the other options are so bad. It's a forced choice, like "your money or your life?" Everyone gives up their money because the other option, one's life, doesn't make sense. In this case we say, "food service or porn." Food service is unattractive and doesn't provide a livable wage, so porn looks good, but only because it's not the worst option. That's not a free choice, that's coercion.

Deer: That's a labor market. You might as well equally say that an employee at Walmart is coerced because it's that or starve, that or poverty, that or food service. A labor market forces those choices, the lack of health care and a livable social safety net forces those choices. In that market why limit women's choices by not accepting sex work as a real alternative? To some it may suit them better than fast-food work. It's only society's idea of women as pathetic, helpless, sexless ciphers that presumes porn to be the "Worst Thing

Ever To Happen To A Young Woman." Sex work is a good way to get paid $200 to $1,000 a day for work that is better compensated and less dangerous than most of the likely alternatives. Sex work has long been a stepping-stone into the middle class for many women, particularly in times of economic dislocation. In what way would either the women themselves or society at large benefit by authoritarian attempts to deny them this opportunity?

When it comes to the concern that women in porn are coerced, as I said, that is how labor works under capitalism, so I simply ask: and this makes porn different from any other working situation how? Employers love depressions and recessions, as people are desperate for work and will put up with any mental torture, any humiliation, just to keep a job. Worker wages as a percentage of gross domestic product have gone down and real wages have been stagnant since the late 1970s or early 1980s. Pension plans have been eliminated, leaving regular people to "manage" their own portfolios to disastrous ends, as what regular person knows how to manage money for retirement? And then they're made to feel guilty for not knowing how. Why is porn singled out as some prime example of worker exploitation? Many people live at the edge or below it, and only a small percentage chooses sex work. If you're talking about "forced" choices, talk about the capitalist system and how it's devalued all forms of labor. Who is looking to hire sex workers at comparable rates to those paid in porn while offering them the same kind of independence?

Comstock: But you say this, again, as though these girls are fully autonomous and are making a fully informed decision. Society has trained them to be sexual in this way. Our sexualized culture taught them to sell themselves from childhood on, and you're reinforcing that. Porn is co-opting female sexuality.[8]

Deer: Who's to say it's a "misconception about her sexuality" that has a woman choose to have sex on camera? My conception of my sexuality is that the camera *is* the place for part of my sexuality to be expressed. I'm an exhibitionist with a message, and I don't like being arrested for being naked in the "wrong" place. Porn was the place where my sexuality emerged and was welcomed. If anti-sex-work feminists *really* wanted to help women, as opposed to further heaping shame and opprobrium on them, they would demand that consensual sex commerce be decriminalized, taking away the opportunity for pimps, "managers," or law enforcement to further exploit women who work on the street without the protections we enjoy in porn.

Again, anti-porn feminists assume that sex work is always bad for women and that no woman in her right mind would ever choose to be in such a "degrading" and "dehumanizing" line of trade. They seem to forget that the terms "degrading" and "dehumanizing" are subjective. They assume that all people experience sex work as radical feminists would experience it in their imaginations. They have shown zero ability or willingness to see women who choose sex work as individuals with individual motivations. I find this intellectually dishonest. It only demonstrates the degree to which anti-porn feminism is rooted in emotion while presenting itself as based on reason and logic.

Audience Member 2: But, if I may . . . the porn industry reinforces the idea that women are products to be sold. Women have been trained to sell themselves from infancy and now you're saying, "go with it." How is that liberating and respecting autonomy, and not just asking women to accept sexism and misogyny because they might get paid a little bit more doing so?

Deer: This is nothing new to pornography. When it comes to being trained to sell oneself, who hasn't been? The anti-porn folk, while they talk a good game about being against "the patriarchy," have fully internalized patriarchal archetypes of "acceptable" women. I've never been more shamed than I have been by fellow feminists. This culture, repressed as it is, values sexuality as a selling point. We use sex to sell cars, guns, beer, makeup, hygiene products, movies, and more. But we can't use sex to sell sex? We can't teach age-appropriate sex education? Anti-porn feminists are as obsessed with sex as any consumers of porn. They get a perverse negative charge over being outraged and disgusted.

Audience Member 2: But you've not answered the question: isn't it disingenuous to claim a career in porn is liberating?

Deer: Those of us who find it so don't generalize that claim to include everyone we work with. For some women, porn is liberating. For others, if they could find a way to make the same money elsewhere, they'd likely do so. Anti-porn feminists give no support to those who want to leave unless a woman is willing to debase herself and admit that she was wrong, wrong, wrong to ever do that nasty job. For an example of how lovely, helping, healing, and supportive anti-porn feminists are, just look at how they treated Linda Lovelace. After parading her around like a show pony, they wanted nothing to do with her when she needed help for her medical expenses. Linda was looking for a comeback in porn to cover those expenses when she died in an auto accident. Unlike the anti-porn feminist camp, the porn business would have welcomed her even though she had allowed herself to be used by its enemies. We're not the ones doing the judging.

Porn is liberating because you can make a living wage on part-time work. Performers can take, or not, the jobs offered them. They have the opportunity to travel, to meet new people, to gain exposure to other options than they might have found in their original small towns. Why is "catering" to male sexuality automatically considered unliberated? Only certain feminists think that most women can, or would want to, do without the sexual attention of men. Most women are heterosexual, making "the male gaze" important to their sense of themselves and their potential happiness. How is it liberating to completely deny an important part of my sexuality, my potential for happiness, by denying that I do, in fact, enjoy sex with men? What happened to the mantra of "my body, my rules?" How is it liberating to be harped upon by women who clearly have contempt for my choices? Why would I want to listen to them any more than I want to listen to a preacher saying that if I don't repent, my soul will burn forever in the pits of hell? Why would I look for help from those who obviously see me as, at best, a pitiable victim or, at worst, a misogynist? Now, do all women who make porn think they made the best choice? No. But most do think and feel that they are making the best choices for them at the time.

Audience Member 3: But, Ms. Deer, Catharine MacKinnon claims that women who claim they enjoy or want to pursue a career in the adult industry suffer from false consciousness, or are in some way indoctrinated or brainwashed, and don't see that they are being exploited and that a career in porn can't possibly be freely chosen, or rewarding.

Deer: I hate this argument. It hasn't changed in thirty-plus years, which shows how shallow it really is. So, somehow, *they* have magically avoided being conditioned by the culture and have super powers to transcend their situation? Who says that my consciousness is "false" and theirs is somehow "real?" Oh, yeah, *they* do. To ascribe our choices to conditioning is to reduce us to lab rats. For anti-porn feminists, any woman who likes male attention, needs male sexuality in their lives, and wants pleasure with men is "indoctrinated." Sorry, ladies. Most women, being, you know, heterosexual, are not willing to become lesbian on political grounds.

Comstock: I think we've come to the heart of our disagreement. Lila, you keep approaching the issue from the perspective of an individual. You think about the women who choose sex work, the individual consumer who buys it, how it influences their lives, and so you are talking always about individual choice, freedom, and liberty.

Deer: And that's what this is about.

Comstock: But the broader social issues are about the place of women in society as a class. And if porn has the effect on culture it does, that is, it influences our views of women, and if it does so in a way that harms them either by limiting their autonomy so they can't exercise control over their own bodies, or by harassing them and fomenting gender inequality, then it isn't just about the individuals, but the impact individual actions have on society as a whole.

Deer: Yet that impact is the result of individual actions, and that's who should be held responsible. Individuals rape, individuals discriminate, individuals get involved in sex work. We need to talk about these individuals because they make up society. And we need to protect their rights, their rights to make and buy and consume porn, their rights to exercise their sexuality. What really gets my goat is that so much of women's social progress over the past 100 years, like suffrage, being able to own property in our own names, getting credit, being able to bring rape charges against a husband, being able to bring assault charges against a husband, gaining custody of children in a divorce, and being able to hold a job, have come about *because* of feminist thinking and action. Not all feminists have porn on the brain. The majority are concerned with gender equity. Porn isn't on their radar. As a sex worker I feel betrayed and abandoned by those women who claim to care about me but only if I subscribe to their way of thinking. What's most infuriating, and has been for years, is that for all of their bloviating about "speaking truth to power," "my body, my rules," and "sexual liberation," when I did what they exhorted me to do, I found that they instead denounced, ignored, demeaned, or deplored every choice I made.

Comstock: But again, it's not about just you. It's about the impact porn has on culture and whether or not it's positive or negative, whether or not we need to deal with it at some point.

Deer: And like I've said, it's like any other media. It simply comes under harsher fire because it is sex, and we have an anti-sex bias in our culture. We aren't talking about how demeaning commercials are, or horror films where the role of the girls is to be pretty, scream, and die. We're talking about sex, and the arguments against porn betray attitudes against sex, or at least against "deviant" sex that some don't view as appropriately mutual or deferential to women's needs, however those get defined.

    Porn is subversive because it shows sex without negative consequences. No one dies. No one goes to jail. No one is hurt. No one gets pregnant. People have sex in groups, with toys, with same-sex partners, with partners of a different race. All that happens is that people have fun, a few orgasms, and go home. Unlike in Hollywood movies, where common social norms are heavily maintained, no woman dies in porn for being sexually "deviant." Women in Hollywood movies routinely experience misfortune if they cross a line: they lose their jobs, kids, partners, freedom, life, sanity, social standing, and more. Porn is countercultural; porn pushes boundaries. It opens up a world of alternative sexualities, of rough sex, lesbian, gay, or queer. It opens up a dialogue on pleasure and sexuality, and in the end people enjoy it, otherwise it wouldn't be such a successful industry. To attempt to kill the industry or attack porn and limit access to it would be to limit access to an open, alternative dialogue on sexuality that most people have access to, and how is that in their best interests? How is it in society's best interests to chill and limit our discourse on sex and desire and promote a monolithic view of sexuality? I do keep focusing on individual liberty, because individuals are the only things that can have freedom and rights, and this whole debate is about how to limit them for the good of culture. Well, news flash, culture is made up of people, and at some point you either trust them and prosecute them when they actually do harm someone, or attempt to control them through dictatorial means.

I think porn can help enable discussion of sexual issues if people are allowed to form their own opinions about it rather than having those opinions dictated to them by people who wish to globalize their personal repugnance and sexual morality. Porn is just one more datum, one more bit of information or material, to introduce into the project of crafting our lives. To claim it's too dangerous, too harmful, or too powerful, is to disparage humanity and artificially construct a social reality engineered to your conception of gender and sexuality. You deprive me of my right to craft my life as I choose with all possible information.

Comstock: Well, I think we're at time. This session was supposed to end almost an hour ago. But thank you all so much for coming, and thank you Ms. Deer. You've definitely given us much to think about, and I think if the point of my presentation was to raise questions about porn, you've done my job for me.

NOTES

1. See Catharine MacKinnon, *Only Words* (Cambridge, MA: Harvard University Press, 1996).

2. See Rae Langton, *Sexual Solipsism* (Oxford: Oxford University Press, 2009). Mary Kate McGowan makes similar claims. A discussion of their work and style of arguments can be found in both Jacob M. Held's and Jennifer Hornsby's chapters in this book.

3. These claims are well articulated and presented in many places, but most notably Gail Dines, *Pornland: How Porn Has Hijacked Our Sexuality* (Boston: Beacon Press, 2010); Pamela Paul, *Pornified: How Pornography Is Transforming Our Lives, Our Relationships, and Our Families* (New York: Times Books, 2005); and Robert Jensen, *Getting Off: Pornography and the End of Masculinity* (Boston: South End Press, 2007).

4. See for example the chapter by Ariane Cruz in this book.

5. See Nadine Strossen, *Defending Pornography: Free Speech, Sex, and the Fight for Women's Rights* (New York: New York University Press, 2000), 237.

6. Catherine Itzin has made this argument. See Catharine Itzin, ed., *Pornography: Women, Violence, and Civil Liberties* (Oxford: Oxford University Press, 1992).

7. For references see American Psychological Association (APA), Task Force on the Sexualization of Girls, *Report of the APA Task Force on the Sexualization of Girls* (Washington, DC: APA, 2007).

8. For more on pornification, see Susanna Paasonen's chapter in this book.

Chapter Eleven

The Gentle Side of Pornography

*A Contemporary Examination of Pornography's
Depiction of Love and Friendship*

Lindsay Coleman

What is most surprising about the debates that surround pornography is how much the various sides agree upon. Pornography is banal, predictable, convoluted, and fundamentally impoverished intellectually. Rarely would a sex-positive academic or practitioner of pornography dispute this. And yet pornography presents both a genre and discourse rich in commentary on human experience despite these obvious limitations. Performers, within the limits of a 20- to 30-minute scene, will engage in oral sex, vaginal penetration, and perhaps anal sex. They may also perform/evoke emotions as varied as concern, affection, jocularity, hostility, contempt, infatuation, even shyness. While there is extensive existing debate on the negative, sadistic, emotionally and physically violent aspects of pornography, this chapter will be dedicated to the more gentle side of pornography, such as it is. In order for this notion to be explored, the working definition of pornography with which I will work is: all adult entertainment that includes unsimulated sex, inclusive of scenes involving heterosexual and homosexual sex.

Two scenes come to mind that in their scenarios, and in the performances of the actors involved, illustrate pornography's potential to depict affection, friendship, and otherwise normative relationships. In the 2013 adult film "*Right Between My Boobs,*" twenty-four-year-old starlet Alex Chance arrives home from a busy day at the office. She appears to be living with her boyfriend, also in his early- to mid-twenties. They make small chat for about five minutes, but Alex soon notices that her lover is in a melancholic frame of mind. He retires to go to bed for a nap. Alex has an idea and playfully rouses him; within a minute she has pounced on his prone figure and they are engaged in hardcore pornographic sex. He ejaculates on her breasts after the requisite interlude and she asks if the sex helped to cheer him up. Energized and exultant he confirms that it has.

Let us consider the context of this scene. A couple, in a seemingly committed relationship, engage in relatively intimate congress, she empathizing with his melancholic state. Her sexual gift appreciated, he expresses a greater joy in life, his melancholy and apathy having lifted, the cathartic sex having served its purpose.

A scene between Nick Manning and Sienna West in *The Making of a Milf* is equally illuminating. After a vigorous bout of sex, fairly unremarkable in and of itself, something surprising occurs. The two actors appear to have enjoyed orgasms. Manning's is naturally obvious thanks to his ejaculation, aimed at West's breasts. West's, as is the common complaint directed at pornography, is likely simulated. Nevertheless the moment depicted is of two humans experiencing intense mutual sexual satisfaction. Their body language is thus all the more remarkable. Where pornographic scenes frequently end awkwardly, trailing off into uncomfortable silence following male ejaculation, in this instance the performers are buoyant, jocular, high-fiving one another. The implication is clear. They are exhibiting all of the traits of friendship, of enjoyment in one another's company, glorying in the pleasure their bodies hold and the pleasure that they have given one another.

This chapter will be expressly concerned with pornographic performers as cognizant, autonomous professionals who bring elements of their personal life to their performance, yet are also businesspeople, expressly engaged in their own commodification. There will similarly be an analysis of the manner in which the sexual scripts of the actors in fact mirror our increasingly pornified society. In turn there will be an examination of the possibility, even within a pornified society, for relationships of warmth and a degree of emotional depth to be borne out in pornographic scenarios by the actors who appear in them. Naturally this view may be contentious, perhaps even offensive to some, and I am well aware of the charge laid by Karen Finley: "We can feel good, moral, and self-righteous in applying our liberal gaze, our self-proclaimed empathetic gaze, to porn stars, when in fact we're creating a place to feel comfortable in our desire."[1] Yet the evidence, such as it is, in the scenes I have described merits surely as much inspection as it does condemnation by those who would point to its obvious corruptions of human love and affection.

BAD PATRIARCHY: MACKINNON AND DINES

Catharine MacKinnon's definition of pornography as a discourse invested in the exploitation of women, in depictions of violence against women, certainly holds true for much of the content found. She goes so far as to state that the roots of this mistreatment, of which pornography is symptomatic, are found in the patriarchal nature of our society: "Women and men are divided by gender, made into the sexes as we know them, by the requirements of its dominant form, heterosexuality, which institutionalizes male sexual dominance and female sexual submission. If this is true, sexuality is the linchpin of gender inequality."[2] The very notion of sexual congress and its depiction effectively places women in a position of subservience. Gail Dines reinforces this notion, in turn repudiating the notion that any other interpretation of pornography's role or influence other than to reinforce white male hegemony is moot: "While [pro-sex] research sheds light on the various sectors of the industry, it cannot stand in for a critical macro-level approach that explores how capitalism, patriarchy, racism and first-world economic domination provides the economic and cultural space for international, mass-scale pornography production."[3] The first scene I described certainly objectifies the actress Alex Chance, yet it is an instance of objectification in which she is being deliberately playful, using her ample bare breasts to rouse her melancholic boyfriend from his slumber. In an amusing point-of-view shot they wobble above his head. It is a moment of humor, ludicrous, teasing, the actress and the character she plays well aware of the singular impact of those breasts on both her boyfriend and the viewer. Chance's character enjoys agency in the scene, and similarly the humor of the moment allows for conceptual breathing room, as it were. It is all for a good cause. His arousal, his orgasm are her gift to him, and her motives are, within this limited context of film sex, loving as depicted in the scenario. The chosen mode of interaction in the Manning/West scene is that of sexual camaraderie. Both scenarios, in short, offer unexpected diversions from the monolithic model MacKinnon offers us. Chance is the instigator in her particular film, and her motivation is not to submit to her partner's desire but rather to supplant his melancholy with desire, he being entirely passive. The connection between Manning and West is contextualized as a sexual act that is part of a friendship, rather than solely an exchange based on West's enforced position of inequality. Friendship, after all, is typically regarded as a kind of relationship shared by equals. What this chapter will explore is the possibility that psychological and sociocultural aspects of male-female friendship create a context in which pornography might be able to depict attitudes of love and friendship.

THE POSSIBILITY OF FRIENDSHIP

Linda Williams cautions against the type of reductive thinking that considers pornography as merely a depiction of men and women reduced to their anatomical parts. First she notes the interpretation Dennis Giles takes of the stag film: "In his view, the male viewer's scrutiny of the vulva is an occasion for (unconscious) identification with the woman herself." This claim itself being a striking counterargument to those put forward by MacKinnon, Williams goes a step further:

> While I do think that this interpretation may begin to describe and explain the greater bisexuality and complexity of the identificatory process for the male spectator of many stag films, I would not extend it to the whole of hard-core pornography. For one thing, the more elaborate narratives of feature-length hard core offer other points of secondary, fictional identification beyond those merely of phallus or hole. [4]

The debate, it seems, can provoke endless interpretive stances. For myself, while pornography is rarely high-minded, or even well-acted, it cannot help but display aspects of the human condition, quite simply because there is more to pornography than a "phallus or hole." Perhaps the fact that human qualities may exist in pornography is because it is human beings themselves, autonomous within the limits of their profession, who perform in pornography, and are the ultimate medium in which its ideas are expressed.

Previously we explored the scenarios in which Chance and West performed, leaving to the imagination what might be motivating the women themselves. And a greater measure of the agency, or lack thereof, of the pornographic performer is possible. It is possible to evaluate the potential for human qualities to be integrated into the production of pornographic films. Even while these performers exploit themselves, they often do so as thinking adults with a measure of emotional and sexual autonomy. West's comments in a recent interview underline this:

> **Author**: Sophia Loren is quoted to have said "Sex is like washing your face—just something you do because you have to. Sex without love is absolutely ridiculous. Sex follows love, it never precedes it." What do you think?

> **Sienna West**: I am a hopeless romantic at heart so I do agree with Sophia. However, she was talking about sex in general not sex in the work place. [5]

Sex, to West, and seemingly the sex she has with Manning, is work. West suggests a divide between sex as it might ideally exist between loving adults, and that which she practices in her profession. She distinguishes between different forms of sex, neither one influencing the other. The answer is a canny one, because with it West strongly implies her own agency and autonomy, and that she has the emotional resources to appreciate sexual love while also being able to rationalize that variant of "professional" sex in which she engages. She also implies that this kind of sex is not ridiculous and absurd in itself, merely distinct from conventional understandings of sexual practice. In short, West upholds her right to be two separate sexual beings: West the worker, and West the romantic. Jodi West, another adult performer, offers a similarly self-aware take on the sex she experiences in the workplace.

> I worked for a couple of other studios to see how this whole pornography thing went and it was somewhat amazing to me that you would meet a guy or girl and then ten minutes later, you'd be banging the heck out of each other. To me, it just seems more natural to have chemistry or at least a friendship with your partner. Desi and I had been friends for about a year (in the swinging community) and I met Levi and Shay through the industry. I would consider them all very dear friends and it's a bonus that I get to have sex on screen with them. That said, you can never have too many friends.[6]

Jodi West here makes clear that the sexual self found in pornography is still an extension of the emotional being who enters into pornography production and then continues on once that production is complete. The human need for friendship, to care about one's sexual partner even in a contrived sexual scenario, remains. The responses of the two actresses certainly suggest as much. However, to better determine the significance of these statements it is necessary to contextualize them further within the notion of the sexual script.

SEXUAL SCRIPTS

The question should be raised as to how demonstrative these statements are of emotional realities of the women involved, and how much they represent a further projection of their pornography persona. Performers such as the two Wests are engaging in what sociologist Erving Goffman has called a "front": "that part of the individual's performance which regularly functions to define the situation for those who observe the performance."[7] Once the actress has her pornography persona, it will be used to negotiate auditions, interviews such as those described in this chapter, casual encounters with fans and, most importantly, performances. The persona will be used when questions are asked about the motivation of the individual for joining the industry, her sexual orientation, and raves such as those many actresses give on how they are "extremely sexual." Pornography, in general, depends on "sexual scripts," learned social interactions/patterns that typify different kinds of sexual interactions, in order to stimulate the erotic fantasies of its audience.[8]

As such it is necessary that much of the public image of the pornography performer, inclusive of their interviews, off-camera persona, and on-camera persona, fulfill certain expectations about the kinds of sexual beings they are, sexual beings first encountered onscreen, yet seen to exist in a similar fantasy paradigm whether they are featured in a print interview, a public appearance at an adult entertainment venue, and so forth. Typically socially available sexual scripts enable the transformation of an actor's filmed sexual performance to be recontextualized as some kind of film narrative, wherein their body's sexual response is given "meaning" from a broader sense of the performers interacting in the wider social world.[9] Jeffrey Escoffier writes:

> But the making of pornography necessarily invokes the culture's generic sexual scenarios—the sex/gender scripts; racial, class and ethnic stereotypes; the dynamics of domination and submission; and various reversals and transgressions of these codes. Pornography video scripts utilize these cultural and symbolic resources.[10]

These codes in turn draw on the performer's private lives and in turn their own emotional narratives. It is worth noting that in the same interview in which she discusses the importance of friendship in the production of pornography, Jodi West also promotes her Forbidden Fruit brand, discusses the real-world prevalence of the incestuous scenarios she enacts in her films, and poses for a series of pornographic nude photos. Similarly one need only watch the 2013 documentary *Aroused*, in which major pornographic actresses engage in acts of both emotional, biographical, and physical exhibitionism as they parade nude for a documentary camera, all while revealing their personal backstories and complex relationships with the pornographic film industry. HBO featured a similar approach in *Katie Morgan: Porn 101*, its own documentary in which the titular pornographic actress is interviewed about her work while nude. In short, there is every possibility that these statements of Sienna West and Jodi West are an extension of their scripts, a means for us, as the viewers, to engage with both our potential for arousal and our personal, human curiosity for these women.

FRIENDSHIP AND SEX

How likely then is the claim that sex and friendship are applicable to one another? In turn how demonstrative is this script of Jodi West's applicable to the emotional realities of our society? Closer than one might think. Sexual interest is a frequent feature in opposite-sex friendships. In fact, sexual attraction is often itself a major initial motive for the formation of an opposite-sex friendship.[11] In one study the majority of participants admitted to physical or sexual attraction towards a friend of the opposite sex.[12] Two out of five students in one college sample reported having had sexual intercourse with at least one person who was their opposite-sex friend at the time. Romantic attraction is also a component of opposite-sex friendship;[13] "52 percent of participants indicated romantic attraction toward an opposite-sex friend."[14] Friendship may effectively serve as "camouflage" for sexual desire. Just as frequently, though, the relationship between sex and friendship is all the more direct.

"Friends with Benefits" (FWB) is a term often used to describe a sexual relationship between those who would otherwise identify as friends. There have been numerous studies that have explored this intriguing modern phenomena. The negotiation of rules between Friends with Benefits has been explored[15] as well as its varied subcategories, the different ways in which men and women experience the category of Friends with Benefits,[16] and the sexual scripts men follow in a Friends with Benefits scenario. It is highly prevalent among university students, with up to 50 percent of students surveyed admitting to such a relationship. In Walid Afifi and Sandra Faulkner's survey study,

> 51% reported having ever engaged in at least one FWB relationship. Of these individuals, 49% had engaged in more than one FWB relationship. In Bisson and Levine's (2009) survey study, 60% of 125 university participants reported having ever engaged in a FWB relationship (36% of whom were currently in a FWB relationship).[17]

The testimony from studies conducted with those in a FWB scenario is intriguing, as it involved a delineation of the relative commingling of the ethos of friendship and the experience of sex:

> I think Friends with Benefits implies someone you were friends with before, whereas Fuck Friends [FBs] is someone you would have met just to fuck and then you would continue. But Friends with Benefits implies that there was a friendship to begin with. (Kristen, female group)[18]

In fact, those in the study even go so far as to integrate the notion of a FWB into a far grander network of social relations, stretching back to foundational relationships in a child's life:

> Well . . . say, if you're in elementary school and everyone progresses and develops. And all of a sudden you guys just hang out one day and sex just happens, right? It's just a random act and then you guys just keep doing it. Or, it could just be a hook up that two friends put together. Like if I went out with friends and I was like "Hey, I have a friend, meet him." And then you have that hook up. And then you become good friends. And then it turns into Friends with Benefits. And then after X amount of time, it stops. (Paul, mixed group)[19]

Indeed, allowances are even made for a semi-platonic attachment, wherein the possibility of desire satisfaction exists, yet equally there exists the possibility of pure regard and companionship:

> I think with Fuck Buddies, the only time you would see that person is when you're having sex. But with Friends with Benefits, you could possibly hang out with them and there would not necessarily be sex. You could hang out with other mutual friends or just have a night without sex. (sex educator group)[20]

What these various testimonials also represent, purely through the words of the participants themselves, is a scenario in which (a) the social world we inhabit has become pornified, what with the permissive, consequence-free sexuality of pornography having come to influence friendships; and (b) friendship and sex may become comprehensively inclusive.

AN OVERARCHING TREND

What does this all indicate? Pornography and the Internet permeate the lives of young men in particular and precipitate attitudes wherein casual sex becomes normal, pedestrian. "The Internet gives teen boys the idea that girls are interchangeable sexual objects at their disposal," says Lynn Ponton, a professor of psychiatry at the University of California at San Francisco and the author of *The Sex Lives of Teenagers*. "So how can they ever be developmentally ready for a real-life relationship?"[21] In turn there is a disconnect that develops from the potentially profound emotional intimacy that sex can create: "But coupled with this apparent disconnection is remarkable frankness about sex, even among friends of the opposite gender."[22] And yet ironically all of these trends in the consumption of pornography by the young, and in turn the co-opting of an entirely casual attitude to sex, occur within a hypersocial context, one dominated by sentiments of friendship and curiosity. The youthful sexual experiments, inspired in part by pornography, the youthful "hookup," mature in college-age students who acquire "fuck buddies" and "Friends with Benefits." And yet this is achieved, as noted, within the context of the experience of friendship, of seeking out companionship with one's peers. Pornography effectively aids in a feedback loop. The young watch pornography and acquire permissive attitudes. These attitudes lead to their concurrent social, sexual, and emotional evolution. By the time they have ended adolescence the notions of sex, pornography, and friendship have commingled. This, coupled with the fact that sexual interest is already a component of male-female friendship, suggests that pornography, in its production and scenarios, is aping a social paradigm it has helped to foster.

Some pornography might explore pro-social, entirely positive emotions such as affection and friendship. This is anathema to much of the discourse

that surrounds pornography. Certain pornographic scenarios may occur between individuals in a relationship, married couples, and so forth. Similarly,
the manner in which performers may interact within pornographic scenarios
would qualify as being affectionate or friendly behavior. Also, pornographic
practitioners themselves are often seeking out those individuals with whom
they are actual friends when making pornographic films. In turn this might be
linked to the fact that the sexual scripts of these productions, and in turn the
scripts performers such as Jodi West follow in interviews, place an emphasis
on friendship. Scripts aside, it is equally possible that West's experience of a
need for friendship is distinct from her pornography persona. Here the possibility is raised that what West describes, her commingled sense of sexual
attraction and friendship, is in fact demonstrative of natural human impulses.
As noted above, intersex friendship itself often contains a sexual component
and in turn our pornography-obsessed society has, via the sexualized intersex
friendships experienced by many, created an unlikely composite of sexual
desire and what might resemble platonic friendship.

CONCLUSION

It must be stated again that the views of MacKinnon, Dines, and Giles are
pertinent and justified. Yet it must be acknowledged that pornography's influence is so pervasive it will inevitably bump up against normative relationships: the college friends, the experimenting teens, the platonic male/female
friends. When it does there will inevitably manifest, within both pornography's production and scenarios, some echo of this sense of emotional nor-
malcy. Sexual scripts naturally problematize any attempts to analyze testimony by pornography's practitioners and consumers. However, the scripts
themselves are ironically consistent with wider social constructs. West's testimony may be false, her thoughts on her work contrived, yet what she
explores in her incest scenarios, for instance, is indicative of wider realities
in society. Indeed pornography is rooted on stronger foundations than the
joyless relief of desire. To Michel Foucault pleasure has history, and as such
the pleasure pornography depicts is inevitably rooted in a wider reality. Giles
goes so far as to claim that the explicit depiction of sex allows the male
viewer to engage obliquely with his own feminine nature. Pornography may
be, in short, a complete workout for the psyche of the viewer. The potential
for the typical, the warm, the everyday to seep into porn, almost invisibly, is
thanks to its unique instability as Williams observes, its fundamentally por-
ous nature. Chance may be objectified in her scene, yet it is simultaneously a
scene which depicts male passivity and female ingenuity and kindness.
Chance is also dominant in the scene through her amusing seduction and

provocation of her boyfriend. Pornography, like the world, is wider and stranger and less formulaic than any might give it credit for.

NOTES

1. Karen Finley, "Make Porn Not War," *XXX: 30 Porn Star Portraits*, ed. Timothy Greenfield-Sanders (Boston: Bulfinch, 2004), 78–79.

2. Catharine MacKinnon, *Toward a Feminist Theory of the State* (Cambridge, MA: Harvard University Press, 1989), 179.

3. Gail Dines, "Dirty Business," in *Pornography: The Production and Consumption of Inequality,* ed. Gail Dines, Robert Jensen, and Ann Russo (New York: Routledge, 1998), 62.

4. Linda Williams, *Hard Core: Power, Pleasure, and the "Frenzy of the Visible"* (Berkeley: University of California Press, 1989), 83.

5. Sienna West, "Sienna West Interview," http://archive.is/JcVKG (accessed 17 Mar. 2014).

6. Jodi West, "Jodi West Interview," http://www.xcritic.com/columns/column.php?columnId=3852 (accessed 17 Mar. 2014).

7. Erving Goffman, *The Presentation of the Self In Everyday Life* (Garden City, NY: Doubleday, 1959), 22.

8. John Gagnon and William Simon, *Sexual Conduct: The Social Sources of Human Sexuality*. (Chicago: Aldine, 1973), 260–65.

9. Leo Braudy, *The World in a Frame: What We See in Films* (Garden City, NY: Anchor Press/Doubleday, 1976), 191–217.

10. Jeffrey Escoffier, "Gay-for-Pay: Straight Men and the Making of Gay Pornography," *Qualitative Sociology* 26, no. 4 (Winter 2003): 550.

11. Suzanne Rose, "Same- and Cross-Sex Friendships and the Psychology of Homosociality,"*Sex Roles* 12, nos. 1–2 (January 1985): 63–74.

12. Heidi Reeder, "'I Like You as a Friend': The Role of Attraction in Cross-Sex Friendship," *Journal of Social and Personal Relationships* 17, no. 3 (June 2000): 329–48.

13. Daniel Kaplan and Christopher Keys, "Sex and Relationship Variables as Predictors of Sexual Attraction in Cross-Sex Platonic Friendships between Young Heterosexual Adults," *Journal of Social and Personal Relationships* 14, no. 2 (April 1997):191–206.

14. Bryan Koenig, Lee Kirkpatrick, and Timothy Ketelaar, "Misperception of Sexual and Romantic Interests in Opposite-Sex Friendships: Four Hypotheses," *Personal Relationships* 14, no. 3 (September 2007): 414.

15. Mikayla Hughes, Kelly Morrison, and Kelli Jean Asada, "What's Love Got to Do with It? Exploring the Impact of Maintenance Rules, Love Attitudes, and Network Support on Friends with Benefits Relationships," *Western Journal of Communication* 69, no. 1 (January 2005): 49–66.

16. Jesse Owen and Frank Fincham, "Effects of Gender and Psychosocial Factors on 'Friends With Benefits' Relationships Among Young Adults," *Archives of Sexual Behavior* 40, no. 2 (April 2011): 311–20.

17. Walid Afifi and Sandra Faulkner, "On Being 'Just Friends': The Frequency and Impact of Sexual Activity in Cross-Sex Friendships," *Journal of Social and Personal Relationships* 17, no. 2 (April 2000): 205–22.

18. Jocelyn Wentland and Elke Reissing, "Taking Casual Sex Not Too Casually: Exploring Definitions of Casual Sexual Relationships," *Canadian Journal of Human Sexuality* 20, no. 3 (December 2011): 79.

19. Wentland and Reissing, "Taking Casual Sex Not Too Casually," 80.

20. Wentland and Reissing, "Taking Casual Sex Not Too Casually," 84.

21. Quoted in Benoit Denizet-Lewis, "Friends, Friends with Benefits and the Benefits of the Local Mall," *New York Times,* May 30, 2004, http://www.nytimes.com/2004/05/30/magazine/30NONDATING.html (accessed 17 Mar. 2014).

22. Denizet-Lewis, "Friends, Friends with Benefits."

Chapter Twelve

Undisciplining Pornography Studies

Katrien Jacobs

This essay proposes a philosophical attitude towards digital media and pornographic immersion, as well as pornography's tendency to provoke mass media scandals and debates. The chapter makes use of queer theory and new media theory to propose a way of consuming, resonating, and reflecting on pornography. First of all, it takes inspiration from Jack Halberstam's notion of "queer art of failure" as a means of rethinking porn usage and arousal by challenging dominant paradigms of economy, culture, and social networking. In developing novel pornographic sensibilities, we step beyond habitual ways of enacting gender and also address a larger crisis within work and leisure institutions.[1] We also test out new modes of being mentally or physically aroused (or stirred) by pornography as "primal media." Pornography becomes a way of sensing and sharing a new type of intimacy and sexual intelligence. It no longer has the unique ability to "subjugate" its viewers by overturning their mental abilities. Rather, as suggested by Susanna Paasonen in her study of Internet pornography and affect, people experience altered sensations of the body and consciousness as "carnal resonance" or a pervasive and constantly negotiated stimulation and affect.[2]

PORN STUDIES AND THE FEAR OF PRIMAL MEDIA

Pornography is defined as a variety of sexually explicit media and aesthetic expressions, while porn studies is the study of representations of sexuality and sex acts within different media regimes. Pornography studies, or the more colloquial term porn studies, is an interdisciplinary academic project, a subfield of several disciplines within the arts and humanities, as well as the social sciences and health sciences. Film and media scholars have been interested in analyzing and debating media aesthetics, changing technologies, and mechanisms of cultural reception, while social scientists have been concerned with analyzing the "media effects" of pornography consumption on individuals or society at large.

Moreover, there is a research tradition that has permeated various academic disciplines, whose glum findings about pornography are morally driven and reinforced by mass media stories about pornography as primal media that damages culture and relationships. In my previous study of Internet pornography conducted in 2006, I described a process of the mass media constructing pornography as primal media and concurrent legislative backlash.[3] I scrutinized a typical news story in the *Financial Times* about UK society's supposed "pornification," in which a reputable journalist describes the effects of Internet pornography on users by featuring "Michael," a typical "addict" of Internet pornography who is a frequent downloader and also has a poor sexual relationship with his wife. To prove the correlation between primal media and sexual neglect, he quotes an academic expert at the University of Pennsylvania's Sexual Trauma and Psychopathology Program, who has found that exposure to porn images directly alters brain waves: "Even non–sex addicts will show brain reactions on PET (Positron Emission Tomography) scans while viewing pornography similar to cocaine addicts looking at images of cocaine." The journalist then alerts readers to the idea that ubiquitous porn industries are actually flooding our homes and media landscapes, our lives and sexual relations:

> [T]alk of pornography flooding into Britain's homes as never before is neither hyperbolic nor judgmental; it's a statement of fact. The internet has released a genie from the bottle. Once pornography had to be actively sought; now it is accessible and affordable for the majority of the population, anonymity guaranteed at the click of a mouse.[4]

Even though the story itself is dated, pornography today is even more so freely available online and "flooding" our home spaces, and nonetheless these claims are systematically flawed as they ignore the fact that porn users do not react to porn in a uniform manner. This type of coverage of pornography tries to evoke a mood of social exasperation about the univocal psychological impact and social force of pornography. Watching porn is erroneously compared to addictions such as recreational drug use, as it would release a chemical in the body that asks for more, and is prone to escalation, including accepting increasingly degrading pornographic content. Another point of inspiration for this kind of argument are neoconservative and religiously inspired studies of porn usage, such as Pamela Paul's *Pornified: How Pornography Is Transforming Our Lives, Our Relationships and Our Families.* Paul came up with an urgent anti-porn message based on a number of interviews with porn users about their sexual relationships. Paul's interviews feature women complaining about their male's excessive consumption and men confessing their lack of interest in marital sex.

Even though Paul's work is based on testimonies about marital problems, it still reinforces a persistent fear of primal porn culture—the idea that pornography would have the power to subjugate audiences to predetermined uncontrollable and socially degraded subjectivities. It is suggested that porn usage and sexual arousal cancel out our rational-critical judgment, just as historically the most vocal academic movement against pornography was initiated by feminists who believed that pornography would universally "subjugate" women, casting them as "victims" of primal media—as receptors of male abuse within pornographic fictions, or as the sex workers of exploitative companies. What is wrong with these suggestions is that they ignore the wide diversity of sexually explicit media and emotive experiences that are currently available. Secondly, they assume that porn/sex workers and porn users are powerless and predominantly internalizing or enacting gender roles of debasement, while sexually explicit media trigger in audiences a much wider range of emotional and philosophical-reflective states.[5]

In trying to frame a response to these accusations, Clarissa Smith has shown in *One for the Girls* that this ongoing essentializing tendency is simply based on a lack of research into actual phenomena, the varying celebrity models, culture industries, and technological infrastructures that constitute pornography. The most famous example of a construction of primal porn culture would be that of anti-pornography activist Andrea Dworkin (1946–2005), who attacked pornography because of its power to dominate females, thereby ignoring "a whole range of differences—not least media forms, textual structures and narrative strategies in favor of a focus on male power."[6]

In short, this tradition is interested in simplifying accounts of actual media experiences and framing pornography as a social ill and aspect of human degradation. At the same there is a tendency to ridicule the work of more serious researchers who get deeply and sometimes personally involved in the study of sexuality. Think for instance about the downfall of pioneering sex researcher Alfred Kinsey (1894–1956), whose reports about sexuality had a massive following, but who was also himself depicted as a victim of sexual addictions. Kinsey rebelled against a tradition of sexual shaming within the academy and society at large that was based on a neglect of empirical data about diversified sexual behaviors. He decided to make a break with morally driven sex research by initiating cycles of interviews with students and wider socioeconomic layers of the population. At a later stage, he wanted to scientifically observe sexual behaviors and organized gatherings that involved the filming of sexual relations, in which he sometimes took part. He quickly became accused of being a morally corrupted individual, seeking sexual pleasure and pornography instead of innovation in health science. He lost a huge amount of his research funding after his approach to sex research was publicly attacked. Kinsey's "unsound" method was valid and trend-setting, in my modest opinion, morally transgressive and sincerely aimed at examining sexual behaviors. But the idea that an individual researcher or collective academic entity could show a deep or "passionate" and personal interest in primal media, has more often than not led to deep trouble for the scholars involved—from institutional stigmas to persistent attacks from conservative organizations and indignant individuals.

As a result of pornography's construction as primal media, academic disciplines have equally been reluctant to accept pornography studies as a valid enterprise. In recent years the field has become more accepted within certain academic departments, and the international academic publisher Routledge has launched a journal with the same name, *Porn Studies*. Yet immediately after its announcement, under the title "Routledge Pro Porn Studies Bias," a large petition was signed by hundreds of people, a fair number of whom were academics, who attacked the journal and its international editorial board for pursuing an unbalanced and morally corrupted mission.[7] As the petitioners against the journal *Porn Studies* stated:

> [W]e ask that you change the name to reflect and make evident the bias of its editors (Pro-Porn Studies) and create another journal which will represent the position of anti-porn scholars and activists and the voices of mental health professionals, porn industry survivors, and feminist scholars whose analyses examine the replication and reification of misogyny, child abuse, and sexual exploitation in mainstream pornography.[8]

The petition was actually initiated by a campaigning group, "Stop Porn Culture," who refer to themselves as "a group of academics, activists, anti-violence experts, health professionals, and educators." Some of these academics (for instance a Comparative Literature professor whose affiliation I have deleted here) are more down-to-earth about their opposition to the subject matter:

> At a time when the humanities are endangered at many institutions, I can't imagine a more self-destructive development than a "pro-porn" academic journal. It hands a supremely useful gift to the opponents of liberal education. Porn makes sexual experience unreal, and destroys the capacity of men and women to form meaningful and lasting relationships.[9]

It is curious that humanities researchers here feel empowered to comment professionally on medical and psychological factors, whereas in actuality they also reveal personal convictions and once again evoke a fear of primal media. It is not just a matter of their personal feelings influencing their ideas, which is indeed also the case with researchers who defend sexual diversity and pornography, but the fact that they want to prevent acts of research into diversified porn cultures and audiences.

Moreover, this type of irate opposition to the study of pornography is indeed part and parcel of its mission. Indeed, this ever-emerging field has always been attacked, even though academic researchers have always been critical of sexually explicit media. Porn researchers do not promote porn culture or pornographic bliss, but they do have to stand up for the right to do research.

A PHILOSOPHICAL MINDSET

It would be easy to argue from here onward that porn studies will slowly get liberated from such controversies, and that academic disciplines are catching up and becoming more tolerant towards academic porn research. Instead, I will argue that pornography research needs to go beyond the academic profession itself to set up alternative embodied practices of reflection. The role of porn studies is to do in-depth research and to document more complex emotional and philosophical experiences. Perhaps a lack of philosophical backdrop is due to the fact that pornographic discrediting is also at work within academic discourses itself, as academic languages are out of touch with contemporary sexually explicit media and its varied industries and aesthetics. This type of discursive incompatibility between academia and pornography is also due to the fact that universities issue censorship measures or firewalls that prevent circulation of sexually explicit media, and that also target noncommercial and educational websites. Again, rash decisions are being made against a potential surfacing of sexually explicit media within public spaces that makes the study of such media landscapes cumbersome. It is believed that pornography is different from other types of media (such as for instance extremely violent or racist media) in that it would indeed have the unique power to corrupt the minds of scholars and students. University administrations rarely discuss their censorship policies and reinforce a fear of primal media rather than encourage advanced research initiatives.

One of the most common side effects of this fear is the idea that pornography usage is getting more extreme and dangerous, especially for the more vulnerable groups of youth and young adults who are now deeply immersed in social media and netporn browsing. Jack Sargeant has given an appropriate retort to this observation. He writes that there has indeed been a tendency in the porn industries to produce ever more extreme and degrading sex acts as licensed obscenities. He zooms in on the example of "anus-to-mouth" videos, in which a male typically pulls his penis from the anus of a female and then sticks it straight into her open mouth and down her throat. Often, the female cavity is cast as the receptor of brutal and excessive male agency, as when multiple penises plunge into an anus, or hordes of penises ejaculate on a female face, or men line up to do the world's biggest gang bang.

Besides the fact that we can crave or hate such depictions of pornographic excess, Sargeant proposes that we think of excess in a more philosophical way, as "all non-reproductive sexual activity belongs to the category of excess expenditure, where the unrestrained pursuit of pleasure becomes in itself both object choice and subject."[10] The more we access porn images as expenditure of resources and desire, the more we may fail to grasp the boundaries between the object of our pursuits and the agencies of desire itself. Pornography becomes agency itself, or a psychosomatic mechanism of processing media landscapes. This condition cannot be halted, but it can be further researched as changing and diversified experiences with media and sex entertainment. It is often blindly assumed this condition will break us apart as social beings or corrupt us as thinkers, but it could also be seen as a social lubricant or even just another thread holding together our social fabric.

Social media environments have encouraged generations of web users to browse through a wide range of products, while managing friendships and affectations around the products of sex entertainment. Wendy Chun's study of cyberculture foresaw that methods of navigating and archiving pornographic excess would be driven by a Foucauldian "will to knowledge," an urge to build a sexual knowledge apparatus within online communities.[11] For example, porn as a downloaded, pirated, and peer-to-peer product par excellence is most aptly shared among young adults, many of whom have amassed collections before entering a university classroom. These ways of accessing porn have also become more common for the target group of male consumers and nontarget groups, who easily glance at and gossip about products as novelty items within their social media spaces.[12]

Hence, rather than thinking that we can halt or curtail states of immersion by means of moral arguments or technologies of censorship, our analysis should be more embodied, more reflective, and socially responsible about this very condition. I thus propose that the field of pornography studies needs to go beyond the boundaries of academic disciplines, and even requires an *undisciplining* of methods of knowledge production. In *The Queer Art of Failure* (2011) and *Gaga Feminism: Sex, Gender and the End of Normal* (2012), Jack Halberstam argues that new languages of social networking and sexual change are interconnected as transnational "climates" or "ecosystems" that transcend disciplinary boundaries. For Halberstam this type of ecology involves a breaking down of normative mechanisms of success, cultural growth, and economic prosperity:

> Heteronormative common sense leads to the equation of success with advancement, capital accumulation, family, ethical conduct, and hope. Other subordi-

nate, queer, or counter-hegemonic modes of common sense lead to the association of failure with nonconformity, anticapitalist practices, nonreproductive
life-styles, negativity and critique.[13]

This capacity to practice idiosyncratic lifestyles is redefined as the "art of
failure," a way of reclaiming differences as self-aware modes of expression
and living. It is not just about sexual relationships but also a way of sidestep-
ping dominant networks of education within neoliberal societies. In asserting
attitudes of failure, people could also reinvent modes of vitality around pornography research, while questioning their daily responsibilities and the
pressures associated with responsible and ethical criticism.

This shift towards self-aware practices of pornography are not only driven
by an outcast mentality, or self-expression for sexual minorities, but can also
be studied "in locations where we presume that the normal is most stable."[14]
For instance, research has shown that divorced middle-aged heterosexual
women now show a tendency towards "hetero-flexibility," or opening up
their sexual preferences to unorthodox relationships or lifestyles. Halberstam's art of failure differs from sectarian identity politics given that the so-
called "normal" populations and relationship models are included within a
larger trend towards nonnormative life choices. The art of failure dissolves
boundaries between "mainstream" and "subcultural" social groups, between
sanctified and disobedient sectors of the culture industry, while pornographic
subject matter is used to question "incarcerated" modules of knowledge production.

I would argue that pornography studies needs to embrace failure to become a discipline that questions itself and its validating sexual knowledge in
refreshing and perverse ways, in the sense that it stands up and intervenes in
ingrained academic research practices. It intervenes not only by recuperating
pornography from ongoing stigmatization and by stimulating research initiatives, but by radically opening up methods of perception, communication,
and networking. Liberal arts disciplines in general have become more aware
of the fact that their fields of study have excluded or normalized minority or
outlawed experiences of sexuality. A call for perversity can be applied to
pornography, as in the Duke University Press book series, "Perverse Moder-
nities," which includes critical introspection by thinking about "disciplinary
infidelities" or how new methods of studying sexuality and perversity will
further question outcomes and "break up" the making of knowledge.[15] Pornography studies can and will take leadership in this self-reflective mission.
Its highly vilified or "raunchy" subject matter is indeed affecting society at
large and cannot be insulated from wider changes in education, culture, and
technology. Pornographic materials should stimulate reflections about how
individual and collective sexual desires and fantasies are nurtured by fluctuating media landscapes. To be vehemently against pornography and porn

studies is to deny these formations of sexual knowledge. Instead, our fields of knowledge should get more sexual and find ways to examine embodied media experiences among the "normal" and "perverse" people. An analysis of how these people sense and judge pornographic materials will challenge the dense and sometimes alienating languages of academic expression and evaluation. We still need to learn how to discuss experiences of the sexual body as they bring to light new and previously discouraged discourses. To that extent pornography studies should include work by nonacademic thinkers—artists, writers, pornographers, investigative journalists, bloggers, independent filmmakers, erotica experts—who have experimented with literary and audio-visual depictions of the sexual body as intellectual enquiry. Certainly mainstream and art-house filmmakers and curators of sex-themed art works have helped in setting up insightful and highly emotive debates about pornographic representation. Pornography studies needs to learn how to fund-raise for such types of symposiums and festivals that can handle frank manifestations and discussions of the sexual body.

While some universities may be opening up to this challenge, it is also the case that this field of knowledge may need to maintain an amount of autonomy from academic thought and expression. Undisciplining pornography studies is not an easy proposition, as the history of radical sex research shows; it would still be a pioneering effort to open up the field of pornography alongside a sense of philosophical reflection and a sense of social change and stylistic overhaul within academic disciplines.

FROM PRIMAL MEDIA TO RESONANCE

Susanna Paasonen has recently introduced a framework of "carnal resonance" that explains how pornography in the digital era may affect and resonate with people in a way that can be distinguished from older paradigms of media. The starting point of her analysis is to speculate how pornography feels to its contemporary users:

> It matters how objects feel since such "feeling" gives rise to different kinds of attachment and resonance. The feel, tactility, and texture of pornography are intimately tied to its technologies of production and distribution—whether the high definition and texture of 35mm film, the grainy authenticity of gonzo and amateur videos, or the apparent immateriality of digital images, videos, and texts that consist of zeros and ones and are open to virtually endless remodification.[16]

In a porn study based on ethnographic interviews with French adult male porn users, Florian Voros further develops Paasonen's notion of materiality and resonance. In his analysis, men access and resonate or "reactivate" por nographic stimuli by downloading, archiving, and commenting on them, and also through bodily techniques such as nipple touching and breast stroking. In this way, Voros believes, pornography and its sexual scenarios no longer overwhelm users. Rather, these products are skillfully and steadily selected and archived, while being "domesticated" amidst every day thoughts and experiences:

> Indeed, surfing for porn on the Internet is a highly interactive process through which we browse, click, interrupt, fast forward, rate, tag or comment on the videos we watch. Apart from moments of surfing, audiences re-produce pornography through a wide range of practices such as uploading their own photos and videos to amateur tubes and cruising websites, or more simply, by reworking mentally, while masturbating, the hottest pornographic scenarios they have recently watched. Parting from the material dimension of the activity, watching porn appears as an active and productive transformation of scripts and objects into pleasure and signification. Through these bodily practices, pornography is subjectively appropriated, transformed and altered.[17]

Even though these ideas about pornographic resonance are primarily based on private porn experiences, my own research seeks to discover if they can be applied to how people process pornography within public screening sites of social debate or education.

The first times that I was part of organizing public symposia about pornography and digital media was in Amsterdam in 2005 and 2007. These were conferences where people presented audio-visually oriented talks and screenings about emerging netporn sites, and in such a way that audiences could watch and process the sexually explicit media being discussed.[18] A novel kind of curating and collectively sensing of sexualized media and sexual knowledge through digital media formats was one way of initiating this field of study. The idea of publicly reflecting on sexually explicit media stems from a belief in properly analyzing cognition and affect. First of all, pornography has indeed suffered from stigmatization, from a lack of public viewing and collective memory. Even though it is easy for people to access and comment on porn movies at their home computers, or when browsing iPhones and tablet devices, there is rarely public discussion of these shared online materials. What we have established with these conferences is that showcasing pornography can indeed intellectually stimulate, entertain, and arouse audiences. Similarly, audiences can get endlessly bored with plotless porn, or they can get disgusted with certain types of "extreme" imagery. It is only fair for researchers to examine these collective emotive and social reactions to global media landscapes.

Even though there are currently very few public physical spaces (like movie theaters) left for porn viewing and education, sexually explicit imagery is widely discussed in the mass media and social media. In this sense, pornography studies should be an educational space to further archive and dissect these manifestations. For instance, in 2008 there was a big Hong Kong sex scandal through which the "DIY" porn collection of a very well-known entertainer, Edison Chen, was released on the Internet. All of a sudden, a bubble of secrecy around pornography burst and many Hong Kong people participated in porn debates through their awareness of this specific collection. In Hong Kong, I closely followed the highly polarized public debates and the formation of collective memory around these images as they attracted responses in the media, in classrooms, and on the Internet. It was a big surprise for me to find out that during these Hong Kong "porn wars," there was an erotically sophisticated and even philosophical perspective at work that would normally have been invisible. During the time of the sex scandal I collaborated with my students to compile these responses and publish an article and documentary about porn culture in Hong Kong.[19] Since the images associated with the scandal had resonated in the public sphere, it became much easier to archive and comment on them as significant technological and sexual changes within Hong Kong society.

In order to continue this kind of research about pornographic resonance, I have set up a series of intercultural workshops entitled "Drifting Eyeballs: A Workshop about Trans-Asian Feminine Pornographic Tastes and Experiences." This recent project intends to instigate and collect women's testimonies regarding sexually explicit media as a type of engagement with new media and about emerging sexual sensibilities. Since this was also a project about feminist uses of social media and the sexual gaze within different cultures, I started out gathering small groups of women in Hong Kong, Japan, and the United States. More specifically, I tried to look for ways to get women's testimonies by means of workshops that consisted of screenings of short video clips followed by discussion. The groups were kept fairly small (about fifteen participants) so that the atmosphere would be comfortable, casual, and allow in-depth dialogues and discussions.

In designing the logistics of the project, women in each of the workshops were asked to watch and respond to video clips, from hard-core pornography to alternative queer and female-friendly pornography produced within different cultures. In this way, the workshops simulated a "hyper-mediated" environment in which web users browse through sexually explicit media as fluctuating genres, fads, and products. As a research project traveling from Hong Kong to the U.S. West Coast, the project archived a wide range of individual and localized reactions to the potential of public screenings. The logistics of finding hosts and public spaces to help organize these screenings was complex, but I managed to set up workshops in several universities, or in sex shops and art galleries and LGBT community spaces that are equally interested in the questions at hand. As stated before, the project had to embrace the art of failure and sometimes leave behind the notion of an "educational institution" altogether, as we gathered in private spaces or motel rooms to watch and discuss segments of movies on a laptop computer. In some sense, the use of smaller screens and tablet devices rather than projection onto a larger screen worked well in allowing people to feel comfortable and at times ignore the oftentimes "crude" and "in-your-face" imagery.

The project also examined the logistics of using public spaces and digital technologies that can help people feel more comfortable and alert while processing sexually explicit media. The project became focused on finding ways to enable these publicly shared expressions of sexual knowledge around multiple selections, or how to have dialogues with a digital generation that is more acquainted with online porn sharing and sexual commentary. The public spaces and digital technologies necessary for basic video editing and data projection are now readily available, while the employment of smaller (computer) screens and tablet technologies gives participants some freedom to be more or less immersed in the porn scenes.

Needless to say, most spaces of education and entertainment would still resist such screenings of sexually explicit media by means of moral objections or licensing laws. Nevertheless, a movement towards pornography studies suggests that sexually explicit media should be part of media education. The workshops suggested that youth do not feel bombarded or subjugated by these sexually explicit media. They are quite willing to share information about their media landscapes—being able to stand up to sexually explicit media while decoding the media selections analytically and emotionally. These types of resonance will never see the light of day if aspects of private and public porn usage are constantly ridiculed and associated with primal fears. While this type of pornography research is gaining ground, the voices against porn studies will be not be dimmed. All we can do is show that our porn immersion is not primal, but underpinned by a complex and embodied philosophical mindset.

CONCLUSION

It is difficult to promote a philosophical mindset towards pornography, since sexually explicit media have long been stigmatized as objects of academic study and mass media commentary. One of the major arguments against any kind of philosophical or cultural studies tradition of pornography is that sexually explicit media have a unique ability to cancel out our ability to critically reflect on media aesthetics or personal-emotive and social impacts. But rather than denying the fact that we are indeed affected by sexually explicit media, this article points out that this condition can be understood or internalized as a type of philosophical libidinal experience. In order to grasp the impact of pornography, we need to "undiscipline pornography studies," to gradually develop innovative methods of immersion and reflection that can grasp how we have indeed become novel beings as desiring subjects and as social beings or researchers. Simply speaking, the engines of pornography studies can been turned on to enhance our knowledge of a wide range of media landscapes, but beyond that we need to use pornography to challenge engrained methods of disembodied judgment or bodily denial within academic thought and expression. While this argument invites a wide range of philosophical rebuttals, it proposes to go beyond well-known methods of disembodied discourse while envisioning a new type of university.

NOTES

The research for this article was partially funded by the CUHK direct grant "Sex, Art, Afterglow: Cross-cultural Reflections on Artistic and Sexual Interventions in Digital Media Cultures." (#4051031)

1. Jack Halberstam, *The Queer Art of Failure* (Durham, NC: Duke University Press, 2011).

2. Susanna Paasonen, *Carnal Resonance: Affect and Online Pornography* (Cambridge, MA: MIT Press, 2011).

3. Katrien Jacobs, *Netporn: DIY Web Culture and Sexual Politics* (Lanham, MD: Rowman and Littlefield, 2007).

4. Adrian Turpin, "Not Tonight Darling, I Am Online," *Financial Times*, April 31, 2006, http://www.ft.com/intl/cms/s/0/c65a4966-bfbb-11da-939f-0000779e2340.html (accessed 15 Nov. 2013).

5. Clarissa Smith, *One for the Girls: The Pleasures and Practices of Reading Women's Porn* (Bristol, UK: Intellect, 2007), 36.

6. Smith, *One for the Girls*, 36.

7. An overview of the recent controversies about porn studies was reported in the *Guardian* on June 16, 2013: http://www.guardian.co.uk/culture/2013/jun/16/journal-editors-attacked-promoting-porn (accessed 15 Nov. 2013).

8. "Routledge Pro Porn Studies Bias," ipetitions.com, http://www.ipetitions.com/petition/porn_studies_bias/signatures (accessed 15 Nov. 2013).

9. "Routledge Pro Porn Studies Bias."

10. Jack Sargeant, "Filth and Sexual Excess: Some Brief Reflections on Popular Scatology," *Media/Culture Journal* 9, no. 5 (November 2006), http://journal.media-culture.org.au/0610/00-editorial.php (accessed 11 Nov. 2006).

11. Wendy Chun, *Control and Freedom: Power and Paranoia in the Age of Fiber Optics* (Cambridge, MA: MIT Press, 2006).

12. Katrien Jacobs, *People's Pornography : Sex and Surveillance on the Chinese Internet* (Bristol, UK: Intellect Books, 2011).

13. Halberstam, *The Queer Art of Failure*, 89.

14. Halberstam, *The Queer Art of Failure*, 82.

15. For an overview of this book series, go to http://www.dukepress.edu/Catalog/ProductList.php?viewby=series&id=39&pagenum=all&sort=newest (accessed 15 Nov. 2013).

16. Susanna Paasonen, *Carnal Resonance: Affect and Online Pornography* (Cambridge, MA: MIT Press, 2011), 99.

17. Florian Voros, "Domesticated Porn: Gendered Embodiment in Audience Reception Practices of Pornography," in *Porn after Porn: Contemporary Alternative Pornographies*, ed. Enrico Biasin, Giovanna Maina, and Frederico Zecca (Milan: Mimesis, 2014), 9.

18. Some of the presentations and papers of these two conferences have been compiled in *Click Me: A Netporn Studies Reader*, ed. M. Janssen, K. Jacobs, and M. Pasquinelli (Amsterdam: Institute of Network Cultures, 2007). Available online at http://www.networkcultures.org/_uploads/24.pdf (accessed 6 Dec. 2013).

19. Katrien Jacobs, "Sex Scandal Science in Hong Kong," *Sexualities: Studies in Culture and Society* 12, no. 5 (2009): 605–12.

Part V

The Possibilities of Pornography

Chapter Thirteen

Sisters Are Doin' It for Themselves

Black Women and the New Pornography

Ariane Cruz

The inferior sex has got a new exterior.—Aretha Franklin and the Eurythmics, "Sisters Are Doin' It for Themselves"

This chapter explores a "new" wave of African American female pornographers currently working to transform prevailing representations of black womanhood in pornography. Negotiating the inequities of a still white male–dominated industry—marginalization of labor, exclusion, rampant stereotyping, racism, and sexism—these pioneers have challenged structural inequalities, altered the material conditions of labor, constructed new sites of distribution and spectatorship, and inspired new audiences while inventing novel images of black female sexuality. All guided by a DIY (do-it-yourself) mission, these women produce pornography that represents a critical intervention in the representation of black female sexuality. Whether using new technology as a platform of empowerment and vehicle of black female sexual autonomy, or more traditional sites of distribution, development, and spectatorship, these women re-envision black female sexuality via their animation of diverse representations of "alternative," nonhegemonic fantasies and pleasure, specifically queer and BDSM (bondage/discipline, dominance/submission, sadism/masochism). Focusing on these overlapping themes—queerness, the architecture of digital and physical spaces of (self) representation, and BDSM— through the work of three highly acclaimed black women pornographers: Shine Louise Houston, Nenna Joiner, and Vanessa Blue, I illustrate the ways black women are changing not only representations of black female sexuality in adult entertainment, but also the face of contemporary American pornography itself. As I argue here, by offering refreshing images of the black female body and figurations of black women's sexual desire that challenge prevailing hegemonic heteronormative constructions of black female sexuality, such as more gender fluidity, body size diversity, queer, and alternative sexual fantasies, these women are challenging dominant visual conventions of black womanhood.

I begin this essay by explaining how I employ the term "new." There are two different ways in which I imagine and enlist it. First, "new" refers to temporal sequence and being recent. Most of the work I am looking at here occurred within the last five years, an exciting era in porn with regard to the growing presence of black woman producers, performers, and directors. Such growth is connected with recent innovations in digital technology that have helped to further democratize the genre.[1] Second, "new" functions as an intervention. Here, new becomes a label designating an ideological shift, a critical transformation. I employ this second conceptualization of "new" quite deliberately to reference an African diasporic cultural tradition. My intention here is to evoke the historical legacy of black cultural production as a matter of reinvention and a political project of not just self-expression, but self-determination.

In his article, "The Trope of a New Negro and the Reconstruction of the Image of the Black," Henry Louis Gates Jr. discusses black representation as a type of urgent rehabilitation in not just the context of the post-Reconstruction New Negro Movement, but the "crux of the period of black intellectual reconstruction" ranging from 1895 to 1925.[2] Gates is concerned with two "antithetical" archetypes: the "New Negro" figure and the "Sambo." While the Sambo represents an anti-black racist figuration via the white gaze, its corrective, corrected trope, the New Negro, symbolizes a restorative act of black self-representation. Gates states:

> Whereas the image of a "New Negro" has served various generations of black intellectuals as a sign of plentitude, of regeneration, or a truly reconstructed presence, the image of the black in what I like to think of as "Sambo Art" has served various generations of racists as a sign of lack, of degeneration, of a truly negated absence. The two sets of figures can also be said to have a certain cause and effect relation, with the fiction of a Negro American who is "now" somehow "new" or different from an "Old Negro" generated to counter the image in the popular American imagination of the black as devoid of all the characteristics that separate the lower forms of human life from the supposedly higher forms.[3]

Similarly, "new" here signifies these three black women pornographers' political investment in a type of reconstruction of black female sexuality from a sign of lack, degeneration, and "negated absence" to one of "regeneration" and "plentitude." As a critical recuperation of black female sexuality, this diverse body of black female-produced pornography represents more than an intervention into the field of pornography; such work can be seen as embodying a "reconstructed presence" in the broader arena of black women's visual (self) representation. In its political project of challenging normative fictions of black female sexual subjectivity, this work represents a transgressive queering of black female sexuality, and its visual renderings in pornography. Often in these women's work, however, queer serves not just as a particular technique of critical inquiry, and/or "as a metaphor without a fixed referent," but designates the authorial gaze and voice, mode of analytical engagement, and primary subjects of representation.[4]

Energized by the emblem of newness, these women work in and against a historical archive of black female hypervisibility and invisibility in contemporary American pornography. Early commercial moving-image pornography featuring black women from the early part of the 1980s, the silver age of porn, generally conformed to a Sambo-type representation characterized by lack, degeneration, an eroticization of racism, black female racial and sexual alterity, and the intense ambivalence of the black female body under the white hetero-patriarchal male gaze. There are two especially egregious examples in the first black video of the early 1980s. In an important yet never-printed trade magazine article, Susie Bright discusses these pioneer videos.[5] Sketching the movement of black pornography from a marginal subset to an important niche within the burgeoning home video industry, and a financially appealing specialization for adventurous pornographers, a "fringe theme that quickly graduated from risky to mandatory requirement in every video store," Bright posits that there were two different types of "black/white theme tapes" in the mid-1980s.[6] One approach, the "one part National Lampoon, a heaping tablespoon of we-are-the-people-your-parents-warned-you-about, and a sprinkling of every racial cliché in the American psyche" was characterized by the work of the Dark Brothers and VCA in the video *Let Me Tell Ya 'Bout Black Chicks* (1985).[7] The second approach, what Bright terms the "'Dis Here Is Black Folks' approach" was pioneered in the video *Hot Chocolate* (1984), written by William Margold and directed by Drea.[8]

Let Me Tell Ya 'Bout Black Chicks is an intensely stereotypical video about a crew of black female maids as they recount their sexual experiences with white men. In one scene, for example, one of the black female leads, Sahara, stars in a double penetration scene with two white men dressed as Ku Klux Klan members. In its employment of the white male Klan figure as a sexual partner for the black female, it recalls a similar scene from a stag film nearly a half a century earlier, entitled *KKK Night Riders* (1939) in which a black woman has sex with a white man dressed in Klan regalia.[9] The "comic" tone of this *Let Me Tell Ya 'Bout Black Chicks* scene—overexaggerated and poorly affected Southern accents—fails to lessen the weight of actual and symbolic historical violence executed against the black female body. Scenes like this reflect the imagined impossibility of sexual violence enacted against the enslaved female, who is, in the words of Saidiya Hartman, "both will-less and always already willing."[10] Highly self-aware of the provocative nature of his work, director Gregory Dark admits, or perhaps boasts, "you will not find one sensitive moment in any of my work."[11]

Coeval pornographer and industry legend William Margold reflects a similar brand of eroticized racism cloaked in caricature in the video *Hot Chocolate* which, unlike *Let Me Tell Ya 'Bout Black Chicks*, has an all-black cast.[12] *Hot Chocolate* also relies on a number of tired racialized tropes and stereotypes of blackness. One scene of a black female performer eating soul food during sex comes to mind. Unable to stop eating, she seems to experience more rapture from the chicken than from her partner. This scene plays on a number of racist stereotypes about black women and their carnal appetites. Margold himself, posturing as a kind of quasi-folklorist pornographer of an essential black sexuality, says the video is "amusingly racist in its own way." Margold states:

> I wrote it with the full intent of basically colloquializing it to the black entity including the scene where, who is it, Sweet Georgia Brown, is having sex on the table and she's eating a rib and dipping white bread in sauce and all that stuff. It's a very, very funny movie in its own way.[13]

Margold's statement reveals how racism in pornography is not just eroticized, but also functions as a kind of comedic device, continuing in a tradition of blackface minstrelsy.[14] This reference to blackface minstrelsy is neither far-fetched nor figurative. In a conversation with the author, Margold recounted a story about the film, when one of the main black male actors could no longer maintain his erection after a long, busy day on set, and the director, a white women, suggested Margold put shoe polish on his own genitals to finish the scene.[15] Though Margold objected, his refusal was not framed in a way that conveyed any sort of protest to the anti-black racism undergirding such an act, the reactions such an exploit might engender on a set of black performers, and/or any kind of general awareness of the complex psychic pain that the humor of the blackface minstrelsy tradition evokes. Furthermore the lighthearted, convivial way in which he recounted the story revealed he was indeed "amused," not troubled, by the suggestion.

I journey back to some of these important, if distressing, moments in the history of black women in contemporary, for-profit, moving-image American pornography to illustrate not a chronological trajectory from negative to positive, but to illuminate the very path itself—the evolution in representations of black female sexuality—as well as to signal the legacy of "controlling images" that this new group of black female pornographers inherits.[16] Revisiting this history shows just how critical these women's work becomes as a political project of recuperation and reinvention. Yet, I want to

Figure 13.1. *Hot Chocolate* (1984) videocassette box cover. *Courtesy of Worth Mentioning Public Relations*

Figure 13.2.   Scene from *Hot Chocolate. Courtesy of Worth Mentioning Public Relations*

be careful to not fall into a kind of essentialist pitfall. I am not contending that because this new body of work is produced by black women, it necessarily reflects "better," less problematic, and/or more humanistic representations of black womanhood. What I am claiming is that it is important to look at the ways in which these women are taking control over their own representations and creating different images of black female sexuality that challenge past presentations. Consequently, I do not read this evolution as one of negative to positive, racist to inclusive, "absence" to "presence," heteronormative to queer, but rather one that signals critical shifts in the landscape of pornography towards a more pluralistic imagining of black female sexuality, one that speaks to the destabilization of dominant hierarchies of desire, beauty, body, power, and spectatorship.[17]

QUEERING BLACK FEMALE PORNOGRAPHIC PRODUCTION

Black lesbian filmmaker Shine Louise Houston has transformed the field of queer pornography production, challenging "formula[s]" of normative black female sexuality in mainstream porn; she states: "There is power in creating images, and for a woman of color and a queer to take that power . . . I don't find it exploitative; I think it's necessary."[18] Houston produces "hardcore indie feminist dyke porn" which challenges perceptions "that porn is exploitation of women and that sex in porn is violence against women."[19] Showcasing beautiful cinematography, inventive narratives, and incredibly diverse performers with respect to race, gender, and body, Houston's work critically queers representations of black female sexual desire, offering modes of pleasure outside of hegemonic, heteronormative representations of black female sexuality in pornography. Houston has produced and directed a number of feature-length porn films including *Superfreak* (2006), *The Wild Search* (2007), *Champion: Love Hurts* (2008), and *Occupied* (2013). Her diverse and imaginative oeuvre complicates trite narratives of female sexuality in mainstream porn. Houston also owns and operates PinkLabel.TV, a fair-trade VOD digital distribution website featuring her own porn, as well as the work of other independent queer pornography filmmakers. In the interest of space, I will focus on her critically acclaimed website, CrashPadSeries.com, launched in 2008.[20]

Houston did not fall into pornography serendipitously, nor is she a filmmaking dilettante. Possessing a BA in fine art film from the San Francisco Art Institute, Houston worked at the legendary San Francisco sex shop, Good Vibrations, a veritable sex-positive pornographer breeding ground since its founding in 1977, for five years prior to producing her own porn.[21] It was here Houston discerned an urgent demand for a *new* and different type of pornography that she believed reflected the fantasies and figures of LGBT people: "That's when I'm like, there needs to be more voices. I believe in my politics. If you don't like it, do what I did. I didn't like what was going on in the porn industry in terms of representation of gay, lesbian, queer, and trans folk, so I made my own stuff."[22] This DIY impetus motivated by a profound disappointment with mainstream porn's offerings is a salient factor running through many of these black female pornographers' work—a desire to create and disseminate *new* images of black female sexuality.

CrashPadSeries.com is based on Houston's first feature film, *The Crash Pad* (2005), a story about an unconnected group of couples, many real-life, who are given a key to a shabby San Francisco apartment that functions as an impromptu venue for their sexual escapades. Behind the closed doors of the mysterious apartment, "a notorious hot bed of queer sex," viewers are privy, via webcam or actual keyhole mediated by the lens of Houston's (the "keymaster") video camera, to a myriad of hard-core sex acts.[23] Now nearly a decade and 170 episodes later, the *Crash Pad Series* is still thriving. CrashPadSeries.com streams live as well as prerecorded *Crash Pad* webisodes, features a characters gallery, directors and performers commentary, blogs, calendar, social media links, and more. The *Crash Pad Series* is not just

Figure 13.3.   Shine Louise Houston. *Courtesy of Pink and White Productions, Inc.*

popular with critics and viewers; another testament to the popularity of the series is the waiting list for future performers. Houston states she never has to recruit performers and has an ongoing waiting list, enough models to book approximately the next five years.

Employing the crash pad narrative of extemporaneous sex in the domestic setting of the random urban apartment, the series is hinged upon a complex and contradictory performance of sexual authenticity, something praised by critics. That is, the *Crash Pad Series* is framed as displaying the "real" sex of "real" lesbians. For example, a pornmoviesforwomen.com description states, "There are no gay-for-pay bottle blondes with scary fake boobs and finger-nails engaged in perfunctory sex here."[24] The authenticity lies not just with the critical reception of Houston's work. Pink and White Productions markets itself as creating pornography that depicts more authentic expressions of queer bodies and desire.[25] CrashPadSeries.com advertises:

> The premise is simple: there's an apartment, and if you're lucky enough to be given the key, you can let yourself in . . . and let yourself go. This isn't fake lesbian porn with pointless high heels and starlets barely able to conceal their distaste as they awkwardly tongue kiss. Real sex, real orgasms, real sweat, real bodily fluids, real laughter—this is the genuine article, so utterly natural that the fact it's being filmed seems nearly incidental.[26]

It is this multifaceted rhetoric of authenticity—*real, genuine, natural, incidental*—here in the context of Houston's work that becomes an important, but problematic, thread purling through the work of this new wave of black female–produced pornography. That is, these groups of women are imagined, and imagine themselves, to be making pornography that caters to the *real* fantasies of *real* black women as well as that which represents *real* bodies, the kind we do not typically see in mainstream porn. The furtive locale of the crash pad provides the ground for an authentically imagined staging of queer sex. The equally mysterious, mythical key opens more than the doors to the crash pad itself; it serves as a powerful metaphorical device symbolizing a broader expansion of racialized sexualities in the landscape of contemporary American commercial porn—enacting a kind of queering itself. As queer porn, the *Crash Pad Series* does more than depict queer relations and sexual fantasy, it is politically invested in a critique of the dichotomies of heteronormativity. Houston states:

> Really it's about a concept of queer and queer sexuality and working outside the binary. . . . These concepts of where you put yourself in the box and where you put yourself on the binary is in fact your choice, that it's not a linear progression. Sexuality is for anybody, and your object of desire or your particular object of desire aren't limited to a certain type of people with a particular body type.[27]

Yet Houston imagines her work as not only reflecting queer sensibility, fantasy, and desire, but also empowering the queer community:

> It creates empowerment by saying yes we are beautiful, we're an art form, we're not all gym bunnies, and that's OK. We're not all super high femme and all this kind of stuff, it's like, hey let's normalize this. These are queer bodies. And hey, we can be just as hot as the models in Penthouse. It's empowering when you can see yourself reflected in an image.[28]

Essential to this empowerment is technology. Houston tells me that technology is "power."[29] The Internet has allowed her to "build something that was going to be able to create content on a regular basis."[30] As such we can understand the medium facilitating not a kind of singular intervention, but an ongoing process of continual permutation reflecting the dynamism and multivalence of black female sexuality itself—the complexity and diverseness of black women's sexual practice and the mutability of black female sexuality. By providing this type of constant content, the technology of the web enables an evolving, not inert, performance of black womanhood.[31]

Having "no fear of the technology," Houston imagines cyberspace as a laboratory for the invention of new and dynamic presentations of black female sexuality.[32] Indeed, as I argue elsewhere, we need to pay critical attention to black female–produced pornography as a salient force in a larger digital renaissance of black female cultural production, and look towards black female pornographers as pioneers in black women's commandeering of new media as a vehicle for critical self-representation.[33] Yet while we need to look more closely, and certainly more seriously, at Internet pornography and the ways it allows for new and different groups of people, often traditionally marginalized, to actively participate in important discourses about gender, race, sexuality, and the body, this examination needs to come with the recognition of the ways this new media has buttressed existing structures of power, and the ways in which the Internet is recycling extant, problematic signifiers of black womanhood. Scholars like Mireille Miller-Young have already cautioned us to be critical of a utopian democratization of cyberporn, exposing the ways in which netporn can be "both transgressive and repressive for Black sexual politics."[34] Despite the work of new black women pornographers, the racial, gendered, sexual ideology of websites (both professional and user-generated) like ghettodoorway.com, ebonycumdumps.com, ghettogaggers.com, ghettobootytube.org, and hoodhunters.com, dominates the cyberscape of black female pornography, rendering a ghettoized black female sexuality often violently objectified by a white and/or black hetero-patriarchal male gaze. It is this visual topography these black women pornographers navigate in their production of *new* images of black female sexuality.

TIGHT SPACES AND POSSIBILITIES OF BLACK FEMINIST PORNOGRAPHIC PRODUCTION

Just across the San Francisco Bay in Oakland, California, Nenna Joiner, another award-winning black female pornographer, produces queer porn featuring black women that similarly challenges racialized and gendered regimes of hegemonic sexuality. However, Joiner has constructed not a digital, but a more concrete space of alternative black female sexual expression and desire, embodied in her adult novelty store, Feelmore510.[35] A similar DIY impetus resonates with Joiner, who is not necessarily trying to produce better pornography, but rather an alternative to mainstream porn offerings of and for black women. She states: "So for me it's doing something different. I don't watch someone else's porn and say ok I can do that better."[36] Like Houston, Joiner strives to counter dominant images of black female sexuality and provide her audience with divergent representations, desires, and fantasies not readily available in mainstream porn and popular media. She states, "Show them something they are not seeing on television. Show them something else."[37] This "something else" is creatively and dynamically reflected in her work as well as in her store. Located in the Uptown district of downtown Oakland (510 is a reference to the Oakland area code), Feelmore510, what Joiner refers to as an "adult progressive retail establishment," opened on Valentine's Day, 2011. Embodying its motto, "It's more than just sex," Feelmore510 sells a variety of products ranging from vibes, lubes, dildos, BDSM accessories, and film, to literature and local artwork in its mission "to inspire people to lead socially and sexually empowering lives."

Both Joiner's pornography and her store function as cultural sites of black female sexual political struggle, where she contests not just the visual "ideology of domination" of black womanhood, but its structural marginalization.[38] As the architect of both *new* images of black female sexuality and a market space for the sale, distribution, and consumption of these images, Joiner and Feelmore510 represent a multifaceted intervention into the face of the American adult entertainment industry and the arena of black women's sexual representation. Yet the store also maintains an important symbiotic relationship to Joiner's porn itself, enabling her to continue to take the pulse of customer desires. Screening her videos at her store, she is able to get important feedback from consumers, informing her future projects and store inventory. Feelmore510 enables her to "capture the market" of the "brown communities."[39] As such it represents a critical material site of black female erotic subjectivity, agency, and self-representation, where Joiner's personal and artistic philosophies of affirmative and heterogeneous queer black fe-

Figure 13.4. Nenna Joiner in front of Feelmore510. *Courtesy of Mike Butler*

male sexuality become embodied. Feelmore510 is a critical space, indeed part of a larger network of critical spaces of and for feminist pornography.

Rooted in the tumultuous sexual politics of the 1980s, owing much to the feminist art movement and the genres of women's, couples, and lesbian pornography, as well as Club 90, a pioneer group of women pornography performers, feminist porn is both "a genre and a political vision," a theory and a practice.[40] Providing a diverse and welcome alternative to mainstream and often heteronormative representations of bodies, sexual desires, pleasures, and fantasies, feminist pornography's political intervention lies in more than its aesthetic and iconographical innovations, but in its transformations with respect to the conditions of sexual labor and the dynamics of porn production. Feminist pornographers recognize the potential empowerment of porn and the principles of its making, providing fair wages, care, safety, choice, and respect, while privileging performer's consent, autonomy, and pleasure. Renowned feminist pornographer Tristan Taormino states,

> I am a feminist pornographer. For me, this means that my process of making porn is ethical, consensual, and respectful. The work environment is safe, and everyone wants to be there. Women and men are given choices: they choose who they will have sex with, the positions they want to be in, and the toys they play with—and it is based on what feels good to them and based on their actual sexuality, not a fabricated script. The movie is a collaboration between director and performer, with the actors' input and ideas about how they want to be represented.[41]

Yet the impetus of the early feminist pornography movement in the United States, as the racial demographics of Club 90 and lesbian pornography trailblazers like *On Our Backs* and *Fatale Video*[42] signal, was largely white women's sexuality, reflecting the dearth of women of color porn performers in the industry at the time, despite their firmly established place in the pornographic imaginary. Decades later in the early- to mid-2000s when feminist porn really advanced in the United States, becoming "an industry within an industry," black women became important, if underrecognized, figures in the field.[43]

Beyond the work she produces, Joiner reflects the vision and praxis of feminist pornography via *Feelmore510*. In her discussion of "feminist sex-toy stores," Lynn Comella reveals that in addition to selling products and helping customers to develop a language for talking about sex, their fantasies, and their desires, feminist sex shops are a vital part of the larger project of feminist cultural production.[44] Inspiring us to read both the texts and contexts of feminist pornography, Comella reminds us that "[f]eminist pornography is not a series of stand-alone texts that exist outside of a much wider context—and history—of sex-positive feminist cultural production and commerce."[45] Shops like Feelmore510 are part of a larger network of what she calls "sex-positive contexts," which beyond functioning as points of sale, avenues of distribution and marketing, and even educational venues, create "favorable conditions of reception."[46] Like Comella, I believe it is important to consider the structures and sites of distribution, not just the products themselves. Yet, I think we also need to think about sites like Feelmore510 and their potential to create not only a sex-positive, female, and LGBTA friendly context, but also a race-affirmative one. As a black-owned and -operated space that fosters the circulation and commodification of counter-hegemonic spectatorship of and texts about blackness, Feelmore510 engenders both a physical setting and a kind of larger theoretical frame of reference or symbolic site, in which black, specifically black queer female sexuality, is not just visible but privileged.

Representing marginalized sexualities in her work, Joiner is also a minority figure in the adult entertainment industry, both as a producer and as a retail owner. As such we can understand the pride she, as a black woman business owner, expresses regarding the Adult Video News's recent crowning of Feelmore510 as "2013 Best Retail Boutique." She states,

> But my store was nominated for an award. Do you get what I am saying? Yeah that's like, even the nomination as a business not just a porn production company, not even a performer, but a business, a legitimate brick-and-mortar business. Like I am up there with the big guys. That's big for a black woman. Can you imagine that? That was the first nominee for a black woman as a business in that category.[47]

For Joiner, it is her "brick and mortar" that will enable her to continue effecting what she terms a "paradigm shift" in representations of black women in contemporary American pornography.[48]

Such a shift is mirrored in her first film, *Tight Places: A Drop of Color* (2010), which won a 2011 Feminist Porn Award for "Most Deliciously Diverse." Reflecting a spectrum of body types, colors, and genders, *Tight Places* reflects Joiner's investment in showcasing the diversity of women's sexuality, particularly queer women of color. *Tight Places* is an "all-queer, all people of color" production that features four performers, who Joiner notes "are all coming from diverse backgrounds and brown communities."[49] Filmed mostly within the domestic space of a small urban apartment (with the exception of one outdoor patio scene), the close quarters, or *tight places*, of the setting engender a feeling of intimacy. In six main scenes, we watch Brooklyn Sky (African American), Vai (Caucasian and Asian), Akira (Native American), and Kohen (Iranian and in the process of transitioning from female to male) as they partner up, then switch partners in various combinations.[50] Like Houston, Joiner casts a racially and gender diverse range of performers—genderqueer, "butch," and "femme," petite, tall, voluptuous—in her documentation of the heterogeneity of queer women of color sexuality

and her challenging of traditional schemas of sexuality in mainstream pornography.

THE DARKER SIDE OF DESIRE: BDSM AND
BLACK FEMALE SEXUALITY

Unlike Shine Louise Houston and Nenna Joiner, Vanessa Blue is not a new-
comer to the industry. Beginning her career circa 1996, Blue boasts a long,
decorated history in the business, both behind and in front of the camera.[51]
Still, Blue represents several key themes of the trope of newness that inspires
the work of this coterie of black female pornographers. Using the Internet as
a platform, she challenges hegemonic hierarchies of desire and racialized
power while representing non-normative, "alternative" sexual fantasies—in
this case, BDSM. In 2004 Vanessa Blue, who also works under the stage
name Domina X, launched her hardcore BDSM-inspired website, fem-
domx.com, "aimed at creating a destination for an audience appreciative of
the sexually aggressive ethnic female."[52] She not only performs on the website, but also directs and films much of the material herself. As the name
signals, the website features femdoms, an abbreviation for female dominatrix
and a BDSM term for sexually dominant women. Femdomx.com illustrates a
complex and contradictory negotiation of pain, pleasure, and power for the
black female performer. Vanessa Blue and the performers on her website
navigate a conflicted, violent terrain of gender, race, and sexuality—travers-
ing antebellum histories of black women's sexual violence and the feminist
(more largely lesbian feminist–led) debates about BDSM stemming from the
late 1970s and early 1980s in which women of color, though marginalized,
played a significant part.[53] Incited by feminists, the questions of sexual morality that charged these debates surrounding BDSM practice were com-
pounded by race, black women's legacies of sexual violence, and the vexed
enactment of BDSM fantasy in which the dynamics of domination and submission were racially cast by the memory of chattel slavery. In its focus on
black women femdoms, femdomx.com represents an engagement with this
discourse *and* a kind of progressive enterprise in terms of its expansion of
roles for black women in the industry.[54] If black women are marginalized in
mainstream porn, they are certainly underrepresented in BDSM pornography. Large mainstream BDSM websites, like kink.com for example, corrobo-
rate this dearth of black women performers. Black women face distinct and
multiple manifestations of racial discrimination in the industry, from blatant
racist remarks and stereotyped and limited roles, to struggling with colorism
and the reign of white feminine beauty ideals. In addition, these actresses
earn half to three-quarters of what their white counterparts earn.[55] Black
women who practice BDSM represent a small but nonetheless heterogeneous

group of women in the already marginalized, and often pathologized, larger kink community. If femdomx.com represents a new direction for Blue in terms of its BDSM niche, it can be seen as a continuation of Blue's past work in the industry and black female empowerment via sexuality.

Though Blue is not typically recognized as producing feminist porn, like Houston and Joiner, foregrounding and making dominant the diverse pleasures, fantasies, and bodies of black women performers is something she has been doing in and through her work for some time. In addition to being a highly acclaimed veteran in adult entertainment, Blue has a reputation for being outspoken about race and discrimination in the industry while also typically employing women of color in her work. Mireille Miller-Young has compellingly presented the ways in which Blue, as both a pornography performer and producer, has expanded the representational field of black female sexuality in pornography and worked to improve the material conditions of black women's sexual labor. Yet it is specifically, as Miller-Young argues, in stepping behind the camera that Blue has facilitated a "more autonomous sexual labor" via her pornography "authorship"—empowering her "[t]o create the terms of one's own performance and to catalyze one's own fantasies into the scene."[56] Such a move from performer to producer represents "a greater mobility that allows sex workers greater agency to traverse the barriers placed around them in the porn business."[57]

Vanessa Blue's femdom vision is definitively one of black female sexual empowerment, what Blue describes as a kind of "fuck[ing] back."[58] She "will never shoot a scene where the girl is anything less than in a position of power. There is enough product like that already."[59] Blue states, "I wanted to totally dig in on the girl power. I was able to take all of my ladies and empower them to fuck the way that they have been getting fucked in previous movies."[60] Motivating female performers to "fuck back" in ways they have not been encouraged to in the past, she seems to posit a self-empowering quality to BDSM, specifically femdom performance and its fostering of sexual agency for black women. Yet despite championing what she calls the "power of the pussy," Blue communicates she is not "interested in pushing any type of pro-black feminine agendas."[61] There is a fascinating juxtaposition here. Well established in the genre of black porn, employing primarily black women performers, vocal about the discrimination of black women in the industry, and articulating a kind of quasi-feminist "girl power," "pro-pussy" philosophy, Blue does not want to "push any type of pro-black feminine agendas."[62] Her reluctance here communicates an important ambivalence. It mirrors the industry's equivocal gaze toward black women as simultaneously desired and disavowed, reflects Blue's careful and strategic negotiation of race within such an industry, and signals feminism's (specifically black American feminism's) historically contentious relationship with porn. Blue, as a black female pornographer *and* as a black woman who produces

BDSM porn, is in somewhat of a doubly precarious position in relation to feminism because of its historical policing of the sexual politics animating the entanglement of pornography, BDSM, violence, pleasure, power, and blackness.

If black feminism has historically produced a particular set of ethical constraints for black women's pornography consumption and production, it has also enunciated moral dictums for black women involved in the practice of BDSM. As Sharon Patricia Holland writes, "[s]omewhere in this moral bathwater, the black female body swirls."[63] Indeed, perhaps some of the most influential black feminist writers have a record of denouncing practices of black female sexuality like pornography and BDSM. Audre Lorde, Alice Walker, and Patricia Hill Collins represent three such scholars. Lorde's groundbreaking conceptualization of the erotic, as "a source of power and information," was one that sharply delimited the erotic from the pornographic.[64] Like Lorde, Alice Walker took a stand against BDSM. However, while Lorde considered it "an institutionalized celebration of dominant/subordinate relationships," Walker believed it to be an especially deleterious practice for black women as a trivialization of the history of chattel slavery, "a fantasy that still strikes terror in black women's hearts."[65] Patricia Hill Collins condemns contemporary pornography as objectifying black women for white male pleasure, and championing themes of violence and black female passivity.[66] While such critiques are typically rooted in the recognition of black women's antebellum legacies of sexual violence and concerns about the complex eroticization of racism, the revitalization of sexual trauma, and oppressive historic images of black female sexuality, such criticisms are problematic insofar as they reinforce normative hierarchies of sexual desire and practice, tether black female sexuality to a particular history, and police purported sexual aberrancies. Dating back to the early- to mid-1980s, these censures are also in response to a certain sociopolitical-sociocultural moment and a particular kind of prefeminist pornography. Pornography, as this new group of black women pornographers illustrates, has evolved, prompting an urgent need for *new* black feminist criticism of this *new* pornography. Furthermore such critiques often fail to take into account the voices of black women producers and performers and/or the lived experiences of black women who practice BDSM. Still, as femdomx.com reveals, anxieties regarding the racialization of violence and sexuality that energized these critiques very much continue to inform black women's enactment of BDSM sexual fantasies.

Blue's femdomx.com loosely interprets the BDSM title, focusing on "fetishism, domination and kink-related activities."[67] The website features videos that range in severity from being invited to smoke a cigarette with partially clothed Blue as she reclines in bed, watching Bella crack a red leather rose flogger, or Carmen give a foot job, to more elaborate, violent scenes of domination, submission, bondage, fireplay, and white male humiliation.[68]

Practices of humiliation in BDSM can range from bootlicking, "cleaning" of various body parts, domestic "slavery," urination, defecation, to verbal degradation. However in femdomx.com race becomes the essential tool in the act of humiliation.[69] I find these scenes of racially charged humiliation to be the most interesting material on the site, not only because such scenes are rare in contemporary American mainstream for-profit pornography, but inasmuch as they hyperbolically illuminate the racialized-sexualized power dynamics and hierarchies of desire undergirding pornography.

Door 2 Door is one example of such racial humiliation on femdomx.com. In what begins as a seemingly fatuous video about a white insurance man, "Major," surprised by his visit to the house of a sketchy, provocatively dressed, and exceptionally horny woman (played by Blue), the story shifts quickly and dramatically to an incisive account of black/white interracial anxiety, aggression, and desire. Soon after Major fails to respond to Blue's sexual advances, she makes an important query—"Are you turned off by my blackness?"—a question that sets the stage for the complex racial machinations of the scene, and incites Blue's physical and verbal aggressiveness. She begins to chastise her white male partner—suffocating him with her breasts and buttocks, deriding him about the small size and wanting ability of his penis. Indeed, the black female body itself becomes a key weapon employed in this cybertheater of BDSM as she commands him to, "[c]hoke between [her] big black tits," while she violently squeezes her breasts around his face. Audio-visually, blackness is represented as superabundant; Blue's body fills the frame of the camera while she repeatedly references herself in oversized terms—"too much," "big," and so on. In turn, this bodily excess of black female sexuality is contrasted with an inadequate white masculinity. Yet black female sexuality emerges ambivalently as both lack and excess—the white male lack of desire for the black female body and her somatic and libidinal superfluity. Such humiliation scenes illuminate ways that race is explicitly evoked and employed as a kind of technology of BDSM. They also signal the complex and contradictory nature of black women's participation in BDSM as complicated by racialized and gendered sociohistorical subtexts: domination and submission, and the binaries of fantasy/reality and black/white.

In femdomx.com, myths of black female sexuality are reinvigorated at the same time they are challenged and their utter performativity and construction made hyaline. Ultimately, in femdom humiliation scenes like *Door 2 Door*, power is not redefined but still legible in the schema of domination and submission. However, power may be reclaimed for the black female who possesses the power to humiliate and vocalize an acerbic critique of both black female sexual alterity and the ambivalence, the binary of lust/disgust,

Figure 13.5.   A scene from *Door 2 Door. www.femdomx.com*

that characterizes black female sexuality especially under the heteronorma-tive white male gaze. Such work might enable us to see the ways BDSM becomes a productive practice for more than, as Foucault says, "inventing new possibilities of pleasure," but for reading these black woman–authored articulations of black female sexuality. [70]

BACK TO THE FUTURE: THE PARADOX OF NEWNESS

At the beginning of this essay, I explained how I used the term *new* as a trope to signal not only recent, but also a type of political intervention in the field of black women's sexual representation. Now I would like to highlight here the paradox of newness as a kind of philosophical apparatus, and the ways in which, while *new* refers to a place in time, and to new technologies of consumption and production, aesthetics, and representational paradigms, there is little new that this group of black women are doing as part of a larger tradition of black women's cultural production. That is, things seem new when we forget what came before and hence we must be mindful of new as a political project often predicated on a certain type of forgetting. Though pornography represents a relatively new arena in which black women are working to disrupt the oppressive fixity of the white male heteropatriarchal gaze, certainly the ways in which black women have turned to visual culture to resist debased images of themselves and their sexuality is nothing new.

In this way, these women illustrate the practice of what Melissa Harris-Perry calls "sister politics." As Harris-Perry argues, a salient political stake for African American women's citizenship lies in the arena of representation, negotiating the powerful mythology of black womanhood and the enduring stereotypes of black female (hyper)sexuality in their struggle for recognition. Sister politics then becomes a kind of critical meta-political practice of black female sexual subjectivity. Harris-Perry states: "Like all citizens, they use politics to lay claim to resources and express public preferences; but sister politics is also about challenging negative images, managing degradation, and resisting or accommodating humiliating public representations."[71] Practicing a kind of "sister politics" or oppositional culture, these women produce what might be viewed as a kind of black feminist activist pornography—that which aims to transform prevailing paradigms and shift how we see black female sexuality, black women's bodies, and black female sexual desire. Varying in their approaches, modes of distribution and production, aesthetic visions, professional training, experience, and relationships with the industry, all these women share a common factor of producing pornography that imagines itself as a kind of corrective to prevailing representations of black female sexuality in porn.

Understanding these women to be practicing a type of "sister politics" in their strategically, financially, and politically motivated negotiation of culture, facilitates a cognizance of the paradox of newness that serves to unite these women with their sisters beyond the pornographic frame, not in opposition to, but in concert with a larger network of black feminist cultural production. [72] Such a recognition might also work towards narrowing the critical chasm between "high" and "low" culture, respectability and deviance, while lifting the silence and stigmatization (particularly within the academy) surrounding black women's sex work, "alternative" sexual practices, and sexually explicit media. Black woman-produced pornography is a critical, if conflicted, site for the expression of black women's sexual agency, pleasure, and power. By focusing on the vicissitudes of production itself—sites and modes of distribution, and the dynamics of labor—both the ideological labor of the pornographic images, and the material conditions of sexual labor, I have illuminated how these black female pornographers engineer the *tight spaces* in which to practice sister politics. [73]

NOTES

1. Do-it-yourself (DIY) technologies like the handheld digital video, editing software, file-sharing and hosting services, webcasting, and webcams have enabled the average person to become, if not a porn star, then a pornographer. Additionally, the onslaught of user-generated porn websites, also called tube sites, has metamorphosized the field of porn production, distribution, and consumption. Tube sites like redtube.com, xtube.com, youporn.com, and pornhub.com, for example, are immensely popular. *Forbes* magazine recently ranked youporn.com and pornhub.com among the top one hundred websites in the world. One of the important things that these user-generated sites have done is mark a shift from professional toward amateur that is a critical transformation in authorial power. See Oliver J. Chiang, "The Challenge of User Generated Porn," *Forbes.com*, August 5, 2009, http://www.forbes.com/2009/08/04/digital-playground-video-technology-e-gang-09-ali-joone.html (accessed 26 Nov. 2010).

2. Coined by Alain Locke, in *The New Negro* (1925), the New Negro Movement (1917–1935) was a cultural renaissance of, for, and by black Americans, a literary, cultural, and artistic movement of black expression. See Henry Louis Gates Jr., "The Trope of a New Negro and the Reconstruction of the Image of the Black," *Representations* 24, special issue: "America Reconstructed, 1840–1940" (1988): 131.

3. Gates, "The Trope of a New Negro," 131.

4. David Eng, Judith Halberstam, and José Esteban Muñoz, "What's Queer about Queer Studies Now?" *Social Text*, 84–85, nos. 3–4 (2005): 1.

5. Susie Bright, "Inter-racial and Black Videos," scheduled to be printed in *Adult Video News* (*AVN*) in December 1986 but never printed, article given to author by Susie Bright. Bright explained to me, as she confirmed in her blog, that *AVN* killed the article because it was essentially too critical and exposed the blatant "racism," "prejudices and superstitions in the business." See Susie Bright, "The History of 'Black' and 'Inter-racial' Porn Videos," Susie Bright's Journal, July 21, 2008, http://susiebright.blogs.com/susie_brights_journal_/porn/page/5/ (accessed 5 Apr. 2010).

6. Bright, "Inter-racial and Black Videos."

7. Bright, "Inter-racial and Black Videos."

8. Margold created the first all-black video, *Hot Chocolate*, writing under the pseudonym Lem Elijah.

9. Film available for viewing at the Kinsey Institute archive.

10. Saidiya Hartman, "Seduction and the Ruses of Power," *Callaloo* 19, no. 2 (Spring 1996): 539.

11. Bright, "Inter-racial and Black Videos."

12. Margold is a long-time fixture in the American adult entertainment industry, boasting over three decades of experience in a variety of different roles such as performer, writer, director, agent, critic, activist, and counselor. For more about William Margold see Robert J. Stoller, *Porn: Myths for the Twentieth Century* (New Haven, CT: Yale University Press, 1991) and/or visit Margold's personal website at http://www.billmargold.com/.

13. Margold, interview with author.

14. For more about the ambivalent performative tradition of blackface minstrelsy, see Eric Lott, *Love and Theft: Blackface Minstrelsy and the American Working Class* (New York: Oxford University Press, 1993), 18.

15. Drea also reflects a similar ambivalent anti-black racist perspective. Despite directing multiple black videos for companies like VCA, Caballero, and VCX, Drea states that "[a]fter every black video I'd make, I'd always say, 'I'll never shoot another Black video again. Never.'" See Bright, "The History of 'Black' and 'Inter-racial' Porn Videos."

16. For more on "controlling images," see Patricia Hill Collins, *Black Feminist Thought: Knowledge, Consciousness, and the Politics of Empowerment* (London: Routledge, 1990).

17. Inspired by black feminist scholar Michele Wallace, I critique the negative/positive critical binary that often frames pornography discourse. Wallace problematizes the negative/positive binary as a prevailing mode of American visual criticism, arguing that it sets the mission of cultural production as a corrective one while privileging reception over production in the realm of representation. Additionally, the negative/positive schema stifles how we look

at and critique images of blackness and asphyxiates our critical visual lexicon. See Michele Wallace, *Invisibility Blues: From Pop to Theory* (New York: Verso, 1990); see also Ariane Cruz, "Pornography: A Black Feminist Woman Scholar's Reconciliation," in *The Feminist Porn Book: The Politics of Producing Pleasure*, ed. Tristan Taormino, Celine Parreñas Shimizu, Constance Penley, and Mireille Miller-Young (New York: Feminist Press, 2013), 215–27.

18. Umayyah Cable, "Let's Talk About Pornography: An Interview with Shine Louise Houston," Feministe.us, April 7, 2009, http://www.feministe.us/blog/archives/2009/04/07/lets-talk-about-pornography-an-interview-with-shine-louise-houston/ (accessed 5 Apr. 2012); see also Pink and White Productions website, http://pinkwhite.biz/PWWP/about/.

19. "Preview: The Crash Pad," CrashPadSeries.com, http://crashpadseries.com/queer-porn/?feature=the-crash-pad-directors-cut (accessed 5 Mar. 2012); "Shine Louise Houston Will Turn You On," interview by Malindo Lo, *Curve*, 2006, http://www.curvemag.com/Detailed/711.html (accessed 5 Mar. 2012).

20. The work of Houston and her production company, Pink and White Productions, is highly decorated. For a list of awards, visit http://pinkwhite.biz/about/awards/.

21. Good Vibrations has been instrumental to the careers of many pioneer luminaries in the landscape of sex-positive women's pornography, such as Carol Queen, Susie Bright, and Candida Royalle.

22. Jillian Eugenios, "Chatting Up Shine Louise Houston," *Curve*, http://www.curvemag.com/Curve-Magazine/Web-Articles-2011/Chatting-up-Shine-Louise-Houston/ (accessed 5 Mar. 2012).

23. *CrashPad Series, Vol. 1: The Top 5 Episodes of Season 1*, Pink and White Productions, directed by Shine Louise Houston, codirected by Shae (San Francisco: Blowfish Video, 2007), DVD.

24. "Porn Movies for Women: The Web's Largest Directory of Female Friendly Porn Films," http://www.pornmoviesforwomen.com/shinelouisehouston.html (accessed 1 May 2012).

25. Houston, interview with author, May 24, 2012.

26. See Pink and White Productions website, http://pinkwhite.biz/PWWP/reviews/the-crash-pad/ (accessed 1 May 2012).

27. Eugenios, "Chatting Up Shine Louise Houston." One of Houston's regular muses, a well-known and highly acclaimed feminist porn star, Jiz Lee, embodies this challenging of binaries. With a preference for the gender-neutral pronouns "they/them," Lee self-identifies as genderqueer, stating "I don't identify as woman, nor do I identify as man. To me genderqueer is a conscious queering of gender or an aware nongendering." Lee is conscious of her own discursive role in the production of gender. Such a sentiment reveals not only Lee's awareness of gender as a social construction, but also as a technology of power, a disciplining of the body. See Jiz Lee, "Uncategorized: Genderqueer Identity and Performance in Independent and Mainstream Porn," in *The Feminist Porn Book: The Politics of Producing Pleasure*, ed. Tristan Taormino, Celine Parreñas Shimizu, Constance Penley, and Mireille Miller-Young (New York: Feminist Press, 2013), 276.

28. Eugenios, "Chatting Up Shine Louise Houston."

29. Houston, interview with author.

30. Houston, interview with author.

31. See Lily Rothman, "Issa Rae of *Awkward Black Girl* on the Future of the Web Series," *Time*, July 10, 2012, http://entertainment.time.com/2012/07/10/issa-rae-of-awkward-black-girl-on-the-future-of-the-web-series/ (accessed 13 Aug. 2012).

32. Houston, interview with author.

33. Ariane Cruz, "Mis(playing) Blackness: Black Female Sexuality in *The Misadventures of Awkward Black Girl*," in *Black Female Sexualities*, ed. Joanne M. Braxton and Trimiko Melancon (New Brunswick, NJ: forthcoming).

34. According to Miller-Young, the problem with net porn is that although it "potentially undermines the hegemonic logic of racial, sexual, segregation in the U.S.," in allowing racially fetishized fantasies to be consumed in privacy and secrecy, it enables them to be "easily disavowed." See Mireille Miller-Young, "Sexy and Smart: Black Women and the Politics of Self-Authorship in Netporn," in *C'lick Me: A Netporn Studies Reader*, ed. Katrien Jacobs,

Marije Janssen, and Matteo Pasquinelli (Amsterdam: Institute of Network Cultures, 2007), 207. Available online at http://www.networkcultures.org/_uploads/24.pdf.

35. Some of Joiner's accolades include the 2012 Eastbay Express "Best Local Film or Documentary," 2012 Eastbay Express Erotic Shorts Brief "Audience Award," and the 2012 Feminist Porn Award "Hottest Dyke Film" for her *Hella Brown: Real Sex in the City* (2011). She was awarded the 2011 Feminist Porn Awards "Most Deliciously Diverse Cast" for her film *Tight Places: A Drop of Color* (2010).

36. Joiner, interview with author, July 14, 2012.

37. Joiner, interview with author.

38. For more see Collins, *Black Feminist Thought*.

39. Joiner, interview with author. In our conversation, Joiner expressed a noted desire to represent the person of color (POC) queer community *and* be acknowledged by them.

40. Tristan Taormino, Celine Parreñas Shimizu, Constance Penley, and Mireille Miller-Young, "Introduction," *The Feminist Porn Book*, 18. Formed initially in 1983 in NYC as a kind of women's pornography support group, Club 90 was comprised of golden age notables Veronica Vera, Annie Sprinkle, Gloria Leonard, Veronica Hart, Kelly Nichols, Sue Nero, and Candida Royalle (who founded Femme Productions in 1984, spearheading the genre of women's porn). In 1984 the group, named after their meeting site, Sprinkle's apartment on 90 Lexington, teamed up with a feminist arts collective to perform "Deep Inside Porn Stars," a performance piece that brought feminist and pornography performers together around the question of pornography from the perspective of women in the industry. Club 90 was an important historical moment, providing a collective site where feminist-identified female performers working in the industry could communicate about their experiences of industry labor, and facilitating a critical shift in representation where women were not just the objects but also the subjects and producers of pornographic images. For more about Club 90 see Annette Fuentes and Margaret Schrage, "Veronica Hart, Gloria Leonard, Kelly Nichols, Candida Royalle, Annie Sprinkle, and Veronica Vera Interviewed: Deep Inside Porn Stars," *Jump Cut* 32 (April 1987): 41–43, and Annie Sprinkle, "Some of My Performances in Retrospect," *Art Journal* 56, no. 4 (Winter 1997): 68–70.

41. Tristan Taormino, "The Danger of Protecting Our Children: Government Porn Regulation Threatens Alternative Representations and Doesn't Save Kids," *Yale Journal of Law and Feminism* 18, no. 1 (2006): 278.

42. Lesbian pornography was instrumental in the feminist pornography movement. The lesbian pornography magazine, *On Our Backs*, was founded by Nan Kinney, Debi Sundahl, and Susie Bright in 1984. In 1985 *Fatale Video*, a company producing and distributing "authentic" lesbian moving-image porn, was also started by Kinney and Sundahl. Latino performer Vanessa Del Rio represents an example of a golden age, woman of color porn star.

43. Originally named *Vixens and Visionaries*, the Feminist Porn Awards, an annual "celebration of erotica focused on women and marginalized people" that began eight years ago in Toronto, has been an important force in feminist pornography. Launched by Good for Her, a sex-positive sex store in Toronto, the awards continue to be instrumental in the feminist pornography movement. For more about the awards, including the nomination criteria, see http://www.goodforher.com/feminist_porn_awards. For more about the "industry" of feminist porn, see *The Feminist Porn Book*, 16. For more about black women in porn, see Mireille Miller-Young, "Putting Hypersexuality to Work: Black Women and Illicit Eroticism in Pornography," *Sexualities* 13 (2010): 227. See also Miller-Young's articles, "Hip-Hop Honeys and Da Hustlaz: Black Sexualities in the New Hip-Hop Pornography," *Meridians* 8, no. 1 (2008): 261–92; "Interventions: The Deviant and Defiant Art of Black Women Porn Directors," in *The Feminist Porn Book*, 105–20; and "Sexy and Smart: Black Women and the Politics of Self-Authorship in Netporn," in *C'lickme: A Netporn Studies Reader*, 205–16.

44. Lynn Comella, "From Text to Context: Feminist Porn and the Making of a Market," in *The Feminist Porn Book*, 80.

45. Comella, "From Text to Context," 91.

46. Comella, "From Text to Context," 86.

47. Joiner, interview with author.

48. Joiner, interview with author.

49. Joiner, interview with author.

50. Joiner, interview with author.

51. In addition to partnering with industry giants like Hustler, in 2005 Blue's series, *Black Reign*, won the Adult Video News (AVN) award for "Best Ethnic-Themed Series." In 2009 she was inducted into the Urban X Awards (which honors the best in ethnic adult video) Hall of Fame.

52. "Vanessa Blue Inks Exclusive Deal with Hustler, Launches Fetish Website," AVN.com, Nov 16, 2004, http://business.avn.com/articles/video/Vanessa-Blue-Inks-Exclusive-Deal-with-Hustler-Launches-Fetish-Web-Site-41181.html (accessed 25 Sept. 2010).

53. Beginning in the late 1970s and early 1980s, the question of BDSM was a hot topic of feminist, primarily lesbian feminist, debate in the tumultuous arena of sexual politics. Samois, a small San Francisco–based collective of lesbian feminist BDSM practitioners, argued that BDSM was not antithetical to being a lesbian or a feminist. Samois argued BDSM to be a productive and pleasurable sexual expression that offers a critique of heteropatriarchy and its naturalization of gendered hierarchies of power with men as dominant, violent, and aggressive, and women as submissive, nonviolent, and passive. In 1979 Samois self-published a 45-page booklet entitled *What Color is Your Handkerchief? A Lesbian S/M Sexuality Reader*. See also Samois, *Coming to Power: Writings and Graphics on Lesbian S/M* (Boston: Alyson Publications, 1981) and *The Second Coming: A Leatherdyke Reader*, edited by Pat Califia and Robin Sweeny (Los Angeles: Alyson Publications, 1996). On the other side, the radical feminist opposition to BDSM did not conceptualize it as a way to theorize gendered and sexualized power outside of the rigid binary of male/female relationships. Instead, these opponents claimed it replicates patriarchal, heterosexist modes of oppression and sexuality. Examples of anti-BDSM texts include *Against Sadomasochism: A Radical Feminist Analysis*, ed. Robin Ruth Linden, Darlene R. Pagano, Diana E. Russell, and Susan Leigh Star (East Palo Alto, CA: Frog in the Well Press, 1982) and *Unleashing Feminism: Critiquing Lesbian Sadomasochism in the Gay Nineties*, ed. Irene Reti (Santa Cruz, CA: HerBooks, 1993).

54. "FemDomX Launches Affiliate Program," AVN.com, Dec 13, 2004, http://business.avn.com/articles/video/FemDomX-Launches-Affiliate-Program-41433.html (accessed 19 Sept. 2010).

55. See Miller-Young, "Putting Hypersexuality to Work," 227.

56. Miller-Young, "Interventions,"106.

57. Miller-Young, "Interventions,"106.

58. "Vanessa Blue Unleashes Fem-Dom Vision on Hustler," AVN.com, February 27, 2005, http://business.avn.com/articles/video/Vanessa-Blue-Unleashes-Fem-Dom-Vision-on-Hustler-42323.html (accessed 25 Sept. 2010).

59. "Vanessa Blue Unleashes Fem-Dom Vision."

60. "Vanessa Blue Unleashes Fem-Dom Vision." Her use of the word "girl" instead of "woman" reflects not so much her own infantilization of the female body, but her adoption of the adult entertainment industry lexicon grounded in the most profitable bedrock of eroticized female infantilization.

61. Blue, e-mail to author on December 3, 2010. Though irresolute, her "pro-pussy" philosophy is, at the very least refreshing in a pro-dick, heteropatriarchal industry. See also "Vanessa Blue Unleashes Fem-Dom Vision on Hustler."

62. Blue, e-mail to author.

63. Sharon Patricia Holland, *The Erotic Life of Racism* (Durham, NC: Duke University Press, 2012), 55. For more about the vexed relationship between black feminist scholarship and pornography, see Cruz, "Pornography: A Black Feminist Woman Scholar's Reconciliation." See also Jennifer C. Nash, "Strange Bedfellows: Black Feminism and Antipornography Feminism," *Social Text* 26 no 4 (2008): 51-76.

64. Audre Lorde, "Uses of the Erotic: The Erotic as Power," in *Sister Outsider: Essays and Speeches* (Berkeley: Crossing Press, 1984), 54.

65. See also "Interview with Audre Lorde: Audre Lorde and Susan Leigh Star," in *Against Sadomasochism*, ed. Robin Ruth Linden, et al., 68. Lorde does express an awareness of how her status "as a minority woman" uniquely informs her familiarity with the politics of "dominance and submission." See also Alice Walker, "A Letter of the Times, Or Should This Sado-

Masochism Be Saved?" in *Against Sadomasochism*, 207. For more about the early black feminist critique of BDSM see Ariane Cruz, "Beyond Black and Blue: BDSM, Internet Pornography, and Black Female Sexuality," article forthcoming in *Feminist Studies*, Vol. 41, Issue 2 (2015).

66. Collins, *Black Feminist Thought*, 167.

67. "Vanessa Blue Unleashes Fem-Dom Vision on Hustler."

68. www.femdomx.com (accessed 12 Nov. 2013).

69. Larry Townsend, author of pioneer BDSM guidebook, *The Leatherman's Handbook* (1972), defines humiliation, a core element of BDSM practice, as "[a] conscious humbling of one partner by the other." See Larry Townsend, *The Leatherman's Handbook II* (New York: Book Surge Publishing, 2007), 43.

70. Foucault's full statement is: "The idea that S&M is related to a deep violence, that S&M practice is a way of liberating this violence, this aggression, is stupid. We know very well that what those people are doing is not aggressive; they are inventing new possibilities of pleasure with strange parts of their body—through the eroticization of the body." See Michel Foucault, *Ethics: Subjectivity and Truth*, ed. Paul Rabinow (New York: New Press, 1994), 165.

71. Melissa-Harris Perry, *Sister Citizenship: Shame, Stereotypes, and Black Women in America* (New Haven, CT: Yale University Press, 2011), 45.

72. Stuart Hall, "Notes on Deconstructing the Popular," in *People's History and Socialist Theory*, ed. Raphael Samuel (London: Routledge, 1981), 239.

73. My thinking here is indebted to Jonathan Eburne's critique of a talk version of this chapter.

Chapter Fourteen

Utopic Futures of the "Other"

Pornography and the Creative Imaginary

Taine Duncan

If we are to "free ourselves," we must do so by liberating the imagination.—
Drucilla Cornell[1]

In 2013, the pornography production world faced three moratoriums on filming due to HIV scares. Most famously, Cameron Bay came out with her
confirmed HIV diagnosis in August, and reported unsafe conditions on the
set where she believed she might have contracted the virus.[2] These production delays renewed discussion of safety on porn sets.[3] The straightforward
question everyone asked was "how to make porn production safer?" but the
question that very few sources asked was "*who* gets to decide what makes
porn performers safe?" The trade agencies circled around this question by
asserting that the government should not be able to mandate condom use on
porn sets. Even in light of the three shutdowns, the Free Speech Coalition
remains staunchly opposed to Los Angeles County's law requiring condom
usage on films made within the county. However, very few sources thought
about asking the performers and the medical community that treats and supports the performers.

At first blush, this absence of recognition for sex workers supports familiar anti-pornography arguments that pornography is not sex-positive and liberatory, but rather relies on coercion and the lack of performer choice and
autonomy. However, in this chapter, I will argue that the relationship between pornography and the liberation of others is much more complicated.
The common feminist pornography debates frequently position the discussion around the freedom associated with autonomy. I contend that emancipatory possibility does not stem from canonical definitions of autonomy, but

from a social creative imaginary—a discourse that enables us to create new visions of the future.

In this chapter, I use Drucilla Cornell's conceptions of natality and imagination to offer this alternative view of subjectivity. In this view, the human subject is necessarily and continuously in the process of creation. To facilitate such creation, a subject must be recognized as a member of an intersubjective community and must be able to participate in the discourses and context that make creativity possible. This view of subjectivity depends heavily on preserving the space and access to a social imaginary. The role of the imaginary is central to the issues and questions surrounding pornography, including potential problems of recognition, abuse, and even the overdetermination of a single view of fantasy. By using the production of intentionally feminist pornography as a touchstone, I argue that the interplay between the imaginary and subjectivity is an important social, existential, and political issue.[4]

WHO GETS TO DECIDE?

If, as I claim above, the conventional debate about pornography centers on autonomy, then that autonomy is generally measured against the perception of free choice. This definition of autonomy depends on understanding freedom in a very particular way, as a sort of negative liberty, wherein individual freedom is measured according to your ability to remain free from constraints and intervention. Autonomy is best preserved, according to this model, by intruding as little as possible into the lives of others. This definition of autonomy also emphasizes the importance of self-determination; once you make your decisions, free from restrictions, your self-identity emerges.

Drucilla Cornell, as a legal theorist in critical theory, is concerned with subjectivity in both juridical and theoretical society. In order to describe how she sees subjectivity she uses concepts that follow feminist readings of the psychoanalyst Jacques Lacan (1901–1981). In these interpretations, the primary difficulty of intersubjective society is the ability to differentiate oneself as a respected Other—as another subject with all the entitlements and accesses thereof. [5]

These two definitions of subjectivity differ from one another in subtle but important ways. Cornell explains that the Kantian autonomous subject of reason is defined as a subject of control and regulation, rather than innovation.[6] In contrast, subjects of relation are defined by their intersections with one another and their ability to find and develop potential.[7] The concept of "natality" is used in political philosophies, including Cornell's, as a challenge to Kantian notions of autonomy. As opposed to autonomy, natality emphasizes the importance of growth and rebirth. Relying on a metaphor of birth emphasizes both a relationship to others and an opportunity for the "I" to self-innovate rather than to absolutely self-determine. Cornell writes:

> There is a distinction, then, between this view of natality and a more tradition-al Kantian understanding of the role of autonomy. In Kant, the subject of reason, the transcendental subject, is the "I", which commands the empirical subject of desire. Reason, in Kant, is pitted against desire, in part because desire itself is relegated to an empirical "property" of the concrete "me." The concrete "me" of empirical desire is a reality. One does not so much change that "me" as control it. What I am suggesting is that Peirce's understanding of the self as "habit" or, as I have interpreted it, as the natality that allows for innovation, means that there is no empirical "me" that is simply there.[8]

For Cornell, then, the implication of a restricted notion of autonomy might apply to questions of subjectivity in relation to issues of pornography, not just in terms of recognition, but also in terms of the potential for pornography to represent greater subjective varieties of desire. If desire is more than an owned property of an autonomous subject, and is instead integral to the fluidity of self-creation, then a business that explores desire may support the growth, innovation, and expansion of subjectivity.

One of the limitations in mainstream pornography's ability to respect performers' agency is not in disavowing autonomy, but in overdetermining appropriate categories. When someone is identified as an autonomous indi-vidual, they must be totalized in this identification process. These totalizing identities create sometimes laughable and sometimes infuriating misrecogni-tions for queer performers. As genderqueer performer Jiz Lee explains:

> Mainstream porn relies on categories and this naturally involves a lot of as-sumptions. A porn website employee in an office somewhere combs through porn scene after scene, clicking various boxes that "describe" the scenes: #lesbian, #big ass, #brunette, #asian, #fingering, #strap-ons. Or maybe: #small tits, #short hair, #white, #lesbian, #doggy-style. My co-stars and I could be perceived many different ways depending on hairstyle, the lighting, the person clicking the boxes. When am I white? Asian? Lesbian? The labels are quick attempts at descriptions I'm not even sure are useful to the consumer, but it's fascinating as a performer to be labeled something you're not, or not complete-ly.[9]

Implicit in Jiz Lee's reflection is an understanding of the fluidity of sub-jectivity that Cornell's natality implies. When Lee claims that they are misla-beled because they are "not completely" lesbian or white, they are claiming that their own personal subjectivity is more expansive than these categories; that it exceeds the restrictions of totalizing categories.[10] Mainstream pornog-raphy appears to trade in categorization that reflects autonomy, sometimes to the detriment of true recognition of a performer's subjectivity.

Although my argument is grounded in Drucilla Cornell's theories of subjectivity and the role of the imaginary, Cornell has written on pornography itself. Her final conclusion on pornography in *The Imaginary Domain: Abortion, Pornography, and Sexual Harassment* focuses on the legal remedies for the heterosexual female viewer of pornography being stripped "forcibly of her self-image."[11] Cornell contends over and against the familiar anti-pornography arguments that it is not that porn as explicit sex is dehumanizing and therefore is both a symbol of violence against women and a precursor to real-world violence, but instead, that the particularities of widespread heterosexual mainstream and industry-produced pornography create a situation in which it is increasingly difficult to self-create.

Cornell contends that there must be a balancing of two countervailing interests; on the one hand, sexual tolerance tends to promote respect and equity in society,[12] but on the other hand, hypersexualized images have a deleterious effect on those being represented. These seemingly opposed interests really do have an intersectional balance: "Women need to have their imaginary domain protected, precisely so that they may continue the arduous journey of finding the 'words to say it,' to develop richer descriptions of their 'sex.'"[13] In other words, when a woman's access to her own imaginary is protected, within the context of sex-positivity, then she is able to articulate, express, and identify with her own embodied desires. Cornell's recommendation for this protection is to create public zones wherein women may be free from unintentional and unwanted exposure to pornographic images; she argues that these zones would be created and enforced by law, but that that should be the extent of legal intervention in pornography.

Although Cornell's recommendation is fairly commonsensical and avoids much of the intrusion and free-speech issues that legal remedies proposed by Andrea Dworkin (1946–2005) or Catharine MacKinnon may face, her solution is stilted in the face of her own rich descriptions of the social and individual importance of a creative imaginary.[14] Cornell argues that this is simply the legal remedy, and that nonlegal remedies must supplement the zoning policy, but she stops short of offering possible frameworks for nonlegal, social remedies. In this way, my argument appropriates her other conceptualizations of the subject, the intersubjective, and social discourse to supplement her arguments surrounding pornography. This response is, therefore, novel insofar as Cornell explicitly limits her response to pornography in terms of legal intervention.[15]

WHAT IS FANTASY?

Linda Williams explains that fantasies—even the normative fantasies of mainstream porn, melodramatic movies, and slasher flicks—are not "wish-fulfilling linear narratives of mastery and control leading to closure and the attainment of desire."[16] Instead, she argues, "They are marked, rather, by the prolongation of desire, and by the lack of fixed position with respect to the objects and events fantasized."[17] Williams and Cornell do not agree about the function and role of current pornographic productions, but Williams here reflects a similar psychoanalytic commitment to Cornell's. The role of fantasy is about displacement, but not simply dislodging the fantasizer from reality, instead displacing the relationship between subject, object, viewer, and viewed. This dislocation may create a situation in which the unwitting woman who sees her sexed body reduced to parts feels as though she has become that object; or, conversely, this dislocation may provide the domain for creating a new sense of self-identity in relation to other subjects and objects. For example, a trans woman may see the sexualized body of a trans performer and identify that desirability with her own sense of self. Cornell explains that much of her critical theory is about explaining the necessary connections between liberation and embracing alternative fantasies.[18] In order to create a world that supports emancipated subjects, you must face discrimination and injustice not as insurmountable obstacles, but as the less desirable possibility for the future.

Although her book ends up being as polemical as the anti-pornography treatises she heartily dismisses, Laura Kipnis does offer a succinct and straightforward account of what theorists mean when they discuss the real effects of pornography's fantasy:

> I've proposed that pornography is both a legitimate form of culture and a fictional, fantastical, even allegorical realm; it neither simply reflects the real world nor is it some hypnotizing call to action. The world of pornography is mythological and hyperbolic, peopled by characters. It doesn't and never will exist, but it does—and this is part of its politics—insist on a sanctioned space for fantasy.[19]

Despite the fact that pornographic fantasies do not directly represent either the now or the not-yet, they are still woven into the fabric of the real. The relationship between the real and the fantastical is often tense, where the fantastical is seen as a radical departure. But as Kipnis indicates, fantasy emerges from culture and within the political space given it. Even though Cornell and Williams indicate that fantasy must offer possibilities of dislocation and change, the potentials are coded by the social and discursive structures bounding our current existence.

The realities of making and producing porn also operate in tension with the fantasies of porn's liberatory potentials. As Tristan Taormino explains about making even intentionally feminist and empowering porn films:

I don't want to paint an unrealistic picture. There are complexities and contradictions inherent in producing porn. . . . I want performers to feel pampered and valued *and* I have a limited budget. I want the atmosphere to be pressure-free *and* I only have this location for a certain number of hours. . . . Sometimes everyone has to make it work within the existing limits, and some days feel more limited than others. But when it all comes together, it feels amazing.[20]

There is a simultaneous tension and symbiosis between the real and fantasy.

WHERE IS THE IMAGINARY?

The power, the risk, and the possibility of liberatory feminist pornography are all related to one central truth in the way in which pornographic films operate on us: "Pornography invokes a suspension of disbelief. It asks us to project ourselves onto the experiences of others we witness, to try to imagine how those experiences would feel, and whether we want to enact them."[21] This process of invocation is the call of the imaginary. The imaginary, then, is a realm that exists beyond the real. Fantasy may be its method of operation, but the imaginary exists to challenge the structures of reality, and gives us the vision to change those structures. Again using the language of psychoanalysis and existentialism, Cornell explains, "The imaginary as a call evokes the beyond of another place and time. It does so by explicitly recognizing the power of metonymy and metaphor to unbind the structures of identification that have created us as sexed and gendered in the limited categories we think of as man and woman."[22] By unbinding the structures that bind us to restrictive and hierarchal notions of subjectivity, the imaginary offers productive resistance. It is what propels us into new social orders and new discursive epistemes.

Because our present reality is often fraught with structural inequality and misrecognition, many feminist theorists have missed the power of the imaginary. Instead, they have seen the way in which current fantasy seems to reflect sexism, racism, and heterosexism in extremely oppressive forms. However, forgetting the potential for imagining alternative futures does not empower the oppressed. Instead, it appears to reify the very structures that determine that oppression; it gives an almost omnipotent power and eternal place to fantasies of discrimination: "To deny the power to rewrite ourselves beyond the wound of femininity is to invest in the imposition of the masculine imaginary upon us as our truth. Feminism begins with that disinvestment."[23]

Reclaiming the space of the imaginary not only opens the space for my own subjectivity; it also allows for recognition of the diversity of the Other.[24] Similarly to the ways in which fantasy is connected to the real, the imaginary operates within a temporal reality. It is a possibility for the future. The generative potential of the imaginary can have real effects, even for political resistance in the present. Chandra Talpade Mohanty's *Feminism Without Borders: Decolonizing Theory, Practicing Solidarity* situates the practical potential of the imaginary as essential for contemporary feminists in address-ing global issues of discrimination. Although she does not address issues of pornography explicitly, Mohanty does argue that "imagined communities" are the best resources for combating sexism that includes sexual political issues.[25] Additionally, Mohanty makes a convincing argument that the prac-tices of solidarity that emerge in imagined communities ensure recognition of meaningful difference. I share Mohanty's concern that many definitions of difference and theories of recognition depend on seeing the Other as either 1) entirely different to the point of unrelatability, or 2) only diverse in the sense that the Other's differences enrich my own experience. Seeing the Other through the lens of the imaginary avoids these misrecognitions by configur-ing the Other as an alternative form of subjectivity, with a history and a future unique from my own, but who shares my potential for growth, change, and reconfiguration in a new social order. The imaginary, therefore, allows me to respect that April Flores's experiences as a performer and model are unique from my own experiences as an academic, but also to imagine a future wherein we both benefit from the end of discrimination against wom-en's bodies.[26]

WHEN DOES UTOPIA COME?

It seems, then, that a radical shift in our understanding of subjectivity, fanta-sy, and the role of the imaginary is necessary for emancipatory possibility. In fact, from the accounts of Cornell, Mohanty, and the insiders of feminist pornography, this shift seems urgent. The alternative vision that begins to emerge is one that I call utopic; however, I do not mean that this shift is utopian in the sense of ideal or transcendent. In fact, following my insistence that fantasy and the imaginary are grounded precisely in the real-lived expe-rience of subjects, the utopic is a vision for a historically possible future reality.

In order for a utopic vision of an emancipatory future to be viable, it must be contained within a legitimating context, a social framework that explains the trajectory that has led us to social inequality and the trajectory that we might be able to follow out of it. This contextualization process is one of the first steps required for pushing us toward that utopic vision. As gender stud-ies theorist Lynn Comella explains, "Finally, the move from text to context is not only an analytic shift in terms of how we talk and think about feminist pornography, it is also a political move that enables us to better account for the ways in which feminist pornography is deeply embedded within a much larger network of sex-positive feminist cultural production."[27] The idea of contextualization hearkens back to Mohanty's idea of an "imagined community," or what I would like to call intentional solidarity. In feminist scholarship, solidarity signifies a form of theoretical and political organization orienting participants around a common outcome, while preserving important differences of their individual identities. It is an attempt to recognize the simultaneous importance of normalization and the practice of recognition.[28]

Providing context to the production of pornography is one step in promoting the practice of recognition. Another is seeing that that context is always in flux. As we—potentially—move toward a utopic future, we recontextualize and reconfigure the meaning, production, and practice of pornography. In describing her own confusing entry into the world of porn production and publication, Violet Blue explains that the source of her ambivalence about pornography was in part due to its *changing* nature. She explains, "Sex is multifaceted, always changing and often unexplainable, as are we. Porn is about sex, and about people, though sometimes it doesn't seem like it, but that makes describing it even more complex. Some people want to make porn seem white, while others want to make porn seem black, and in reality it's gray."[29] One notable way in which pornography's meaning changes in a feminist context has to do with even the definitions of pornography. Producers of mainstream pornographic film have relied on familiar visual tropes to signify male arousal and sexual satisfaction to the detriment of creating alternative visual narratives of sexual excitement and fulfillment, most notably of female sexual excitement and fulfillment. Feminist pornographers frequently use images of the controversial practice of female ejaculation to challenge the unquestioned masculinity of the "cum shot" or "money shot."[30] However, it is precisely because female sexual experience is less obviously visually apparent than a tumescent penis, that many feminists regard nonfilmic and even nonvisual erotic productions as pornography. For example, Deborah Shamoon explains that pornographic comics marketed to women in Japan frequently use a technique wherein bodies are drawn to be transparent, to show penetration from within the female body experiencing it.[31] Another example reflects the context of the experience of many trans individuals who have a variable relationship with their changing bodies. For them, written erotica better matches the sexual fantasy than pornographic films that crystallize certain bodily configurations.[32] These alternative definitions of pornography reflect the ways in which feminist pornography can affect contextual change.

Intentional solidarity need not only include women and sexual minorities. It is clear to me, and to many gender theorists, that because patriarchal discrimination relies on untenable and artificial definitions of gender, heterosexual men may also face harmful expectations for their bodies, sexuality, and gender performance. Mainstream heterosexual porn, for example, frequently features male performers with abnormally large genitalia. And, through the magic of editing, those same films often make it appear that men can become tumescent immediately upon arousal and stay that way for extended periods of time. Bobby Noble argues that feminist pornography interrogates assumptions about masculinity as well as femininity. By definition, feminist pornography positions porn in terms of female and feminine desire, but as Noble explains, the current trend in feminist porn is to embrace and explore masculine desires from a variety of perspectives as well:

> It features different kinds of masculine subjects as objects of desire in its productions—FTM, trans, genderqueer, butch, and cisgender—but it also rethinks the consumption practices of masculinity, refusing to accept a feminist politic that assumes that heterosexual cissexual male performers or spectators or desires are dangerous. In fact, what trended at the 2011 Feminist Porn Awards, both in terms of content but also in terms of culture, was an entirely reconfigured epistemological proximity to, and desire for, masculinity.[33]

Noble is not alone in seeing innovation in collaboration across multiple differences, including sex and gender. Feminist philosopher Rosi Braidotti also argues that her work "rests on the firm belief that we, early third millennium posthuman subjects in our multiple and differential locations, are perfectly capable of rising to the challenge of our times, provided we make it into a collective endeavor and joint project."[34]

The expansion of collaboration and embracing intersubjectivity can reflexively help to expand individual subjectivity. Although Audre Lorde is critical of pornography itself, she agrees that there is power in the erotic experience that cultivates a radical expansion of the self. And, further, this radical expansion challenges the normative structures of hierarchy by empowering women and the marginalized. She writes, "The erotic is a measure between the beginnings of our sense of self and the chaos of our strongest feelings. It is an internal sense of satisfaction to which, once we have experienced it, we know we can aspire. For having experienced the fullness of this depth of feeling and recognizing its power, in honor and self-respect we can require no less of ourselves."[35]

WHY CARE ABOUT PORNOGRAPHY?

I am certainly concerned with what pornography does in the present. I believe in solidarity for promoting the safety and recognition of sex workers and performers. I find myself frequently facing hypersexualized and normalized versions of the female form, and feeling the personal stings of alienation and objectification spurred by those images. I am concerned with the normalization of a specific untenable form of white, cisgendered, heterosexual, and aggressive masculinity that can only stabilize its illusion of supremacy through the binary disavowal of the Other. I am worried that dominant forms of pornography are so pervasive that sexuality and sexual expression may be increasingly figured in terms of the commodification of young girls and women. However, at its core, critical philosophy is not about simply enumerating the problems of the present; it is about theorizing a process through which practical change is possible. It is fundamentally oriented toward a future. It is this futural potential that has been my primary concern in this chapter. What is our utopic vision for the not-yet achieved emancipation of subjectivity, for the not-yet realized mutual recognition of intersubjectivity?

Pornography is uniquely oriented to engage with these issues of utopic vision. Through its manifestation and coproduction of fantasy, pornography can be a lens for vision. By depending on fundamental relationships between vulnerable bodies, pornography can be a site for witnessing intersubjectivity. In its tendency to tarry with the liminal, the taboo, and the boundaries of norms, pornography may be able to serve as one of many gateways into greater social emancipation, particularly for marginalized Others.

I am not arguing that pornography will inevitably produce these effects, nor am I contending that pornography is the only source for expanding our social creative imaginary. Instead, following Cornell's conceptualization, I envision a social project that expands our understandings of freedom and subjectivity. I share in Braidotti's vision for this type of project:

> Shifting an imaginary is not like casting away a used garment, but more like shedding an old skin. It happens often enough at the molecular level, but in the social it is a painful experience. Part of the answer lies in the formulation of the question: "we" are in this together. This is a collective activity, a group project that connects active, conscious, and desiring citizens. It points towards a virtual destination: post-unitary nomadic identities, floating foundations, etc., but it is not utopian. As a project it is historically grounded, socially embedded, and already partly actualized in the joint endeavor, that is, the community, of those who are actively working toward it. If this be utopian it is only in the sense of the positive affects that are mobilized in the process: the necessary dose of imagination, dreamlike vision, and bonding without which no social project can take off.[36]

Returning to the issue of safety in pornography, then, a social creative imaginary would emphasize that performers need the space to create communal action, but that they would also need our social participation in creating the vision to imagine otherwise. One example that comes close to this idea put into practice comes from Tristan Taormino, whose response to 2013's HIV cases was twofold. First, she began to require condom usage on all her film sets for all her performers. But rather than simply making a universal and unilateral decision for performers, she began to record their anonymous responses to the issue of condom use on sets. This record of their thoughts after the year's heightened concern reflects sensitivity to changing dynamics. She was not preoccupied with the autonomy of individual performers; instead, she recognized that many voices must be heard and placed in context. Additionally, she acknowledged that despite making a decision to require condom usage on her sets, this decision was contextually determined and may be contextually overturned. In other words, she recognizes the possibilities of the future.[37]

NOTES

1. Drucilla Cornell, *The Imaginary Domain: Abortion, Pornography, and Sexual Harassment* (New York: Routledge, 1995), 158.

2. Marisa Gerber, "Porn Performer Tests Postive for HIV; Industry Group Seeks Shutdown," *Los Angeles Times,* December 7, 2013, http://articles.latimes.com/2013/dec/07/local/la-me-ln-porn-performer-tests-hiv-positive-shutdown-20131207 (accessed 17 Dec. 2013).

3. It seems quite callous to say that the production delays renewed the safety discussions rather than the diagnoses, but there are conflicting reports for how many cases of HIV were actually associated with porn performers. The trade union halts production based on possible cases, rather than simply confirmed diagnosis.

4. I want to thank the editors of this volume, Jacob Held and Lindsay Coleman, for their insight and patience as I worked through this chapter. As allies of feminist thought, they asked thoughtful questions that helped me to clarify feminist concepts for uninitiated audiences.

5. Throughout this article I use the concept of "Other" to signify another member of society whose difference becomes a primary marker of individuating that person. Using the capitalization of other is a common conceptual tendency in feminist philosophy, although its meaning can vary from universalized other, to the inaccessible parts of the self, to a marker of alienation and objectification. Each of these definitions has resonance with my own operational usage, as the common thread between these definitions is difference.

6. Drucilla Cornell, *Transformations* (New York: Routledge, 1993), 42.

7. Cornell, *Transformations*, 44.

8. Cornell, *Transformations*, 42.

9. Jiz Lee, "Uncategorized: Genderqueer Identity and Performance in Independent and Mainstream Porn," in *The Feminist Porn Book: The Politics of Producing Pleasure*, ed. Tristan Taormino, Celine Parreñas Shimizu, Constance Penley, and Mireille Miller-Young (New York: Feminist Press, 2013), 277.

10. Jiz Lee's preferred gender pronoun is a singular "they." As a genderqueer person, Lee does not identify with either side of a restrictive gender binary, and therefore does not feel represented by singular pronouns "he" or "she." Persons whose gender identity and birth sex match are identified as cisgendered, whereas persons with variant gender identities and birth sexes are identified as genderqueer, transgendered, or simply trans.

11. Cornell, *Imaginary Domain*, 148.

12. As Cornell explains, "There is evidence that societies and communities in which there is sexual tolerance, in which the proliferation of sexual imaginaries are encouraged, are safer places for women." Cornell, *Imaginary Domain*, 153.

13. Cornell, *Imaginary Domain*, 153.

14. Dworkin and MacKinnon are the most infamous of all radical anti-porn feminists, and critiques of their extreme legal interventions are widespread and varied. Espousing or arguing against their positions has so limited feminist philosophy on the issue of pornography, that I am intentionally avoiding engagement in this chapter.

15. This also means that my argument is explicitly social and not juridical in nature. I am not making any claims related to legal issues of censorship, sexual harassment, or distribution. I

am, however, making arguments that depend on expanded inclusion of participation in social discourses that make democratic participation in legal remedies possible.

16. Linda Williams, "Film Bodies: Gender, Genre, and Excess," *Genre, Gender, Race, and World Cinema: An Anthology*, ed. Julie F. Codell (Malden, MA: Blackwell, 2007), 33.

17. Williams, "Film Bodies," 33.

18. "Fantasies themselves are not separate from reality. My entire argument against one brand of linguistic philosophy has been that it does not adequately address the way in which social fantasies, particularly those about how one is gendered or sexed, are the basis of our symbolic order and therefore our form of life" (Cornell, *Imaginary Domain*, 157).

19. Laura Kipnis, *Bound and Gagged: Pornography and the Politics of Fantasy in America* (Durham, NC: Duke University Press, 1996), 163.

20. Tristan Taormino, "Calling the Shots: Feminist Porn in Theory and Practice," in *The Feminist Porn Book: The Politics of Producing Pleasure*, eds. Tristan Taormino, Celine Parreñas Shimizu, Constance Penley, and Mireille Miller-Young (New York: Feminist Press, 2013), 263.

21. Keiko Lane, "Imag(in)ing Possibilities: The Psychotherapeutic Potential of Queer Pornography," in *The Feminist Porn Book: The Politics of Producing Pleasure*, 172.

22. Cornell, *Imaginary Domain*, 162.

23. Cornell, *Imaginary Domain*, 163.

24. "As we rewrite ourselves, we open up the psychic space to know ourselves differently and to know the other woman as different from ourselves." Cornell, *Imaginary Domain*, 163.

25. Chandra Talpade Mohanty, *Feminism Without Borders: Decolonizing Theory, Practicing Solidarity* (Durham, NC: Duke University Press, 2003), 46.

26. The most well-known work featuring April Flores is the book *Fat Girl* (Los Angeles: Rare Bird Books, 2013).

27. Lynn Comella, "From Text to Context: Feminist Porn and the Making of a Market," *The Feminist Porn Book: The Politics of Producing Pleasure*, 92.

28. Hilde Lindemann argues that this is a feature of all feminist ethics, in fact, not just of solidarity. She writes, "All the same, feminist ethics is *normative* as well as descriptive. It's fundamentally about how things ought to be, while description plays the crucial but secondary role of helping us to figure that out." Lindemann, *An Invitation to Feminist Ethics* (Boston: McGraw Hill, 2006), 14.

29. Violet Blue, ". . . On Experiencing Boot Camp on the Road to Becoming an Adult Video Expert," in *Naked Ambition: Women Who Are Changing Pornography*, ed. Carly Milne (New York: Carroll and Graf Publishers, 2005), 28.

30. The most often referenced video that serves as the exemplar for this feminist porn technique is *How to Female Ejaculate* (1992) starring and produced by Debi Sundahl as Fanny Fatale. I refer to the practice of female ejaculation as controversial, since medical experts and sex professionals are still unsure of how stimulation of the G spot may or may not lead to a necessary ejaculation of the urethral sponge through the vaginal canal.

31. Deborah Shamoon, "Office Sluts and Rebel Flowers: The Pleasures of Japanese Pornographic Comics for Women," in *Porn Studies*, ed. Linda Williams (Durham, NC: Duke University Press, 2004), 88.

32. See, for example: *Take Me There: Trans and Genderqueer Erotica*, ed. Tristan Taormino (Berkeley, CA: Cleis Press, 2011).

33. Bobby Noble, "Knowing Dick: Penetration and the Pleasures of Feminist Porn's Trans Men," *The Feminist Porn Book: The Politics of Producing Pleasure*, 317.

34. Rosi Braidotti, *The Posthuman* (Cambridge: Polity, 2013), 196.

35. Audre Lorde, "Uses of the Erotic: The Erotic as Power," in *Feminism and Pornography*, ed. Drucilla Cornell (Oxford: Oxford University Press, 2000), 570.

36. Rosi Braidotti, "Affirmation versus Vulnerability: On Contemporary Ethical Debates," *Symposium: Canadian Journal of Continental Philosophy* 10, no. 1 (Spring 2006): 244.

37. See Taormino's website for her record of this decision and those interviews:http://puckerup.com/category/feminist-porn/ (accessed 17 Dec. 2013).

Chapter Fifteen

In the Arms of the Angel

Playfulness, Creativity, and Porn's Possibilities

Joy Simmons Bradley

In a "behind the scenes" video with porn stars Buck Angel and Lyla Lei, viewers are invited to watch as Buck and Lyla are photographed while having sex in various positions. Buck is muscular and tattooed, with a neatly trimmed horseshoe mustache. He wears a tank top, which shows off his brawny arms, and a pair of leather pants that are straining at the crotch with the requisite enormous bulge. As things get hot and heavy between Lyla and Buck, he starts to unbuckle his pants, warning her apologetically, "My dick is kinda big." He laughs as he reaches into his pants. The viewer expects him to pull out an impossibly large penis. Instead, as he smiles at the camera, he says, "Look! This is called a blooper." He pulls a pair of balled up socks out of his pants, drops them and kicks them away from the stage. He is then handed an enormous strap-on penis from off-stage, attaches it to a harness inside his leather pants, and the scene continues. This video gives the viewer a sense for the playfulness with which Buck Angel approaches his non-normative embodiment in his pornography work. Buck is a female-to-male transgender porn star who markets himself as the "Man with a Pussy." With his clothes on, his gender presentation is normatively masculine. With his clothes off, the observer's desire to fit him neatly into a gender category is unsettled by the presence of his vagina, juxtaposed against a myriad of normatively masculine features. It becomes yet more difficult during his porn performances to understand his embodiment with reference to normative categories of gender and sexuality. He eludes classification as a "gay porn star" or a "straight porn star," due in part to his transgender embodiment and the new sexual practices that such an embodiment makes possible.

For decades, there has been an ongoing debate in feminist philosophy over the effects of pornography. Catharine MacKinnon is one of the most notable anti-pornography feminists. Working from the premise that gender and sexuality are social constructs, MacKinnon argues that pornography provides much of the material out of which gender and sexuality are differentially constructed with reference to power. Men wield social power, while women do not. According to MacKinnon, this power differential is largely created by the way that women are depicted in pornography: as desiring to be used and dominated. MacKinnon writes, "Pornography is a means through which sexuality is socially constructed, a site of construction, a domain of exercise. It constructs women as things for sexual use and constructs its consumers to desperately want women to desperately want possession and cruelty and dehumanization."[1] Pornography "teaches" men how to be men, which means using, possessing, and objectifying women. According to MacKinnon, "Pornography defines women by how we look according to how we can be sexually used. Pornography codes how to look at women, so you know what you can do with one when you see one."[2] For MacKinnon and other anti-pornography feminists, there is a direct correlation between pornographic representations of male and female sexuality and the raping, beating, killing, and general disenfranchisement of women. When reading MacKinnon discuss pornography in this way, one is tempted to assume that she is referring only to BDSM pornography and not talking about "regular" or "soft-core" porn. Jeffrey G. Sherman cautions against such a misconstruction in his discussion of anti-pornography feminists, including MacKinnon: "A common misreading of the feminist critique implicates only manifestly coercive or violent pornography in the maintenance of patriarchal subordination. In fact, the feminist critique is a good deal more radical; it concerns the social construction of sexuality, not violence, and a narrow focus on violent pornography trivializes the feminists' point."[3] For MacKinnon, pornography that depicts women being beaten, raped, cut, bound, or gagged is not the only pornography that (re)produces the gender hierarchy that is responsible for the disenfranchisement of women. All pornography is implicated.

Since discussions of pornography by MacKinnon and other anti-pornography feminists revolve almost exclusively around porn that depicts heterosexual sex, one wonders how gay, lesbian, and transgender porn is implicated in the construction of harmful gender dynamics. That MacKinnon and others all but ignore the burgeoning field of gay, lesbian, and transgender pornography in their writing and in their presentations weakens their thesis that *all* pornography creates and sustains the subordination of women to men. To argue convincingly that all pornography harms women and therefore ought to be censored would require a sustained and in-depth critique of queer pornography, one that MacKinnon and other anti-pornography feminists do not offer. It is conceivable that images of nonnormative sexualities and/or involving nonnormative bodies could disrupt the heterosexual power differential. However, MacKinnon does not seem to make room for such disturbances in pornography. In fact, she claims that sexually explicit materials that eroticize *any* form of hierarchy are responsible for women's subjugation and ought to be eschewed. MacKinnon writes:

> Pornography's multiple variations on and departures from the male dominant/ female submissive sexual/gender theme are not exceptions to these gender regularities. They affirm them. The capacity of gender reversals (dominatrixes) and inversions (homosexuality) to stimulate sexual excitement is derived precisely from their mimicry or parody or negation or reversal of the standard arrangement. This affirms rather than undermines or qualifies the standard sexual arrangement as the standard sexual arrangement, the definition of sex, the standard from which all else is defined, that in which sexuality as such inheres.[4]

According to MacKinnon, in pornographic sexuality (which constructs sexuality in the "real" world) there is always one who is active and one who is passive, one who is "using" and one who is "being used," a subject and one who is being subjected. The masculine role is the role of the subject while the feminine role is the role of the subjected. In MacKinnon's view, this constitutes paradigmatic sexuality. Sexuality is constructed such that viewers experience pleasure when they see this power differential played out in sexually explicit ways. Male domination is thus produced and reinforced by pornography. Any departure from, or reversal of, this heterosexual template of feminine subordination, such as one might see in lesbian, gay, or transgender pornography, produces pleasure in the viewer simply because it references or "mimics" the original male/female hierarchy of domination and submission. Queer pornography is nothing more than a reiteration and reinscription of gender inequality. For MacKinnon, there seems to be no place for queer pornography with feminist aims, or *any* feminist pornography, for that matter.

MacKinnon's argument that pornography is directly correlated with the routine objectification and violation of women underpins much of the current feminist anti-pornography activism. Stop Porn Culture is a fairly new organization, created in response to the explosion of readily available pornography on the Internet, and has updated the anti-pornography slide shows presented in the 1970s. They regularly hold international conferences and workshops utilizing these slideshows. Any anti-porn activist can download these slide shows in the form of a PowerPoint presentation from stoppornculture.com in order to hold his or her own workshop. Feminist activist and scholar Gail Dines is a founding member of Stop Porn Culture, and much of her work builds on MacKinnon's thesis that pornography is harmful to women. MacKinnon's influence can be seen throughout the presentations, and in some cases, she is even directly quoted. Conspicuously absent in the slide show discussion of pornography is gay, lesbian, transgender, or queer pornography. The focus of these slide shows is exclusively sexually explicit depictions of women that appear to be produced for male consumption only. The existence of queer pornography is effectively erased. "Pornography" becomes synonymous with sexually explicit material that is heterosexual in content, featuring normatively gendered bodies. Depicting pornography in this way ignores the raidly growing area of gay, lesbian, transgender, and queer pornography, some of which has explicitly feminist aims.[5]

The possibility of feminist pornography is given a cursory nod in the "Talk Back: FAQ and a Q&A" section of Stop Porn Culture's website. The question, "Can there be a feminist pornography?" is answered with the assurance that, yes, there is a place for the feminist struggle for gender equality in the arts. However, the activists at Stop Porn Culture write, "The rush to imagine 'good' pornography can be a way to avoid contemplating the nature of the actual pornography we live with."[6] The assumption here seems to be that feminist pornography does not yet exist and that it is not yet part of the landscape of "actual pornography we live with." Since feminist pornography supposedly has yet to be realized, "responsible" feminists are called upon—not to create "better" pornography—but to eliminate pornography altogether, thus eradicating one of the root causes of gender hierarchy. Because pornography is thought to be an essential element in the construction of women's gender and sexuality as subordinated to men's—the "what" out of which gender and sexuality is constructed—we cannot eliminate the subjugation of women until we do away with pornography. A "good" feminist ought not to be concerned with attempting to resist dominant constructions of gender and sexuality from within pornography. Such opposition from within is framed as ineffective at best and, at worst, a distraction from the *real* work with which feminists ought to be concerned, which is the eradication of pornography that can then lead to the transformation of gender and sexuality as we know it. Such an unnuanced characterization of feminist pornography as "good," over and against all other kinds of "bad" pornography, is deeply problematic. It also ignores the existence of decades of feminist pornography whose aim is to resist and transform mainstream notions of sexuality and womanhood while harnessing the power of pornographic representations to affirm non-normative expressions of gender and sexuality. These sexually explicit, non-normative expressions of gender and sexuality have the potential to trouble the binary gender system on which the subordination of women to men is premised in the first place.

In what has been termed the feminist "porn wars," the most prominent argument opposing MacKinnon and the censorship of pornography has been the free speech argument. Nadine Strossen was a notable proponent of the position that censorship is more likely to harm women and minorities than it is to help them, and she argued convincingly to this effect.[7] However, Clarissa Smith and Feona Attwood contend that this line of reasoning merely requires that pornography be tolerated by adults, because free and open debate ought to be valued in U.S. society. It does nothing to call into question the characterization of pornography "as a singular form in which the degradation or subordination of women is played out or as irredeemably harmful to children who see it 'too early.'" Smith and Attwood go on to say:

> Free speech arguments merely require that sexually explicit materials should not be censored for adults, and that in free and democratic societies pornography should be tolerated. . . . But this toleration is always an unstable achievement for any minority grouping or interest, open to reassessment and redefinition at any time. And in making arguments for free speech, its proponents often cede the ground that *some* forms of pornography are indeed awful, damaging, and to be abhorred, thereby confirming the basic analysis that there is something intrinsically problematic about both the cultural forms of sexual representation and those who seek them out.[8]

Rather than simply tolerating pornography as a form of free speech, problematic though it may be, there is value in showing how pornography itself, as a "cultural form of sexual representation," can pose a powerful challenge to normative and compulsory sexualities and gender presentations. Pornography, even BDSM pornography, need not reinforce male hegemony. In fact, it might undermine it in significant ways.

If masculinity and male sexuality means having power and femininity and female sexuality means being "defined by what male desire requires for arousal and satisfaction," as MacKinnon claims, and if pornography both produces and reinforces this unjust distribution of power, then the only solution to women's condition of subordination is to overthrow pornography entirely as a step towards a new construction of gender and sexuality that is premised on equality, where women are finally free from subjection.[9] Certainly, in some mainstream pornography, we spectate as normative gender identities are reinscribed and women are portrayed as tasty treats for the consumption of the male viewer. However, the situation is much more complex and interesting than this. To reduce pornography to a practice that *only* produces and sustains male hegemony is to ignore the myriad ways that pornography can call attention to, and creatively resist, normative constructions of gender and sexuality. In porn performances, normative gender and sexual practices may be reiterated in uncritical ways, but they may also be called into question and deeply troubled. To suppress pornographic expression altogether would not mean the beginning of an overthrow of an unequal gender system. Instead, it would mean foreclosing the powerful critiques of the binary gender system and compulsory heterosexuality that pornography has to offer.

What MacKinnon misses is the Foucauldian insight that power produces its own possibilities for resistance and that there is no position outside of power relations from which we may resist. For Michel Foucault (1926–1984), power is not exercised only from the top down. Rather, "Power plays a 'directly productive role,' 'it comes from below'; it is multidirectional, operating from the top down and also from the bottom up . . . it is not in a position of exteriority to other types of relationships."[10] What this means is that there is no utopia after the death of pornography, where we will find ourselves outside of power relationships. Given this definition of power, Foucault's description of resistance in *The History of Sexuality, Volume I* is worth quoting at length:

> Where there is power, there is resistance, and yet, or rather consequently, this resistance is never in a position of exteriority in relation to power. Should it be said that one is always "inside" power, there is no "escaping" it, there is no absolute outside where it is concerned, because one is subject to the law in any case? . . . This would be to misunderstand the strictly relational character of power relationships. Their existence depends on a multiplicity of points of resistance. . . . These points of resistance are present everywhere in the power network. Hence there is no single locus of great Refusal, no soul of revolt, source of all rebellions, or pure law of the revolutionary. Instead, there is a plurality of resistances, each of them a special case: resistances that are possible, necessary, improbable.[11]

For Foucault, power is everywhere. But this does *not* mean that we are in a position of total domination, where there are no possibilities for resistance or liberation. In fact, power often produces its own possibilities for resistance. Rather than circulating from the "top down," power is diffused throughout society. There is no single place in society from which power originates, rather, power emanates from multiple locations. As Brent L. Pickett explains, because "power is spread through society and not localized in any particular place, the struggle against power must also be diffuse."[12] Since there is no single locus of power, there is no single locus for struggle against power. The workings of power can be challenged from multiple locations.

Pickett elaborates on the point that power, as something that organizes human multiplicities, is productive rather than simply being restrictive:

> This [organization of multiplicities] happens on an individual level, such as organizing an aimless flux of impulses, sensations, and desires into a skilled worker. It also happens on a larger level, for instance by integrating that worker into a divided, hierarchical factory space. . . . Indeed, resistance can be made effective, in a sense, by the very power which has opposed it; for instance, by forging a group of skilled workers and bringing them together, disciplinary techniques create the possibility of large strikes.[13]

The very organizational and disciplinary techniques that power employs can be used as tools for resistance and struggle against oppressive hierarchies. Power provides the conditions for the possibility of resistance. We see this demonstrated in Buck Angel's porn scenes where he plays with normative conceptions of masculinity and femininity. Masculinity and femininity are produced by power and are used to organize bodies in hierarchical configurations. Normative conceptions of masculinity and femininity also discipline bodies: a "real man" dresses himself, comports himself, and otherwise "fashions" his body in ways that affirm his masculinity while repudiating femininity. In Buck Angel's porn scenes, "masculinity" and "femininity" provide the tools for resisting the hegemony of the binary gender system when Buck Angel calls their presumed "naturalness" into question. It is imperative that masculinity and femininity retain their claim to naturalness so that they may maintain their normalizing force. Buck Angel troubles their claim to naturalness, by displaying a masculine body that retains traces of the feminine (the "Man with a Pussy"), thereby disrupting their normalizing power. While it seems true that some mainstream pornography reiterates, reinscribes, and reinforces dominant and oppressive constructions of gender and sexuality, it would be a mistake to treat the anti-pornography position as the main "locus of great Refusal," from within which we can finally be freed from harmful gender hierarchies and the problem of violence towards women. While pornography can be identified as a locus from which power emanates in that it disseminates sexually explicit images that reiterate the subordination of women, pornography also creates the possibility for struggle *against* both the subjugation of women and the inadequate and exclusionary binary gender system that renders such subjugation possible. In producing an industry that can reinforce harmful gender hierarchies, power also creates the possibility for resisting this hierarchy from within the pornography industry itself. While some of porn's sexually explicit imagery is problematic, to categorically condemn all pornography and strive for its eradication is also to seek to eradicate a potent site of resistance to oppressive constructions of gender.

In an interview with the *Advocate* magazine in 1982, Foucault was asked by the interviewers to elaborate on his claim "that resistance is never in a position of externality vis-à-vis power" and to explain how we are not therefore "always trapped inside that relationship."[14] Foucault responded by saying,

> It is a struggle, but what I mean by *power relations* is the fact that we are in a strategic situation toward each other. . . . It means that we always have possibilities, there are always possibilities of changing the situation. We cannot jump *outside* the situation, and there is no point where you are free from all power relations. But you can always change it. So what I've said does not

mean that we are always trapped, but that we are always free—well, anyway,
that there is always the possibility of changing.[15]

So for Foucault, the point is not to get rid of relations of power altogether.
This is impossible. Rather, freedom means finding ways to creatively resist
from *within*, which may mean exposing as contingent relational structures
that have been naturalized and invested with normative power, such as the
nuclear family structure or the binary gender system. This kind of resistance
opens up new ways of doing relationships so that there is a proliferation of
relational possibilities and new potential for pleasure.

For Foucault, there is no "outside" of power relations, toward which we
may strive. MacKinnon seems to imagine a state where sexuality and gender
are constructed such that men and women are finally freed from relationships
of power. But any redefinitions of the categories "man" and "woman" will
carry with them their own sets of exclusions. What must be disavowed in
order to be a "good man" and a "good woman" under this new system of
gender equality? For Foucault, to resist power effectively is to take up that
which power produces and to subvert those things—or play with them—in
creative ways. The point is to multiply pleasures and invest parts of the body
with new and creative meanings that fly in the face of the normative. This is
made clear in Foucault's discussion of sadomasochism (S&M), which appears in Foucault's 1982 interview with the *Advocate*, where power relations
are eroticized in creative ways. In this interview, Foucault suggests that S&
M practices have liberatory possibilities. This stands in striking opposition to
the position of anti-pornography feminists, which is that S&M pornography
is particularly heinous and objectionable. For Foucault, however, the practice
of S&M can effectively open up possibilities for pleasure beyond those that
are directly produced by power. Foucault elaborates his position in the following way:

> I think that S&M is . . . the real creation of new possibilities of pleasure, which
> people had no idea about previously. The idea that S&M is related to a deep
> violence, that S&M practice is a way of liberating this violence, this aggres-
> sion, is stupid. We know very well what all those people are doing is not
> aggressive; they are inventing new possibilities of pleasure with strange parts
> of their body—through the eroticization of the body. I think it's a kind of
> creation, a creative enterprise, which has as one of its main features what I call
> the desexualization of pleasure. The idea that bodily pleasure should always
> come from sexual pleasure as the root of *all* our possible pleasure—I think
> *that's* something quite wrong. These practices are insisting that we can pro-
> duce pleasure with very odd things, very strange parts of our bodies, in very
> unusual situations, and so on.[16]

Foucault objects to the notion that we harbor S&M tendencies deep within our psyches that are brought to the surface and relieved through S&M

practice. Instead, S&M practices are useful and interesting because they trouble the conflation of pleasure and sex. Foucault points out that, traditionally, pleasure comes from a very limited number of activities: "drinking, eating, and fucking."[17] S&M practice, however, is capable of generating intense pleasure outside of the traditionally paradigmatic pleasure-producing activities. We are invited to think of the relationship between bodies and pleasures in new and creative ways. This is accomplished through "playing" with power relations and parts of the body that are generally neglected in erotic situations. S&M practice opens up "the possibility of using our bodies as a possible source of very numerous pleasures."[18] Foucault is evidently concerned with the multiplication of pleasures and practices that trouble normative assumptions about bodies and pleasures, rather than their suppression. Following Foucault, we should be suspicious of projects that seek to limit creative pleasures and practices, such as the feminist anti-pornography project.

Current anti-pornography feminism has created a situation where relational possibilities are foreclosed, rather than allowed to proliferate. In the slide show produced by Stop Porn Culture entitled, "It Is Easy Out Here for a Pimp," we observe a discourse that differentiates "healthy sexuality" from "unhealthy sexuality." In a list entitled, "Do You Know the Difference?" "Healthy sex" is juxtaposed with "Porn-related sex" (read: "unhealthy sex"), drawing from work by Malt and Malt in *The Porn Trap*. "Porn-related sex" is defined as "using someone, doing to someone, performance for others, public commodity, separate from love, emotionally distant, can be degrading, can be irresponsible, involves deception, compromises values, feels shameful, and impulse gratification." "Healthy sex," in contrast, is portrayed as "caring for someone, sharing with someone, private experience, personal treasure, an expression of love, nurturing, requires certain conditions, always respectful, approached responsibly, requires honesty, involves all the senses, enhances who you really are, and lasting satisfaction."[19] Clarissa Smith and Feona Attwood point out that such a characterization of "healthy sex" perpetuates quite a few exclusions:

> Casual sex, kinky sex, rough sex, and even monogamous, straight, vanilla sex that might be the product of routine, boredom, fun, or thrill-seeking, does not meet these standards. A proper purpose for sex is assumed and there is no consideration of the variety of sexual practices that people engage in, diverse understandings of what sex is, or the multifarious reasons why people have sex. Although they vehemently reject being characterized as "antisex," [anti-porn feminists] foreclose the possibilities of sexuality as plural and in process.[20]

This kind of discourse is an attempt to regulate sexuality, rather than allowing for the proliferation of pleasures. Rather than creating new ways of relating to one another, this binary opposition between "healthy" and "un-healthy" sexuality actively excludes a variety of sexual relationships. The dichotomy between "healthy" and "unhealthy" sexual practice becomes a way of disciplining bodies by delimiting the sexual practices in which they should or should not engage.

A great example of feminist pornography that calls into question our normative assumptions about gender and sexuality is the work of Buck Angel, the self-described "Man with a Pussy." This porn star highlights for his viewers the insufficiency of our categories for describing sexuality and gender by overflowing these categories and rendering them unstable. Buck is a female-to-male (FTM) transgender porn performer who has undergone testosterone therapy and "top" surgery, which is the removal of the breasts and the male contouring of the chest. To see Buck Angel fully clothed—and even in various stages of undress—is to see someone who is normatively masculine. Buck's muscular physique very much fulfills the viewers' expectations for the "ideal man"—until Buck takes his pants off. Fully undressed, his embodiment is uncertain. It lacks coherence. To be coherently male is to have all the gender markings of a man, including a flesh-and-blood penis. Buck Angel has all the bodily gender markings of a man, both visual and aural—from hair length, to chest shape, to muscle definition, to the deep timbre of his voice. But instead of a penis, he has a vagina. While clothed, it is fairly unproblematic to classify Buck as normatively male. However, when Buck is stripped naked and playfully engaged in sexual acts, he troubles categories of gender and sexuality that purport to be natural.

Following Foucault, Judith Butler understands gender identity and sexual identity to be effects of power. Gender identity—our identification as *either* male *or* female—is the effect of discursive practices and is the condition for the possibility of our visibility as human beings in society. Until a fetus can be identified as a "he" or a "she," it is merely an "it." To confer a normative gender identity on someone is to have humanity and social visibility simultaneously attributed to him or her. When a normative gender identity is conferred on someone, part of the social expectation is that his/her sexual identity and desire will be coextensive with his/her gender identity. If your body is identified female at birth, the normative expectation is that you will grow up to dress and act like a woman, you will desire to have sex with men and you will engage in heterosexual sexual practices. Butler writes,

> "Intelligible" genders are those which in some sense institute and maintain relations of coherence and continuity among sex, gender, sexual practice, and desire. In other words, the spectres of discontinuity and incoherence, themselves thinkable only in relation to existing norms of continuity and coherence, are constantly prohibited and produced by the very laws that seek to establish causal or expressive lines of connection among biological sex, culturally con-

stituted genders, and the "expression" or "effect" of both in the manifestation of sexual desire through sexual practice.[21]

So in order to have a "coherent" gender identity, one's sexual desires and practices must correspond in socially acceptable ways with one's gender. The expectation is that, if a person is assigned female at birth, she will naturally desire to have sex with men. Here, "biological sex" is thought to be a causal force on her sexuality. To be "intelligible" as a woman is not only to perform femininity, but also to be heterosexual. Of course, this very notion of "coherence" produces its own possibilities for transgression.

For Butler, drag performances reveal that gender itself is something that must be constantly reiterated through performance. She writes,

> Drag constitutes the mundane way in which genders are appropriated, theatricalized, worn, and done; it implies that all gendering is a kind of impersonation and approximation. If this is true, it seems, there is no original or primary gender that drag imitates, but *gender is a kind of imitation for which there is no original*; in fact, it is a kind of imitation that produces the very notion of the original as an *effect* and consequence of the imitation itself.[22]

For Butler, gender is nothing more than the *performance* of gender. Drag is interesting because it calls into question the reality of gender. It destabilizes our belief that certain kinds of dress and comportment naturally follow from a certain biological sex. Butler emphasizes that there is "no original" in the above quote because gender is a cultural creation—there is no such thing as a "man" or a "woman" apart from the way these categories are created and established by discourses of power. The apparent "naturalness" of these categories, and the heterosexuality that appears to be coextensive with them, is an effect of their "compulsive and compulsory repetition."[23]

In addition to drag performances, Butler also writes that transgender bodies, in whatever stage of transition they might be found, call into question normative gender categories. Transgender bodies cannot be easily "read" by viewers who are looking for markers of normative masculinity and femininity. Butler writes,

> The moment in which one's staid and usual cultural perceptions fail, when one cannot with surety read the body that one sees, is precisely the moment when one is no longer sure whether the body encountered is that of a man or a woman. The vacillation between the categories itself constitutes the experience of the body in question. When such categories come into question, the *reality* of gender is also put into crisis: it becomes unclear how to distinguish the real from the unreal. And this is the occasion in which we come to understand that what we take to be "real," what we invoke as the naturalized knowledge of gender is, in fact, a changeable and revisable reality.[24]

Encounters with transgender bodies can be quite unsettling for cisgender people precisely because they may be bodies that refuse to be easily categorized as *either* male *or* female. Buck Angel's body is a prime example of this. When Buck is fully clothed, the spectator can be comfortable—he or she may be certain that Buck is a man, due to his sculpted, muscular physique, facial hair, narrow hips, masculine comportment, deep voice, and masculine attire. The category "man" is not yet troubled. However, when Buck undresses, revealing his vagina (or rather, the absence of his penis), the category "man" becomes troubled. His body vacillates between gender categories, destabilizing the binary gender system, revealing it as a cultural creation that cannot sufficiently contain all the bodies we might encounter.

The situation becomes even more complicated when Buck Angel has sex. In his porn videos, Buck Angel approaches sexual practice with quite a bit of creativity and playfulness. For example, in a scene with costar Nikki Brand, their sexual encounter begins with Nikki sucking Buck Angel's strap-on penis while he is fully clothed. This beginning is not the least bit unsettling. Buck and Nikki both appear to be normatively gendered and their sexual practice appears to be coextensive with their gender identities. Their genders are socially coherent at this moment. The scene concludes, however, with Nikki wearing a strap-on penis and fucking Buck in the vagina. This no longer appears to the spectator as a heterosexual sexual encounter between two normatively gendered people. Buck's embodiment, while quite masculine, defies easy categorization as male since he is being fucked in the vagina (though he is quite clearly also not female here). His body bears traces of both genders.

Normative categories for sexual identity are also troubled by this sexual encounter between Buck and Nikki. While it can easily be categorized as a heterosexual encounter at the beginning of the scene, the end of the scene, in which "a woman fucks a man in the vagina," cannot be easily and neatly categorized as "heterosexual," "homosexual," or "bisexual." The perceived reality of gender, and the assumption that gender is coextensive with desire and sexual practice, are called into question by this scene. In other scenes, Buck Angel has sex with men. In these scenes, Buck routinely fucks other men with strap-on penises and is also fucked in the vagina by cisgender men. These practices, too, defy easy categorization as "homosexual" encounters since Buck Angel's body still carries traces of his past as a woman. Buck's embodiment renders his encounters with other men as not quite homosexual, but also definitely not heterosexual. As a spectator, one feels the need for a new kind of taxonomy through which one may understand Buck's sexual encounters. Perhaps Buck's embodiment, playfulness, and creativity open up the possibility of the proliferation of gender categories and ways to understand sexual orientation.

Buck Angel's porn scenes trouble binary gender categories by calling into question their naturalness. These are the very categories that, according to MacKinnon, are constructed in such a way that women are deeply harmed. It stands to reason that MacKinnon would support any effort to call these categories into question. The denaturalization of the binary gender system is imperative to the feminist project. Buck Angel's pornography also decouples gender and sexuality, which are generally thought to be coextensive. His porn scenes highlight the insufficiency of our categories for sexual orientation: it is difficult, if not impossible, given our system of classification of sexual acts, to categorize coherently an act that involves a man being fucked in the pussy by a woman with a penis. Such an act not only disrupts our expectation of heterosexuality, but also entirely defies categorization in terms of sexual orientation. Buck Angel highlights the insufficiency of our taxonomies when it comes to both gender and sexual orientation. Buck Angel's gender presentation and sexuality overflows our normative categories that claim to describe, not only what is "normal," but also what is "natural." Disrupting the binary gender system's claim to naturalness is central to a feminist project that seeks to undo a gender hierarchy that privileges men at the expense of women, as well as people with nonnormative embodiments. On the contrary, MacKinnon, along with other anti-pornography feminists, undermine the aims of their own feminist project through their narrow focus on mainstream heterosexual pornography, which effectively erases the existence of decades of queer pornography. The "reality" of porn, according to Stop Porn Culture, is that men are subjugating and using women. Somehow, feminist porn and queer porn with feminist aims are not part of "the actual pornography we live with." This discourse of erasure and refusal to critically engage the transformative possibilities of feminist pornography actually sabotages, rather than nurtures, the feminist agenda. The eagerness of anti-pornography feminists to foreclose the opportunities for creative resistances within the pornography industry is frightening: critical resistance to power ought to be cultivated rather than stifled. If pornography were to be censored and the categories of "man" and "woman" as we know them were to be reconstructed, what hegemonic constructions of gender and sexuality would take their place? What would need to be excluded and disavowed, such that we could perform "ideal masculinity" and "ideal femininity"? It is imperative that opportunities for resistance not be foreclosed so that exclusionary constructions of sexuality and gender are not simply replaced by equally restrictive categories. In their haste to discourage feminists from working in the porn industry to create feminist porn, anti-pornography feminists run the risk of replacing one hegemonic construction with another. We particularly see this in their effort to differentiate "healthy" from "unhealthy" (read: pornographic) sexuality. Much that can be liberatory and transgressive is excluded from their definition of "healthy" sexuality.

MacKinnon and other anti-pornography feminists seek to disrupt the gender hierarchy by calling into question the social construction of masculinity and femininity. Buck Angel does just that, in a pornographic context. Because of this sexually explicit context, his work will never be acceptable to anti-pornography feminists. Nevertheless, what Buck Angel does in front of the camera is central to the feminist agenda. He takes the elements of gender and sexuality produced by power, and plays with them in ways that disrupt the claim to naturalness that gender and sexuality generally possess. He disrupts binary gender categories by being fully masculine at times (with his clothes on) and then "slipping" between masculine and feminine at other times, while his transgender body is engaged in sexual acts. At times, his body refuses categorization in terms of both gender and sexual orientation. Our taxonomies are troubled and destabilized during his porn performances. The refusal of anti-pornography feminists to critically engage with—or even acknowledge—the value of Buck Angel's performances to the work of feminism is problematic. To ignore Buck Angel's transgressive and transformative work, as well as the work of so many artists like him, is an unfortunate reminder of the erasure of queer artists throughout history, whose valuable contributions have been ignored and suppressed. As feminism's third wave has striven to acknowledge, exclusion and erasure does feminism's transformative project no favors.

NOTES

1. Catharine A. MacKinnon, "Sexuality, Pornography, and Method: 'Pleasure under Patriarchy,'" *Ethics* 99, no. 2 (January 1989): 327.
2. Catharine A. MacKinnon, *Feminism Unmodified: Discourses on Life and Law* (Cambridge, MA: Harvard University Press, 1987), 173.
3. Jeffrey G. Sherman, "Love Speech: The Social Utility of Pornography," *Stanford Law Review* 47, no. 4 (April 1995): 664, n. 19.
4. MacKinnon, "Sexuality, Pornography, and Method," 332–33.
5. Work can be "feminist" by my definition to the extent that it seeks to undermine hierarchies and norms that perpetuate oppressions and exclusions of all kinds, including, but certainly not limited to, gender hierarchies that privilege masculinity; racist hierarchies and norms of beauty that privilege whiteness; compulsory heterosexuality that excludes all kinds of nonnormative sexualities; the privileging of cis-gender bodies that perpetuates the erasure of transgender bodies; norms that marginalize bodies that are "disabled"; and class hierarchies that privilege the rich.
6. "Talk Back: FAQ and a Q&A," Stop Porn Culture, http://stoppornculture.org/activism-and-projects/faqs-and-a-qa/#13 (accessed 15 Aug. 2013).
7. See Nadine Strossen, "A Feminist Critique of 'the' Feminist Critique of Pornography," *Virginia Law Review* 79, no. 5 (August 1993): 1099–1190.
8. Clarissa Smith and Feona Attwood, "Emotional Truths and Thrilling Slide Shows: The Resurgence of Antiporn Feminism," in *The Feminist Porn Book: The Politics of Producing Pleasure*, ed. Tristan Taormino, Celine Perreñas Shimizu, Constance Penley, and Mireille Miller-Young (New York: Feminist Press, 2013), 47.
9. MacKinnon, "Sexuality, Pornography, and Method," 318–19.

10. Herbert L. Dreyfus and Paul Rabinow, *Michel Foucault: Beyond Structuralism and Hermeneutics* (Chicago: University of Chicago Press): 185.

11. Michel Foucault, *The History of Sexuality, Volume I: An Introduction* (New York: Vintage Books, 1990), 95–96.

12. Brent L. Pickett, "Foucault and the Politics of Resistance," *Polity* 28, no. 4 (Summer 1996): 458.

13. Pickett, "Foucault and the Politics of Resistance," 458–59.

14. Michel Foucault, "Sex, Power, and the Politics of Identity," in *Ethics: Subjectivity and Truth*, ed. Paul Rabinow (New York: New Press, 1997), 167.

15. Foucault, "Sex, Power, and the Politics of Identity," 167.

16. Foucault, "Sex, Power, and the Politics of Identity," 165.

17. Foucault, "Sex, Power, and the Politics of Identity," 165.

18. Foucault, "Sex, Power, and the Politics of Identity," 165.

19. "It's Easy Out Here for a Pimp: How a Porn Culture Grooms Kids for Sexual Exploitation," slide show, Stop Porn Culture, http://stoppornculture.org/activism-and-projects/spc-presentations/ (accessed August 15, 2013).

20. Smith and Attwood, "Emotional Truths and Thrilling Slide Shows," 51.

21. Judith Butler, *Gender Trouble* (New York: Routledge, 1999): 23.

22. Judith Butler, "Imitation and Gender Insubordination," in *Inside/Out: Lesbian Theories, Gay Theories*, ed. Diane Fuss (New York: Routledge, 1991): 21.

23. Butler, "Imitation and Gender Insubordination," 21.

24. Butler, *Gender Trouble*, xxiii.

Index

About the Editors and Contributors

Lindsay Coleman is an academic, independent film producer, and private tutor based in Melbourne, Australia. In 2004 he achieved graduate entry to the Notre Dame School of Medicine in Fremantle, ultimately accepting a scholarship to study for his doctorate in Media/Film Studies at the University of Melbourne. Lindsay has been published in such books as *The War Body on Screen*, *Taking South Park Seriously*, *Undead in the West*, *Gilmore Girls and the Politics of Identity*, *Doctor Who in Time and Space*, and *Bloodlust and Dust*. He is the editor of *Sex and Storytelling in Modern Cinema*. He is also currently working on a sequel to the 1993 documentary *Visions of Light*, as well as books on film composing, film editing, and cinematography.

Jacob M. Held is associate professor of philosophy in the Department of Philosophy and Religion at the University of Central Arkansas. His primary research interests focus on legal and political theory, nineteenth-century German philosophy, and applied ethics. In addition, he works extensively at the intersection of philosophy and popular culture, most recently editing *Roald Dahl and Philosophy: A Little Nonsense Now and Then* (2014).

***

Louise Antony is professor of philosophy at the University of Massachusetts, Amherst. She earned her BA in philosophy at Syracuse University in 1975, and her PhD in philosophy at Harvard University in 1982. She has research interests in the philosophy of mind, epistemology, feminist theory, philosophy of language, and the philosophy of religion. She recently edited *Philosophers without Gods: Meditations on Atheism and the Secular Life* (2007). She was coeditor, with Charlotte Witt, of *A Mind of One's Own:*

Feminist Essays on Reason and Objectivity (1990), and contributed to that volume her essay, "Quine as Feminist: The Radical Import of Naturalized Epistemology." She is currently at work on a monograph about reasons for action and reasons for belief.

Joy Simmons Bradley is a PhD candidate in philosophy at Duquesne University in Pittsburgh, Pennsylvania. Her areas of interest are critical philosophies of race, feminism, queer theory, and existentialist phenomenology. Her work has been published in the *APA Newsletter on Philosophy and the Black Experience*, *Simone de Beauvoir Studies*, and the *Journal of Theoretical and Philosophical Criminology*.

Susan J. Brison is associate professor and chair of the Philosophy Department at Dartmouth University. She is the author of *Aftermath: Violence and the Remaking of a Self* (2002) and numerous scholarly articles on sexual violence and freedom of expression.

Ariane Cruz is assistant professor in the Department of Women's Studies at the Pennsylvania State University. She holds a PhD from the University of California, Berkeley, in African Diaspora Studies with a designated emphasis in Women, Gender, and Sexuality. Her teaching at Penn State includes classes on feminist visual culture, racialized sexuality, and representations of race, gender, and sexuality. Her research interests include images of black female sexuality, black visuality, and pornography. She is currently working on a manuscript exploring black women, BDSM, and pornography. Her work appears in *Camera Obscura*, *The Feminist Porn Book: The Politics of Producing Pleasure* (2013), *Hypatia*, and *Women & Performance*.

Taine Duncan is assistant professor of philosophy and director of the Gender Studies program at the University of Central Arkansas. When she is not teaching and researching, she remains committed to community and public activism for issues of gender, sex, and sexuality. She also loves books, film, and television, so she likes thinking about the ways in which gender, identity, and media representation (or misrepresentation) interact.

Matthew B. Ezzell is assistant professor of sociology at James Madison University. His research, teaching, and activism focus on the reproduction of and resistance to inequality and oppression. He has a background in Women's Studies and has been active in the rape crisis and anti-violence movements for over seventeen years.

Nina Hartley is a pioneering feminist worker, using her body in the service of promoting a sexually sane and literate society. She is thrilled to see a new generation of sex-positive performer/activists spread the good news about sex. For the past thirty years her commitment to the importance of sexual autonomy has fueled her career in adult entertainment. As a performer, director, writer, educator, public speaker, and feminist thinker she's traveled the world to deliver her message. She believes that sexual freedom is a fundamental human right and welcomes the new social media opportunities for spreading her message to the widest number of people. Hartley is the author of *Nina Hartley's Guide to Total Sex* (2006). Putting to use her BS in nursing, she and her husband, I. S. Levine, have produced the million-selling sexed video series collectively known as *The Nina Hartley Guides*. Still active in front of the camera, she and her husband live in Los Angeles.

Jennifer Hornsby is professor of philosophy at Birkbeck, University of London, and codirector of the Centre for the Study of Mind in Nature, University of Oslo. Her main interests are in philosophy of action, mind, and language, metaphysics, and feminism in philosophy; she has published work in all these areas.

Katrien Jacobs is associate professor at Chinese University of Hong Kong. She has lectured and published widely about pornography, censorship, and media activism in Hong Kong and global media environments. She is also working on long-term research projects in visual anthropology that detail the impact of Japanese animation on Southeast Asian youth cultures and social networks. She is the author of three books about Internet culture, art, and sexuality: Libi_doc: Journeys in the Performance of Sex Art (2005), Netporn: DIY Web Culture and SexualPolitics (2007), and People's Pornography: Sex and Surveillance on then Chinese Internet (2011). Her work can be found on www.libidot.org/blog.

Robert Jensen is a professor in the School of Journalism at the University of Texas at Austin and board member of the Third Coast Activist Resource Center in Austin. He is the author of *Arguing for Our Lives: A User's Guide to Constructive Dialogue* (2013); *All My Bones Shake: Seeking a Progressive Path to the Prophetic Voice* (2009); *Getting Off: Pornography and the End of Masculinity* (2007); *The Heart of Whiteness: Confronting Race, Racism and White Privilege* (2005); *Citizens of the Empire: The Struggle to Claim Our Humanity* (2004); and *Writing Dissent: Taking Radical Ideas from the Margins to the Mainstream* (2002). Jensen is also coproducer of the documentary film, *Abe Osheroff: One Foot in the Grave, the Other Still Dancing* (2009), which chronicles the life and philosophy of the longtime radical activist.

Natalie Nenadic is assistant professor of philosophy at the University of Kentucky. Her research is in the history of philosophy (especially Heidegger, Arendt, and Hegel), social and political philosophy, and philosophy of law, especially global justice; she brings these resources to the contemporary ethical challenges of sexual violence, pornography, and genocide. The recipient of a 2013–2014 American Association of University Women Fellowship, her recent publications include "Heidegger, Arendt, and Eichmann in Jerusalem" (*Journal of Comparative and Continental Philosophy*) and "Genocide and Sexual Atrocities: Hannah Arendt's Eichmann in Jerusalem and Karadzic in New York" (*Philosophical Topics*).

Susanna Paasonen is professor of media studies at the University of Turku, Finland. With an interest in media theory, sexuality, and affect, she is the author of *Carnal Resonance: Affect and Online Pornography* (2011) as well as coeditor of *Pornification: Sex and Sexuality in Media Culture* (with Kaarina Nikunen and Laura Saarenmaa, 2007), *Working with Affect in Feminist Readings: Disturbing Differences* (with Marianne Liljeström, 2010) and *Networked Affect* (with Ken Hillis and Michael Petit, 2014).

Shira Tarrant is associate professor in the Women's, Gender, and Sexuality Studies Department at California State University, Long Beach. She is the author of several books including *Men and Feminism* (2009); *Fashion Talks: Undressing the Power of Style* (2012); *When Sex Became Gender* (2006); *Men Speak Out: Views on Gender, Sex, and Power* (2013); *New Views on Pornography* (forthcoming); and *21st Century Sex: Contemporary Issues in Pleasure and Safety* (forthcoming). Her commentary is featured on global media including the Canadian Broadcasting Corporation, NBC, *Forbes*, *Chicago Tribune*, *Baltimore Sun*, *Denver Post*, *Sydney Morning Herald*, and on radio stations in Los Angeles, New York, Berkeley, Houston, and elsewhere around the country.